EDUCATIONAL FACILITIES

PLANNING, MODERNIZATION, AND MANAGEMENT

SECOND EDITION

BASIL CASTALDI

EDUCATIONAL CONSULTANT

ALLYN AND BACON, INC.
BOSTON   LONDON   SYDNEY   TORONTO

Library of Congress Cataloging in Publication Data

Castaldi, Basil.
  Educational facilities.

  1. School plant management. I. Title.
LB3241.C37 1982   690'.7   81-17652
ISBN 0-205-07745-5   AACR2

Printed in the United States of America

Printing number and year (last digits):
10 9 8 7 6 5 4 3 2 1   86 85 84 83 82

To my wife Angela, to my daughter Linda, and son Paul for the countless hours spent away from them during the preparation of this text.

Contents

Preface

As was true of the first edition, this book is a comprehensive treatise on the planning, design, remodeling, and maintenance of educational facilities. It is intended to serve the needs of students and practitioners. It is organized so that it can be used as a basic textbook by the student in educational administration, and as a resourceful guidebook for the school practitioner. The fundamental concepts and associated theory concerning the planning of educational facilities are of equal importance to both groups. The difference lies primarily in the emphasis placed on theory or on practices by each group. The student is perhaps a little more interested in the theory than in the practices. The practitioner, on the other hand, must often produce concrete solutions to the real problems of educational administration and attaches far more importance to the practice than to the theory. The difference between these two groups lies in the point of view. The student examines practices to better understand the theory, while the practitioner utilizes theory to justify practical solutions. It can be seen, therefore, that theory and practice are not mutually exclusive. They strongly supplement each other depending upon whether the reader is a student or practitioner.

This book is organized to facilitate this dual purpose. The first two sections of this text deal with the theory and principles associated with school plant planning. They contain detailed discussions of educational survey techniques, and the principles of educational psychology that are applicable to educational facilities. These theoretical considerations serve as a basis for the development of a long-range educational plan for any school district. In this part of the book, practices are introduced only as needed to illustrate the operational aspects of the theory.

Parts III and IV of the book include detailed suggestions pertaining to the planning, maintenance, and updating of educational facilities. These practices are described in specific terms and can often be used in a given situation with just a few minor adjustments. In other cases, the practices presented in these sections may suggest solutions to more complicated problems. In either case, the information contained in this part of the book can be extremely helpful to the school principal, the school superintendent and the staff members, the board of education, and the school architect.

The author wishes to state at the very outset that no statement contained in this book should be construed as favoring one sex over the other. Any role described in this text can be played by either men or women of equal competence. Specific reference is made to the function of students, teachers, school administrators, architects, consultants, clerks-of-the-works, citizens, and other persons involved in the planning of educational facilities.

In order to avoid the dilemma described above, the author applied the existing rules of "standard English," *with the understanding that any function described in this text can be performed by any qualified person regardless of sex.* Even the use of "it," instead of "he" or "she," was examined, but the result seemed to depersonalize the narrative and weaken its intended impact. Until a new vocabulary is developed and fully accepted in the English language, the author finds it more desirable to employ current "standard English" with stipulated reservations.

B. C.

1

Theory and Principles of Planning

CHAPTER 1

The Evolution of Educational Facilities

Space for learning has undergone dramatic changes over the past two thousand years. In the beginning, there were no educational facilities at all. There were no classrooms and there were no desks and chairs for students. Plato and Aristotle met with students to exchange and discuss ideas in the open air at any convenient location, perhaps in the shade of a temple, wall or other building. It was not an enclosure but a space for learning. Since then, educational facilities have become effective laboratories of learning where teachers and students benefit from the latest advances in educational technology and instructional methodology. The rudimentary space for learning has become a complex enclosure that controls the environment and supports the learning process.

INTRODUCTION

It should be stated at the outset that this book is envisioned as a broad-based guide for school officials, members of boards of education, school administrators, school maintenance personnel, educational consultants and school architects. The text is organized so that the reader may refer only to the sections that are of interest to him or her. Parts of this publication deal with curriculum development, principles of learning applicable to the planning of school facilities and promising innovations in educational methodology. Another part is concentrated on the process and activities related to the identification of educational needs for the foreseeable future. A third focus of this publication is on the actual planning of a specific type of school facility that has been recommended by the Board of Education. Such a recommendation by school officials may involve the construction of a new facility or the modernization of an existing school building. And finally, this text includes material on the maintenance and operation of a school building, and on techniques for saving energy.

This book offers a comprehensive treatment of educational facilities from a theoretical and a practical point of view. It is aimed at meeting the needs of the student and the practitioner. From the standpoint of the student preparing for a position in educational administration, this presentation provides many of the basic principles that underlie the suggested application of the theory. When viewed by a practicing school administrator such as a superintendent of schools, college president, school principal, or dean of administration, this book offers a wide variety of specific and pragmatic suggestions that are of immediate value to the professional in the field. This dualism of purpose, however, should not be construed to mean that students are not interested in practice or that practitioners see little or no value in theory. But as a practical matter, the student frequently has more time to examine the "why" of the practice, while the hard-pressed practicing administrator is often required to provide solutions to problems with little time to deal with theory.

In the first case, the primary objective is to arrive at feasible ideal solutions through the application of accepted principles. In the second instance, school administrators are seeking to find practical answers in the shortest possible time using the theory and principles to support their recommendations to their respective boards. Principles and concrete solutions to problems are not mutually exclusive. Each potential user of this text will place a different emphasis on theory or practice presented in this book, depending upon the individual situation. For example, the school principal who is asked to submit a set of recommendations to the superintendent of schools within a few days as to how he could best use his present school building under a given set of circumstances would find it very helpful to focus immediately upon the suggested practices that apply to his problem in developing his response. In preparing this report, however, he would find it advantageous to review the principles and theory appropriate to his situation in order to support his recommendations to higher authority. From this illustration, it can be seen that theory and practice are mutually supportive. Since the student needs some knowledge of the practices to better understand the theory, and the practitioner can take advantage of certain basic principles to bolster his recommendations, the principles and practices presented in this book can serve both the student and the practitioner.

THE "THINGS" OF EDUCATION

For centuries, very little attention was given to the *"things* of education." Education was envisioned primarily as people—teachers and learners. School buildings were incidental to the learning process. Wherever the Athenian teacher could conveniently hold a discussion with a small group of learners, that was where the school was. Education was primitive and uncomplicated in those days. Parents simply selected a teacher and sent only their *boys* to him. Oftentimes the school was nothing more than a teacher and a few students meeting on the open stairs of an ancient temple.

Recent advances in the field of educational psychology and electronic programming have stimulated the development of a wide variety of effective teaching aids. These new instructional tools have had a profound effect on modern educational thinking about the "things of education." They have made school buildings more sophisticated in design and function. Presently, the school building is much more than a shelter for its occupants. It is a complete educational tool. The well-conceived educational facility of today should be capable of supporting a wide variety of learning experiences. Consequently, the design elements of the modern school building go far beyond the functionally planned school building of yesteryear. They include many innovations caused by the electronic revolution. The availability of sophisticated teaching aids has introduced a multitude of exciting features in the design of futuristic school buildings—from kindergarten to graduate school.

These new teaching devices are important additions to the collection of educational hardware. Hardware alone, however, is educationally useless. It must be coupled with an ample supply of related educational software in the form of magnetic tapes, films, and transparencies.

Excellent school facilities and dedicated teachers are the basic ingredients of a good educational program. As important as "the things of education" may be, they do not, per se, produce first-rate instruction. It cannot be assumed that functionally designed school buildings containing a wide variety of modern teaching aids will automatically improve the quality of the educational program. The importance of skillful teachers cannot be overstated. Hardware alone cannot and will not produce the desired educational outcome. On the other hand, a skillful teacher working in a well-designed and highly functional school building, supplied with a wide array of electronic and visual teaching aids, can achieve a level of instructional effectiveness that far exceeds what is possible when the necessary "things of education" are not provided.

EXTENDED USE OF EXISTING BUILDINGS

During the period of increasing birthrates and expanding school enrollments immediately after World War II, the solution to overcrowded classrooms was, in most cases, a new building. The major questions, under those circumstances, were what new building and where should it be located. Today the problem assumes an entirely different form. With the significant drop in birthrate, the former problem of overcrowding is less pressing. In a few suburban areas, there is still a little residual overcrowding, but for the most part, the major educational challenge stems from obsolescence. To be sure, obsolete school buildings existed even during the most recent period of high birthrates, but the need for new capacity was so great that it was often fiscally impossible to replace obsolete schools and construct new ones simultaneously.

With taxes rising higher and higher, and with a significant increase in taxpayer resistance to the construction of new school buildings, it might be extremely profitable to explore the ways and means of making existing buildings more educationally effective. A way must be found to overcome obsolescence and to provide for a moderate increase in building capacity without overburdening the taxpayers of the school district. We must begin to look more seriously at the buildings we have. These represent a sizable capital outlay and every conceivable avenue should be explored to protect this investment without "shortchanging" the education of the people housed in such facilities.

As will be discussed in detail in Chapter 16, remodeling is not always the most economical solution to the problem of obsolescence and additional capacity. On the other hand, we can no longer afford the luxury of abandoning school buildings simply because they are old, educationally obsolete, or both. It is strongly suggested that no existing school buildings be recommended for disposal by a school district until a study in depth is made as to the wisdom of this course of action.

There will undoubtedly be situations in which the cost of remodeling would not be in the best financial interest of the school district over a fifty-year period, but would adequately meet the short-range needs of the district under a given set of circumstances. For example, a heavily bonded school district might have two options. It could remodel an existing building for one million dollars with an expected useful life of fifteen years, or it could construct a new one for three million dollars with an expected useful life of sixty years. Straight logic would dictate that the new three-million-dollar building is the "better buy." However, let us, for a moment, look beyond the long-term economic picture and examine the financial impact on the school district when these options are considered. This study might show that the school district is already heavily in debt and is paying for a number of recently constructed school buildings. Taxes for other services may also be high. Its tax leeway is approaching an alarming level. Under these circumstances, would it be better to consider some form of install-ment purchasing to provide for its educational needs? Build what is needed in the foreseeable future for the least amount of capital outlay and accept the penalty that must be paid because the school district is not in a position to take full advantage of long-range financial benefits.

Admittedly, this approach is pragmatic, but more and more school districts will be confronted with a situation similar to the example cited above in the not-too-distant future. The recent period of rapid enrollment growth has left many school districts in precarious financial straits. For some time to come, such school districts must make the best use of existing facilities until they can recover some of their borrowing potential. Several sections of this book deal directly with the ways and means of getting the most education out of existing school buildings.

PROTECTING THE CAPITAL INVESTMENT OF THE SCHOOL DISTRICT

Maintaining the educational efficiency and the aesthetic attractiveness of school buildings is a matter of considerable concern to both educators and boards of education. New buildings do not always fare too well in this regard. For understandable reasons, the public often assumes that such ultramodern facilities require little or no further attention from the standpoint of maintaining educational effectiveness and aesthetic appeal. This attitude is natural but unrealistic. Actually, a building is assumed to be new when the keys are turned over to the Board of Education. From that day forward, it starts to get old. The mechanical equipment begins to wear, the intensity of the artificial lighting visibly declines, the metal surfaces commence tarnishing, painted areas start accumulating a film of condensed air pollutants, and the well-known aging process sets in.

These changes are slow, subtle, natural, and cumulative. In addition to natural changes, the normal use of the building by its occupants greatly accentuates the problem of maintenance. Students contribute to the normal soiling of floors and walls and the expected wear and tear on the surfaces accessible to them. Also, they cause a substantial amount of unpredictable damage due to abuse or misuse of the building or the teaching equipment housed in it. Consequently, a new school building is not immune to educational deterioration due to the lack of proper maintenance.

A good building maintenance program is necessary to protect the initial capital outlay investment made by a school district. A long-range program of preventive and restorative maintenance is definitely needed in any school district. It is important that maintenance be conceived as an ongoing activity designed to keep the educational function and environmental conditions of a school building at peak efficiency. This course of action is more likely to result in a maximum educational return per maintenance dollar expended than would be possible under other approaches. Various suggestions concerning the maintenance and operation of a school building are presented in Chapter 17.

A HISTORICAL PERSPECTIVE OF EDUCATIONAL FACILITIES

It is difficult to imagine that school buildings are not as old as education itself. In fact, today's educational facility is a relatively new concept that gained momentum immediately following World War II. To be sure, there were many structures called schools where teaching and learning occurred prior to that time, but they were generally unsophisticated structural envelopes that simply protected teachers and pupils from the elements. In essence, they were shelters in which teachers cited and pupils recited, and where the "things of education" consisted primarily of benches, tables, books, pencils, paper, pens, and perhaps a slate blackboard.

At the risk of reiterating certain historical facts that are quite familiar to many educators, it is fascinating to examine the development of educational facilities over the centuries of recorded history in relation to the corresponding educational practices over the same period of time. It will be seen that until recently there was little or no attempt made to design school buildings for specific educational functions. It may take some of the readers by surprise to learn from this documentary that school buildings did not become architectural entities until the middle of the twentieth century!

For centuries, architects envisioned architecture as an overall science of building construction without placing any significant emphasis on school design. Until recent times, architects felt that school buildings were not primarily vehicles of architectural expression. In fact, school buildings did not attract the serious attention of architects until mass education was established in many countries about a century ago. The development of architecture in relation to school buildings is traced through three periods in history. The first is the Hellenistic era. Although there was some development of church grammar schools in Italy, France, Germany, and England during the fifteenth and sixteenth centuries,[1] a review of the historical literature reveals no special interest in school facilities as a form of architecture at that time. Consequently, the second phase of this study jumps to the early American and post-Civil War period. The date of the third phase of this review is the Twentieth Century.

THE HELLENISTIC AND ROMAN PERIOD

The Status of School Buildings (500 B.C.-200 B.C.)

According to McCormick and Cassidy,

> As teachers were supported by fees from their pupils, only the well-paid (teachers) could furnish schoolrooms for their classes. The teachers of the poor held their sessions in the open air (Figure 1), usually in the shelter of public buildings such as temples . . .[2]

Butts points out that it would be "more correct to speak of Athenian teachers than of Athenian schools—where the teacher was, there was school. Parents selected a teacher and sent their boys to him."[3]

[1]Ellwood P. Cubberley. The History of Education (New York: Houghton Mifflin Co., 1948), p. 280.

[2]Patrick McCormick and Francis Cassidy. History of Education (New York: Catholic Education Press, 1953), p. 105.

[3]R. Freeman Butts. A Cultural History of Education (New York: McGraw-Hill, 1947), p. 55.

FIGURE 1.1 The open air classroom—model 500 B.C.

The educational program of the Greek boy of this period was quite simple. It comprised three basic areas of learning requiring only three teachers, the *chitharist* or teacher of music, the *grammaticist* or teacher of reading, writing, and arithmetic, and the *paedotribe* or teacher of gymnastics.[4] What little educational equipment there was (Figure 2), the pupil supplied. It consisted of:

    a. Plaques of baked earth upon which the alphabet was written
    b. Several styli
    c. Wax tablets
    d. A counting board using pebbles of different colors for thousands, hundreds, tens, and units.
    e. Quills, ink, and papyrus.
    f. Simple musical instruments, such as the lyre or the flute.[5]

[4]William A. Smith. *Ancient Education* (New York: Philosophical Library, 1955), p. 133.

[5]Cubberley, *op. cit.*, pp. 26–29.

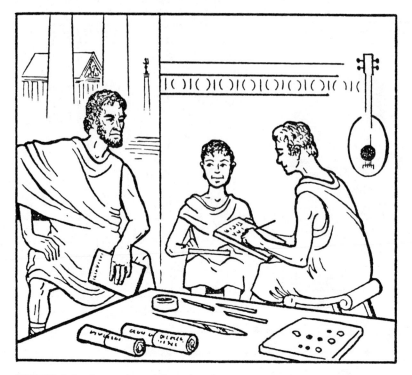

FIGURE 1.2 An early grade school.

According to Cubberley,[6] the grammaticist and the chitharist originally occupied the same room for instructional purposes, but later separated and taught in two adjoining rooms. The palaestra was usually found in another building where pupils reported for instruction in gymnastics.

Educational facilities during the Roman period (about 100 B.C.) had not greatly improved over those found in Greece one or two centuries earlier.[7] Classes might well have been held under a portico, in a shed, in a booth in front of a house, or in a recessed corner shut in by curtains as shown in Figure 3. The equipment found in these spaces for learning usually consisted of a chair for the master, benches for the pupils, and a bundle of rods (ferula) for the instruction.[8]

School buildings as we know them today did not exist in the Greek and Roman world. Even in those days, the teaching station was in use, operating in the open air or in any enclosure that would protect the pupils from the elements. The meeting place of the pupils and teacher was incidental to the instructional process.

[6]*Ibid.*, p. 30.

[7]*Ibid.*, p. 66.

[8]Russell Sturgis. *History of Architecture* (Doubleday, 1916), p. 142.

FIGURE 1.3 The Roman school—model 100 B.C.

The Status of Architecture (500 B.C.-200 B.C.)

In the meantime, architecture was focused upon the design of the early forms of Doric temples found in Italy and Corinth[9] (Figure 4). When choosing the materials used in the construction of these temples the builders be-

FIGURE 1.4 Architecture—500 B.C.

[9]*Ibid.,* p. 129.

gan with softer stone that could be easily shaped and later used marble only as its great superiority became more important than the ease of working.[10] From the vantage point of architectural development, school buildings did not seem to be of interest to the architects during this era.

THE EARLY AMERICAN PERIOD (SEVENTEENTH CENTURY)

The early American schoolhouses were neither charming nor comfortable, and most of them were located in surroundings inviting neither to the body nor the mind . . . . Generally, the schoolhouses in rural districts were located in waste and wild spots which the plow had deserted to broom, sedge and rabbits. The records abound in accounts of ugly cheerless places as school sites.

Seventeenth-century American schools were usually one room structures with benches and long tables for the pupils and a raised podium for the teacher[11] (Figure 5).

FIGURE 1.5 A 17th century American classroom.

[10]*Idem.*

[11]Edgar W. Knight. *Education in the U.S.* (3rd ed.; Boston: Ginn and Company, 1951), p. 413.

These schoolhouses were frequently crowded, poorly ventilated and drab, and equipped with a whipping post.

Seventeenth and eighteenth century American schoolhouses had progressed very little beyond the ancient notion that they were simply shelters in which pupils and teachers might come together. They did include some furniture—benches and tables for the pupils and a podium for the teacher.

Early American Architecture

Early American architecture followed whatever was in vogue in England at the time. The lack of trained architects, the inexperience of the builders in working with classical forms, and the necessity of using wood and bricks instead of stone produced an architecture which was interesting but undistinguished.[12]

Architectural interest at that time was focused primarily on public buildings (Figure 6), such as Craigie House in Cambridge, the old State House in Boston, and Independence Hall in Philadelphia.

American school buildings were so simple and so utilitarian in this period that they failed to attract the attention of architects. In all probability, the practical and resourceful citizen in the seventeenth century felt no need of architectural advice in planning a schoolhouse anyway. To him, a school was a simple structure—usually one large room with a fireplace at one end and windows at the other.

THE POST-CIVIL WAR PERIOD

American School Buildings

As late as the middle of the nineteenth century, American schools were still in a deplorable state as depicted in Figure 7. According to Knight:

> The great majority of the schools of New York state in 1844 were officially described . . . as naked and deformed, in comfortless and dilapidated buildings with unhung doors, broken sashes, absent panes, stilted benches, yawning roofs and muddy mouldering floors . . . . Only one third of the schoolhouses were reported in good repair, another third in only comfortable circumstances, while more than 3,300 were unfit for the reception of either man or beast.[13]

The battle for free public schools in the United States was fought and won between 1820 and 1850. Through the efforts of Horace Mann, Henry Barnard, and others the value of free public education came to be recog-

---

[12]Lewis Pilcher. *Encyclopedia Americana*, 1948 Ed., Vol. 2, p. 183.
[13]Knight, *op. cit.*, p. 416.

FIGURE 1.6 17th century American architecture.

FIGURE 1.7 The 19th century American school.

nized, and in time the *public school* became an accepted institution in the United States. Schoolhouses of many types began to rise throughout the country. The more elaborate schools were, of course, erected in the cities, simple one- or two-room structures sufficed for the rural areas. By and large, the school building itself was still viewed as a place where the teacher could instruct pupils in a sheltered environment. The schoolhouse was still a long way from a learning laboratory. In fact, as noted above, a few school buildings were still "unfit for the reception of either man or beast."

Post-Civil War American Architecture

Roth points out:

> During the second half of the nineteenth century, the decline of architectural conception and creative thought was approaching the lowest possible level characteristic of a deeply uprooted and contradictory epoch. The architects in that period held on to certain vague traditions which in no way correspond to modern times. The fact that school buildings became a state concern (during this period) furthered their erroneous development from the start.[14]

No evidence of any distinct relationship between schoolhouse design and architecture appeared until the latter part of the nineteenth century. In big cities, where the structurally complex buildings needed could no longer be planned by laymen, the advice and services of architects were sought at last.

[14]Alfred Roth. *The New School* (New York: Frederick Praeger, 1957), p. 24.

In its incipient stages, school architecture was more or less an adaptation of other forms of architecture without much regard to the needs of education. As Roth says: ". . . The design of the ordinary school building took no account of its nature or various functions. The solution adopted was nothing but an addition of classrooms, one exactly like the other."[15]

During the latter part of the nineteenth century, schools were designed as architectural works of art rather than as educational facilities. Schoolhouses of that period were outsized buildings, characterized by unfunctional and undifferentiated space organization, and unfunctional and non-creative design.[16] Many such schools are still in use with their large corridors and imposing lobbies, stately columns, and useless parapets. Architectural emphasis was clearly on shape, form, and style, not on the functional aspects of school plants.

THE TWENTIETH CENTURY

School Buildings and Architecture

At the turn of the century,

> . . . Schools were either castles or palaces and their architectural style either Gothic, Renaissance, or Baroque, or a combination of styles. Whatever their shapes or forms were, they in no way resembled a school (in the functional sense). The child's own scale was not taken into consideration, either practically or emotionally. Out-sized entrances, corridors, stairways seem to be particularly selected by the architect for his "artistic" effects with the well meant aim of contributing to the child's education in art.
>
> It would be wrong and unfair to blame the architect alone. The absence of unbiased pedagogical conceptions, and of a curriculum based on them were as much a cause of mistaken evolution, as was the lack of close collaboration between the architect, educator and building authorities.[17]

During this period, schoolhouses were, for the most part, not architecturally exciting. The effect of European architecture was noticeable in some school buildings (Figure 8), and a few schools built earlier in the century did reflect the classical influence, but the majority of them were structures without architectural character. Many looked like large boxes enclosed by red brick walls and covered by a steep slanted roof. The large boxes were subdivided into four or eight smaller, uniform, cubicles called classrooms. Sometimes, the attic space under the slate roof was used as an assembly hall. At that time, these buildings undoubtedly represented the best conceivable answer to the school housing problem, but, as Roth points

[15]Ibid., p. 24.
[16]Ibid., p. 26.
[17]Idem.

FIGURE 1.8 The classical American school.

out, neither the architects nor the educators really had a clear understanding of the educational tasks to be accomplished.[18]

Today many educators and architects are aware of the need for functional planning of school buildings. Unfortunately, some boards of education and school administrators have not yet recognized the need for cooperative action between educators and architects. Some school districts still ask an architect to design a school on the basis of the information listed on a single sheet of paper. This information may include the grade level and number of pupils to be housed in a school and, perhaps, the number of the various types of spaces desired. To ask an architect to design a school without giving him a complete set of educational specifications requiring perhaps fifty or sixty pages of educational information is ridiculous and unfair. Until it is generally recognized that school plant planning is a team operation involving architects, educators, and boards of education, schools will continue to be built to meet housing rather than instructional needs, and many will include the shortcoming of the schools of yesterday and today. According to Roth: "The development of school buildings up to the present time must be considered faulty for, indeed, it has not achieved the standard required by sound and valid pedagogic principles."[19]

During the latter part of the twentieth century, the development of school buildings was rapid, innovative and dramatic. Immediately following World War II, architects became quite excited about "bringing the outside into the building." Accordingly, large expanses of window-walls were built into school buildings. Beautiful vistas and natural light in great quan-

[18]*Idem.*
[19]*Ibid.*, p. 24.

tities were the order of the day. This development created problems of controlling heat build-up within the buildings during certain parts of the year and glare from direct and reflected sunlight. The 1960s ushered in the era of the "finger design." Perimeters were long and energy losses were high. But with a plentiful supply of inexpensive energy, this design posed no significant problems. During the 1970s, air conditioning of school buildings was widely accepted. But due to the large amounts of energy required for air conditioning, architects became deeply concerned with the heat gain of a school building during hot days when air conditioning was required. In order to solve this problem, architects introduced the controversial "windowless" school. These and other developments that have occurred recently are discussed in detail in various parts of this text.

CHAPTER 2

Educational Psychology and Educational Facilities

Every educational facility should be designed to support, stimulate, and strengthen learning and yet, as stated in Chapter 1, American school buildings have "not achieved the standards required by sound and valid pedagogic principles." While there has been a strong emphasis on functional planning, there seems to be no appreciable evidence of a *systematic and conscious* effort to design schools in accordance with accepted principles of educational psychology. To be sure, school buildings have housed psychologically sound practices for decades, but the application of psychological principles directly related to learning to school planning has been only incidental. This aspect of school plant planning offers a challenging opportunity for the design of psychologically exciting school buildings.

The primary objective of this chapter is to establish a relationship between some accepted principles of learning and school building design. In a sense, we shall attempt to answer the question, "What implications do the findings of educational psychologists have for school plant planning?" Each applicable psychological consideration will be divided into three parts: (1) a summary of the findings related to a given principle of learning that may have some bearing on school building design; (2) a discussion of its implications for the educational program; and (3) specific ideas related to building design to guide educators and architects in their quest for school buildings that are pedagogically sound and educationally functional.

This chapter is not intended to serve as a short course in educational psychology. It is conceived simply as a compilation of research findings in the psychology of learning pertinent to the planning of educational facilities. The ideas illustrating the application of certain psychology principles in the design of school facilities are offered in the hope that they will suggest many other solutions that will satisfy psychological requirements.

19

Implications of Educational Psychology for the Educational Program

In applying the principle of conceptual planning described in Chapter 3, it is necessary to establish and define a set of conditions, requirements, or goals stemming from pedagogical needs as an antecedent to functional school planning. To proceed logically from psychological principle to school plant, it is essential that an intermediate step be introduced. Psychological concepts should first be translated into human activities or needs before serious thought is given to school plant design. Conceptual planning demands freedom of thought, open-mindedness, and creative thinking; it also must be founded firmly on a set of realistic and necessary conditions for effective learning. Therefore, the implications of the various concepts of learning presented later must be translated into activities, conditions, and requirements that will serve as a basis for the eventual design of a school building.

SOCIAL NEEDS

Psychological Aspects

It is generally agreed among educational psychologists that the feelings of belongingness and of security are of paramount importance in the learning process. The rejected child and the insecure student, for example, have certain psychological needs that must be satisfied before learning can take place effectively. According to Ruch:

> Man everywhere seems to have certain basic psychological needs which he expresses through the social patterns of his particular culture. Among these are the *need for security*, the need to respond to others through the exchange of love and esteem, the need for new experience and greater knowledge, and the need for approval and some degree of prestige.[1]

In this same connection, Jersild also feels that belongingness is an important aspect of the well-being of a child. He says: "In time, through a combination of many factors, one of the strongest motives of a child's life is the desire to be accepted, to belong. . . ."[2] And finally, Horrocks comments on the principle of belongingness and security in relation to the needs of adolescents. "There seems to be general agreement that the peer group is

---

[1]Floyd L. Ruch, *Psychology and Life* (Chicago: Scott Foresman and Company, 1958), p. 138.

[2]Arthur T. Jersild, *Child Psychology* (New York: Prentice-Hall, 1950), p. 185.

good because it may give the adolescent security, an opportunity for status and a feeling of belonging."[3]

Some psychologists also believe that human beings have a basic need for social situations and opportunities that will give them a sense of belongingness. Horrocks stresses the importance of group membership in adolescents:

> Thus, as the adolescent mingles more and more with his age mates and participates in group activity with them his feeling of belonging to the group becomes greater and greater and may reach the extent of transcending nearly everything else in importance.[4]

A number of educational psychologists believe that social activities are of extreme importance in the lives of children and adolescents.[5] They suggest that constructive group activities are essential in developing a feeling of belongingness within an individual. Psychologists also seem to agree that the feeling of belongingness and the sense of security are vital to the well-being of the individual, indeed that they represent two basic psychological needs that must be met if the individual is to become well adjusted to his environment and to the expectations of the culture in which he lives. In relation to education, Blair, Jones, and Simpson point out that students "will need to feel important and to have their accomplishments admired by others, and they need to feel that they are a part of a group—that is, have a sense of belonging."[6]

From the foregoing discussion, a few inferences may be drawn. If, as is quite evident, social activities underlie the development of feelings of belongingness and security among individuals, and if human beings become better adjusted to their social environment, as these two psychological needs are met, then a wide variety of sensibly planned social activities and groupings in school will tend to produce well-adjusted students.

School Facilities for Social Development

Social development in school requires a variety of spaces for group activities. For example, a conference room for the use of small groups might be located in the library area. Such a space could serve as a meeting place for ten or twelve members belonging to various school organizations, or as a headquarters for the school literary club. This room might be designed so that it could be easily supervised by the librarian through the use of

[3]John E. Horrocks, *The Psychology of Adolescents* (Boston: Houghton Mifflin, 1962), p. 137.

[4]*Ibid.*

[5]Laurel N. Tanner et al., *Classroom Teaching and Learning* (New York: Holt, Rinehart and Winston, Inc., 1971), pp. 148–150.

[6]Glenn M. Blair, R. Stewart Jones, and Ray H. Simpson, *Educational Psychology*, 4th ed. (York: The Macmillan Company, 1975), p. 313.

double-glazed vision strips. If this room is located in the library complex, it should have direct access to a corridor so that its use will not interfere with the normal operation of the library.

There could be great social value in an outdoor assembly area, planned perhaps around a simple fireplace, for "sing-along" sessions, for large school gatherings, for picnics, and for musical programs. Such an area could be attractively landscaped and perhaps be provided with a shallow pool and fountain.

The school could provide a few small spaces for highly specialized activities. Such spaces might be large enough for half a dozen to a dozen students interested in projects in photography, science, radio, television, repair of home appliances and other special interests.

Group programs might be expanded by locating an observation laboratory for approximately fifteen students on the roof of the school building. Here students might pursue studies and investigations in meteorology, astronomy, astronautics, and techniques of celestial navigation. Such a space could be supervised easily by use of closed-circuit television. It might also be desirable to locate space near the homemaking room. Such a room could be large enough to accommodate about ten girls who may wish to form a "gourmet club," or it might be utilized by a few girls for homemaking projects that cannot be completed during the normal class period. For these purposes, this special room would contain a kitchen unit, storage spaces for food and supplies, and it should be located and designed to permit easy supervision by the homemaking teacher.

Social and instructional advantages can be enjoyed by students who love the out-of-doors. A quarter of an acre of land near the school could be developed as the "School Gardens" under the sponsorship of the "Plant Lovers Club."

The feeling of belongingness can be intensified in a large elementary school by subdividing the school into clusters of distinctly separate spaces. There might be the red, the green, and the blue schools with corresponding colors in each of the clusters. Each cluster might consist of seven rooms housing pupils in kindergarten through Grade 6, or each cluster of fewer rooms may house pupils in the same grade. A single space for assembly and work projects serving each cluster of rooms would add to the feeling of unity of the pupils housed in each unit.

There may be some educational advantage in providing for school-wide social activities of the students. Lobby areas might be designed for dancing during the lunch hour, and the cafeteria could be planned for informal meetings of large groups. A snack bar might also be included in order to encourage socialization under informal conditions.

School officials might also plan spaces for informal learning-recreational activities for small groups of students. It might be desirable to design spaces that serve about a dozen students in music appreciation, creative art, astronautics, rocket and automobile models, art appreciation, and other fields.

INDIVIDUAL DIFFERENCES AND GROUP SIMILARITIES

Psychologists have accumulated a wealth of information about the nature and character of individual differences, but there is still a scarcity of knowledge concerning the psychological similarities that exist among human beings.

Psychological Aspect

Individual differences.   A few general viewpoints related to this aspect of the learner are presented in this section. Cronbach observes that "students differ in interests, long term goals, ability, social effectiveness, personality and other respects."[7] In discussing student performance in the light of individual differences, Blair, Jones, and Simpson add another interesting dimension to expected student behavior. They indicate that "such a wide range of difference in all types of school work make attempts to achieve 'standardized performance' futile."[8] There are also distinct differences in learning among individuals. Hughes observes in this respect: "The method and rate of learning depend upon the qualities of each individual."[9] There is also a marked difference among individuals in physical development, as Cronbach notes, "Children grow at different rates and develop different physiques."[10]

Individual differences vary over a wide range of human characteristics. For the purpose of this writing, however, only individual differences related to the learning process have been considered. It may be concluded that a student may differ from his fellows in rate of learning, physical development, sensory perceptions, speech, social-emotional adjustment, attitudes and interests, general intellectual ability, and his response to the various stimuli related to the learning process. It can be seen, therefore, that attention to the individual is of paramount importance in the design of the educational experiences that pupils undergo under the guidance of the school.

Group similarities.   Individuals do differ from one another, but at the same time there are also identifiable similarities among them. Because of the dearth of information regarding similarities among individuals, the existence of such similarities can only be inferred from the literature on educational psychology. According to Blair et al., students have similarities related to both physical and psychological needs. They mention that all students need ". . . food, air, liquid, activity and rest. In addition to these

[7]Lee J. Cronbach, *Educational Psychology*, 3rd ed. (New York: Harcourt, Brace Jovanovich, 1977), p. 104.

[8]Blair et al., *Educational Psychology*, p. 121.

[9]A. G. Hughes and E. H. Hughes, *Learning and Teaching* (New York: Longmans Green and Company, 1959), p. 410.

[10]Cronbach, *Educational Psychology*, p. 151.

biological needs, every child in our society possesses certain social and personality needs."[1] Hence, some similarities exist among all individuals. The full import of group similarities is probably not widely recognized at the present time. At first glance, it might be assumed that it is knowledge of this principle that influences the various forms of pupil grouping found in the schools today. Upon further investigation, however, it becomes quite clear that such grouping is based more on reducing the range of individual differences within the group than it is upon the recognition that certain similarities exist among large numbers of human beings. Nevertheless, the principle of group similarities has definite implications for curriculum development and school plant planning in the future, and should be viewed as separate and distinct from the concept of individual differences.

School Facilities for Individual Differences and Group Similarities

School districts that take cognizance of individual differences among their pupils must offer them a wide variety of learning experiences. School plant planners might locate a number of teaching devices in the instructional materials and information resources center where pupils may be supervised by noncertified staff working in the library complex. Each teaching station might be designed to facilitate the use of audiovisual equipment, charts, models, and materials. The school building might also contain one or two small workshops where creative teachers may design and construct simple teaching devices.

A comprehensive testing program is essential for the identification of individual differences and group similarities. Facilities for the program would include a suite of spaces where tests may be stored, scored, and studied. The scoring could be done by one clerk and the record-keeping by another who might also record the information for data-processing machines. A small conference room might be located in this area for the use of teachers and guidance personnel who wish to confer on test results, or to formulate changes in curriculum and pupil grouping in the light of the individual differences revealed by diagnostic testing.

Individual differences suggest individual treatment of pupils. There may be some merit, therefore, in planning small private faculty offices where teachers may offer individual instruction when it is warranted. Small private offices may also be provided for the guidance counselor, the school psychologist, the school nurse, the speech correctionist, and the teachers for remedial instruction.

Group similarities call for spaces that serve the needs of both small and large groups. It might be advisable for a school district to provide a

[1]Blair et al., *Educational Psychology*, p. 48.

few rooms where a teacher can meet with a half-dozen students who are experiencing similar difficulties in learning. These small spaces could also be utilized for program enrichment activities for more advanced or talented pupils. It might also be practical, for example, to design self-contained elementary grade classrooms so that two small spaces could be formed at one end of the room by use of folding partitions. These small rooms could be utilized for remedial instruction and program enrichment.

THE MULTISTIMULI EFFECT ON THE RETENTION OF LEARNING

Psychological Aspects

Broadly defined, learning is a process which brings about a change in the individual's way of responding as a result of practice or other experience.[12] In learning, the individual responds to various types of stimuli that impinge upon him. The stimulus is always perceived by one or more of his senses. For the most part, such stimuli are perceived visually and aurally. In a few instances, the stimulus may involve the sense of touch and taste; only rarely is the sense of smell employed in the learning process. The multistimuli effect refers to the application of several stimuli to produce a designed change in the individual. The different stimuli utilized in the learning process may vary in form, in time of application, and in technique of application. Educational psychologists have been deeply concerned with the relationship of retention of learning to the type and number of stimuli applied during the learning process itself.[13]

　　Two other laws of learning are related to the strengthening of learning when more than one stimulus enters the learning situation. *The Law of Facilitation:* The strength of a reflex may be increased through the presentation of a second stimulus, which does not itself elicit the response. *The Law of Conditioning of Type R:* If the occurrence of an operant is followed by the presentation of a reinforcing stimulus, the strength is increased.[14] Cronbach also alludes to the importance of reviews of learned knowledge. He says ". . . reviews are required to keep knowledge alive."[15]

　　From the foregoing discussion, it can be inferred that multiple stimuli can improve the retention of learned skills and knowledge. It can also be

[12]Ruch, *Psychology and Life*, p. 297.

[13]Robert M. Gagne, *Conditions of Learning* (New York: Holt, Rinehart and Winston, Inc., 1970), pp. 181–182.

[14]William K. Estes, *Modern Learning Theory* (New York: Appleton-Company-Crofts Inc., 1954), p. 312.

[15]Cronbach, *Educational Psychology*, p. 468.

implied that the effectiveness of the learning is substantially improved if learning experiences are designed so as to expose the learner to several related stimuli during the learning process. Although review was the method most frequently mentioned by psychologists, other techniques could be employed to accomplish the same purpose.

School Facilities for Multistimuli Instruction

School buildings can become more effective tools of education if they expose the pupil to learning experiences that embody several types of stimuli. School facilities might be devised so that students receive the initial learning stimulus through one sense and a second stimulus later through another. For example, an illustrated presentation by the teacher could be followed by a second presentation, one involving the sense of touch and smell, which could be conducted in a specially designed laboratory space. It might also be possible to plan instructional spaces so that learning could be improved by appropriate lighting effects—spot lighting, color, and changes in light intensity—and by the ingenious use of sound effects. Even the atmosphere of a room could be used to add another dimension to learning. For example, it might be quite impressive to raise both the temperature and the humidity in a social studies room in order that students might feel the simulated effect of a tropical climate, a dry climate, a hot and dry atmosphere. The imaginative use of equipment can improve learning by increasing the number of stimuli to which the pupil is exposed. It might be desirable, for example, to introduce a cathode ray oscilloscope and a sound amplifier in a mathematics room so the pupils can see and hear a sine wave.

Repetition of the same group of stimuli represents another aspect of multistimuli effect. It might be possible, in a well-equipped school, for a teacher to record a presentation on videotape and reproduce it later during a review session.

ATTENDING AND LEARNING

Psychological Aspects

The relationship between attention and learning has been recognized for centuries. Not until recently, however, have psychologists explored this relationship scientifically.[16] Their findings have dispelled many previously held notions about attending and the attention span. A few of these misconceptions are still prevalent. Several aspects of attending are presented below from the viewpoint of the educational psychologist.

[16]Robert M. W. Travers, *Educational Psychology* (New York: The Macmillan Co., 1973), pp. 119–121.

The length of time that an individual can concentrate on a single object is extremely short. However, when a problem or activity is involved in the task, the attention span can last for several minutes. Attention span also varies with age. As a child becomes older, his attention span increases.[17] According to Jersild, "Except in response to urgent physical demands, a young child's concentration span tends to be brief. When he fixates an object with his eyes, his regard is likely to be fleeting at first and to lengthen with time."[18] A. G. Hughes points out that "experimenters have shown that we cannot attend to *simple objects* for over a few seconds, about 5 or 6 seconds at a time."[19] This finding seems almost incredible. However, a simple experiment that can be quickly performed by the reader is presented to illustrate this point.

EXPERIMENT

1. Fix attention upon the center of Figure 2.1.
2. Observe closely the perspective or change of perspective that is being perceived.

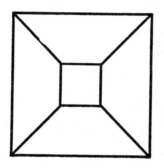

FIGURE 2.1 Attention Span.

It is found that the diagram in Figure 2.1 appears to change in perspective from concave to convex or vice versa every few seconds for most persons performing this test. Psychologists attribute this phenomenon to the length of the attention span of the individual. According to their explanation, Figure 2.1 would appear concave or convex as long as attention is given to it without interruption. When the attention period is terminated, the individual receives another perspective. The crux of this experiment is that attention is fixed upon a *simple object*.

On the other hand, the attention span is increased from a few seconds to a few minutes when the task at hand is more complex. Hughes

[17] Jersild, *Child Psychology*, p. 359.

[18] *Ibid.*, p. 357.

[19] Hughes and Hughes, *Learning and Teaching*, p. 121.

says: "We often say we have concentrated our attention on a particular problem for an hour or two. A little reflection will show us that the object of our attention was by no means the same throughout. We attend first to one aspect of the problem, then to another."[20] Griffith also pointed out that objects in school are more ". . . complex than that encountered by concentrating on a single object. The story being read, for example, moves from word to word and from event to event." Griffith concludes that the attention span for complex objects varies with the kind of material.[21] A. G. Hughes makes an interesting observation regarding young children:

> Young children, being interested in activity and in concrete objects rather than ideas, attend more readily when there is something to see, taste or smell. When they try to attend to ideas of other people expressed in words, they find it necessary to reinforce the listening by looking at or touching the speaker.[22]

And finally, Edwards believed that "the best attention is had with slight distraction."[23] He maintained that "this disturbance seems to be necessary to arouse one to real effort." Edwards offered the rationale that the overcoming of some difficulty brings forth more earnest endeavor on the part of the student. Also, he points out that students should acquire the ability to pay attention to the task at hand in the presence of slight distractions.

School Facilities for Attending and Learning

Since the attention span of individuals is relatively short, variety in the learning situation can improve the quality of the learning. Teaching spaces might be deliberately designed to permit teachers to shift easily and quickly from one type of activity to another. The ease with which such changes can be made encourages the teacher to limit the duration of classroom activities to periods that are well within the attention span of the pupils. It might, for example, be possible to design a classroom with movable partitions and with strategically placed work benches and utilities so that within a few moments the teachers could shift from an activity involving the entire class to one that could be conducted in three or four small groups.

The attention of pupils is improved when the character of the activity alternates between mental and physical efforts. It might be advantageous,

[20]Ibid., p. 120.

[21]Coleman R. Griffith, Psychology Applied to Teaching and Learning (New York: Farrar and Rinehart, Inc., 1939), p. 367.

[22]Hughes and Hughes, Learning and Teaching, p. 121.

[23]A. S. Edwards, The Fundamental Principles of Learning and Study (Baltimore: Warwick and York, 1925), p. 198.

therefore, to design elementary schools with direct access to a well-devel oped outdoor instructional area. The teacher could then alternate between physical and mental activity at will during favorable weather.

It is believed by psychologists that incidental and minor distractions tend to improve learning. There might be some merit, therefore, in providing horizontal strips of fenestration so that pupils could benefit from the incidental distractions provided by nature and man outside of the school building.

TRANSFER OF LEARNING

Psychological Aspects

According to Blair, "Transfer of learning exists whenever a previous learning has influence upon the learning or performance of new responses."[24] In the past, a few erroneous views regarding the transfer of learning have been espoused. It was, for example, incorrectly assumed that instruction in Latin would improve the writing of English. It was also erroneously presumed that geometry teaches the student to reason. Recent studies by educational psychologists have disproved these beliefs and set forth new principles related to the transfer of learning. A few of these findings are presented here.

Effective transfer of learning can exist under certain specific conditions. According to Blair, "Transfer occurs when there is a similarity betwen two activities either in substance or procedure."[25] Cronbach offers some insights into the nature of learning. He states: "Learning is cumulative to a far greater extent than the student realizes."[26]

The similarity between an earlier learning situation and the one to which transfer of learning is desired does not, per se, guarantee a transfer of learning. For such transfer to occur, the student himself must *recognize* the similarity between the two situations. Psychologists have also investigated the conditions required for transfer of learning to occur in relation to stated educational goals. Campanelle points out that "the closer the (learning) activity is to the goal, the more effective the learning. Here again, we see a perfect explanation of association or the connective postulates of Thorndike. It may be a formalized way of stating Thorndike's Law of Contiguity."[27] It can be concluded, therefore, that the greater the simi-

---

[24]Blair et al., *Educational Psychology*, p. 272.

[25]*Ibid.*, p. 292.

[26]Cronbach, *Educational Psychology*, p. 584.

[27]Thomas C. Campanelle, *Psychology of Education* (New York: Chilton Company, 1960), p. 159.

larity between the learning situations and the situation outside of school for which the student is being prepared, the greater will be the transfer of learning.

School Facilities for High Transfer of Learning

The more nearly the learning experience resembles the real situation, the greater the transfer of learning. There may be educational advantages, therefore, to designing the learning situation in school to resemble the situation for which the student is being trained. For example, it might be desirable to design homemaking rooms with an apartment-type, a corridor-type, a galley-type, an L-type, or a U-type kitchen similar to those likely to be found in a home. It might also be worthwhile to construct office practice rooms to resemble secretarial offices. Shops, laboratories, and special rooms that have a counterpart outside of the school might also be made more realistic.

Once the several motor skills that are common to more than one area of learning have been identified, a special room could be designed to train students in these skills. Perhaps this space could be located in a room adjoining the gymnasium play area.

Specific facts, generalizations and broad concepts, and techniques of analyzing situations transfer quite readily. Instructional spaces could be planned so that charts, models, and drawings revealing related facts could be displayed in the classroom over relatively long periods of time. It might also be possible, for example, to strengthen the retention and transfer of broad concepts, if such generalizations were taped and later reproduced in the classroom as part of review sessions. Techniques of analyzing situations could be videotaped and shown later to improve learnings that are transferable.

READINESS FOR LEARNING OR ACTION

Psychological Aspects

The principle of readiness is perhaps one of the most fundamental considerations in both teaching and learning. Usually associated with the learner, readiness is also applicable to the teacher, the school administrator, the board of education, and even to the citizens in a community. For the purposes of this presentation, however, the principle of readiness is applied only to the learner. Educational psychologists have spent a great deal of time, effort, and energy in exploring the numerous conditions that promote a readiness for learning. Only a few of their findings are mentioned in this presentation.

Readiness is a rather complex concept that does not readily lend itself to a simple definition. According to Simpson:

> In the broad sense of the term, readiness to learn requires that the child be prepared not only in the mental prerequisites—materials of the curriculum—but also in the emotional, social and physical prerequisites . . . Lack of all-around readiness for learning constitutes a formidable barrier to a child's efficiency in school.[28]

Readiness is determined partly by the physical, social, emotional, and intellectual development of an individual. To be ready to learn, therefore, the individual must be in a state of readiness in other interrelated respects. Blair, Jones, and Simpson add another dimension to the concept of readiness: "Children are more ready to respond to (instructional) material which meets their needs and fits their already established interests."[29] A. G. Hughes approaches the matter of readiness from a different, but interesting, point of view. Human beings have an inborn desire to learn, to query, and to explore; accordingly, Hughes asserts that "the best time to teach children is when they feel the need for being taught."[30] This point of view is related to the belief that a child should not be "pushed into" a learning situation, but ushered into it when he is ready to learn.

Cronbach deals extensively with the topic of readiness. He conceives the problem of readiness very broadly as one of development of readiness, identification of individual differences in readiness, and the assessment of readiness. Each aspect of the problem, as stated, has certain implications for the school plant planner. Cronbach points out that student readiness involves not only readiness for certain skills and knowledge but also the situation and environment in which the student finds himself. He states, "Readiness is not merely for certain subject-matter. The learner is ready or unready for the total learning situation . . ."[31]

School Facilities that Nurture Readiness

Readiness for learning can be accelerated by providing for suitable pupil activities in a school building. Since the state of readiness for learning varies among pupils, there might be a substantial advantage in designing a school building for nongraded classes. Designing spaces for elementary

[28]Robert G. Simpson, *Educational Psychology* (New York: J. B. Lippincott, 1949), p. 153.

[29]Blair et al., *Educational Psychology*, p. 128.

[30]Hughes and Hughes, *Learning and Teaching*, p. 357.

[31]Cronbach, *Educational Psychology*, p. 149.

schools in clusters of four rooms, for example, would centralize four grade levels in one area. Specially planned spaces for instruction of emotionally disturbed and socially immature children might be of great value. And finally, it might be advisable to include flexible spaces that can be subdivided into smaller spaces in which pupils may begin new learning experiences as soon as they are ready for them. The pneumatic partition is admirably suited for this purpose. Newly formed spaces could be used by small groups of pupils who become ready for experiences in independent project work, music appreciation, and independent reading. This flexibility also enables the teacher to match the learning experiences of the pupil to his readiness for such experiences (Figure 2.2).

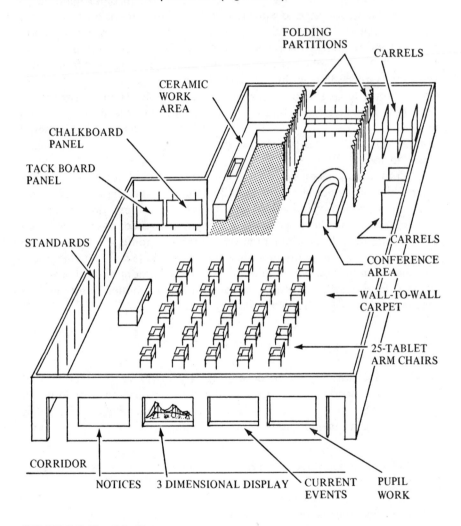

FIGURE 2.2 Flexible Spaces.

MOTIVATION

Psychological Aspects

Extrinsic motivation.   Extrinsic motivation for learning exists when the forces motivating the pupil bear no inherent relationship to the task to be learned. In school, pupils may be extrinsically energized by report cards, honor rolls, gold stars, eligibility for the athletic team, recognition, etc.

Intrinsic motivation.   Intrinsic motivation for learning occurs when the energizing force stems from the desire of the pupil to learn the task for its own sake. Intrinsic motivation, therefore, requires that the teacher build interest in the material to be studied. According to Ruch, ". . . both learning and remembering tend to be better when the motivation is intrinsic."[32]

In practice, both extrinsic and intrinsic motivation play an important part in the learning process. Although intrinsic motivation produces a higher quality of learning, extrinsic motivation may often supply the spark that leads to fruitful learning.

Blair, Jones, and Simpson conceive motivation as those "forces which energize and direct behavior." They also point out that, contrary to widespread belief, the teacher does not motivate the learner. They continue: "Motivation, contrary to popular usage of the term, is not a bag of tricks the teacher uses to produce learning."[33] Thus, motivation is not something that is done to the learner but a force within him that impels him toward a certain goal. Motivation occurs when a person endeavors to satisfy a certain need. In this regard, the school plays an important part in causing pupils to learn of needs that would never have developed otherwise. The importance of motivating in the learning process is strongly emphasized by Symonds, who asserts, "A child learns only when he is motivated."[34] In describing motivation, Woodruff explains, "A motive is any condition within the learner (1) that arouses and sustains activity. (2) It is always within the learner and never exists apart from his own mental process. (3) It is not put there by the teacher, but grows within the person as a direct result of his experience throughout life."[35]

School Facilities that Promote Motivation

School facilities can be designed to promote the growth and development of both extrinsic and intrinsic motivation. Extrinsic motivation can be stimu-

[32]Ruch, *Psychology and Life*, p. 326.

[33]Blair et al., *Educational Psychology*, p. 198.

[34]Percival M. Symonds, *Education Has to Learn From Psychology* (New York: Bureau of Publications, Teachers College, Columbia University, 1958), p. 1.

[35]Asahel D. Woodruff, *The Psychology of Teaching*, 3rd Edition (Greenwood Press., Westport, Conn., 1974), pp. 244–245.

lated by providing situations in which the pupil enjoys a feeling of accomplishment, recognition, or approval. In this connection, there might be some merit in placing three-dimensional displays along the corridors where the work of pupils may be exhibited. An "honor bulletin" could be installed in the main lobby for display of notices, articles, and materials that reflect pupil achievement.

Intrinsic motivation can also be significantly influenced by the design of a school building. Instructional spaces could be designed to facilitate the construction of specially prepared teaching materials, and the use of electronic instructional devices and audiovisual equipment. The specific means of stimulating intrinsic motivation are limited only by the ingenuity of the school planners and by the creativity of the teacher after the spaces are completed. There might be some educational advantage in exposing selected units of the mechanical and electrical system of a school plant so that students could examine and study these applications of the scientific principles presented to them in the classroom. The interest of the student might also be aroused, for example, if he could see automatic controlling devices at work by looking at one or two units through a clear plastic cover. The application of electronics could be emphasized if the public address and televison systems were not enclosed in opaque boxes. A tour of the boiler room might stimulate interest in chemistry, physics, electronics, or cybernetics. It might be feasible to leave certain important structural design elements of the school exposed to view so that students could see an application of the principles of static equilibrium and the various techniques employed in structural engineering.

THE ANOMALOUS STUDENT

Psychological Aspects

As mentioned earlier, individual differences exist throughout the entire spectrum of human characteristics. However, some characteristics are common to most people. Many practices in mass education are predicated upon the presence of human similarities and upon group arrangements that reduce the range of certain individual differences within that group. Unless an individual is abnormal, this type of grouping is perhaps an acceptable compromise in universal education.

Psychologists are becoming more and more concerned with the extremes of abnormality—the slow learner and the gifted, the pupil who matures slowly and the one who develops very rapidly, the student who is socially retarded and the one who is socially advanced. There is also a great awareness of special learning difficulties of individuals who deviate greatly from a so-called average or norm. Pupils may be slow in learning because they lack ability, interest, or experience. Learners may not re-

spond normally to schoolwork because of sensory or speech defects, or because of orthopedic problems or social-emotional maladjustment.

The problem of the anomalous pupil is quite serious in the public
schools. Blair, Jones, and Simpson comment on the magnitude of the problem:

> "The extent of this condition is indicated by the fact that approximately 14%
> of twenty-four million children from ages five to seventeen are not in
> school."[36]

School Facilities for the Anomalous Student

School buildings can be planned to meet the special needs of students with
various types of physical impediments. School exits, thresholds, elevators,
walks, and loading zones might be designed for the needs of the paraple-
gic. School planners might also concentrate on the special requirements of
the pupil with a heart condition, the one who has partial sight, and the one
who is hard-of-hearing. For example, it might be possible to install a low-
power broadcast system in the school so that pupils with hearing difficulties might hear the teacher through the use of transistor-type receivers. In
this case, a pupil's mobility would not be limited to the confines of his
desk.

It might be possible to provide carrels and autotutorial aids for the
slow learner and for the gifted pupil. Self-instruction could supplement the
formal instruction received by the student. One small room adjoining each
major type of instructional space in a secondary school could be used for
remedial instruction for slow learners and for project-type activities for
talented students. There is also a need for well-equipped and appropriately designed spaces for remedial instruction in speech, reading, and
physical development.

ACTIVITY AND LEARNING

Psychological Aspects

Psychologists believe that purposeful activity is an essential element of the
total learning process. In discussing the need to teach a wide variety of
meaningful concepts in order to stimulate discovery, Schwartz points out
that "To teach these various concepts to learners, you can provide a multitude of materials for manipulation and subsequent discovery."[37] Educators
have been long aware that students should be given the opportunity to explore and learn by discovery. The learning situation should include a wide

[36]Blair et al., *Educational Psychology*, p. 332.

[37]Lita Linzer Schwartz, *Educational Psychology*, 2nd Edition, (Holbrook Press, Inc.,
Boston 1977), p. 277.

array of educational materials and equipment that will arouse the curiosity of the students and encourage them to probe into the unknown. In this connection, Cronbach offers a few words of wisdom; he says, "You cannot learn by discovery if you fail to discover."[38] This observation has deep implications for school plant planning.

Another aspect of the learning process concerns the relationship of activity to the quality of the learning that occurs. Skills must be learned while being put into practice if retention of learning is to be strengthened. In this connection, Woodruff states that "Skills are acquired by drill or practice. . . . The higher the skill sought the more drill or practice is required."[39] In discussing the goal that students should be motivated to like school activities for their own sake, Blair, Jones, and Simpson observe that "Only when the school offers activities that satisfy the needs of all the pupils will this goal have been approached."[40] Psychologists are also in fairly good agreement that students have a need for activity that stimulates curiosity, increases bodily movements, and promotes an interest in exploration, games, and problem-solving. Thus, pupil activity serves to satisfy a basic need and results in improved learning. Griffith maintained that activity also serves to increase the efficiency of learning.

> . . . Too much emphasis cannot be laid on the fact that learning is promoted by action. It follows that the speed and precision of learning would become more effective in direct proportion to the amount of activity that is aroused during the process."[41]

Pupil activities may supply experiences that reward them and thus intensify the learning. The introduction of relevant pupil activities in the learning process promotes learning by discovery and encourages learners to explore and probe more deeply into the unknown.

School Facilities that Promote Activity Programs and Meaningful Learning

School buildings can be planned to facilitate *activity-type* learning and thus to lend greater meaning to the "book-type" learning found in all schools. Spaces for instruction in subject-matter areas, such as language arts, mathematics, and social studies could be designed for activity-oriented learning experiences. For example, the mathematics room could be designed with a work and project counter, including hot and cold running water, for pupils working on the development of mathematical surfaces. The room might include features that facilitate project work in trigo-

---

[38]Cronbach, *Educational Psychology*, p. 548.
[39]Woodruff, *The Psychology of Teaching*, pp. 252–253.
[40]Blair et al., *Educational Psychology*, p. 199.
[41]Griffith, *Psychology Applied to Teaching and Learning*, p. 202.

nometry and in wave mechanics. And special attention could be given to planning a space that strengthens mathematical instruction in probability and solid geometry through pupil projects. Also, school planners might try to design teaching spaces that encourage the use of the discovery method, which often calls for some type of pupil activity. A wide variety of instructional supplies and equipment and well-located and properly designed space in which to store them are essential in any activity-centered program.

FATIGUE AND LEARNING

Psychological Aspects

Psychologists have found that, contrary to common belief, mental fatigue simply reflects the somatic or physical conditions that produce it.[42] Physical fatigue stems from the expenditure of additional energy by the individual to overcome physical obstacles or disturbances. Mental fatigue may, indeed, be caused by physical fatigue, but it may also be the result of a "feeling of fatigue" which stems primarily from psychological or pedagogical sources. Regardless of its cause, psychologists agree that fatigue is deleterious to learning. The causes of fatigue are basically physical, psychological, or pedagogical.

Physical causes of fatigue.   Pupil fatigue can be induced by an improper visual environment, including illumination of low intensity, improper brightness differences, glare in any form, nonuniform distribution of light, poor sight lines, and viewing angles that produce distortion. Unsuitable and uncomfortable equipment also produces fatigue. The most frequent sources of discomfort are improperly selected and adjusted tables and seats. Instructional equipment and work spaces that are not well designed add to student fatigue. And finally, "distracting noise contributes to a feeling of fatigue among many school children."[43] Improper temperature and ventilation are also sources of discomfort that induce fatigue.

Pedagogical causes of fatigue.   Ill-conceived school curricula contribute significantly to fatigue or a "feeling of fatigue." Textbook-centered programs, together with a multitude of other school conventions, can produce either a psychological or a pedagogical basis for fatigue.[44] Lecture and catechetical methods are instructional techniques that frequently cause fatigue.

[42]Simpson, *Educational Psychology*, p. 317.

[43]George Hartman, "Effect of Noise in School Children," *Journal of Educational Psychology*, 27 (1946), 149–160.

[44]Simpson, *Educational Psychology*, p. 321.

Psychological causes of fatigue.   Psychologically induced fatigue has its roots in monotony, boredom, lack of intrinsic motivation, and learning tasks that are not matched to the readiness, interests, and basic needs of the pupil. Teachers can also prevent unnecessary fatigue by designing experiences that will provide pupils with a sense of self-confidence and security.

Depletion of oxygen and fatigue.   Research does not support the popular belief that fatigue is caused by a depletion of oxygen. A study conducted in England indicated that fatigue is not caused by depletion of oxygen in the classroom and the accumulation of excessive amounts of carbon dioxide. It is known, however, that a high concentration of carbon dioxide under certain conditions of temperature and humidity can induce drowsiness, which adversely affects learning.

School Facilities that Reduce Fatigue and Improve Learning

Every design feature of a school building that lessens fatigue may help improve learning. Any increase in the comfort and convenience of teachers and pupils tends to reduce fatigue. School planners should design schools with suitably controlled thermal environments, quiet and well-regulated ventilating systems, good visual environments with appropriate brightness balances and high-quality illumination, and attractively decorated interiors. Schools should be free from "cross-talk" (through ventilating systems), fan noises, and distracting sounds and vibrations.

Psychological fatigue results from boredom and monotony, both of which can be diminished in instructional spaces that are uniquely designed to stimulate pupil interest in the subjects being taught in these rooms. Attention might be concentrated on shape, color, flexibility of teaching activity and essential instructional materials.

GROUPING FOR EFFECTIVE INSTRUCTION

Psychological Aspects

For many decades educators and educational psychologists have tried to discover the optimal group size for effective instruction, but still they do not agree as to what it is. The practice of teaching pupils in groups of twenty-five to thirty is being challenged. There is a growing belief among both educators and psychologists that there is no magic number indicating the perfect or best group or class size. On the contrary, there is a significant trend toward pupil groups that vary in size in accordance with the purpose of the group or the type of instruction to be offered. Groupings in the schools of the future will not be formed solely on the basis of chronological age, but will be influenced to some extent by matters such as ability, social maturity, pupil readiness, interests, and aptitudes.

The principle of least-group size.   According to Thelan, the optimal group size should be: '. . . the smallest group in which it is possible to have represented as a functional level all the socialization and achievement skills required for the particular learning activity at hand.'"[45] This principle underlies many changes anticipated in the schools of tomorrow. In effect, it postulates that pupil groupings may vary from two to several hundred students. By inference, "groups" might consist of one pupil. Grouping, according to this principle, is not determined by a conventional group size or the subgroups within a traditional class, but rather by the function and purpose and social characteristics of the group.

School Facilities for Effective Group Instruction

The concept of least-group size demands appropriately designed spaces for each type of grouping that is possible under this principle. It might be educationally desirable to plan a school for the instruction of groups in excess of 100 students. It might even be possible to accomplish this grouping electronically. For example, four quasi-conventional classrooms could be located contiguously in a sector of a circle, each separated from the other by a wall including a double-glazed vision strip. Panels of chalkboard or tackboard could be installed to slide vertically in front of the vision strips. Further, each room could be subdivided by a partition. For large-group instruction, the panels could be raised, microphones could be activated in each room, and television receivers could be operated over a closed-circuit television system. The large-group effect would be enhanced by joining the four spaces together visually through the use of vision strips, and aurally by means of sound amplifiers. A student in any room, therefore, could see and hear what is taking place in any other room. The teacher could be located near the center of the circle, visible to all of the rooms directly and through television. When it is desired to instruct pupils in groups of twenty or twenty-five, the panels could be lowered and the microphones would be deactivated. For teaching smaller groups, the folding partitions could be closed in any of the classrooms, as shown in Figure 2.3.

Smaller spaces for groups of five or six students might also be planned. These small instructional spaces could be located in the instructional materials and information resource center where they can be easily supervised.

[45]H. A. Thelan, "Group Dynamics in Instruction—The Principle of Least Group Size," *The Social Review*, 57 (1949), 139–148.

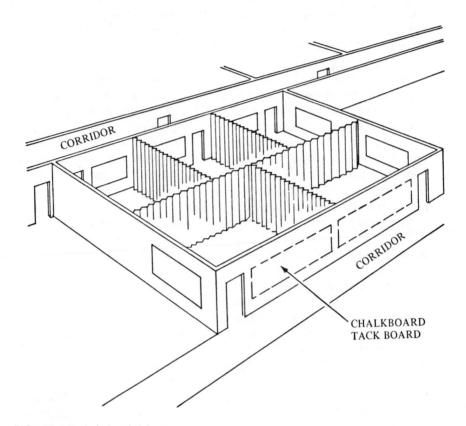

FIGURE 2.3 Subdividable Spaces.

INCIDENTAL LEARNING

A great deal of learning takes place unconsciously outside of the formal setting of the classroom. The potential value of this phenomenon is yet to be realized in our schools. According to Shaffer, "The concept of unconscious learning represents a very great discovery of modern psychology, for which we are mainly indebted to Sigmund Freud."[46] Individuals are capable of learning without realizing that learning is taking place. Under certain circumstances, incidental learning can become a significant supplement to formal learning.[47]

[46]Lawrence Shaffer and Edward Shoben, Jr., The Psychology of Adjustment (Boston: Houghton Mifflin, 1956), p. 139.

[47]See Francis J. Kelley et al., Educational Psychology (Columbus, Ohio: Merrill Publishing Co., 1969), p. 170, and Michael J. A. Howe, Understanding School Learning (New York: Harper and Row, 1972), pp. 85–91.

School Facilities for Incidental Learning

Incidental learning represents an educational bonus in any school. The ingenious design of a school building can stimulate "unconscious" learning immeasurably. For example, in designing a school, scientific instruments could be stored so that they can be viewed from the corridor. A brief description of the equipment placed beside the instrument would allow students to learn about Geiger counters, sphygmomanometers, Tesla coils, van de Graaf machines, etc. Cakes, together with recipes, could be shown in the homemaking area; maps and photographs related to current events, together with a commentary on the happenings of the day, could be displayed near the social science rooms; new books could be exhibited near the library; poems and notable quotations might be shown near English rooms.

It might also be practical to design chalkboards in panels that slide on tracks so that each panel could be moved vertically and horizontally. This arrangement would permit a teacher to write basic principles and diagrams on a panel during the initial presentation, after which he could store it in a location where it would remain for the rest of the week, month, semester, or year. Each time the student casually glances at it, he will be reminded subconsciously of the principle as it was originally presented.

CHAPTER 3

Educational Technology, Promising Concepts, and Innovative Practices

It can be assumed, *a priori*, that the design of educational facilities reflects the educational thinking and architectural philosophy at the time when school facilities are proposed, planned, conceived, and constructed. The end product at any given time represents a blending of prevailing architectural concepts, dominant educational practices, and promising curricular innovations. The well-planned educational facility not only provides for the accepted and conventional educational practices that are widespread at that time but also includes features that can accommodate a few of the more promising foreseeable educational concepts of the future. School plant planners should consider the innovations and practices that are described in this chapter as well as others that may be brought to their attention during the design stages of new or modernized school buildings.

CREATIVE ADVANCES IN EDUCATIONAL TECHNOLOGY

The number and variety of electronic teaching devices available for a multitude of educational uses are amazingly large. One of the first forms of teaching aids appeared at the turn of the twentieth century in the form of the arc lattern. This projector was extraordinarily simple. It consisted of a slide holder, a relatively large lens, and two rods of carbon that produced a very bright electric arc. While this bulky device worked fairly well, it was noisy, not conveniently portable,and somewhat troublesome to operate.

The next generation of teaching aids marked the beginning of the widespread use of supplementary instructional devices. The development of high-intensity light bulbs inaugurated a new era in projection techniques. The arc lantern was soon replaced by the slide projector, and the movie projector became a common piece of educational equipment. Most schools owned at least one movie projector, which was shared by several teachers in a school building. During this same period, a group of enterprising scientists invented the vacuum tube, which made it possible to produce a powerful distortion-free record player suitable for classroom use. Enterprising educators exploited these relatively simple educational tools to the maximum.

Today, electronic teaching devices have become extremely sophisticated and highly specialized. A few of them are programmable and many are completely automated. Once the starting button is depressed, the equipment requires no further attention by the user. To be sure, the movie projector and slide projector have been significantly improved. They are lighter in weight, simpler to use, and brighter in intensity of image. While the record player is still widely used, the tape recorder-player is gradually replacing it in the classroom. The ingenious overhead projector is supplementing the chalkboard, and its application is far more effective than the chalkboard in the presentation of materials in a sequential pattern. Also, the capability of superimposing transparent overlays on the overhead projector to depict changes in situation, statistics, or statements makes it far superior to the traditional chalkboard in many respects.

The most exciting electronic devices, however, have yet to be fully exploited. To be sure, educators are aware of their capabilities and potential, but their future use depends upon the adaptability of the teachers and upon the ingenuity of school administrators to provide staffing, equipment, and the necessary software. The more promising electronic teaching aids are discussed in the following sections.

COMPUTERS

Little did George Boole, a mathematics professor in Ireland, realize that his "Investigation in the Laws of Thought" in 1854, establishing formal logic and creating a new algebra known as Boolean algebra,[1] would ever have any practical application in the real world. He and other mathematicians of that era were primarily engaged in developing abstract algebra. It was not until the middle of the twentieth century that Boolean algebra attained great prominence in the development of computers. His work was rediscovered and applied by scientists and engineers in designing complex logic circuits for modern digital computers.

Computer Development and Its Relation to Education

The computer is well recognized as one of the most sophisticated electronic marvels of the twentieth century. Its development has been continuous,

[1]Carl B. Boyer, A History of Mathematics (New York: John Wiley and Sons, 1968), pp. 634–635.

rapid, and unparalleled over a period of several decades. In the beginning, the digital computer was simply an instrument for computing numerical data at phenomenal speeds using the binary system of numbers. But, with the introduction of programmed logic circuits, the computer has become one of the most versatile instruments in the world. It is ideally suited for educational purposes. It is capable of drawing diagrams on paper or displaying them on a video screen. It can present learning material to the student. It can pose questions and supply answers orally on a video screen as well as on paper. It can generate tests, correct them, and prepare and print a diagnostic report for both the student and the teacher. It is admirably equipped to maintain a continuous and up-to-date record of student progress. And it is well-adapted for monitoring and prescribing the learning experiences of each student on an individual basis.

The computer can perform many routine educational tasks flawlessly, efficiently, and at super-human speeds, but it is pedagogically inadequate and unsatisfactory in some respects. In its present stage of development, it is extremely unlikely that the computer of today will ever replace the teacher. After all, the computer is nothing more than a piece of sophisticatedly designed hardware. It has no judgment, no feelings, and no heart. It is simply an electronic aid that slavishly responds to the instructions that were programmed into it by some human being. The computer itself is stupid. It is never more creative nor more knowledgeable than the human being who gave it its instructions through a process called "computer programming." Consequently, the computer becomes an invaluable instructional aid only when it is properly and imaginatively programmed by a person who is a master teacher in his or her field and also very knowledgeable about the learning process, the learners for whom the program is designed, and the capabilities of the computer itself.

Size and Capacity of Computers

The early computers were generally designed as large computers. As the state of the art developed, smaller and less versatile computers were developed for a wide variety of specialized uses. Large and small computers have an important place in education. The uses of each type will be discussed in the latter part of this chapter.

The large or macro-computer is the ultimate in digital computers. It can accomplish tasks that transcend human capability from the standpoint of speed, memory, information retrieval, sequential thought processes, and control systems. The macro-computer has tremendous memory capabilities and a reaction time that is measured in "millionths of seconds." The macro-computer is so fast that it can outrun its output capabilities. For example, it can process huge amounts of data in short periods of time. Since its output is much slower than the computer unit, the output from the computer unit is stored on memory banks and subsequently released to the output devices over a period of several hours or days depending upon the speed of the computer, its storage capacity, and the volume of the material. For educational purposes, the phenomenal speed of the computer makes it possible for the same computer to be serving a large number of students at what appears to be the same time through a process known as "time sharing." The computer is so fast that students are seldom aware that the computer is putting them on a "temporary hold" while it is serving other students. The sections describing "Computer Assisted Instructior" and "Computer Managed Instruction" apply primarily to large computers.

The smaller computers known as micro-computers are attracting the attention of many educators. Although their capability and speed are quite restricted compared with those found in macro-computers, their potential for individualized instruction is extremely promising. The use of small computers as educational tools are discussed in the next section.

Micro-Computers for Instructional Purposes

As indicated earlier, the micro-computer is a relatively recent development in computer technology. The units are small, completely programmable, highly versatile, and potentially of great value to education. The speed, memory bank, number of logic circuits, and programming capacity of micro-computers are limited but adequate for educational uses. And, if disc capabilities are added to the system, micro-computers can be used as teaching aids for both Computer Assisted Instruction (CAI) and Computer Managed Instruction (CMI) in much the same way as full-scale computers.

One of the most appealing advantages of micro-computers is cost. A basic unit with a 16 K RAM (Random Access Memory), plus tape cassette and a video monitor costs about the same as two high-quality electric typewriters. A second desirable feature of micro-computers is their adaptability for increased capacity and expanded functions. For example, the 16 K RAM unit mentioned above can be readily expanded internally to 32 K RAM. Its memory can be greatly increased by acquiring a disc expansion system. The output can be printed on paper by attaching a printer to the unit. Obviously, the more accessories and capacity that are added to the system, the higher will be the cost. Thus, the cost of a micro-computer can range from the price of two electric typewriters to that of seven such typewriters. For educational purposes a 32 K RAM unit with a printer, video monitor, and one mini disc drive would be quite adequate. If the programmed computer material used by the students is not too lengthy or complicated a 16 K unit would suffice.

The space required for a complete micro-computer system is quite modest. The keyboard, video monitor, printer, and cassette units require about ten square feet of flat table space. Disc drives may be placed on the floor under the table. Each drive requires about one-half of a square foot of floor space. A semicircular or V-shaped table should be provided so that the user is conveniently located with respect to the keyboard, printer, and cassette player. The table should be about thirty inches high and include knee space for the operator. In general, mini-computers are made up of a number of independent units, each of which requires a separate power outlet. It is suggested that at least six 120 Volt A.C. outlets be provided on a strip in each carrel where mini-computers will be located. In designing carrels for mini-computers, it should be remembered that students also need working surfaces for recording data and writing reports. Accordingly, it is suggested that an additional six square feet of flat surface at table height be provided for these functions. And, finally, school facility planners should pay some attention to temperature and humidity in spaces where micro-computers are in operation. The temperature in such spaces should range between 60 degrees Fahrenheit and 85 degrees Fahrenheit. The micro-computer generates a relatively modest amount of heat which must be dissipated, but the primary problem is caused by the effect that temperature and humidity have on the cassette tapes that are often used for loading and saving computer programs. During periods of low humidity, sparks are often generated by the movement of people in contact with substances that produce electrostatic charges, such as carpeting and some plastic materials used for furniture and furnishings. The discharge of electrostatic electricity introduces unwanted impulses into the computer through its tapes and the system breaks down. Either the loaded program is faulty or the computer "freezes," in which case the computer becomes inoperative and the entire loading procedure must be repeated from the beginning. When the temperature falls between the range mentioned above, the air can absorb and retain more of the moisture generated by the occupants of a room and the humidity problem is substantially reduced. If the room is ventilated, the relative humidity should be kept above 50 percent.

Some of the early model micro-computers produced annoying television interference on some channel frequencies. The manufacturers of such equipment have since taken steps to correct this problem. Nevertheless, as a precaution, it is suggested that micro-computers that are to be purchased for school use be checked with respect to television interference on sets located in the same room or in any of the learning spaces adjoining the micro-computer center. For the most part, well-shielded closed circuit television systems are less likely to be affected by micro-computer radiation, but it is far better to eliminate the interference at the source than to try to cope with it after it is generated.

The micro-computer, like the large computer discussed earlier, is an ideal teaching aid for individualized instruction. While the full size computer has a vast memory for storing educational materials that are later retrieved and utilized by students on demand, the micro-computer can perform essentially the same function through the use of several diskettes. Individualized educational programs can be programmed into the micro-computer for each student in relation to the specific needs of such student, utilizing the same instructional management techniques that are associated with large computers. These and other computer-oriented teaching strategies are discussed in detail in a subsequent section of this chapter entitled "Computers for Personalized Instruction."

Computers for Data Processing and Information Retrieval

In addition to its use as a teaching aid discussed in the preceding section, the computer has the capacity of storing enormous amounts of information that can be retrieved on a highly selective basis. The computer is inherently capable of locating and reproducing millions of bits of stored information almost instantaneously. If desired, it cannot only locate but also process such stored data in any way that it is programmed to do so before it appears as output either on the cathode ray tube or on its printer. And it performs this often tedious task on command and with lightning speed.

This computer capability can be exploited advantageously by educators in many ways. The use of the computer for information retrieval and data processing in education is limited only by the ingenuity and creativity of the computer programmer, and the extent of his knowledge and understanding of teaching, curriculum development, and educational administration. The computer is ideal for assembling pertinent information about any student for guidance and job placement purposes. It is useful for providing teachers with an analysis of student achievement, and noting strengths and weaknesses. It is an excellent device for scoring standardized tests and printing out a diagnostic summary for each student. It is helpful in making longitudinal studies on student progress in the basic skills. It is well-suited for assembling health information about a student for use by the school nurse, guidance counselors, athletic directors and coaches. And finally, such computers are most useful for administrative purposes for such tasks as accounting, payroll-making, inventory control, purchasing, maintenance scheduling, and budgetary estimates for the foreseeable future. There are also a few less common administrative applications, such as projecting future school enrollments and determining whether it is more advantageous to modernize an existing school building or to abandon it as a school facility. These, and other applications are left to the discretion of local school administrators and their respective computer programmers.

It is not suggested, however, that this complicated information retrieval system be installed in a proposed school facility at this time. The system is not judged to be cost-effective in its present stage of development. The potential application of this system is mentioned only from the standpoint of making provision for its possible use in the future. For the present, it is recommended that a space of about 150 square feet be provided for the computer and related storage and that approximately 15 percent of the carrels in the instructional resources center be designed to accommodate a computer terminal unit, which is about the size of a large dictionary, in addition to space normally provided for other functions associated with such carrels. These special carrels should be wired for sound and television. The cost of computers is dropping very rapidly and the day may soon be at hand when computers can be used economically as a part of an information retrieval and data processing system. The cost of some micro-computers with large memory capability is already within the reach of a few school districts.

VIDEOTAPE RECORDERS

Scientists and engineers have recently succeeded in recording television programs on magnetic tape. This development augurs well for education. Educators are just becoming aware of the potential of this electronic break-through. At first glance, it appears to be another form of recording images for showing at a later time, similar to photographic films that produce mo-tion pictures. To be sure, both of these methods record images for future showing. But this is the point at which the similarity ends. Videotape re-corders capture images on magnetic tape and can reproduce them instan-taneously. No processing is required. This procedure provides immediate feedback that can strongly reinforce learning in some selected situations. For example, the process of heating a beaker of water, bringing the liquid to a boil, and converting the substance from liquid to vapor can be re-corded on videotape during a science demonstration by the teacher. The televison camera could also include in its view a thermometer whose bulb is immersed in the water and a stop watch that was started at the moment the heat was applied. Immediately following the demonstration, the teacher could "play back" the tape in slow motion. Students could see the formation of bubbles within the water, their movement toward the surface of the liquid, and then bursting into the atmosphere, including the effects of surface tension. They could notice time and temperature at which all of these phenomena occur. There are many other ways in which videotape recorders can be used in order to give greater meaning to learning ex-perience. This educational tool has countless applications in the learning process. It can also be used by teachers in making a self-analysis of their teaching techniques and methods of delivery. Creative teachers and imaginative curriculum directors can use this relatively new educational tool very advantageously for the improvement of both teaching and learn-ing.

CABLE TELEVISION

In addition to broadcasting television signals through the air, signals can also be transmitted by cable. At the present time, atmospheric transmission of television signals is generally confined to thirteen channels in the very high frequency range (VHF) and eighty-three channels are available in the ultra-high frequency (UHF) range. Most of the programs in these frequencies are free to the public. A few channels, however, are allocated to a system known as "Pay Television." In these instances, the broadcast signal is scrambled. It can be unscrambled only by those subscribers who rent the unscrambler from the broadcaster. Cable television, on the other hand, transmits its television through shielded cables. In order to receive a television program, the subscriber to this service must have a direct cable connection on his own television set. This system has a number of features that are worthy of note. First of all, the system is private. Only those television sets attached to the cable can receive the television signals. And secondly, many programs can be transmitted simultaneously over the same cable. Herein lies the great advantage in the use of cable television for educational purposes. One cable can deliver many television programs to any school facility.

The implications of cable television for education are quite clear. Since numerous television programs can be received at the same time, several subject areas can be served simultaneously. Or, a number of different levels of the same subject can be viewed by groups of students corresponding to the level for which the television presentation is desired. It should also be mentioned that if a school facility is wired for closed circuit television, each program can be channeled to the proper classroom once it is received by the master television set which is attached to the cable. New and modernized school facilities should make provision for cable television by providing a closed circuit television system throughout the building and planning a small room where the cable television signals will be received from the cable and be distributed to selected parts of the building.

TEACHING DEVICES FOR INDIVIDUALIZED INSTRUCTION

The concept of individualized instruction is undoubtedly as old as teaching itself. As stated in detail in Chapter 1, a great deal of the teaching of the Greeks during the Hellenistic period was conducted on an individualized and small-group basis. As education became more universal, however, the need for teaching in groups became an economic necessity. The optimum size of the group or class is open to serious question and has often become a controversial item in discussions between teachers and boards of education. With the development of new instructional aids, the movement toward personalized instruction[2] has been gaining momentum at an accelerated pace.

The educational technology has reached the point at which teaching can be conducted on an individual basis within the economic ability of

[2]Basil Castaldi, "Personalized Instruction and Programs," CEFP Council of Educational Facility Planners Journal, January 1981.

most school districts. As this trend develops, however, the teacher will certainly not be replaced by some electronic device. The role of the teacher, of course, will be changed somewhat. The teacher will be teaching students instead of classes. For those who would advocate the increased automation of the teaching-learning process, a word of explanation is in order. Educational hardware is not likely to ever replace the teacher. Regardless of their degree of sophistication, computers or similar electronic devices are quite impersonal. They all lack the ability of exercising judgment at strategic points during the teaching-learning process. It is true, of course, that the computer is capable of decision making under predetermined conditions. Unfortunately, these conditions are frequently programmed into it by a human being who knows neither the student nor the specific circumstances under which he or she is required to learn. On the other hand, the use of educational hardware can substantially improve the quality of learning in our schools by allowing the teacher more time for personalized instruction, while the programmed educational aids can provide much of the routine material for a large number of learners at individualized rates.

The widespread interest in individualized instruction is also continuing in directions that do not require special educational hardware. While these approaches are not entirely new, renewed efforts are being made by innovative teachers to make learning more meaningful for the student. This thrust takes the form of negotiated learning and independent study, modular scheduling, team teaching, and prescriptive learning. These and other innovative approaches are treated at length in this chapter.

COMPUTERS FOR PERSONALIZED INSTRUCTION

For some time the use of the computer for various types of educational applications has been researched in depth. There is no question whatsoever that the computer is most effective in dealing with the administrative aspects of education. It has great value in producing class lists, scheduling students, computing grade point averages, and in identifying students on various criteria, such as students coming from minority groups, students who have dropped out of school, those who meet certain criteria for academic honors, and those who have failed two or more courses and should receive special attention. These are only a few examples of what the computer can do in educational administration. The actual number of applications depends upon the size of the school and the school district policies regarding the extent to which individualized attention will be given to students.

The instructional uses of the computer are currently focused on two basic applications. The first is called Computer Assisted Instruction (CAI), which is an extremely effective method of providing personalized instruction. Under this concept, the teacher becomes directly involved in the instruction only when the computer has failed to register reasonable student progress. The student may also seek teacher assistance whenever he feels the need for it, regardless of the instructions given to him by the computer. The other prevalent educational use of the computer is in the management of instruction. This application comes under the label of Computer Managed Instruction (CMI). As will be seen later, this application has a much more promising future than CAI.

The most exciting utilization of the computer, however, is still in the embryonic stage. The computer, with its vast memory and selecting capability, is an ideal device for generating individualized tests for students. The random-generated test is a basic ingredient in the development of personalized instructional systems based on student performance objectives. Once the performance objectives have been determined, test questions are formulated, designed specifically to determine whether or not one or more objectives have been achieved by the student. Once the validity of the testing has been determined, using appropriate statistical methods, the student can take and retake tests designed to measure a given level of achievement without the repetition of specific test questions. The computer, under this application, is programmed to generate a specific set of test questions for a given student, at a certain achievement level. The test is scored by the computer and both the student and the supervising teacher receive the results immediately and automatically for a given situation.

Computer Assisted Instruction

One of the most promising advances in educational technology has been made through the use of computers. The research is still continuing on the effectiveness of computers in the teaching-learning process. Results thus far seem to indicate that in areas involving cognitive learning, the *computer* is capable of producing instructional outcomes that compare favorably with those obtained by conventional methods.

The prospect of using computers as an aid to instruction is quite exciting. This feeling of exhilaration must be experienced to be appreciated. It is fascinating to carry on a dialogue with the computer. It feels as though this inanimate object suddenly becomes alive. In a recent demonstration by one of the manufacturers of computers, the magic of the computer on a twelve-year-old boy was clearly revealed. In a matter of fifteen minutes, this boy learned how to solve a simple equation in an introductory unit on algebra. It might be helpful to describe this demonstration in greater detail.

The boy who participated in the demonstration was selected at random. The purpose of the exercise was to show the procedure involved in the use of the computer as a teaching aid. A portion of the dialogue will be presented to describe the action and interaction between the learner and the computer.

Computer: Hello. What is your name? Please type it for me.

Boy: My name is Paul.

Computer: Good, Paul, are you ready to go? If you are, type the word "yes."

Boy: Yes.

Computer: (Explains an idea in about 100 words and asks the boy to respond from time to time in the process.)

Computer: (Asks a question) Paul, please type A, B, C, or D, whichever you think is the best answer to the question.

Boy: (Types his answer.)

Computer: Paul, you have answered correctly again. You now have earned 22 points toward the final score of 50. Are you already for more learning?

Boy: Yes.

The computer has a great potential for individualized instruction, but there are still a number of problems to be solved. First and foremost is the lack of "software." The program outlined above was meticulously prepared by an expert in microinstruction and the psychology of learning. Although the number and variety of programs for computers are increasing rapidly, there is still a wide gap between those available and those needed. Some school districts feel that their own instructional staff can prepare tailor-made programmed instruction for the pupils of the school district. This point of view is natural, but the level of sophistication required to develop unit-centered programs is a competency for which only a handful of teachers are trained.

Such persons must possess a mastery of psychology of learning, an understanding of microinstruction, a skill in the art of asking questions, and, most importantly, a full command of the subject field being programmed. Unless these conditions are recognized, "homemade" programs may not achieve the desired results. Obviously, a large school district with adequate financial resources could well employ such persons as part of the staff and produce its own programs for computer assisted instruction. The greatest hope in the production of software for the computer lies in private enterprise, which is set up to do the task on an economically sound basis. This situation is analogous to the idea that every school district should prepare and publish its own textbooks. Hopefully, we can look to private industry for the software in computer instruction as we have done in the past regarding textbooks, films, slides, and tapes.

The financial aspect of computer assisted instruction is still a matter of some concern. The cost of purchasing, leasing, or sharing the hardware (the computer) is still beyond the reach of many school districts. However, rapid advances are being made in the design of less costly and more efficient computers. The rapid advances in computer technology are substantially reducing the cost per student-hour of computer time. Also, there is a corresponding development in the shared-time use of computers that could dramatically further reduce the cost of computer assisted instruction. Under the shared-time approach, a single computer can simultaneously serve many students. Since the computer works in microseconds and the student responds in macrotime, several other students can be served by the computer while it is "waiting" for a given student to respond. In actual practice, the computer is so fast that the student is never even aware that the computer was "busy" when he happened to make his input.

The computer should not be viewed as a universal tool. It certainly has high potential as an instructional aid, but it should not be assumed that it is equally effective in all areas of learning and for all purposes. Also, computer assisted instruction is not appropriate for all students and may be lacking in economic efficiency. A well-planned educational institution should include several learning options for its students. It would be unrealistic for a school district, college, or university to rely entirely on computer assisted instruction for achieving its educational objectives. Some students must be taught in classes where group activity and teacher initiative are present. For others, it might be necessary for the teacher to be quite direct and to proceed step by step in a structured situation. But for a large number of students, a balanced combination of traditional approaches with computer assisted instruction can be quite effective.

Implications of computer assisted instruction for school plant planning. Once the decision has been made by educational authorities to provide individualized computer assisted instruction as a learning option, it will be necessary to establish the manner in which this decision will be implemented. The answers to the following questions will help to shape the physical facilities that will house the program of instruction.

1. In what subject matter areas will the computer assisted instruction program be offered? From what level to what level?
2. Will students be scheduled in the computer laboratory or will an open laboratory concept be adopted?
3. Will students be assigned to specific teachers or will they simply report to the teacher in the laboratory when the student is working with the computer?

4. Who will be responsible for student progress, advisement, and evaluation?
5. Will students be required to "cover" a given number of units in a given semester or will they work entirely at their own rates?

The specific design of the spaces to house computer assisted instruction will depend somewhat on the desired procedure. But a few of the major functional needs of the program can be delineated in sufficient detail to assist educational planners in the task of providing appropriate facilities for computer assisted instruction.

a. *The computer learning laboratory.* This space is the center for computer assisted instruction. A carrel, with sound-absorbing walls, should be provided for each student station. Each student station for computer assisted instruction needs space for the carrel itself, for a chair, and for student circulation. In general, an allocation of about twenty square feet per student station is sufficient to accommodate these functions.

b. *The size of the laboratory for computer assisted instruction.* Since the student activity is individualized, the number of students concentrated in a given area is not critical. The limit is determined by the amount of teacher instruction that is required to augment the computer assisted instruction. This amount depends upon the nature of the subject matter, the readiness of the students for that level of instruction, and the clarity of the programmed instruction.

Guidelines for computer assisted instruction.   For planning purposes, it is suggested that a flexible approach be considered, using the "rules of thumb" listed below:

1. The present Experimental Practices suggest that students should work with the computer for twenty minutes at a sitting about three times per week. Thus, one student station containing a computer terminal can serve approximately thirty students per week based on a six-hour school day. In colleges, the number could probably be increased to about forty-five per week, assuming 100 percent efficiency in both cases. Under the open laboratory concept, an efficiency of 70 percent is about as much as can be expected.

2. In planning the number of carrels needed, a figure of twenty-five students per carrel per week is quite reasonable. Thus, once the number of students to be enrolled in computer assisted instruction is determined, the number of carrels can be established by allowing twenty-five students per carrel.

3. An instructor in each subject-matter area offered in the computer assisted instruction laboratory should be available at all times. Consequently, the scheduling of the laboratory becomes a very important cost consideration. If it is scheduled for one subject area at a time, only one or two teachers competent in that subject would be needed during that

scheduled period. On the other hand, under the open-laboratory concept, any student could utilize the laboratory in any of the subjects offered at any time. Thus, at least one teacher in each of the subjects offered should be on duty at all times. Unless the institution is large enough to justify about 200 carrels, the open-laboratory concept is economically questionable.

4. Ideally, the computer assisted instruction laboratory should consist of a relatively large room with carrels so arranged that they can be supervised from a central point where the teachers are stationed. Perhaps an arrangement of rows of carrels as spokes of a wheel with glassed-in offices for teachers at the hub would satisfy the functional relationship between the students and the helping teachers in the laboratory. While visual contact between the students and the helping teachers is desirable, the use of a signal light activated by the student when assistance is needed could also be used where visual contact is not practical.

5. The helping teacher or teachers should be readily accessible to the students. A double-glazed office should be provided for each teacher. The helping teacher may confer with the student in his office or he may go directly to the student carrel and assist him when the computer has failed. One teacher office should be provided for each fifty student stations in the laboratory, plus one additional office for flexibility. Each office should contain about 120 square feet including space for two four-drawer files and a storage cabinet for instructional supplies.

Computer Managed Instruction

The computer is ideally suited for the management of instruction. The basic difference between computer assisted instruction and computer managed instruction is that the computer in the latter case does not become a direct tool of instruction. Under computer managed instruction, the computer simply provides the student with directions, "administers" tests, and, on the basis of the student's answers, gives him or her further directions.

Let us briefly outline the major features of computer managed instruction. The student sits at a carrel containing a computer terminal similar to that used in computer assisted instruction. Upon proper activation the computer may instruct the student to go to the library, read a specified section of a given book, and return to the computer upon completion of the assignment. When he or she returns, he is asked a number of questions by the computer based on that assignment. If the student responds correctly, the computer may instruct the student to study a series of audiovisual tapes and return to the computer for testing and further directions. In the event that a student does not answer the question correctly, the computer gives the student alternative assignments on the same general topic and retests him. Traditional class instruction may be an important part of the assignments the students receive under computer managed instruction. Clearly, under this concept, the computer serves only as a control mechanism for individualized instruction. The primary responsibility for the instruction rests entirely with the teacher.

Unlike computer assisted instruction, most teachers are capable of preparing the instructions that can be programmed into a computer. In a sense, such directions could be taken directly from lesson plans that are an essential part of traditional methods of teaching. The testing associated with computer managed instruction, however, requires both skill and ingenuity on the part of the teacher. There is a definite change of emphasis in the preparation of tests under computer managed instruction. Ordinarily, testing is focused on student achievement. Under this concept, however, the focus is on the diagnostic potential of the test. Unless this potential is painstakenly built into the test, the effectiveness of computer managed instruction is substantially reduced.

Implications of computer managed instruction for school plant planning. The space requirement for each student station is similar to that suggested under computer assisted instruction. The basic difference lies in the space needed for supervisory staff. Under the computer managed instruction concept, no teacher is required in the laboratory. A paraprofessional person, such as a teacher aide, is sufficient. The primary function of this person is to oversee the operation, making certain that the equipment is functioning properly and assisting students in activating the computer.

It is suggested that a single glassed-in office be provided in each laboratory, irrespective of capacity. If this office could be elevated about five feet above the floor, the supervisory function could be significantly improved. About 100 square feet of space is sufficient for this office, since the teacher aide does not become involved in the instructional process. Under this concept, students are assigned to qualified teachers who serve as advisors. Such teachers need not necessarily be stationed in the computer managed instruction laboratory for the effective operation of this concept. These teacher-advisors maintain records of test results, student achievement, and student progress. Thus, it is essential that such a teacher-advisor be provided with an office containing about 100 square feet and supplied with one four-drawer file in addition to a desk and three chairs.

THE DIAL ACCESS LABORATORY

This facility consists of a fully automatic electronic device which activates a given tape upon demand by a student or any other person, and sends the audio signal to a carrel where the student is waiting for the information. By simply dialing a number, the student can listen to tapes of a lecture that was recorded in the classroom earlier, a play recorded by professionals, music for pleasure, foreign language recordings, and any special instructional material supplementing basic instruction conducted by the teacher.

The dial access laboratory can also be used as a language laboratory by simply adding a teacher console to the system. When the console is under the control of the teacher, the independent access feature at each carrel may be temporarily deactivated. A word of caution is in order at this point. If the educational program calls for the full-time use of a language laboratory, it is less costly and educationally more efficient to plan a separate language laboratory convenient to the classroom where instruction is offered in the foreign languages.

Although it has been suggested that the dial access laboratory be placed in the Learning Resources Center complex, it is feasible and practical to locate listening carrels in any appropriate alcove in the building or in other buildings on the campus. There is a definite trend to provide study areas for students outside of the library or the study halls. Semi-quiet areas are often strategically located throughout the building or campus for this purpose. In situations where it seems to make sense, it would not be unreasonable to install carrels with a dial and earphone plug in study alcoves or study areas in various parts of the building. A student could be loaned an earphone for an indefinite period of time and use it for all of his audiovisual work in the school—in the laboratories, in the Learning Resources Center, and in the semi-quiet areas. In order to minimize vandalism, these alcoves should be surrounded by faculty offices or be supervised by a video camera with signs clearly indicating that such video equipment is in operation. The physical features of a dial access laboratory should be built into the design of the building. Space will be needed for student carrels, for the automated switching equipment, for the storage of cassettes, and for the repair and maintenance of the software. The size of the total space for the carrels obviously depends upon the number of students to be served. Allow at least 25 square feet per carrel. If the school district has had no previous experience with a dial access laboratory, it is suggested that the capacity of the dial access laboratory be about 5 percent of the school enrollment. In secondary schools, the American Library Association has suggested that the seating capacity of the library be at least 15 percent of the school enrollment. If we define "library work" as any activity whereby the student retrieves information from stored sources, all tapes, slides, motion picture films, and transparencies assume the same position as books and other printed materials. Thus, the capacity of the dial access laboratory can be included within the 15 percent recommendation mentioned above. A space of approximately 300 square feet should be allocated for the switching equipment and a storage room containing about 350 square feet should adjoin the space for the equipment. If the laboratory serves more than fifty students, an office, preferably with vision strips, should be included for a staff member who can provide assistance and supervision.

SELF-CONTAINED TEACHING DEVICES

Most of the electronic equipment mentioned in this chapter is designed primarily for program enrichment and is viewed as a supplement to the teaching normally conducted by the instructor. Because this equipment is considered a school-wide facility, serving all teachers, all students, and all programs, it is usually located in the Learning Resources Center and placed under the jurisdiction and control of the director of the Learning Resources Center.

Early Teaching Machines

Teaching devices initially gained much favor as a result of the work of Pressey in Ohio and Skinner at Harvard. Many different types of machines were developed. Essentially, they all depend upon the principle of programmed learning. Students are exposed to sequential and logical bits of information, and then at predetermined intervals they are required to answer one or more questions. Depending upon the type of machine, the student either continues linearly after answering a question incorrectly or is shunted into a branch which contains a supplementary series of bits of information. If he masters the material in the branch, he then returns to the major track of the program. In passing, it should be mentioned that the ordinary textbook is an elementary form of programmed learning. Because it does not provide for student response and reward, the textbook is not classified as a teaching machine even though it is a self-instructional device. Computers are now replacing teaching machines of the past.

Tape and Record Players, Film Projectors, and Television

While tape recorders, film projectors, record players, and television are commonly used for group instruction, they are equally well suited for individualized instructional activities. The application of these electronic devices depends upon the manner in which the instructional material recorded on the tapes and films is organized, structured, and presented. These tapes and films are generally called "software," as opposed to "hardware," by the manufacturers and marketers of audiovisual equipment or the producers of tapes and films for such equipment.

The educational uses of simple audiovisual equipment for individualized instruction is limited only by the availability of the desired software. Today, this limit is of little concern. There is an abundance of software on the market for this purpose in all of the basic disciplines, such as reading, mathematics, and language arts. There is also a wide variety of software for students to use on an individual basis in science, social studies, the practical arts, and the fine and performing arts. The material recorded in the software is presented in two major forms. The most common form of recording is descriptive, resembling a well-organized type of lecture. This form of software is extremely useful as a supplement to classroom instruction. The second type of software is highly structured and serves as a sort of "teacher aide." The material is programmed and divided into self-contained learning units similar to those described under computer assisted instruction. The software, under this concept, includes testing material at various points in the series of independent learning units. This approach does not replace the teacher in any way. It simply provides a little extra time for the teacher to plan the instructional activities of each student over and above his regular teaching duties. Under an individually oriented instructional setting, the teacher manages all of the instructional activities and provides the necessary basic instruction wherever and whenever it is needed.

PRACTICAL APPLICATIONS OF PORTABLE AUDIOVISUAL DEVICES

The application of audiovisual equipment for individualized instruction is limited only by the creativity of the teacher and the availability of the software. In some instances, the teacher can prepare magnetic tapes for certain uses of the equipment. A few examples illustrating some of the ways in which audiovisual equipment may be utilized in certain learning situations are presented below.

For Use in Science Laboratories

Tapes prepared by the classroom teacher can be used advantageously in a science laboratory. For example, a class of twenty-four students in a physics laboratory may be conducting five or six different experiments in electricity at the same time. This practice is often necessary in order to minimize the amount of test instruments and expensive equipment that may be required for certain experiments. Thus, by subdividing the class into, let us say, six groups of four students each, only one-sixth of the equipment would be needed. Each student group would rotate from experiment to experiment every week until all of the experiments are completed by all of the students.

Under this arrangement, the teacher could prepare a tape giving complete instructions and appropriate cautions for each experiment. A group of four students would check out a tape cassette for, let us say, experiment A. They would listen to it at their laboratory station. If sound is a problem, earphones could be used. The students would follow the instructions on the tape which could be as follows: "Ask one student in your group to check out one 6-volt battery, a 1000-OHM resistance box, 10 feet of single conductor #22 wire, one ammeter and one volt meter. Stop the player until the person returns with the material." Upon the return of the student with the necessary supplies and equipment, the tape recorder would again be activated for further instruction until experiment A is completed and the report on the experiment is prepared.

For Supplementary Instructions for Gifted Students

The descriptive type software mentioned earlier is well suited for supplementary instruction for gifted students. This information could be provided by short subject reels of motion picture film or by tape recorder cassettes. The equipment would probably be located in the Instructional Resources Center where it would be available to all students in the school.

Assistance to Slow Learners

The use of audiovisual equipment for slow learners can be most rewarding. Routine exercises could be practiced by the student on an individual basis using the appropriate type of software. For example, if a student has not fully mastered the skill of subtraction in arithmetic, he or she could sit at a carrel in the classroom or in the Instructional Resources Center and practice doing a large and varied number of subtractions with instructions from a tape recorder and using pencil and paper to perform the calculations.

Reinforcement of Learning for Some Students

For a large number of students, the use of audiovisual equipment at a time of their choosing could strongly reinforce the regular classroom instruction, particularly those students who have just mastered certain skills or who have been introduced to new concepts for the first time. These students would be permitted to use the equipment at certain times of the school day when they have some free time, such as study periods or their equivalent in the lower grade levels.

For a Full Program of Personalized Instruction

It should be stated at the outset of this discussion that individualized instruction is not for all students. Many students feel much more comfortable in a group instruction setting. There are others who can profit from an individualized instructional program under certain conditions.

All of the audiovisual equipment and associated software can be used most advantageously under the guidance of a creative teacher, providing the students are receptive to this individualized form of instruction.

If such a program is instituted, it would be housed in a specially designed learning laboratory which might be located adjacent to the Instructional Resources Center, but not under its control or supervision. This laboratory is envisioned as a specialized classroom similar to any other instructional space, such as a science laboratory, homemaking laboratory, business machine laboratory, music room, and art studio. Consequently, it would be an integral part of the teaching program of the school under the direct supervision of the respective instructional units.

LARGE GROUP INSTRUCTION

The term "large group instruction" is relative and may have a meaning that differs from person to person. For the purpose of this discussion, large group instruction refers to groups of students of fifty or more. The figure is selected arbitrarily for the convenience of the reader. Actually, the concepts discussed in this section are not particularly sensitive to group size, whether it be 15, 30, 90, or 900.

Programmed Student Response System

Electronic equipment designed to improve group instruction has been available for the past decade. Due primarily to cost, student response systems have not been widely used. The fundamental concept, however, is basically sound and its potential educational effectiveness is high. The simplest form of the student response system consists of four buttons installed at each seat in an auditorium. With this simple installation, the instructor functions as he has in the past with one exception. From time to time, at strategic points, he asks a multiple-choice question. The students respond by depressing button A, B, C, or D. A rapid specially designed calculator instantly informs the instructor of the percent of all the students answering correctly. Also, the actual responses of students are recorded by seat number for future analysis by the teacher. This simplified system keeps the teacher continually informed of the extent to which he is reaching the students during his presentation, provides for active participation by the students, and records individual student progress for diagnostic purposes by the instructor.

Student response systems more sophisticated in design and function are currently on the market. The teacher can, if he so desires, preprogram his entire presentation. The electronic heart of this equipment is capable of controlling the lights within the room, two movie projectors, one slide projector, and one tape recorder. In addition, it can keep a record of individual student responses and give the instructor instantaneous feedback on the percent of students answering each test question correctly, similar to the results using the simple student response system. As mentioned above, the teacher can program the entire presentation utilizing movie projectors, slide projectors, and tapes sequentially at times desired by the teacher. For example, the presentation may begin with a slide containing the title of the subject under study and a tape recorder reproducing introductory remarks prepared by the instructor. This phase can be followed immediately by showing a five-minute sound movie film, followed by a question and student response. If the response is acceptable to the teacher, the programmed presentation continues. On the other hand, if an excessive percent of the students have answered incorrectly in the judgment of the teacher, he temporarily interrupts the programmed presentation and makes a new "live" presentation on the same point missed by a large number of students. At the completion of his second attempt, he asks a second test question that is equivalent to the original. If he has succeeded, as indicated by the student response, he reactivates the automatic operation of the system, which resumes the programmed presentation prepared by the teacher.

In planning for a student response system, it is essential that the architect be informed well in advance of preliminary plans of the desire to provide such a system. A small cable must be installed at each seat during the construction. Sometimes conduits are installed in anticipation of providing the wiring and equipment at a later date. The best time, economically, to install a student response system is during the original construction of a large-group facility. It is suggested that one or two manufacturers of this equipment be contacted early, so that certain specifications for wiring can be included in the official specification prepared by the architect.

Radio—Telephone—Television

Educators have yet to fully exploit the powerful and effective learning potential of radio, telephone, and television. As soon as this concept is put into operation somewhere and an efficient procedure is developed, the goal of mass education will be brought much closer to reality. The granting of the External Degree in England and elsewhere is an excellent example of mass education. What is needed to accomplish this worthwhile goal is a means of educating hundreds of people at a time without expending large sums of money for capital outlay. The proposed use of radio, telephone, and television represents one practical and financially feasible approach to mass education particularly at the college and university level.

In educating adults and post-high school students, it is proposed that radio, telephone, and television be used for large-group instruction for further education. Under this concept, a student might earn college credit toward a degree, or become sufficiently proficient for a diploma or certificate. Each institution would determine its own procedure and standards for the nature of recognition it wishes to give for such extramural instruction.

The proposed procedure is as follows: A presentation is made over a local television station or over an educational television station for one hour by a recognized authority in the field or a member of the college or university staff. Upon the termination of the telecast, a panel of three or four faculty members from a given department at each of the institutions granting awards for this program would receive telephone calls from students at home. Students registered in the course could call the institution, using an ENTERPRISE number at no cost to them. A moderator would keep about ten students in contact with the panel at a time. This discussion involving ten students and three panelists at any given time would be simultaneously broadcast by radio. The discussion period by radio could cover a period of about two hours. If the moderator would allow each student calling to remain on the "open line" for five minutes, over 200 students could participate in the discussions while all the other students registered in the class would benefit from these discussions by radio. Under this concept, large numbers of students could receive a major part of their instruction at home. They would take whatever tests might be required on the campus and use laboratories and libraries on the campus specifically designed for this type of learning activity.

Television and Videotape

Television is a powerful medium for group instruction. The use of this instructional aid is growing very rapidly as the number of educational television broadcasting stations increases. The content and nature of the educational television programs is increasingly focused on the special needs of the public schools. In some instances, the programs that are broadcast from educational television stations are coordinated with the instruction that takes place in the school districts within their range of coverage. Some of these stations employ educational coordinators who work directly with the local school districts for the purpose of maximizing the impact of their television programs on the education of the students in their respective areas.

Videotape recording has greatly enhanced the effect of educational television on the schools. Videotape recording makes it possible to record a program which is broadcast by educational television at any time during the day or night. After a program is recorded on videotape, it can be reproduced immediately after it is recorded or at any later time.

Videotape recording offers great challenges and opportunities for classroom teachers. Since educational television programs can be recorded on tape for twenty-four hours during the day, the number of programs that are available to the school districts has almost tripled. Once a program is recorded on videotape at any school facility, it can be rebroadcast throughout the building over a closed circuit television system or it can be directed to one classroom at any predetermined time. Thus, the classroom teacher is no longer dependent on the time in which a particular program was broadcast from the educational television station. Through the magic of videotaping, the teacher can introduce any television program at the most appropriate time during the instructional process. Stated differently, the teacher can show a television program whenever the class is ready for it.

Teachers may also use videotaping for self-diagnosis of their teaching techniques. The teacher may ask the staff from the instructional resource center to set up a television camera and videotape recorder in his or her classroom. The teacher would activate the equipment and record all of the classroom activities for a period of time. Later during the day, in his or her own privacy, the teacher could play the videotape and make a self-evaluation of his or her performance. This use of videotape equipment often leads to self-improvement without any fear of embarrassment on the part of the teacher.

PREVALENT EDUCATIONAL CONCEPTS AND INNOVATIVE PRACTICES

There are many exciting concepts that are being introduced from time to time in various school districts. Some are the product of imaginative classroom teachers who are on a never-ending search for more effective teaching methods. Others are conceived in a more theoretical setting in colleges and universities. Regardless of the origin of new educational concepts, some of them eventually become an accepted part of the curriculum in many school districts and should be considered in planning school facilities.

Innovations are being proposed in quick succession. The application of educational concepts seems to be in a constant state of flux. Some are terminated, some are continued, and new ones are introduced. Educators sometimes jokingly point out that if one makes no changes for a sufficiently long time, present practices will someday be seen as promising innovations. Under this recycling concept, it is conceivable that a traditional school system could become a pioneer in education by simply waiting for all of the others to complete the cycle. For this reason, many educators compare changes in curriculum to a pendulum that moves back and forth. To be sure, as public attitudes and values change, the school curriculum changes with it. It should not come as a complete surprise when old concepts are revived and reintroduced in the school curriculum.

It is sometimes assumed that all innovative practices or imaginative concepts must be good because they are new and exciting. This position is not always tenable, however. Some innovations are readily accepted and persist over a number of years. Some are tried and dropped without much fanfare. These are often called fads. And others continue in practice in an atmosphere of uncertainty and controversy. In recent times, "the windowless school concept" and "the open space plan" have been subjected to considerable controversy. Their fate is apparently not yet been decided.

The design of functional futuristic school buildings requires super-human capabilities. School plant planners should not only be superbly endowed with creative powers but they should also be able to clearly distinguish between those educational concepts and practices that will persist for a long time and those that are likely to be short-lived. Obviously, it is humanly impossible to perform this task with any degree of certainty. At best, school building planners can study a large number of concepts and practices and identify those that best fit into the philosophy of the people who will be served by the proposed school building. In order to facilitate this process, a few selected concepts that are judged to be educationally sound and administratively feasible have been included in this book. There are, indeed, many other outstanding and exciting innovations that should be considered by school officials and architects when a school building is being planned.

There is no established taxonomy for various types of educational concepts and practices. For the purpose of this presentation, they have been grouped into three arbitrary categories. Group I includes those practices that are primarily associated with changes in the method of instruction. Group II is comprised of concepts that are likely to produce changes in student grouping and scheduling. And Group III contains concepts that are related to possible changes in school organization. Obviously not all concepts fits neatly into predetermined categories. In this presentation, each innovation has been placed in the group where it would seem to have the greatest impact.

In considering these concepts, it is suggested that school plant planners not limit themselves to this small list of innovative practices. Other ideas should also be considered when a new educational facility is being planned or when an existing school building is being modernized. On the other hand, innovations should not be incorporated in the design of a building simply because they appear to be new and exciting. In some instances, it might be wise not to introduce new practices upon the completion of a new or modernized school building, particularly if the community, the staff, and the students are not yet ready for such changes. In these instances, school plant planners should design the school building so that these features can be added at a later date.

GROUP I—CHANGES IN METHOD OF INSTRUCTION

Negotiated Learning

Negotiated learning is not a new concept. It is a revival of learning methods familiarly known as the "Contract Method," "Independent Study," or "Multi-Option Instruction." The application of this concept has much merit for those students who can profit from it. In general, the success of this approach to individualized instruction depends upon the skill of the teacher in preparing and using well-conceived units of instruction, and upon the initiative and resourcefulness of the student. When both of these elements are present, the results from this approach to learning can be gratifying both to the teacher and to the student. Negotiated learning allows the student to participate in shaping the learning experiences that he will undergo in achieving certain predetermined educational outcomes that may be in harmony with his personal goals.

Implications of this concept for school plant planning.   There are not many special design features associated with this concept. Obviously, a teacher office or faculty work station, having an area of about 120 square feet, is needed for this type of individualized instruction. The present national trend is to provide offices for teachers even at the secondary level. Thus, where this facility is provided, nothing special is required to accommodate the negotiated learning approach.

If the student is to learn on an individual basis, he needs space in which to study, experiment, and discuss. Students enrolled in this program are assigned to a carrel for an indefinite period of time. The inference from this requirement is simply that the number of student carrels included in a proposed school plan should be increased by an amount equal to the number of students anticipated in this program. Normally, carrels are not assigned. Students using the Learning Resources Center simply find a vacant carrel and use it at that time. Under the concept of negotiated learning, a student station is reserved for that student. These carrels should contain lockable drawers and lockable bookshelves where students can store their books and work materials.

The Open Laboratory Concept

The open laboratory concept can be applied to any learning situation requiring the student to perform experiments, gain skills, or conduct demonstrations of basic principles. The most likely application of this concept in the schools of today is associated with the science laboratories, secretarial science laboratories, and engineering science laboratories.

The open laboratory approach is neither too involved nor overly complicated. The student is free to do his laboratory work at his convenience provided he reserves the use of the space in advance. A faculty member is always on duty in each of the open laboratories to assist the student when the need arises and to make certain that all safety and health precautions are taken by the students.

Implications for school plant planning.   The spaces that are most affected by this concept are the laboratories where this method of instruction is desired. The size of the respective laboratories must be increased to accommodate the carrels where students primarily listen to tape recordings. It is recommended that the number of carrels provided in these spaces be approximately 50 percent of the laboratory capacity. Some planners feel that a one to three ratio is sufficient, and it often is, but during the busy periods, laboratory experiment stations often remain vacant because the lack of a sufficient number of carrels causes a bottleneck. For this reason, the 50 percent figure is suggested.

If space is at a premium, the amount of area allocated to each carrel can be kept at a minimum by omitting chair space associated with the carrels. Except for physically handicapped students, it is not unreasonable to expect a student in a laboratory to stand in front of a carrel and listen to a tape for five or six minutes at a time. Under these conditions, the area for each carrel can be reduced from about 20 square feet to approximately 12 square feet. Consequently, it would require an additional 150 square feet of space in a biology laboratory, for example, serving twenty-four students, to accommodate the suggested twelve carrels. These could be located in an alcove or along a wall that is not exposed to heavy student circulation. Also, these carrels should be supplied with local lighting and a 120-volt outlet for tape players and other audiovisual equipment.

The Nongraded School

The nongraded school concept has special significance for the planning of elementary and secondary school facilities. In its application to secondary schools, this idea revolves more closely around a well-developed guidance program than it does around any special features that might be built into a secondary school. Although school facilities in themselves strongly influence the quality of the educational program, it is felt that the cooperative efforts of administrators, staff, and guidance personnel are fundamental to the success of the nongraded system at both the elementary and secondary levels of education. Obviously, under this concept, the number of guidance counselors must be sharply increased.

Basically, the nongraded-school concept depends upon the organization of groupings within the various "year of school" levels. The major requirement in this connection is that rooms housing students in sequential year levels be contiguous. In schools or subject-matter areas having more than one room per "year level," the spaces should be sequential within a given group. For example, in a six-grade elementary school building, one group of instructional spaces would house "year level" 1—6 in sequence. A second group of spaces would contain a second sequence of six rooms, etc. Such an arrangement facilitates the movement of students from one room to the other for certain aspects of their instruction. In addition, the nongraded school should contain one seminar-type room having an area of about 350 square feet for each group of about six teachers.

The Epideikic Method of Instruction in the School of the Future

The epideikic method of instruction, defined as the demonstration-inquiry method of teaching, relies heavily upon the combination of teacher demonstration and student inquiry. In this age of science and advanced technology, it is appropriate to introduce the demonstration type of instruction whenever possible in the school curriculum. Students should be able to observe demonstrations of basic principles in the sciences and the humanities and then to make inquiries stemming from their observations. As pointed out in Chapter 2, the inquiry method of instruction, used judiciously, has a definite place in the school curriculum. The epideikic concept is basic to both the inquiry and the presentation forms of instruction. The school of the future can encourage and facilitate both by including features that support, encourage, and stimulate demonstration.

This concept is applicable to all areas of instruction. Whenever the word demonstration is mentioned in education, it is generally envisioned as applying to the physical sciences. To be sure, many demonstrations do arise from the physical world about us, but the teacher may often use the demonstration method to reinforce instruction in the social sciences. For example, a colony of ants may be viewed through a glass in order to show the distribution of labor and specialization of activity in an organized society. A group of imaginative teachers working with a receptive planning committee can suggest many ingenious features that will promote the demonstration type of instruction. One obvious suggestion would be to provide a demonstration area in the classrooms or large-group instructional spaces. The minimum requirement in an elementary school building, for example, would be one demonstration table with sink, utilities, and electricity in each instructional space. In instructional spaces having a capacity of more than ten students, a closed-circuit television unit should be provided with one 21-inch monitor per twenty-five students. The school of the future would probably include television monitors in the same ratio in spaces where large-group instruction is conducted. The epideikic concept should also play a part in the design of spaces that can be converted into large teaching areas through the use of operable partitions.

As mentioned in Chapter 2, the teacher does not motivate the pupil; this he must do for himself. But the teacher can play a major role in this endeavor by providing those experiences that are most likely to energize the pupil to the extent that he then becomes motivated to learn. This objective has been consciously or unconsciously foremost in the thinking of successful teachers for centuries.

In planning school buildings, both architects and educators can do much to assist the teacher in stimulating the pupil's desire for learning. Provision should be made for every reasonable type of demonstration and simple experiment in the physical and social sciences. The demonstration concept can be a powerful stimulation to pupil motivation and can be the means of arousing intellectual curiosity at the elementary school level. Both the method of presentation and the content of instruction must arouse and hold the interest of the learner if we expect to awaken pupils from their frequent classroom lethargy. School plant planners and architects should explore many ideas pertaining to the demonstration concept in the hope of activating pupil motivation.

GROUP II—CHANGES IN STUDENT GROUPING AND SCHEDULING

Variable Group-Size Teaching for Secondary Schools

One intriguing concept being considered for secondary school and college-level instruction could virtually eliminate the conventional instruction of students in classes or sections.

Under the variable group-size concept, primary attention is given to the curriculum and the individual learning experiences that it includes. The entire curriculum is analyzed to determine the most effective group size for each of these learning experiences. Such an analysis would clearly indicate that for some experiences, a one-to-one ratio is best—one teacher instructing a single student. For other types of learning, the ratio might well be one teacher for three or four students, or one teacher to fifteen learners. For still others, the ratio could be one teacher to as many as 150 or 300 or 500 students. This approach treats learning in a realistic and sensible fashion, providing for tutoring where it is needed and for large group instruction where it is effective. The overall cost of instruction to the school district is not changed materially under this plan. The increased cost of teaching groups smaller than the conventional twenty-five or thirty students is offset by the saving in instructional time when a single teacher teaches large groups of 150 or more students. School plant planners should give serious thought to this concept in designing the schools of the future. The concept goes much farther than the mere installation of randomly scattered, movable partitions throughout the building. Such half-measures are not justifiable in school plant planning. It would be wiser to include destructible partitions rather than costly movable ones in the design of a school building.

A school building planned for variable class size must contain spaces that can be divided and subdivided easily by the teacher at any time. The major requirement, in this instance, is a system of interlocking operable partitions having a noise reduction coefficient of about 38 decibels. Spaces should be capable of accommodating groups of 6, 15, 30, 60, 90, 150, and 300 students.

The number of spaces required for groups of a given size depends upon the nature of the educational program. It is suggested that the following formula be used to determine the requisite number of instructional areas (*not* rooms).

$$T = 1.25 \frac{E}{C} \cdot \frac{n}{N}$$

where

> T = Number of areas needed (rounded off to the closest whole number)
> E = *Total number* of students requiring space for a given group size
> C = Number of students in a given group or class
> n = Number of minutes that a given group size meets per week
> N = Number of minutes in the school week

Example: Let us assume that an elementary school program calls for 275 students to meet in groups of 16 for 10 percent of the time. Suppose further that there are 300 minutes in the school day. The students would meet about 30 minutes per week (10 percent of the time) in groups of 6.

$$T \cdot (1.25)\frac{275}{6} \cdot \frac{30}{300} = (1.25)(45.8)(0.1)$$

$$= 5.7 \text{ or } 6 \text{ spaces of this size}$$

This means that six areas will be required on a full-time basis to satisfy the needs for this grouping of six students. The computation is repeated for all of the other groupings. The total number of areas needed equals the sum of the individual computations.

The Variable Class Size Concept for Elementary Schools and Middle Schools

Many educators agree that certain learning experiences can be imparted just as effectively to groups of 300, 150, 75, and 50 pupils as they can to the conventional group of 25 pupils. On the other hand, there are some learning situations in which the traditional group of 25 is far too large. In fact, a ratio of one pupil to one teacher is required for transmission of certain knowledge or skills from the teacher to the pupil. There may be other learning experiences where the group should consist of 2 or 3, 6 or 8, or 12 to 15 pupils.

In view of the growing acceptance of the belief that grouping for instruction should vary according to the character or complexity of the learning activity, educators are beginning to plan school buildings to accommodate groupings of various sizes. Teachers are being provided with offices where they can work with individual students. A few small seminar-type rooms that can be subdivided by operable partitions are being included in elementary schools to meet the need for small group instruction. And conventional classrooms are being designed so that three or four of them can be joined to form a large instructional space for a single group.

Modular Scheduling

For many years educators have shown a keen interest in some form of modular scheduling. Under this concept, the unit module may vary in length from 15 to 20 to 22½ or 30 minutes. The number of minutes contained in the unit module is immaterial, but the number of modules included in each block of time is a matter of considerable educational significance. Variations in the size of time blocks are achieved by grouping two or more unit modules in a single time block for a given teaching period on certain days of the week. Consequently, the length of time a student spends in a given class may vary from day to day, depending upon the nature of the learning.

From time to time, educators have expressed fears that high school pupils would become confused under a schedule that varied from hour to hour and from day to day. In practice, however, these fears are unfounded. In one school district, for example, modular scheduling was introduced in the middle school. When the author inquired how the pupil managed to remember his schedule as it changed from day to day, the response revealed an idea that was ingenious. Each pupil was asked to make a copy of his schedule and paste it inside of his locker door. Thus, every morning the pupil could quickly remind himself of his schedule for the day.

At various times in the recent past, the idea of instant rescheduling has received serious attention. This plan calls for the instantaneous rescheduling of students, spaces, teachers, and supplementary instructional services whenever the need arises. Unfortunately, this desirable goal is more theoretical than practical. Unless the present pattern of master-scheduling four or five teachers for each student at predetermined times changes drastically, instant scheduling and rescheduling are not feasible. On the other hand, the prospect is brighter in schools where team teaching involving the entire program of a given group of students is in full operation. Although the probability of success of instant rescheduling is somewhat improved under these circumstances, the problem of communication still remains to be solved. If there were a system of instant communication among all persons involved in the rescheduling of all related teaching activities for a large group of students, the instant schedule concept could be seriously considered. Unfortunately, the present state of the art in instant communication is not yet sufficiently sophisticated to permit the instant rescheduling of students, teachers, spaces, and related supplementary services.

The introduction of modular scheduling does not pose a serious problem for the educational facility planner, provided a predetermined, fixed weekly cycle is adopted. For example, if a 15-minute unit module were adopted, a course in the teaching of Spanish could be scheduled as follows:

a.	Monday	3 modules	45 minutes
b.	Tuesday	4 modules	60 minutes
c.	Wednesday	3 modules	45 minutes
d.	Thursday	3 modules	45 minutes
e.	Friday	2 modules	30 minutes

The daily schedule could be repeated each week.

Schedule rotation is as easy to accomplish under modular scheduling as it is with conventional scheduling. It is quite simple to rotate the modular time sequence from day to day. This capability can benefit both the teachers and the students because it makes it possible for the teacher to conduct each class at a different time of the day from day to day. Consequently, the same students and teachers are not continually holding the same classes at the end of the day when both students and teachers are more likely to be fatigued. An example is presented to illustrate the case with which the modular scheduling can be adapted to a rotating time sequence.

Using a 15-minute module, the school day could be divided into twenty-four modules. Starting the cycle on Monday, module 1 would occur between 8:15 and 8:30. Module 2 would fall between 8:30 and 8:45 and so on to module 24, which occurs between 2:15 p.m. and 2:30 p.m. On Tuesday, module 6 could be scheduled between 8:15 and 9:30. All of the other modules follow in sequence, with module 24 followed by module 1, which which would fall between 1:30 and 1:45 p.m., and ending the day with module 4, between 2:15 p.m. and 2:30 p.m.

When the rotating feature is applied to a modular schedule, however, care should be exercised to make certain that some of the larger blocks of time do not become fragmented. For example, if modules 1 through 6 were scheduled as a science laboratory period for some students, it is possible, and indeed very likely, that on a certain day this block of 90 minutes could be split, through the rotation process, so that modules 3 through 6 (one hour) could occur in the morning and modules 1 and 2 could be scheduled for the end of the day. When rotation of periods is coupled with modular scheduling, the shift in rotation should be planned so that large blocks of time are not dichotomized. It may be necessary to design the master schedule so that large time blocks can be rotated as a whole unit of time.

The effect of modular scheduling on space utilization depends upon the degree of flexibility built into it. Obviously, the highest utilization of space is achieved when all the blocks of time are equal in length, as is the case with the traditional schedule. If each large block of time could be interwoven with a corresponding small block so that the two could fully utilize a teaching station, the difference in space utilization between the modular schedule and the conventional would disappear. In general, this delicate balance is difficult to achieve. The price of flexibility, using modular scheduling, is a possible drop in space utilization. A good rule of thumb to follow in this regard is that the greater the variation in the length of the blocks of time, the less will be the efficiency of the utilization of the building. In situations where modular scheduling is contemplated, an allowance for a loss in pupil station utilization of 5 percent should be included in the computation of the number of spaces required by the educational program.

The Multi-Structured Schedule

The multi-structured schedule is a simpler form of modular scheduling. It represents only a small departure from conventional scheduling and is, therefore, less threatening to those seeking a less rigid scheduling method. In the discussion of the variable group-size concept, attention was focused primarily upon variations in group size without considering the time element associated with them. Time was introduced peripherally when it was mentioned that the cost of instruction did not necessarily increase as a result of variable size grouping. It was noted that the cost of instructing smaller groups of learners could be balanced through savings in teacher time per student during large-group instructional periods. In fact, it can be demonstrated that a teacher who instructs a traditional class of thirty learners, five periods per day, five days per week, can spend the same number of contact minutes per week per learner in about 75 percent of the conventional teacher time.

In addition to improved utilization of teachers, it is possible to instruct groups of about fifteen students for approximately 40 percent of the teaching time. Table 3.1 shows the difference between the conventional and

TABLE 3.1   Comparative schedules

| | Traditional Schedule | | | | | | Proposed Schedule—Type A | | | | |
Period	M	T	W	Th	F	Period	M	T	W	Th	F
1	30*	30	30	30	30	1	150*	17	150	17	150
2	30	30	30	30	30	2	×	17*	17	17	17
3	30	30	30	30	30	3	×	17	17	17	17
4	30	30	30	30	30	4	×	17	17	17	17
5	30	30	30	30	30	5	×	17	17	17	17

*Group size.

potential utilization of teacher time for a given course. The teacher, under the proposed schedule—Type A, spends about 80 percent of the conventional time for total instruction. He may use the remaining 20 percent of his time for preparation of instructional materials. According to the traditional schedule, he simply uses all of his class contact time, repeating many of the same words period after period with a fixed group of 30 students. The proposed schedule, on the other hand, allows the teacher to meet five periods per week with each learner for the same length of time included in the conventional schedule but with two major differences. The teacher has a bonus of about 20 percent of his time in which to prepare materials, and he meets with classes of only 17 learners rather than 30, for about 85 percent of his total instructional time. Each student spends approximately 60 percent of his time in large groups, and 40 percent in small groups of 17 students.

In some subject-matter areas, such as mathematics, it might be desirable to spend three periods per week in small groups and only two in large groups. Table 3.2 indicates the resulting class sizes, if a teacher of mathematics having a traditional load of 125 students in high school were to introduce a multi-structured schedule. In this case, each student meets two periods per week in a group of 125 pupils and three times per week in groups of approximately 18.

The multi-structured schedule can be introduced into any school with facilities for instruction of both small and large groups. Under the traditional schedule, classes of twenty-five to thirty students are scheduled to meet four or five times per week. Sometimes there is a trace of multi-scheduling even in the traditional high school. For example, when pupils are scheduled for physical education three days per week and for study during the remaining two periods of the normal five-period-per-week cycle, a simple form of the multi-structured schedule is in operation. Modular scheduling embodies the multi-structured concept.

Under the multi-structured schedule, the school may operate several schedules simultaneously. For some courses, it may continue the conventional schedule in which each class meets five times per week. For some courses, students or pupils can meet three times in large groups and twice a week in small groups. For others, students or pupils may assemble in large groups only twice per week and in small groups three periods per

TABLE 3.2   Variable class-size schedule

| Period | Proposed Schedule—Type B | | | | |
	M	T	W	Th	F
1	18	125	18	125	18
2	18	18	18	18	18
3	18	free	18	18	18
4	18	18	18	18	18
5	18	free	18	18	21

week. Other schedule structures are also possible. The author has found that if the three-large—two-small group combination is properly related to the two-large—three-small group structure, the use of instructional spaces can be dovetailed and a high-level of space utilization can be attained.

Team Teaching

The idea of team teaching goes much farther than most of the cooperative efforts of teachers in the conventional school today. The structure and procedures associated with the implementation of this concept will receive greater attention in the future. A team of teachers with talents and abilities in different fields of instruction can develop the curriculum and methodology most likely to achieve the objectives set cooperatively by the team itself and by the school administration. The school of the future designed for team teaching should provide space where three or four teachers can plan together, space where a single teacher can prepare materials for large-group presentation, work space where other types of instructional materials can be produced, and space where 90, 120, 180, or 300 students can be instructed as a single group as well as in groups of 30 or fewer.

The implications of the team-teaching concept for school plant planning are quite clear. A seminar room about 300 square feet in area should be provided for each two teams. An office should be planned for each teacher. A workroom having an area of approximately 400 square feet should be planned, preferably near the library. And classrooms should be grouped so that the opening of a number of movable partitions would convert several of them into a single relatively square space with good sight lines to the podium. Team teaching can also be effective in a school which cannot convert several traditional classrooms into a single large one. When large-group instruction is desired, such schools can use the auditorium, multipurpose room, or cafeteria for this purpose. Schools designed for convertibility of ordinary spaces into larger or smaller ones, however, possess an extraordinary flexibility that is essential to application of the concept of variable class size, as discussed in the following section.

GROUP III—CHANGES IN SCHOOL ORGANIZATION

The Open Campus

Many secondary schools are introducing the open campus concept in order to provide greater student freedom. Under this concept, students are treated as adults and are allowed to engage in a wide variety of activities within the building and, in some cases, students may even leave the school if they have no classes at any given period. Admittedly, there is considerable merit in the philosophy of giving students greater freedom and making them responsible for using their time wisely.

The introduction of the open campus concept in a number of secondary schools has become a virtual nightmare. In one particular secondary school, students were permitted complete freedom within the building during their "free periods." While students could work in the library, go to a study area, or confer with a faculty member, most of them, in this instance, chose to socialize in the corridors. These corridors became so noisy that teachers conducting classes in these areas soon discovered that teaching under these conditions was becoming quite difficult. Some of the students engaged in all sorts of pranks in the corridors. It was reported that a teacher in a room adjoining a noisy corridor heard a loud pounding noise coming from the direction of the corridor. Upon investigation, the teacher discovered that two or three boys had stuffed a girl in one of the large corridor lockers reserved for faculty storage. Vandalism also became a new problem with which the school was forced to cope, simply because students were given a greater latitude of freedom without providing for student activities in advance. This picture seems gloomy. It is. The above details describe an actual situation. The lesson to be learned from this narrative is, "Don't institute an open campus in a facility that is not designed for it." In the above-mentioned secondary school, it was not the philosophy of giving students greater freedom that was faulty, but the lack of facilities that would permit students to use this freedom wisely.

When a school facility is in the planning stages, special consideration should be given to the special needs of the open campus concept if it is to be adopted. In existing school buildings, however, the introduction of the open campus concept should be delayed until the proper facilities can be provided. Without such spaces, the open campus concept can become a real disappointment.

The open campus concept requires spaces for a wide variety of activities. These spaces can provide educationally enriching experiences for many students enrolled in a secondary school. A secondary school housing the open campus concept should:

1. Provide two or three classrooms where films are shown throughout the school day. Any student who has a "free period" should have the opportunity of viewing a film of his choice.
2. Include two or three television-reviewing rooms. Each room should have televisions turned to one of the major network stations.
3. Provide a student lounge where students can socialize. This space should be planned for some form of passive supervision.
4. Include a snack bar where students may obtain nourishment.
5. Feature a recreation room with Ping Pong tables and other similar recreational equipment.

6. Be designed so that noisy spaces do not interfere with the instructional process in other parts of the building.

7. Be planned so as to minimize vandalism where students may congregate in isolated, out-of-the-way alcoves, rooms, or corridors.

8. Take full advantage of glass walls that provide for the isolation of noise, but maintain visual contact among students.

The Open Space Plan

There has been a great deal of interest nationally in the design of school buildings without partitions. Some educators are beginning to have second thoughts about this concept. There are many strong arguments favoring the "open space plan" and an equal number of good reasons against it. The objective school plant planner usually finds himself having "mixed feelings" as to whether or not to recommend the open space plan. As a result, schools are designed with compromise features in relation to this concept. The compromise solution modifies the single large space interrupted only by supporting columns, by including a number of partial walls—floor to ceiling—supplemented by folding partitions. Both sides of this issue will be discussed in considerable detail in the subsequent paragraphs.

For the open space plan. The large expanse of space is psychologically liberating. One gets a feeling of freedom of both movement and thought in schools containing large open spaces. Since partitions are often light, movable visual screens, the spaces for instruction *can* be changed in size and shape—at will and at once. The omission of walls allegedly reduces the cost of the building substantially. The "open space plan" lends a feeling of informality to the learning process. Students feel less regimented in the "open space plan." There is likely to be a greater intermingling of both students and teachers. The open space plan facilitates the grouping and regrouping of students. The open space plan tends to encourage change, experimentation, and innovation.

Against the open space plan. Confusion and a laissez-faire attitude is often present in the "school without walls." As one observes such a school building, it soon becomes apparent that students roam from area to area. Since there are no corridors under the open space plan, students simply pass from one teaching area to and through another in traveling from one point in the building to another. Although there are yet no validated research findings regarding the quantity and quality of the learning that takes place in the open space plan, it can be hypothesized that the amount of learning occurring under this concept is open to question. From a first-hand qualitative study of the open plan school, the author found himself "straining" to hear the teacher from a position in the rear of the room. After two or three hours of this "extra straining," the author felt a sense of fatigue.

In discussing the open space plan with students, all seemed to like it, but both the writer and the students identified two major shortcomings of the open space plan. Subjects that require deep concentration are more difficult for the student to master under this plan. Students complained particularly of mathematics. The subject matter was not usually very exciting, while the topic discussed by the teacher on the other side of the screen seemed to be more interesting. It was also reported by some students in mathematics that sufficient chalkboard for student work was lacking. The other serious drawback of the open space plan deals with the use of audiovisual materials. The latter is incompatible with the "open space plan." Questions were raised with the school administration regarding the difficulty of using audiovisual materials. They had a ready-made solution: construct three audiovisual rooms. When it is realized that the open "classroom" is not used while the class is in the audiovisual room, it becomes abundantly clear that much, if not all, of the savings in walls is expended for the construction of audiovisual rooms to supplement the open space plan.

Many of the teachers liked the "liberated" feeling they experienced in the open space plan, but stated that the constant background noise forced them to concentrate on hearing and consequently left them somewhat physically fatigued at the end of the day. The open space plan is a mixed blessing. Ideally, it would be desirable to plan space in such a way that the open plan atmosphere and informality could be produced whenever it was desired, and that effective teaching spaces could be created through the simple operation of folding partitions when it was educationally advantageous to do so. Imaginative school planners may wish to face the challenge of designing a school facility that contains the advantages of the open space plan without its deficiencies.

The proponents of the open space plan also extol the virtues of flexibility in space. While this is theoretically possible, faculty members using the open space plan indicated that the space allocated to a given class activity is rarely changed. From a practical point of view, the "flexible" space becomes almost inflexible. In a given high school, the open space plan consisted of the space normally occupied by twenty-nine conventional classrooms plus space for corridors. Spaces for classes were loosely related to patches of colored tile on the floor. The colored patches also served an aesthetic function. Classes were located randomly within the open space. A mathematics class, for example, could adjoin an English class, a social studies class, and a foreign language class. Under these conditions, increasing the space in one class could not be done without encroaching on the space occupied by another group of students. Thus, the potential flexibility that was built into the open space plan could not be realized under normal operating conditions. In fairness to the open space plan, however, if a comprehensive team teaching approach were employed in the instructional program, the flexibility of space utilization inherent in the open space plan could be achieved. On the other hand, the degree of flexibility in a conventional building is also limited by the number, length, and arrangement of folding partitions and the configuration of the walls in a given area.

The School-Within-a-School Concept

For at least a decade, the school-within-a-school idea has been gaining considerable support at the high school level. In areas where the population is so concentrated that enrollments in excess of 1,500 students must be educated at one location, this concept should be seriously explored. This concept is sometimes called the "House Plan." A word of caution is in order, however. Some school districts resort to the school-within-a-school concept, not because of high population density, but because they want a single football or basketball team—clearly an indefensible rationale for planning any kind of high school. After all, some students must be transported over fairly long distances if, let us say, 2,500 students are to be enrolled in one school. The money spent in transporting pupils from home to school represents a necessary but noneducational expenditure, and such funds, whether they are from state or local sources, might be better utilized in direct support of the educational program. Consequently, when a secondary school is likely to have an enrollment of more than 1,500 students, the board of education and school planners should seek to provide multiple school plants in two or more parts of the school district, except in highly congested areas such as New York, Los Angeles, Chicago, Dallas, Boston, and Philadelphia.

A superintendent of schools once defended the planning of a single large high school in a sparsely settled school district by pointing out that pupils were bussed anyway. So, "What difference does it make?" Actually, it makes a considerable difference in cost—much more than the superintendent implied. In this situation, two secondary schools would have cut the bus mileage almost in half, not to mention the time spent on the buses by the pupils. Unless there is a compelling reason for building secondary schools with capacities greater than 1,500, the planning of one or more 1,200-student secondary schools should be given serious consideration. Under the school-within-a-school concept, a large secondary school is envisioned as two or more secondary schools operating independently on the same school site. Each school has students randomly assigned to it at all grade levels. Each school has its own administrative guidance and teaching personnel, and each is planned to operate as though it were located separately in another part of the school district.

BROADLY-BASED PLANNING CONCEPTS

The concepts and practices discussed thus far in this chapter are relatively narrow in scope and are confined to limited areas of educational activities and school organization. Admittedly, the consideration of such concepts is imperative in the planning of school buildings that are advanced in educational function and forward-looking in architectural design. But effective school building planning goes beyond the review and consideration of these types of concepts and practices. School plant planners must also be concerned with broad concepts that affect the physical operation and educational function of the entire school facility.

In planning school facilities of advanced design, it is prudent to give serious attention to those concepts and practices that are likely to have a positive influence on the function of the school plant as a whole or on the long range cost-effectiveness of capital outlay expenditures. A few examples of broadly-based concepts are presented in this section. Some of them are simply reminders of traditional practices that are fairly well-known among school officials and architects. Others are a little more subtle and less widespread. In any case, school plant planners should seriously weigh the advantages of concepts that are focused on the macroscopic aspects of school plant design as well as those that involve microscopic, but highly important, features of a well-planned school facility.

Planning Functional School Buildings

In 1880 Louis Sullivan, an eminent American architect, enunciated a fundamental principle of modern architecture: "Form follows function." This new principle, coupled with the influence of Richard Morris Hunt and Henry Hobson Richardson, men thoroughly trained by European study in architecture, hastened the revival of an architectural style that was destined to have a significant impact on the design of school buildings in the United States.

The planning of functional school buildings has been the primary goal of both architects and educators since the end of World War II. But, as mentioned earlier, the influence of this fundamental concept has been quite limited in the planning of school facilities. To be sure, there are outstanding schools in Wayland, Massachusetts; in Norridge, Illinois; in San Angelo, Texas; in Greenwich, Connecticut; in Lexington, Massachusetts; in San Mateo, California; and in Tucson, Arizona, to mention only a few. But the number of educationally imaginative school buildings in this country is still a very small percentage of those built since World War II.

The future holds much promise for the planning of educationally creative schools. A number of emerging educational concepts seem destined to make radical changes in the design of schools in the United States.

The remaining sections of this chapter will be devoted to new dimensions in school plant planning. Each major concept will be introduced in this chapter, and then discussed fully in subsequent chapters.

Image-Building Through Education

Little thought has been given to the image-building aspect of education. The image that the community projects to the world is important to the social and economic growth of that community. Although "Good schools build better communities," many local school districts make little effort to improve their overall image through education. A high-quality educational program is a vital feature of a favorable community image, and so are well-planned school buildings that contribute to the attainment of that program.

The school building enhances the community image in two ways —through its contribution to the educational program and through its visual appeal. Architects are very conscious of this feature of school design, but unfortunately, boards of education and school officials sometimes override their judgment in this respect.

Silently, but forcefully, school buildings create favorable or unfavorable impressions upon those who view them. To someone exploring the community as a prospective industrial site, an attractive building on a well-landscaped site may speak more eloquently than thousands of words spoken by the local chamber of commerce.

Curriculum-Oriented School Planning

If educationally effective school buildings are to be planned in the future, educators must explore and develop school planning in an entirely new dimension—curriculum development. To be sure, curriculum development is neither new nor unfamiliar to educators. Before an architect designs a school building, the local school officials should acquaint him with specific information related to the curriculum, the actual experiences that pupils undergo under the guidance of the school. For example, it means very little to an architect to tell him that a space is desired for general science. But if he is told that for about 30 percent of the time twenty-five pupils watch demonstrations by the teacher, about 20 percent of the time twenty-five pupils perform simple experiments using water, gas, and electricity at work benches, about 10 percent of the time fourteen pupils work on the chalkboard, about 30 percent of the time the instructor lectures and discusses material with twenty-five talented pupils, and that special projects are done in a separate room by about five talented pupils, the architect can begin to relate pupil activities or experiences to spatial requirements.

Information about the curriculum is indispensable to the architect. It might be helpful to place ourselves in the position of the architect. What would we do, as architects, if we were asked to design a general science room? We might think back twenty years to the one we used in junior high school and design one like it. We might read about the desired features of a general science room listed by the National Association of Science Teachers. We might travel to many schools and look at many science rooms in order to design a science room that contains what we think are the best features of all of them. If we were architects, we would be forced to design a science room of some kind, but we would never know whether or not we had designed the type of room our client needed unless we had a detailed description of the curriculum for general science.

Planning Schools for People

The human aspects of school plant planning are beginning to receive attention from educators and architects alike. Currently, primary emphasis is on functional planning of schools, that is, on designing the building to serve its intended functions effectively. Admittedly, functional planning is important, but it is equally important to plan for the needs of people. These needs transcend those that are met when a proper thermal, visual, and acoustical environment is created.

The concept of planning schools for people introduces a new dimension in school plant planning, which is discussed in Chapters 6 and 8. This concept calls for design of a school that meets the physical, psychological, and social needs of people, and protects their health, safety, and well-being. Basically, of course, the school must be planned to accommodate and facilitate the activities of students, teachers, clerical workers, custodians, and administrators. Naturally, these matters are consciously or subconsciously considered in the design of some of our most advanced schools, but little effort has been made to conceptualize these needs in a systematic and logical fashion.

Planning Schools for Effective Learning

No competent school planner would, in good conscience, permit the design of a school that would not promote effective learning. And yet, Roth, an international authority on schools,[3] felt prompted to say that the development of school buildings up to 1957 had been "faulty" because their design had not been based upon "sound and valid pedagogic principles." According to some architects currently engaged in planning schools, the situation has not changed significantly since Roth made this statement. A survey of the literature on school buildings published during

[3]Alfred Roth, The New School (New York: Frederick Prager, 1957), p. 26.

the past two years seems to support this view. Many educators are planning schools for team teaching, for variable grouping, for television, for teaching machines, but relatively few are consciously concerned with the direct application of accepted learning principles that should affect the design of entire buildings. The glamor surrounding educational innovations seems to obscure the fundamental principles of learning that should underlie the planning of every instructional element of school building.

Conceptual School Planning

It is difficult to express the full meaning of conceptual school planning. It is an intellectual activity that scans the universe of human thought in order to retrieve groups of related ideas for further study. It may be viewed, at times, as the end product of a search into the depths of knowledge for new and promising concepts related to the educative process.

Conceptual planning is perhaps one of the most important ingredients in the design of *educationally imaginative* school buildings. Conceptual school planning may be defined, in this connection, as the creative intellectual activity that precedes and contributes to the preparation of the educational specifications. It is the process whereby fundamental educational concepts are formulated, developed, expressed, evaluated, and incorporated in the design of the school. The steps associated with conceptual school planning lead from the intellectual to physical. Once the concept is developed to the point at which it can be verbalized, it must be carefully evaluated in relation to psychological principles of learning, principles of administration, and local and state educational policies before it can then be included in the educational specifications.

The Concept of Gradualism

Evolutionary changes in educational methodology are more likely to be effected than revolutionary revisions in school practices. Since the readiness principle applies to teachers as well as to pupils, it cannot be assumed that all teachers will be ready for proposed changes in instructional methods simultaneously. School buildings must be designed, therefore, for a smooth and gradual progression from existing teaching methods to those that may be proposed. Furthermore, it should be possible to vary the rate of such changes within the same area of instruction in accordance with the readiness of the teachers and students for proposed modifications in teaching methods. The application of the principle of gradualism in school plant planning has many implications for school design which transcend those of the well-established principle of flexibility.

The need for gradualism, however, should not in any way interfere with or interrupt the introduction of promising innovations into the school program. On the contrary, the concept of gradualism is viewed as an accelerator of desired change. Recognizing the existence of at least one major deterrent for change, it provides for it in a constructive and positive manner. Thus, the architect should plan a given school facility as though a desired new practice or practices were to be instituted on the day on which it is occupied, but design it so that the contemplated innovations may be introduced slowly over a period of time. Accordingly, a board of education and superintendent of schools should plan a school plant that can accommodate many bold and promising educational innovations without disturbing the security of its occupants or the serenity of the taxpayers or alumni financing it.

The Concept of Reversibility

The principle of reversibility is another new dimension in school plant planning. Educational practices that seem to hold much promise when a school is designed may prove to be ineffective or inappropriate later. There must be ample provision to move gradually in a desired direction, as mentioned in the previous paragraph, but there must also be an equally efficient procedure for reversing the direction of the change at any time. Although no school can be planned for reversibility of every change, the principle of reversibility should be applied in planning school buildings whenever possible.

The Concept of Contractibility

In the late 1960s, contractibility was given little or no consideration in the planning of school facilities. The emphasis was mostly on expansibility since school enrollments were increasing from year to year. The enrollment trends have reversed since that time and many school districts are confronted with excess building capacity.

In those school districts where new or expanded school facilities are needed, serious consideration should be given to contractibility of educational use. Under this principle, a school building should be designed so that a predetermined part of the facility could be used for other than educational purposes. In the event of a substantial decrease in school enrollment, the school district would be in a position to allow part of the school facility to be used by other public agencies or nonpublic enterprises whose activities are compatible with the educational function conducted in the remainder of the building. Thus, when planning new construction, school plant planners should ask the question, "How can this proposed school facility be used, if only about one-half of the capacity is needed at some future time?"

2

Procedures and Criteria for Long-Range Planning

CHAPTER 4

School Surveys

Education is a product of the dynamic culture in which we live. Like the changing society in which it thrives, education must continually change in response to the educational demands of our people. School districts are confronted periodically with the question of whether or not their schools are satisfying the current needs of society, a question that is often difficult to answer. The school survey method offers educators a promising technique for determining the extent to which our schools are meeting our nation's needs.

School surveys vary in profundity, in subject matter, and in method of execution, but they all have a number of elements in common. All surveys require relevant information about the school district, gathered and assembled in an orderly manner. School surveys usually include an interpretation and analysis of all pertinent data. They all contain a number of conclusions and a set of suggestions for the consideration of the board of education, and some suggest a step-by-step plan of action.

THE NATURE AND CHARACTER OF SCHOOL SURVEYS

A school survey is the *sine qua non* of educational planning. No school district can play intelligently for its future without first making a survey of its school system. A school district cannot be assured that it is spending public funds wisely nor can it really know with certainty whether or not its students are being properly educated without making a school survey. And no school district can know whether it is receiving a reasonable educational return for the tax dollars it expands without some form of professional study. In fact, a school district that fails periodically to review its educational program, operating procedures, and future needs never really knows whether or not the educational goals set forth by the board of education are being achieved.

Enlightened school administrators and forward-looking members of boards of education are beginning to recognize that the school survey represents an intelligent and sound approach to educational planning. In fact, the school survey could be viewed as an essential element of the decision-making process in education. Long-range planning that stems from a school survey is more likely to be soundly based than are decisions made without the benefit of a systematic study of the school district and the education it offers. According to Huxley, "Irrationally held truths may be more harmful than reasoned errors."[1] The survey technique provides a powerful means of removing many irrational notions from consideration in the development of a long-range plan. Yet it does not restrict action on matters than seem reasonable and logical, although some of these actions will inevitably fall into the category of "reasoned errors."

The school survey is not uniformly perceived by all educators. Some view it as a study in depth of any or all matters related to education. Some regard it simply as an educational inventory of the school district. Others may use it to evaluate present practices within the school district for the purpose of effecting educational improvement. Some educators utilize the school survey as an objective and systematic approach to future planning; indeed, as an application of the scientific method to the development of long-range educational plans. To still others it is a public relations device whereby the attention of members of boards of education, citizens, faculty, and staff becomes focused upon the goals of the school and the degree to which they are being attained by the school district. Educators generally agree, however, that a well-designed school survey reveals as objectively as possible the educational status of the school district and specifies the action required if the educational objectives of the school district are to be realized.

The principal purpose of most school surveys is to develop a long-range plan of action based upon an objective and systematic study of needs, resources, and educational goals of the school district. The findings, conclusions, and recommendations resulting from a school survey are presented in a written report to the board of education. A realistic plan of action should be part of this report. According to Moser, "The purpose of many surveys is simply to provide someone with information."[2] In a school survey, that *someone* may be a school official, a board of education, or a citizen.

DISTINCTIVE FEATURES OF SCHOOL SURVEYS

There are a number of compelling arguments for making a school survey. Many of the potential benefits of school studies are not rapidly apparent to school officials or members of boards of education. Nevertheless, the case for the school survey is quite impressive from the standpoint of improved

[1]Thomas Huxley, "The Coming of Age of the Origin of the Species," *Science and Culture,* v. 12.

[2]C. A. Moser, *Survey Methods in Social Investigation* (Toronto: Heinemann, Ltd., 1958), p. 2.

education and the more efficient use of tax dollars. The survey method is a logical approach to the ever-present task of devising a well-reasoned plan of action that serves the best interest of the students, the public, and the taxpayers of a school district. A few of the fundamental considerations related to school surveys are presented below.

1. *The school survey creates a favorite psychological climate for making an objective study of the educational affairs of a school district.* A school study is generally perceived as a scientific and impartial approach to the examination and evaluation of matters related to education. Such studies should contain objective, professional judgments and a well-reasoned analysis of the educational operation. The psychological climate for educational progress is most favorable during a school survey. Local school officials and members of the board of education usually maintain an open mind during a school survey. Action on major educational issues is often postponed pending the outcome of a survey, and decisions are more likely to be made on the basis of fact than emotion in school districts where school surveys have been conducted by competent people.

2. *The school survey offers an effective process for systematically assembling and analyzing data.* The survey process demands that meticulous attention be given to the gathering and analysis of all data. The validity and soundness of the survey recommendations are directly related to the care with which all of the basic data are assembled, compiled, analyzed, and evaluated. This methodical approach is an important aspect of the survey process.

3. *The school survey is an application of the scientific method of inquiry to educational problems.* In most school surveys, the data are gathered, analyzed, and evaluated. Then conclusions are drawn, and recommendations are formulated on the basis of these conclusions. Purposes and goals of the school system are clearly specified. In the school survey, existing educational practices in a school district are compared with those considered acceptable and desirable nationally. Recommendations developed in the survey are designed to correct any differences between observed and desired educational performance and to provide for any special educational needs of the community.

4. *The recommended long-range program resulting from a school survey is built almost entirely upon facts and logic.* In a school survey emotional forces are kept to a minimum. Expert-type surveys can be conducted without being unduly influenced by emotional attitudes related to local issues. Consultants working on expert-type surveys usually treat emotionally oriented information simply as one factor that must be taken into account in formulating a logical and realistic long-range plan for the school district.

5. *The school survey looks toward the future.* All too often, school districts live in a glory of their past. Some are interested in the present, and a few focus their attention on the immediate future, but only rarely do school districts plan in detail between five and ten years in advance.

Though the survey relies heavily on past experience and performance in the school district it is concerned with both immediate and long-range needs. Through the process of extrapolation, it is possible to identify the educational needs five or ten years hence. The school survey rests solidly on the past, is shaped by the present, and projects logically into the future.

6. *The school survey views all parts of the educational enterprise in proper perspective.* A school survey looks at all pertinent aspects of the educational undertaking. It includes an analysis and evaluation of all relevant information, viewing each bit of information in relation to other bits of information. A school study can disclose the status and quality of the educational program at the elementary, junior high school, and senior high school level at a given time. It can also reveal the articulation and relationships existing among these schools. Since a survey examines all facts that shape the overall effectiveness of the school system, each part of the educational enterprise may be viewed by itself and in relation to other parts of the school operation.

7. *The school survey may reveal inequalities of educational opportunity within a school district.* The comprehensive school survey, described later, includes an examination of every classroom, every subject, and every course in the school district. In such a study, the differences between similar activities in different parts of the school district are readily apparent. For example, there may be two second-grade classrooms in two different buildings. One class may be taught in a small, poorly ventilated classroom in the basement, while the other is housed in a well-designed classroom that provides a wide variety of pupil experiences. The differences in the quality of educational opportunity are quickly revealed when such facts are presented in a survey report.

8. *The school survey enables boards of education to plan on the basis of facts.* As has been mentioned earlier, the recommendations contained in school surveys stem from a professional analysis of the facts, not from opinions, hearsay, or public perceptions.

9. *The school survey represents a sound, business-like approach to school operation.* In 1977, over 81 billion dollars were spent in the United States to educate about 44 million pupils.[3] Any enterprise that costs over 20 billion dollars per year to manage and operate fits into the category of big business. Because of the decentralization of education in the United States, however, the enormousness of school business is not always recognized. Although not a profit-making enterprise, school business does represent a large investment of our national resources.

In any well-operated corporation, where success is measured in profits, long-range planning is of paramount importance in the future development of that business. Surveys and long-range planning are accepted as standard operating procedures in business, and, it would seem that such practices would be equally good for school business.

[3]U.S. Office of Education.

THE SCHOOL SURVEY PROCESS

The school survey process has been significantly improved since the end of World War II. The construction deferred during the war years and the rapid increase in pupil population after the war created a substantial disparity between building capacity and anticipated enrollments. Local boards of education were confronted with overwhelming problems caused by obsolescence of school plants, increased enrollments, and rising costs. As a result, the accelerating demand for school surveys soon outstripped the supply of school surveyors.

State departments of education and state universities responded to this need by establishing service divisions within their administrative structures. By and large, the state universities, where service bureaus were instituted, made the greatest contribution to the development of a sound school survey process. The various offices of field services in the state universities have contributed significantly to the development of the school survey techniques that are in use today. The work of John Herrick and Marion Conrad at Ohio State University and the efforts of Harold Church at Indiana University have made a noticeable impact on the survey process. For example, the percent of survival technique commonly used in making enrollment projections is frequently called, "The Ohio State Method." Merle Sumption and Basil Castaldi concentrated mainly on the development of citizens school surveys at the University of Illinois. Don Leu and Floyd Parker at Michigan State University have added survey techniques that are peculiar to studies made in very large school districts. Some of the private schools of education have also played an important part in furthering the knowledge and application of survey techniques. Cyril Sargent and Donald Mitchell, formerly of the Center of Field Studies at Harvard University, developed noteworthy techniques in projecting pupil enrollments, in assessing community characteristics and growth, and in viewing school problems from the standpoint of the community planner and the sociologist. At Stanford University, James MacConnell made a great contribution to the survey process, before he began a promising program in school research under the sponsorship of the Ford Foundation. Men such as Conrad Briner, formerly at the University of Chicago; Jack Childress, formerly at Northwestern University and Boston University; W. D. McClurkin, Peabody College; and Henry Linn and Felix McCormick at Teachers College, Columbia University, deserve much credit for the development and improvement of techniques and instruments employed in the survey process. No account of the development of the school survey process would be complete without mention of the late Nicholaus Engelhardt, who, as a professor at Teachers College, Columbia University, was among the first educators to devote his energies to the problem of the school survey. During the thirties, he laid the foundation for the survey techniques that are being used in the United States today. We are also indebted to his later work in his firm of Engelhardt, Engelhardt and Leggett, where he not only applied the techniques he had developed but constantly refined them and made such improvements available to education at large.

The survey process can be divided into four distinct sequential operations. The initial step of the survey method involves the systematic gathering and *organization of basic data*. All pertinent information is then subjected to *professional interpretation and evaluation*. The analysis, synthesis, and evaluation of the basic data lead to the *development of professionally sound conclusions*. And finally, the conclusions form the basis for the *preparation of recommendations* designed to chart the future course of the school district. Each phase of the survey process is discussed in the order that it would normally appear in any school survey.

THE DATA-GATHERING PHASE

The validity, quality, and usefulness of any school survey depend entirely upon the sufficiency, accuracy, and appropriateness of the basic data assembled during the study. No survey recommendations can be considered valid if the data upon which they are based are faulty in any way. A few simple guides for the data-gathering process should be kept in mind.

Selection of Necessary Data

Survey data should be relevant, necessary, and sufficient.   The selection of appropriate data for a school survey is crucial to the success of the study. Before embarking on the data-gathering phase of the survey, each member of the study group should spend some time determining exactly what information is needed. The experienced school survey consultant often begins by mentally reviewing every detail associated with the purpose, content, and scope of the school survey to be undertaken. He carefully analyzes the objectives of the survey and lists the nature of the basic data required for the study. He imagines, as accurately as possible, the field of inquiry that must be pursued in view of the topics that may be included in the recommendations, which are related in turn to the concerns expressed by the board of education, and the nature of the problem itself. He also envisions the *topical* aspects of the conclusions likely to be included in the survey report. At this point, the surveyor is not concerned at all about the content or specific nature of the possible conclusions and recommendations. He is interested only in the subjects or topics about which recommendations are likely to be developed. This plan of action enables the consultant to prepare a list of the kind of specific data required for the study before he actually begins the data-compiling process.

It should be emphasized that the school surveyor does *not* begin a school study by setting forth the desired theoretical solutions for which he later develops the rationale to substantiate his biases. Rather, he should anticipate the *topics* that may be included in the recommendations but *should not* concern himself with specific answers to problems. To illustrate this point, let us cite a typical situation. A board of education has requested a building survey of a school district. The surveyor reviews the topics that might be included in such a study. In so doing, he would probably ask himself a number of questions. Which buildings should be abandoned immediately? Which schools should be expanded? Which buildings should be remodeled? Which structures should be modernized? What is the maximum amount of money that should be spent in each school being remodeled? How much capacity should be added to the expanded schools? Where will new schools be located? What should be their capacity? What safety hazards should be avoided in locating new schools? What grade organization is best for the school district in view of the desired educational program and the adequacy of the present buildings? Where should mentally handicapped pupils and special education be housed? Where should the central administration be located? Should there be centralized warehousing and centralized kitchens? These and many other questions could be raised. As can easily be seen, these questions are not recommendations or answers to problems. They are simply topics that might be included in the recommendations. By studying questions such as those listed above, the school surveyor can begin to list the specific types of information that should be gathered. This preliminary overview of the study will enable the surveyor to prepare forms and checklists that will assist him in gathering the data systematically and efficiently, and help him to avoid gathering superfluous and irrelevant information.

Information about Community Mores and Attitudes

Survey data should include information on local attitudes and underlying community forces.   Some educators and professional persons conducting surveys would argue that the mores of a community and the way people of a school district feel about educational matters may be ignored in a school survey, but such forces, though intangible, are real and must be taken into account. This point of view, however, does not suggest that the emotional forces within the school district should be allowed to dominate survey recommendations. Instead, it views the emotional forces and the mores of a community as the setting within which sound educational action may be planned. With a knowledge of these intangible forces, a new dimension is added to long-range planning strategy and timing.

Organized Data-Gathering Procedure

The data-gathering process should be efficient and well-structured. After a list of needed data is prepared, the logical source of information for each item should be determined. Efficiency in data-gathering demands that the number of visits to the same source be kept at a minimum, not only to conserve time, but also to promote goodwill. Persons in a position to dispense information may become annoyed if they are subjected to repeated visits. Also, when surveys are made a group of citizens, goodwill of those supplying information often is shattered when different survey people repeatedly ask them for the same data. Not only do such practices adversely affect human relations, but they also reveal inefficiency in the data-gathering process.

DATA ANALYSIS, INTERPRETATION, AND EVALUATION

The second phase of the survey process, which involves the analysis and interpretation of the data that have been gathered, is critical in any study.

Data Organization and Analysis

Accurate data must be organized logically and set forth in a meaningful and useful form. Figures should be arranged in tables. Material related to the educational program should be organized around subject matter, courses, or activities. All ideas and explanations of the facts should be clearly stated. There should be a well-substantiated *descriptive* analysis of all matters related to the educational aspects of the school district. In a sense, this phase of the study consists of a detailed description of the present status of the school facilities, the educational program, and the operational aspects of the school districts.

Data Evaluation

Once the data are organized into a logical pattern, they must be evaluated and interpreted before they can contribute to the conclusions derived from a study. The process of evaluation involves judgment; judgment that depends upon the values, experience, knowledge, and background of the person making the judgment. The appraisal and interpretation of data should be made only by persons competent to do so. While this statement may seem superfluous, educators often allow technical decisions to be made by citizens in the name of democratic action on the assumption that everyone has a right to express an opinion, which overlooks the fact that there is a vast difference in validity between an opinion and a professional judgment.

All data related to *operational* and *instructional* aspects of education should be analyzed and evaluated by professionally trained persons. The strengths and weaknesses of the educational program and of the administrative organization should be identified and lucidly stated. The educational adequacy of all facilities should be covered in detail. All matters that work a hardship on the teacher-learning situation should be clearly noted. Any feature of the school that endangers the safety and health of those occupying the building should be strongly emphasized. In view of the wide array of topics that may be covered in a school survey, it is often necessary to employ a professional team whose members are capable of rendering professional judgments on matters related to structural engineering, community planning, fire safety, educational program, school plants, educational finance, school operation, and architecture.

TYPES OF SCHOOL SURVEYS

Although there appears to be a wide variety of school surveys, each is a specialized version of the comprehensive school survey. Specialized school surveys are generally conducted within a specified area of study for two main reasons. The first is related to cost. Specialized surveys are less costly and usually require less time for completion. The second reason for selecting a specialized survey is need. Often, the greatest need for a survey lies in one area of investigation only. For example, a school district confronted with a declining enrollment may wish to make a study of community growth and pupil population in order to plan its personnel needs for the future. It may have a lesser need for studying the educational program at such time. Each type of survey will be discussed in some detail in the subsequent sections of this text.

THE COMPREHENSIVE SCHOOL SURVEY

The comprehensive survey contains all of the specialized surveys described below. This type of survey could also include an energy audit like the one presented in Chapter 9. As its name implies, the comprehensive survey of a school district is quite broad. It includes a study of the community and its population, business procedures, budgets and capital costs, educational programs, staffing and in-service training, board policies, educational facilities. Only the types of school surveys that are most likely to be encountered in a school district are discussed in a subsequent section entitled, "Specialized Surveys." The school building survey, which is an essential element of educational facility planning, is described in detail in Chapter 5. While a comprehensive survey is an ideal process for achieving overall educational improvement, very few school districts select this type of survey. Thus, educational surveys are usually conducted in limited areas of inquiry based on the felt needs of the school district.

SPECIALIZED SCHOOL SURVEYS

Although a wide variety of specialized school surveys is possible, there are four major categories that include practically all types of surveys likely to be conducted in a school district. There may be instances where a school survey includes more than one type of the specialized surveys described in this section. Regardless of the scope of the survey, the same general principles apply to all types of school studies.

The Community and Pupil Population Survey

Studies in this category are concerned primarily with changes in pupil population and with the growth potential of the school district. This type of survey includes an examination of the geographical growth potential of the school district, a study of the population growth pattern of the community, a careful analysis of past pupil enrollments, and the computation of a statistically sound, grade-by-grade, year-by-year, enrollment projection.

Projection of Anticipated Pupil Population.   The preparation of an enrollment projection is indispensable to long-range educational planning. Although several techniques for making enrollment projections are currently in use, the perfect method for accurately predicting future enrollments has not yet been invented. Nevertheless, current methods are extremely helpful in planning for the future, even though the results are only reasonable approximations of anticipated future enrollments. As crude as our present methods seem to be, however, it can be reasonably expected that deviations from actual enrollments later should not exceed plus or minus 10 percent under normal circumstances. On the other hand, school surveyors also point out that if the projected enrollment agrees with the actual number of pupils four or five years hence, such agreement should be attributed more to coincidence than to skill.

The most widely used technique for projecting pupil population is the percent of retention method. The basic concept of this method is very simple. For each year and each grade in the past five to ten years[4] the percent of retention is computed. For example, what percent of the number of pupils in the first grade this year will appear in the second grade next year? The average percent for each grade, properly adjusted for factors foreseeable in the future, becomes the percent figure used in computing future enrollments. If, on the average, 98 pupils appear in the second grade in any given year for each 100 pupils in the first grade during the previous year, then this 98 percent plus an adjustment for foreseeable factors will determine the enrollment in each second grade if we know the enrollment of the first grade in the preceding year. This procedure is followed for each grade. A more detailed version of this method is described in *The Road to Better Schools*.[5] Work sheets and instructions are provided for the numerical computations associated with this type of enrollment projection. (See also Appendix A.)

[4]The number of years selected, which is based upon the type of growth pattern, requires professional judgment.

[5]Basil Castaldi, *The Road to Better Schools* (Cambridge, Mass.: New England School Development Council), 1955.

The Finance Survey

The finance survey includes a study of the business practices of the school district, a review of the disbursements and income, and a determination of the expenditure trends of the school district. The finance survey analyzes in detail the cost of operating the school district, using nationally accepted classifications of expenditures such as administration, instruction, operation of plant, attendance and health services, pupil transportation, maintenance of plant, and fixed charges. Financial figures should also be presented on a cost or income per pupil basis, so that it is possible not only to compare the cost or income per pupil with that in other school districts, but also to make comparisons among the various educational centers within the school district.

Survey experts also probe other aspects of school finance. They conduct an intensive search for all possible sources of school revenue and try to determine whether or not the school district is receiving all of the revenue to which it is legally entitled from local, county, state, federal, and private sources. The finance survey also contains an analysis of present indebtedness and bonding potential, as well as a projection of the bonding capacity of a school district for the foreseeable future. Such a survey includes future trends of wealth, pupil load, and financial ability of the school district as well as a look at assessment procedures and their effect on school revenue.

The finance survey may also contain a study in depth of the school business affairs of the district. The organization of the business services and the efficient use of all nonacademic personnel in the school district are scrutinized. The planning and procedures related to budget-making are evaluated in terms of educational soundness and financial efficiency. The accounting system and record-keeping functions are examined and studied. Purchasing procedures are judged in relation to sound business practices. The existence of adequate safeguards in the school system is also explored—safeguards to protect honest people from being falsely accused for malfeasance of duty and safeguards for the school district to protect it from being deceived or defrauded by persons or groups who are not acting in the public interest.

Educational Program Survey

Ideally, every school survey should include a comprehensive expert study of the educational program offered by the school district. The educational program of a district, after all, is the heart of the educational system in the United States. Unfortunately, school surveys often do not include an expert study in depth of the educational program. Perhaps the two principal reasons for the frequent omission of such studies are: (1) the cost of the program study is often higher than the school district is willing to pay, and (2) the need to employ outside experts for such a study is not readily acknowledged. The belief that a local staff survey of equal value can be conducted without outside assistance and at no additional cost to the school district tends to neutralize the desire of boards of education to have experts make a study of the educational program.

Regardless of who conducts the study, the educational program survey examines a wide variety of instructional materials and techniques. The program study also reviews and analyzes the specific educational goals of the school district and appraises the extent to which these goals are being met. The survey is designed to discover and identify shortcomings in the educational program and to include suggestions that will overcome such deficiencies. Properly conducted, a program study is a systematic and penetrating study of each element of the existing program in relation to the most advanced and effective instructional practices.

The program survey covers all of the instructional experiences that pupils undergo in a school. The course content, its sequence, and its depth are closely examined. The methodology and instructional techniques are scrutinized, and the textbooks and instructional materials used in the schools are examined from the standpoint of appropriateness and educational effectiveness. Finally, the overall program and related activities in each area of learning are judged in terms of the practices of today and the probable techniques of tomorrow. It should be pointed out that the degree of excellence of an educational program is difficult to determine objectively. Most of our evaluations are subjective, and many of our judgments must, of necessity, be inferential. For example, if we observe a practice that appears to be outstanding, we infer, often without proof, that good learning is taking place as a result of this practice. This conclusion is not necessarily valid in all situations.

Ideally, outside experts from the various areas of instruction should be employed to work with teachers and school staff in making a program study, but for financial reasons, this cooperative venture is not always possible. Consequently, the success of the teacher-staff study must rely heavily upon the competence of the school administrators and the resourcefulness of the teachers involved. With vision, cooperation, and mutual respect between the teachers and members of the administrative staff, it is possible to conduct a staff school program survey that can result in modernization of the curriculum in any school district.

The School Building Survey

One of the school surveys that is most often demanded and conducted is the building study. In many school districts, the need for a building survey often supplies the required spark that results in a much broader study. The building survey, in such cases, starts a sort of chain reaction in the thinking of members of boards of education regarding the educational areas that should be covered in a survey of the school district. While a program study, a community study, and a finance study can be made independently, since the facts needed are self-contained in the study, a building study cannot be made intelligently without a knowledge of future enrollments (community study), educational program (program study), and the financial ability of the school district (finance study). Consequently, whenever a valid building survey is made for a school district, the surveyors must take into account the findings resulting from other types of school surveys. The school building survey is discussed in detail in Chapter 5.

THE PRODUCERS OF SCHOOL SURVEYS

This section is devoted primarily to people who are involved in conducting school surveys. It is revealing to learn of the wide variety of groups that are commonly engaged in making educational recommendations that may have long-lasting effects on the quality of education in a school district. Boards of education are often confronted with a number of questions concerning the people who should conduct the school survey. Are professional persons the only people who make school surveys? Can citizens conduct school surveys without expert assistance? Is the school staff generally best qualified to make school surveys? Are surveys performed by experts more likely to be accepted by the community than those conducted by the administration and local professional staff? The answer to all of these questions is generally "No." There are advantages and disadvantages associated with surveys done by different groups of people. Each school district must decide for itself how it wishes to proceed in conducting a school survey. It is hoped that the information presented in this chapter will be helpful to school officials and boards of education in arriving at a decision regarding the people who should become involved in making a school survey. The choice depends entirely on the local situation at the time a school survey is considered. For example, if community attitudes on certain aspects of education are diversified, and some issues have become controversial and emotional, the citizen school survey becomes a very attractive option. Each alternative will be described in detail.

School Survey by Experts

The expert survey is directed and executed by experts in education who are usually from outside of the school district. Such surveys may be conducted by organized teams employed by state departments of education or universities, or they may be undertaken by private firms that conduct expert surveys.

Qualified survey groups are generally well trained, highly experienced and very well organized. After a preliminary review of the survey objectives, they are able to determine quite specifically most of the basic data required and where they are most likely to be available.

The expert-type survey is sometimes judged in terms of the amount of time that the experts spend in the field. The critics of expert studies may erroneously conclude that the validity of such studies is lower than that of locally conducted studies because the experts have had only a brief contact with the local situation. A study conducted by the former Office of Field Services at the University of Illinois revealed no foundation for such a conclusion. The study concluded that the recommendations of the expert studies were more consistently sound educationally than those resulting from locally conducted studies. The experts have a wealth of experience and background upon which to draw, while persons conducting local surveys are more apt to have limited experience. The expert devotes full time to the study, including periods when he is energetic and creative, while local persons usually work on a survey after school when they are normally tired.

The expert survey has much in its favor. It is conducted by an efficient and reliable method. It contains, for the most part, an impartial appraisal of the school district. It can be objective because the experts can "call them as they see them" without fear of personal consequences, since they do not usually live in the school district. Another advantage of the expert survey is that it can usually be completed in a shorter period of time than the local staff or citizens school survey.

The expert-type survey also possesses a number of disadvantages. As a school official once said, "An expert is one who blows in, blows off, and blows out." The statement contains a number of important implications. One weakness of the expert study is that the "expertness" is not and does not become part of the school district. All that the expert leaves in the school district at the completion of a study is a survey report. Since practically no local citizens participate in the expert survey, there may be no feeling of ownership or strong support for the recommended plans of action on the part of local citizens including the members of the board of education. Consequently, implementation of the recommendations made by experts is somewhat more difficult to achieve than implementation of the results from other types of surveys. In spite of these weaknesses, however, the expert-type survey can be most effective if it is followed by some form of citizen participation as soon as it is completed. And it can have an even greater impact on the community if some of the members of the expert survey team can work with citizens during the transitional period between the time when the study is completed and the time when community action is planned by local citizens.

The survey, of course, is only as good as the degree of expertness of the experts. While this might appear to be self-evident, if often escapes school officials and the boards of education who employ the experts. Even if the experts are on the staff of a university or a state department of education, boards of education should not confuse the prestige of the institution with the desired expertness of the individuals. When survey services are rendered on a fee basis, and they usually are, the board of education should assure itself that the experts possess the necessary competencies for the task at hand. When a prospective educational consultant or survey group is being interviewed, it is good business to require a statement, in writing, of the training, background, and experience of each member of the survey team.

School Survey by Local Professional Staff

A school survey may be conducted by the local superintendent of schools and his administrative and instructional staff. In this case, the outside experts mentioned in the preceding section are simply replaced by local talent. This type of survey is often called a self-study of the school district or is referred to as a form of the "do-it-yourself" survey.

The advantages accruing from this type of study are limited. The major benefit derived from such a study is financial. Since the personnel are already employed by the school district, only the additional cost of supplies and reference materials is involved. Another significant advantage of the local school staff survey is the participation of many local professional persons in the survey. The facts uncovered by the study, the conclusions drawn from them, and the recommendations set forth in the report represent the combined effort and thinking of local people. There is full understanding of the report and a strong feeling of interest in and support for the findings among a number of people living or working in the community. This group could become a nucleus for the planning of community action designed to implement the recommendations in the report.

Before a local staff survey is authorized, however, it is essential that its disadvantages be carefully weighed. It is important to realize that local staff personnel do not usually possess the same level of competence as do outside experts, nor do they usually have the technical competencies required for a school survey. For example, demographers, or men competent to make enrollment projections, are frequently not available at the local level. In all probability, there is no one at the local level who can make a professional evaluation of the adequacy of school facilities, in terms of future changes in instructional methods or equipment. It is also very rare that someone on the local staff has had the experience of extrapolating assessed valuations, revenues, and school operating costs for five to ten years. On the other hand, in studies involving the educational program, it is possible to identify a number of outstanding local teachers who can make a significant contribution in this type of school survey. But even in this area of investigation, some of the local staff may not be as up to date or as competent in some respects as outside experts. A second disadvantage is that local personnel would very likely be asked to conduct a staff survey on an overload basis, i.e., the survey would be one more responsibility added to an already full schedule. Obviously, the amount of energy that could be devoted to such a study would be quite limited. Third, the prestige of local people is usually not as great as that of an outsider. For some unknown reason, local people are seldom considered experts by the community. Therefore, the recommendations in a local survey report do not always carry as much infleunce as those found in the expert survey. Fourth, the local school staff is often accused, rightly or wrongly, of empire-building. Citizens may view local school surveys with suspicion; after all, they reason, the school staff has an educational axe to grind. Also, a local school staff survey is colored by the built-in biases of the various staff members in relation to the power structure and mores of the community. And finally, the local staff survey is more time-consuming than the expert survey.

Admittedly, studies of the educational program undertaken as a joint responsibility by teachers and staff have significantly improved education in many school districts. While the quality of such studies is usually good, the attention of the teachers and staff is concentrated primarily on the best-accepted practices of today without the benefit of the knowledge of changes that are likely to occur in the future.

It must not be concluded that surveys of the school program conducted by the local staff do not have a place in our educational scheme of things. It is well known that whenever studies of the educational program are conducted jointly by staff and teachers, curriculum improvement usually occurs. These studies are largely responsible for the updating of existing programs. There is often a lag between the time when educational innovations are accepted as good practices and the time when they appear in most of the schools. The work of teachers and staff on educational program development is indispensable to the introduction of accepted practices in the schools and the improvement of pupil experiences in the classrooms.

School Survey by Citizens

For the purpose of this discussion, a citizens school survey is a comprehensive study of the school district and educational matters conducted by a group of selected citizens *under the guidance of experienced professional personnel*. This definition excludes school studies made by a self-appointed group of citizens or surveys conducted by citizen pressure groups. A well-conducted citizens school survey can be a powerful, constructive, educational force in any school district. Citizens school surveys should be welcomed rather than feared by local school officials, provided the board of education and local school administrators are thoroughly familiar with the scope of such surveys, proper selection of members of the citizens committee, organization of the groups, procedures, and operating principles associated with this type of study and with the specific roles played by professional personnel as resource persons. Citizens can and should delve deeply into educational matters concerning *what the schools should accomplish* and into educational problems that *reflect the values and mores* of the community. On the other hand, they should not be asked to undertake studies of educational matters requiring technical and professional competence. Briefly, it is the responsibility of a citizens school survey committee to examine and evaluate *what* the schools should do but *not* to define *how* it shall be done. In a good school system, it is the duty of professional educators to determine *how* the results desired by the citizens shall be best achieved.

The citizens school survey is often responsible for significant changes in attitudes. In a citizens survey of school district reorganization in central Illinois, the change in attitude that occurred over a nine-month period was quite pronounced. During the first meeting of the study committee, fewer than 25 percent of the committee members were in favor of consolidating the two school districts in question. Nine months and twenty-two meetings later, the survey committee unamimously recommended that the two school districts form a single educational unit. According to social psychologists, such changes in attitudes are not at all surprising. They can be explained on the basis of socio-psychological principles. In discussing attitudinal mutability, Newcomb[6] attributes such changes in attitude to "increased familarity with the problem or object." Attitudinal changes are more likely to occur "when existing attitudes about it [the problem] are relatively weak" or when increased familiarity with the problem is brought about "by firsthand experiences." In a school survey both of these principles are operating. There are usually a few persons on a citizens survey committee whose attitudes about the issues to be examined are weak when the study is initiated. Also, the citizens school survey encourages citizens to gather basic data firsthand whenever possible.

In citizens school surveys when the line of demarcation between the responsibilities of lay citizens and those of professional personnel has not been clear, confusion has often resulted. There have been instances where professional personnel have dominated citizens groups to the point that the citizens merely "rubber stamped" the plans of the educators. On the other hand, there have also been situations where citizens have improperly involved themselves in technical matters related to education, such as methods for teaching reading and writing, or whether laboratory experiences are needed for effective instruction of science in junior high school. Citizens committees have on some occasions expressed their views on whether or not a three-year or a two-year junior high school should be established in a school district. This problem is complex and highly technical, requiring a knowledge of child development, educational psychology, and educational administration. It is not one that can be intelligently solved by laymen without technical guidance from professional educators.

[6]Theodore M. Newcomb, *Social Psychology* (New York: Dryden Press, 1950), p. 202.

An analogy will illustrate the line of demarcation between the responsibility of citizens and that of professionals. Let us suppose that a bridge must be built over a river. It is the responsibility of the citizens to decide where such a bridge shall be located and to specify its load, its capacity, etc. Once this determination is made, it becomes the responsibility of engineers to decide upon the length of the spans and the technical specifications of materials and design. Again, the citizens state *what* is needed and the professionals decide *how* best to achieve the desired results.

It should be emphasized, however, that citizens have much to contribute to a citizens school survey. They have the right and duty to describe what kind of educated individual they hope the school will produce. Citizens have every right to demand that certain areas of learning or skills be included in the school program. Citizens have the right to request the schools to impart attitudes and values to the students consistent with our culture and with our democratic way of life. These matters are not for the professionals to decide. In practice, school officials have made decisions in these matters under the guidance and direction of the board of education. Citizens committees can play a major role in shaping the education of the future in any school district, through the use of a well-conducted citizens school survey.

Principles Underlying the Organization and Function of Citizens School Surveys

The results of citizens school surveys will be most gratifying for boards of education, school personnel, and citizens if each person concerned can feel that he has made a worthwhile contribution to the study. The quality of a citizens school survey is directly related to the degree of participation of each member of the committee. The considerations listed below are drawn from the results of research on citizens school surveys conducted by the former Office of Field Services at the University of Illinois. Since a detailed description of procedural matters relating to citizens school surveys has been published by Sumption,[7] information regarding the details of organization, operation, and techniques will not be covered in this text.

Citizens school survey committees should be established on an ad hoc basis. A citizens committee should be organized to assist the board of education with a specific set of problems. The purpose of the citizens group should be stated clearly and precisely, and when that purpose has been achieved, the group should be dissolved. The practice in some school districts of establishing a citizens advisory committee as a continuing group is not in the best interest of the school district or the citizens. Standing committees seldom experience the satisfaction of completing a job and receiving due recognition for it. The advantages of the ad hoc citizens committee far outweigh its disadvantages in regard to a citizens school survey.

[7]Merle R. Sumption, *How to Conduct a Citizens School Survey* (New York: Prentice-Hall, 1952).

The members of the citizens survey committee should represent the total educational community.[8] It is essential that the study group selected be a valid sample of the community, and that the individuals in the group, insofar as possible, be those whose opinions and views are respected. Contrary to common belief, influential people are not necessarily those from the elite group. It might well be that the waitress at the hotel dining room is just as influential in her segment of the voting public in matters related to education as the bank president who lunches there is among his contacts on similar matters.

The citizens committee should be directly commissioned by the board of education and report directly to it. Citizens who are expected to give generously of their time, energy, and skills in conducting a school survey should be invited to participate in such a study by the highest educational authority in the school district. Also, the board of education should impress upon the citizens that their advice and assistance are genuinely desired. Citizens school study committees should not be used to promote a point of view or a plan of action that has been developed outside of the committee. On the contrary, the committee is responsible for the development of a plan of action which is transmitted directly to the board of education for its study and consideration.

The citizens survey committee should be organized so that competent resource persons are assigned to each area of study. The success of a citizens school survey depends almost entirely upon the ingenuity and creativity of the citizens and the quality of professional assistance and guidance available during the study. From the direct observation of many citizens groups in action, it has been found that a citizens survey committee is more likely to make a significant contribution to the educational program of the school district when it is assisted directly by competent resource persons. It has also been observed that citizens school surveys may have a negative or regressive influence upon the quality of education in a school district when professional resource personnel is completely lacking.

The overall span of time for a citizens school survey should not exceed one year. Experiments in which the overall time span of a survey was varied from three months to two years revealed clearly that citizens studies that extended over the long summer vacation into another school year lost their initial impact, and that the enthusiasm of the citizens waned noticeably with the passage of time.[9] These experiments also indicated that the optimum time span was between eight months and a year from the time the study group was selected to the completion of the survey report. Too short a time span apparently does not allow sufficient time for the committee to reach its peak performance as a group, and too long a time span causes frustration among the more impatient members of the group, increases dropouts, and increases the number of absences from the survey committee meetings.

[8]Ibid., p. 6.
[9]Office of Field Services, University of Illinois.

Citizens survey committees should meet once or twice a month. Experimentation on the frequency of regular meetings of citizens survey groups also revealed that if the full committee met more often than once every two weeks, the subgroups did not have enough time to complete their work between these regular meetings. It was also observed that if regular meetings were held less frequently than once a month, the continuity of the study was adversely affected. There was also an observable tendency to devote too much time to recapitulation at subsequent meetings when the time interval between survey committee meetings exceeded one month.

The formulation of recommendations in a citizens school survey should be the result of a joint effort by citizens and resource persons. The development of recommendations is one of the most important tasks of a citizens survey committee. The proposed recommendations should *not* be formulated by the professional resource persons and imposed upon the citizens. Nor should the citizens formulate recommendations without the guidance of professional personnel. The procedure suggested for the development of survey recommendations is discussed later in this chapter. It is sufficient to state here that the quality of the recommendation contained in a citizens survey report is directly related to the degree of cooperation between the citizens and the professional consultants when the recommendations are formulated.

The citizens survey committee should be organized so as to provide opportunities for maximum participation on the part of all its members. As was noted earlier, the quality of a citizens school study is related to the degree of participation of the citizens. The organization and the procedures of a citizens school survey should be designed to facilitate maximum participation by committee members. Whenever possible, additional citizens should be involved in the study at appropriate points. For example, the PTA could participate by taking a census under the guidance of the Pupil Population Subcommittee. Or, additional citizens could rate school buildings under the direction of the building subcommittee. A strong feeling of interest in the study is generated through such participation. With more people actively interested in the results of the study, a larger nucleus of informed citizens will be available in the school district when the time of community action approaches.

The board of education should give prompt recognition to the citizens who worked on a school survey. The board of education should formally accept a citizens survey at a public function. A letter or certificate from the board may be used as a form of recognition. It is important, too, that the board of education seriously consider each recommendation made by the citizens group. In the event that certain recommendations are not favorably received by the board, it must, as a representative of the people, explain to the satisfaction of the citizens group why it cannot act favorably on them. The board of education should not dismiss lightly any results of a study on which citizens spent many months.

Any delay by the board of education in giving recognition to the citizen survey committee for its work or in accepting the survey report can produce a potentially explosive situation. It should be realized the citizens have spent considerable energy in completing the study, and that they are apt to have paternalistic feelings toward the results of their study. In a sense, the survey may appear to be a masterpiece to the citizens. It is easy to understand, therefore, that any delay on the part of the board in accepting the report can be, and often is, interpreted as board disapproval of the study. Two basic principles should be borne in mind by the board of education: (a) *The more promptly a citizens report is accepted, the greater the goodwill generated by the school board among the citizens participating in the survey.* (b) *The greater the number of citizens recommendations that can be favorably acted upon by the board of education, the greater will be the citizens support for the improvement of the schools in the district.* Application of the latter principle makes it imperative that the board of education state clearly why it cannot follow citizen recommendations, if such is the case.

Organization, Process, and Procedures in Citizen School Surveys

A citizens school survey should not be employed by local school officials or boards of education until they have gained a complete understanding of the citizens survey process. Unless tested procedures and techniques are employed, the results of a citizens school survey may be disappointing and even disastrous. It should be pointed out that a citizens school survey is not always the best type of survey. In general, the more technical the area to be studied, the less desirable it is to organize a citizens survey. For example, it would be inappropriate to ask a group of citizens to offer recommendations as to the best method of teaching set theory in high school mathematics, but it would be quite proper to seek their help in determining the character of the Christmas program in the public schools. The citizens school survey is highly suited to situations involving community attitudes, values, and aspirations. Also, in school districts that have repeatedly lost school referenda, the citizens school survey becomes an excellent method of developing citizenry that is informed on educational matters. The school survey in such cases also provides the mechanism for valuable feedback to local school officials.

The Committee on Recommendations

As stated earlier, it is extremely important in citizens school surveys that the citizens themselves play a major role in the formulation of recommendations. According to Sumption,[10] the survey committee is subdivided into study groups. The four major divisions are:

[10]Sumption, *How to Conduct a Citizens School Survey*, p. 23.

    a. The community and its people
    b. The school finances
    c. The present school plant
    d. The educational program

These work groups are responsible for gathering, analyzing, and interpreting data in their respective areas. Each group acts almost independently during the first few meetings of the survey. As the survey progresses, each subcommittee in turn presents its report to the entire survey committee. The creation of a committee on recommendations (CORE committee) during the subcommittee reporting stage greatly facilitates the formulation of recommendations.

    The CORE committee consists of a representative from each subgroup, the consultant to each subgroup, the chairman and secretary of the overall school survey committee, and the survey director. The superintendent of schools and other school officials serve as resource persons for the CORE committee. This committee is not conceived as an executive body, but as a work group that prepares a set of tentative recommendations and presents them to the full committee for its consideration. The full committee may accept individual recommendations, reject them, or modify them. In some studies, the operating rules of the study may require that all modifications of the recommendations submitted by the CORE committee be approved by the appropriate subcommittee before such recommendations are adopted by the survey group as a whole.

    Although citizen participation in educational affairs has been generally supported by both school administrators and boards of education over the past few decades, the need for such participation has been greatly intensified recently through the efforts of the National Community Education Association with headquarters in Washington, D.C. A number of centers for community education have been established throughout the United States, including the Council of Education Facility Center in Ohio. Dwayne Gardner, executive director of the Council of Educational Facility Planners, set the tone in an issue of the *Community Education Journal*[11] featuring various aspects of edcational facility planning. With dwindling school enrollments and an increased interest in reducing taxes, community education activities are assuming a new and constructive role in society.

Guides for Deciding Whether to Make Citizens School Surveys

As indicated earlier, the citizens school survey is not always the best solution for all situations. While it is true that all citizens are familiar with education because they have all attended school, it does not follow that all citizens have the competence to deal with technical matters related to edu-

---

[11]*Community Education Journal*, January 1980, Community Education Association, Washington, D.C.

cation. A citizens school survey does hold an important and esteemed place in education in the United States and can serve as a powerful and constructive means of improving education.

A citizens school survey is most appropriate in situations where:

1. The perceived educational problems involve community values and local attitudes.
2. There is a lack of community understanding of what the schools should accomplish.
3. Repeated defeats of school referenda indicate that the public is not fully informed about the educational needs of the school district.
4. Public apathy has been responsible for a stagnant educational program.
5. The board of education is desirous of developing a sound long-range building program.
6. School district reorganization is being explored.

A citizens school survey is unsuitable in situations involving:

1. The planning of specific school buildings.
2. A study of content and methodology in any subject-matter field.
3. Studies of grade-level organization.
4. Studies of administrative procedures, organizations, and operational school policies.
5. Studies where less than six months can be devoted to a survey.
6. Studies requiring technical competence in the field of education and educational psychology.

School Survey by Citizens Assisted by Experts

This type of survey differs from the full-scale citizens school survey in that outside experts are not part of the study group, but are invited by the chairman of the citizens committee when they are needed. This type of study has impressive advantages and formidable shortcomings, and involves a calculated risk. Unless the local superintendent of schools has had previous experience with the citizens school survey and is prepared to assume full responsibility for directing the study, it is very unwise to undertake a modified citizens school survey. In some situations, such a survey has jeopardized the position of school administrators and reduced the effectiveness of the educational program in the school district; hence it should be undertaken with extreme caution.

Strengths and weaknesses.   The modified citizens school survey technique is one that should be approached very cautiously. School officials and members of boards of education should become familiar with the risks inherent in this type of study. Unless strong, positive leadership exists among the local school administrators and in the board of education, the risks in the use of the modified citizens school survey are greater than the potential value of such a study.

Advantages.   The primary advantage of the modified citizens school survey over the full-scale citizens survey is lower cost. The modified survey utilizes local school people as resource persons, and thus entails no additional cost for personnel. The full-scale citizens survey, discussed earlier, would require between 50 and 60 man-days of professional service paid for by the school district on a per diem of contract basis. It can be seen, therefore, that a medium-sized school district having an enrollment of about 5,000 pupils could save several thousands of dollars by conducting a modified citizens survey rather than a full-scale citizens survey.

Other arguments frequently offered in favor of this type of study are not conclusive. Some educators maintain that the employment of local school personnel as resource persons to citizens subcommittees makes available to the study groups information that is directly related and applicable to the local situation. It is further argued that local professional persons are also locally oriented and are, therefore, more sensitive to the local problems than outside consultants would be. These arguments, of course, cannot be refuted. What is often overlooked in comparing the modified and full-scale citizens survey, is that local resource persons are also used in the full-scale survey to supplement the services of the outside consultants. Consequently, it cannot be claimed that the use of local professional persons is an argument *for* the modified study and *against* the full-scale citizens survey.

Disadvantages.   The modified citizens school survey has a number of serious weaknesses that should be carefully considered before such a study is undertaken. The major disadvantages of the modified study school survey are listed below:

Citizens rarely request expert assistance, even though it is made available to them. In studies of this type, citizens are not always aware that they need professional assistance. As a result, they act or make decisions on the basis of ignorance, rather than knowledge. The writer hastens to add, however, that to the best of his own knowledge in such instances, the citizens acted in good conscience. In each situation, it was evident that the citizens simply were not cognizant of the complexities of the problem or issue at hand, and hence did not realize that technical assistance was required.

More specifically, citizens do not always realize their limitations in coping with problems related to modern education. For this reason, they are likely to draw erroneous conclusions and make unsound recommendations. In all fairness to citizens who give generously of their time, energy, and effort on such committees, it should be pointed out that they are sincere, conscientious, and well-intentioned. The only question that can be raised is whether or not citizens groups possess the necessary technical competence to conduct a school survey and to make recommendations that are educationally sound, financially possible, and administratively feasible.

Citizens seldom receive proper guidance in the organization, procedures, and content of citizens surveys. In a "do-it-yourself" survey such as this, there is, in all probability, no local person, professional or otherwise, who has the know-how for organizing and conducting a citizens school survey. Only in rare situations does a school district have among its professional personnel a person who has had broad experience in school surveys, in the use of group dynamics, and in applying the principles of social psychology to educational improvement.

There is a real danger that citizens will make decisions more on the basis of emotion, tradition, and loyalties than on the basis of facts. While this danger exists in any type of citizens school survey, the lack of experience among the local consultants assigned to the modified citizens school survey makes it difficult for them to cope with the problem. Also, since the local consultants live in the community, they tend to carry less influence and status than a resource person from outside the community. Experienced consultants working with citizens are extremely sensitive to group feeling and perceive the direction of thought in the group long before ideas begin to crystallize. It is during this crucial period that a consultant can be extremely effective as a resource person by raising fundamental questions at the appropriate time. This high-quality guidance is usually lacking in a "do-it-yourself" survey.

The modified survey may be quite provincial. Since the modified survey utilizes local personnel, local problems are viewed in a rather narrow perspective. Promising ideas and practices in use in other parts of the country are not always considered by such a group, simply because they know nothing about them. In all fairness to local resource persons, it should be pointed out that most of them probably have full-time duties as teachers or administrators, and must carry the committee assignment as an overload. Also, many promising educational innovations initiated in local school districts are not widely publicized, and educational research findings are not systematically disseminated. It is not at all surprising, therefore, to find that local professional people do not have so broad a perspective as experienced consultants, whose primary responsibility it is to be up-to-date on educational matters.

The modified citizens survey could create a negative educational force in the community. There are a few instances where a "do-it-yourself" survey has no impact, positive or negative, on the education of the school district. There are also a few cases in which the modified citizens school survey became a liability to the board of education and to school officials. A modified citizens survey was recently completed in an Ohio city. The citizens committee spent two years on the study. During that time they requested no expert assistance, other than to have a demographer make an enrollment projection, and they did not communicate either with the board of education or with school officials. The citizens simply studied the educational problems of the school district independently and rejected the services of local resource persons when such assistance was offered. When the study was finally completed and submitted to the board of education, its recommendations were found to be neither financially nor educationally sound. The recommended grade organization was quite impractical for the school district in question. The board of education, in good conscience, could not accept the citizen recommendations, whereupon the members of the committee took it upon themselves to make speeches throughout the city promoting their own point of view. The board of education and superintendent of schools became the target of public criticism, even though their position was educationally sound and financially efficient.

The writer does not intend to demonstrate that there is no place for the modified citizens school survey in education in the United States, but rather to emphasize that the "do-it-yourself" survey is *risky* unless strong and positive leadership is exercised by the local board of education or school administrators in conducting it. To be sure, there have been successful surveys of this type. But, without exception, strong local leadership and conscientious citizens were associated with these successful surveys. When a spirit of cooperation and understanding exists between the citizens group and the school officials and board of education, a modified citizens school survey can be undertaken with some degree of confidence, provided the local school officials are prepared to furnish competent and positive leadership in conducting such a study.

PRODUCT OUTCOME

In pursuing the scientific method of inquiry, no recommendations are possible unless they are preceded by the development of well-founded conclusions. Although the process of forming conclusions from data assembled in school surveys is complex and sometimes difficult, by examining many small pieces of related educational information, it is often possible to arrive at valid conclusions. This approach demands logic, common sense, and professional judgments, together with objectivity and understanding of the situation. Admittedly, conclusions in school surveys cannot always be derived from completely objective information and from a precise mathematical analysis of the available data. But there is no justification for substituting clichés or biases, opinions, and hearsay for logic and sound reasoning. To ignore well-considered professional judgments in arriving at conclusions in school surveys in the absence of more exact information is to destroy the very foundation of the survey process.

CONCLUSIONS

Conclusions Supported by Facts and Sound Professional Judgment

Conclusions included in a school survey must be substantiated by irrefutable evidence or sound professional judgment. It is extremely important that the relationship between the conclusions and the facts or judgments be clearly established and easily recognized by the reader of the survey report.

The care with which conclusions are formulated can also have an impact on school-community relations. Citizens are less likely to disagree with professional conclusions when such conclusions stem directly from valid professional judgments, objective data, and intelligent reasoning. If school officials can present conclusions that many citizens can understand on the basis of information included in the survey, the superintendent of schools and the board of education will encounter less opposition to the implementation of recommendations.

Conclusions in a school survey suggest a plan of action. Any study that leaves the reader with the feeling of "so what" defeats its purpose and represents a waste of both effort and money on the part of the school district. On the other hand, a survey containing sound recommendations can be invaluable to the educational growth and development of the school district. The essential characteristics of survey conclusions and recommendations are discussed in the following paragraphs.

Conclusions Avoid Educational Clichés and Shibboleths

Again, if a conclusion cannot be made on the basis of the evaluation and interpretation of the facts or professional judgments, it might better not be made at all. One weak conclusion that is questioned by citizens can cast doubt on other conclusions that are perfectly sound. The use of educational jargon to substantiate a conclusion does not particularly impress the citizens of a school district.

Analogies may be introduced to emphasize a conclusion, but they should not be used to substitute for the factual basis supporting it. Citizens may get the impression that educators must resort to analogies because the facts of the situation are not strong enough to support the conclusions.

Conclusions Focussed on Strengths and Weaknesses of a School District

Many school officials and school board members have the erroneous impression that the purpose of a survey is solely to find out what is wrong with a school district. This version of a school survey is correct as far as it goes, but it is too limited. The survey should also recognize and give due credit for the strengths and superior characteristics of the school program.

No school district is all bad or all good. The writer has found, without exception, that several positive statements can always be truthfully made about any school district. The positive approach to school surveys demands that evidence of excellence be given the same emphasis as evidence of inadequacy, inefficiency, and inferiority. Obviously, very little, if any, improvement can be expected from a survey report that accentuates the positive and eliminates a discussion of the negative. On the other hand, the shotgun approach that tears mercilessly into the negative aspects of the school district is also damaging. It tends to build up resentment among those affected by the study and often places school officials and boards of education on the defensive. What is really needed, of course, is a well-reasoned, factual, and firm presentation of the shortcomings discovered during the study which, if possible, implicates neither individuals nor groups. In any effective school survey, it is essential that both praiseworthy and uncomplimentary features be given equal consideration.

Conclusions Tactfully Stated

Conclusions that reflect unfavorably on the people of a school district are always unpopular. Many citizens may already recognize the deficiencies of their school district, but for some reason, no one dares to raise questions about them. In this respect, the school survey can serve a most useful function by bringing the truth out into the open for wide discussion. Without distorting the truth or minimizing the shortcomings of a school district, conclusions can be carefully prepared to make the needed impact upon the reader in language that does not arouse him to the immediate defense of his pride or school district. There is sometimes a tendency for school officials and school surveyors to de-emphasize the defiencies observed in a school district. This is not justifiable, because boards of education pay substantial fees for school studies, from which they hope to gain a complete picture of their districts so that improvements can be effected. It is a disservice to the boards of education to withhold or minimize the negative aspects of a school district. On the other hand, there is no point in antagonizing members of boards of education, school officials, and citizens by stating conclusions in an offensive or tactless manner. A judicious choice of words is appropriate in expressing conclusions that are not complimentary in nature.

Conclusions and Recommendations Clear and Concise

Conclusions, as well as recommendations that are discussed in the next section, should be clear, concise, and to the point. Conclusions may reflect a positive, negative, or neutral position. It is not uncommon to encounter conclusions that tend to confuse the reader. In their attempt to be fair, educators sometimes present more than one position related to a single point in one concluding statement. This technique should be avoided, if possible, since it only bewilders the citizens. If no definite conclusion can be drawn from the facts on a point of interest to the citizens, it should be stated in the conclusions.

It should be emphasized, in this connection, that every conclusion will not necessarily include a positive or negative statement on the issue. A neutral conclusion is possible and sometimes desirable. While a neutral conclusion does not usually lead to recommended action, other than perhaps suggesting further study on the issue in question, the inclusion or exclusion of a neutral conclusion in a survey depends upon the importance and nature of the issue under consideration.

Complex recommendations frequently confuse the readers and are likely to result in misunderstanding. It is true that many recommendations are inherently complex, but these can often be broken down in such a manner that two or three simple recommendations can replace a single complex statement.

RECOMMENDATIONS

Recommendations consist of a series of statements designed to achieve the goals and purposes of the school survey. Recommendations serve many purposes. They are instrumental in correcting deficiencies uncovered during the study. They promote improvements in the educational program. They focus on economic efficiency. And they suggest viable solutions to educational problems confronting the school district. Regardless of the intent of a recommendation, it should not be proposed unless it is the direct outcome of a well-documented conclusion. A valid recommendation, therefore, is one that can be traced back to one or more conclusions that can, in turn, be substantiated by the facts stated in the report. As indicated above, recommendations should be unambiguous, concise, and clear-cut. They should be expressed in tactful language. On the other hand, recommendations should not be worded so evasively or so conditionally that they lose their effectiveness. Each recommendation should focus on a specific type of action and each set of recommendations should apply to one option. It is possible for a survey report to include several options, but each option should be educationally sound. If the team conducting the survey believes that the alternative recommendations, though educationally sound, vary in quality from one another, it is within the prerogative of the survey team to list the alternatives in priority order and to give reasons for its choice of priority. This information is helpful to the school officials and boards of education who will be making final decisions after they have had an opportunity to study the survey report.

Recommendations—Realistic, Educationally Practicable, and Financially Feasible

Unless a recommendation appears logical, reasonable, practicable, and feasible to those responsible for taking action, it is doomed to failure. Educational soundness and financial feasibility are two fundamental consider-ations in the formulation of recommendations in school surveys.

Recommendations—Evolutionary in Nature

The application of the principle of gradualism is essential in recommenda-tions that involve changes or the introduction of innovations. Fundamental changes often demand changes within and outside of people. When recommendations provide for evolutionary changes, the desired results are more likely to be achieved because gradual change seems to be more acceptable to most people.

Recommendations—Sensitive to the Values and Attitudes of the Community

In school surveys, recommendations are designed to correct educational deficiencies, to effect essential improvements, and to provide for future needs, but any recommendation that contains ideas that are contrary to the feelings and attitudes of the people responsible for taking action on educa-tional matters will probably receive little, if any, consideration. The school surveyor thus finds himself in a dilemma. Should recommendations be de-signed to improve the educational ills of the school district or to please those empowered to act on the recommendations? It would be ideal if all recommendations could accomplish both purposes, but with regard to recommendations dealing with highly controversial educational topics, it is unlikely. In such instances, only his knowledge and understanding of the values and attitudes of the people enable the school surveyor to express sensitive recommendations tactfully.

CHAPTER 5

The School Building Survey

The school building survey report contains an evaluation of existing buildings in relation to the educational functions desired by the school district, including a calculation of building capacities, a statement of unmet educational needs, and a recommended long-range building program.

Knowledge of the Educational Program and Curriculum

While the building surveyor does not necessarily evaluate the educational program, nor does he formulate it, he must, nevertheless, be well acquainted with all of the programs, activities, and student experiences that should exist in a given school.

Formal educational offerings. As a first step in appraising the educational adequacy of a school building, the surveyor must develop a detailed mental image of a model school plant against which to compare existing buildings. In creating the mental image of the model school facility, he should have in his posession a detailed description of the educational program. It is not enough, for example, for local school officials to indicate that "art" will be taught in a high school. The course organization and content should be described briefly. The major types of pupil activities included in each course and the approximate number of students participating in each type of learning experience should be noted.

Informal educational offerings. The cocurricular opportunities available to students in a well-conceived educational program are designed to satisfy their individual interests and to supplement the formal instructional program. Accordingly, the building survey should evaluate the suitability and adequacy of existing school buildings for these instructional activities. Again, it is imperative that the school surveyor have a complete description of these supplementary activities to assist him in developing the image of the model school facility for the district.

Supplementary instructional activities.   Not all instructional activities occur in classrooms or laboratories. Self-instruction, for example, is carried on in the library, in the study halls, in the carrels where teaching devices are used, and in the sound laboratory through the medium of tapes. The school surveyor should build into the mental image of the model school building those features that facilitate additional activities, such as assembly, remedial instruction, group library work, dramatics, music, and art exhibition. He should also envision a school facility that can house other programs desired by the school district such as adult education, special education, and summer education.

Noninstructional activities.   All schools provide some type of service activities such as administration, health, and guidance. The major functional features of all noninstructional services supplied in the various types of school buildings should be noted by the school building surveyor. Other services that might be considered in a building survey include hot lunch, book rentals, secretarial, curriculum material preparation, audiovisual, and public relations.

Board of education policies affecting school plant.   The school surveyor should be aware of all board policies governing the manner in which school buildings are to be utilized. Knowledge of board policies serves two purposes. It permits the school building surveyor to determine the extent to which existing school facilities limit the implementation of established board policies, and guides him in developing recommendations designed to facilitate implementation of board policies on matters such as grade organization, maximum class size, nursery school, kindergarten, post-high school training, adult classes, night school, and summer school. Board policies related to the maximum distance pupils are required to walk to school, the maximum time pupils may ride on school buses, and the optimum size of the various types of schools are also of primary concern to the building surveyor.

Educational Adequacy of the Building Design

After the pertinent facts about a school building have been studied, the surveyor must answer the question, "Is the building under consideration designed to satisfactorily house the desired educational program?" To answer it, he turns to the mental image of the model representing the school capable of accommodating the desired educational program, and then compares the actual school with it. School buildings do not always possess every feature contained in the mental image, of course. Consequently, the building surveyor specifies whatever excellent features the real building may have and also lists its deficiencies. This evaluation enables him to arrive at a well-reasoned conclusion regarding the educational adequacy of the school.

It might be advantageous for the building surveyor to translate into words the mental image of his model building. He might prepare a checklist of such characteristics as size, shape, location of instructional spaces, and environmental conditions. He might also decribe any special features related to the school as a whole or to any space contained in it. Special work areas, unusual equipment, storage requirements, and certain display facilities might also be specified. Circulation patterns within the school and desirable space relationships could be mentioned. The checklist should be the product of an analysis of the desired educational program which has been imaginatively translated into reasonable and necessary space requirements.

Sufficiency of Instructional Spaces

The educational adequacy of a school can be adversely affected by any deficiency in either the number or size of available teaching spaces. Theoretically, capacity represents the largest number of students that can be instructed in a school building without curtailing the desired educational program. In practice, however, the capacity of a school has different meanings to different people. To some educators, the capacity of a building is simply the number of students that can be accommodated for "homeroom" purposes. To others, it is the number of pupils for which the architect originally designed the building. To many, the capacity of a school is the sum of the capacity of individual spaces multiplied by a pupil station utilization factor (see Chapter 6) of 0.80 for secondary schools and 0.90 for elementary schools. Note, however, that in none of these conceptions of capacity is any mention made of the school curriculum, administrative policy, or organization of the school day.

According to Conrad,[1] Knezevich,[2] and Castaldi,[3] ideally the number and type of instructional spaces contained in a school building should be those necessary and sufficient to accommodate the desired educational program for the total number of students enrolled in the school. A properly computed capacity of a school provides a measure of the spatial adequacy of the building in relation to the program housed in it. Consequently, if the capacity of a school is substantially lower than its student enrollment, the

[1]Marion J. Conrad, "Technique for Determining the Operating Capacity of Secondary School Buildings," doctoral dissertation, Ohio State University, 1952.

[2]Stephen Knezevich, "When are Schools Overcrowded?" *American School Board Journal*, 134 (January, 1957), pp. 46–48.

[3]Basil Castaldi, "The Concept of Dynamic Capacity," *School Executive* (August, 1959), pp. 44–45.

building is restricting the educational programs in some respects. Under these conditions, often characterized as "overcrowding," it is the quality of the educational experiences that usually suffers. The extent of the educational deficiency of a school with respect to capacity is directly proportional to the differences between its capacity and enrollment.

In any school building survey, the calculation of student capacity for each serviceable building is a prerequisite to long-range planning. To specify the type and size of additional school buildings needed in the foreseeable future, the capacity of all usable existing buildings must be accurately determined. Thus, the computation of building capacity provides information that is fundamental in the evaluation of the educational adequacy of a building and in the development of a long-range building program.

Secondary School Capacity

The most logical and meaningful approach to secondary school capacity to date was developed by Conrad[4] in 1952. The Conrad Technique directly relates capacity to educational program. His procedure is based on the principle that the building should fit rather than determine the program. Accordingly, the effective capacity of a building for a given educational program is determined by the number of pupils that can be properly accommodated in the subject-matter area where overcrowding would first occur.[5] For those who may wish to compute secondary school capacity using this method, a manual describing the application of the Conrad Technique is available.[6]

Although the Conrad technique is undoubtedly the most precise procedure for determining the operating capacity of secondary schools, the method of successive approximations[7] employing the "concept of dynamic capacity" will also produce satisfactory results. In using this method, the number of each type of space needed to house the desired educational program for any selected school enrollment is compared with the number of corresponding spaces available in an existing building. The trial-and-error method may be employed to determine the capacity of a school building by repeatedly comparing needed spaces with available spaces. A computation of the number of the various types of spaces needed for the current school enrollment adjusted for the desired rather than the present educational program may be a logical starting point. According to the

[4]Conrad, "Technique for Determining Operating Capacity."

[5]John H. Herrick et al., From School Program to School Plant (New York: Holt and Company, 1956), p. 70.

[6]Marion J. Conrad, A Manual for Determining the Operating Capacity of Secondary School Buildings (Columbus: The Bureau of Educational Research, Ohio State University, 1954).

[7]Castaldi, "The Concept of Dynamic Capacity."

method of successive approximations, the spaces needed for the desired educational program are computed for each selected total enrollment. The selected enrollment figure is repeatedly revised and space needs are re-computed until there is a fairly good match between spaces needed for the program and spaces available in the building. The total enrollment produc-ing the best fit between needed and available spaces becomes the capac-ity of the building. Only in rare situations will there be a perfect match be-tween available spaces and those needed for a given educational program and total enrollment. At best, the stated capacity will be a compromise in which there will be a deficiency in some types of spaces and an excess in others, and thus the stated capacity is usually qualified.

As an example, let us assume that the number of the various types of space in a given building is in close agreement with the corresponding spaces required by the desired educational program for a selected enroll-ment of 500 students. Let us assume that the existing building lacks one room for general science, 0.5 of a room for instruction in art, and contains three regular classrooms more than are needed for a total enrollment of 500 students. The capacity of this building, therefore, would be 500 pupils with an excess of three regular classrooms and a deficiency of 0.5 teaching station for instruction in art and one teaching station for instruction in science. Additional information on secondary school capacity is presented in Chapter 14.

A rule of thumb is sometimes utilized in making an approximate esti-mate of the capacity of a secondary school, but this approach is neither exact nor meaningful. On the other hand, it is sometimes necessary to make a rapid capacity computation for nontechnical purposes. The capac-ity of a conventionally organized secondary school can be roughly approximated by multiplying the number of *teaching stations* by 23. A teaching station is defined as any space where one teacher (conventional school) instructs a group of students. Thus libraries, study halls, cafeterias, and auditoriums would be excluded from the enumeration of teaching sta-tions, but a gymnasium designed so that four classes can be taught in it simultaneously would be recorded as four teaching stations.

Elementary School Capacity

The capacity of an elementary school (K-6) organized in accordance with the self-contained classroom concept is relatively simple to compute. The acceptable class size at the elementary level ranges between twenty and twenty-five pupils in kindergarten and between twenty-two and twenty-seven in grades 1–6, provided the floor area of the classroom exceeds a minimum size of 1,100 square feet for kindergarten and 850 square feet for the remaining grades. The minimum figures have been reduced slight-ly from earlier accepted sizes for economic and energy conservation reasons.

This matter is discussed more fully in Chapters 13 and 14. Two factors affect the capacity of conventionally organized elementary schools. One is related to school district policy regarding maximum class size and the other to limitations imposed upon the desired class size by the lack of space in the classroom. In determining the capacity of an elementary school, the school surveyor simply uses either the maximum class size established by the board of education or the maximum class size that may be effectively instructed in a space of limited size or improper shape, whichever class size is lower. Since there are no standards, as such, the school surveyor must use professional judgment in determining the number of pupils that can profitably participate in the learning experiences intended for the space in question. For purposes of long-range planning, the capacity of an elementary school may be taken as the sum of the capacity of the individual spaces less 10 percent. Some educators simply regard the sum of the capacity of the individual self-contained classrooms as the capacity of the school. The additional 10 percent, however, allows some leeway for the annual variations in grade enrollments. Of course, it is often extremely difficult to balance class sizes in school districts where only one or two sections per grade may be in operation, and class load equalization can be a troublesome problem in school districts of any size.

In the less conventional elementary schools, where team teaching, large and small group instruction, and departmentalization are used, capacity computations are made in accordance with techniques described earlier under the heading Secondary School Capacity. A simple method of approximating the capacity of nontraditionally organized elementary schools consists of converting existing spaces into "equivalent self-contained classrooms" and applying the technique described in the preceding paragraph.

Safety and Health

Every school building survey must include a close examination of all features of the school that affect the safety and health of its occupants. Any school that endangers the safety or health of those using the building should be closed, unless the deficiencies can be corrected.

Although school surveyors are not expected to possess all of the technical competencies required to evaluate the safety and health characteristics of a schoolhouse, they should, at least, be sufficiently familiar with such problems to recognize the need for further study by experts. A few of the major aspects of safety and health are mentioned below.

Fire safety.   The danger resulting from fire is of primary concern to school officials, boards of education, and school surveyors. Points to be considered in evaluating the fire safety of a school include heating plants, escape of combustible gases, the rapidity with which fire may spread through the structure, electrical wiring and overloaded circuits, storage of combustible materials, fire alarm systems, condition and serviceability of fire extinguishers, and safety of emergency egress from the building. Whenever feasible, a school surveyor should engage the services of an authority in fire hazards to assist him in assessing the fire safety of a school.

Structural soundness.   The evaluation of the structural safety of a school lies strictly in the province of structural engineering. Unless the school surveyor is a structural engineer, he would be well advised simply to report all observable structural deterioration without an evaluation of its possible consequences. If, in the judgment of the school building surveyor, the structural deterioration has reached the point of endangering lives, he should urge that the building be examined by a structural engineer without delay.

Environmental conditions.   Healthfulness is closely related to a number of environmental factors that are of primary interest to the school building surveyor. For example, lack of cleanliness; improper disposition of garbage, trash, and ashes; insufficient control of rodents, flies, and insects; and improper storage of foods are all matters of concern. Also it is essential that the school surveyor examine the visual environment of the school, including the quality of illumination, brightness balances in the instructional areas, and freedom from glare in the visual sphere of the students. The building survey also includes a study of the performance of heating and ventilating systems and an appraisal of the acoustical environment, particularly in very quiet or extremely noisy areas.

Other safety considerations.   The school survey should take careful note of safety conditions both inside and outside of the school. The improper location of doors, worn stair treads, loose plaster, slippery floors, and unprotected plate glass represent only a few examples of possible hazards within the building. Outside of the building, safety considerations may be concentrated on matters such as the layout of driveways, the location of pupil bus-loading zones, the type and condition of play equipment, the various play surfaces, and the presence of unprotected high-voltage electrical transformers.

Development of the Long-Range Building Program

Long-range planning is the process whereby the actions of the past and present are logically and sensibly related to those planned for the future. Because of the permanent and fixed nature of both school buildings and instructional equipment, it is essential that future planning be based upon sound reasoning and desirable educational objectives.

Before a sound long-range plan can be developed, the conclusions related to educational program, existing buildings, pupil population, and finance must be examined and carefully considered. A valid long-range building program is the product of many factors. Logically, conclusions pertaining to the desired educational program and anticipated pupil enrollments establish the overall housing need of a school district. Conclusions about the adequacy of present facilities indicate the extent to which present buildings can meet the overall need. And conclusions concerning finance and rate of population growth determine the rate at which new facilities will be needed and the extent to which construction of new buildings can be financed.

Principles of Long-Range Planning

Sometimes, of course, a board of education must deviate from a well-conceived long-range plan because of public sentiment or the necessity for gaining public support. However, before yielding to a less desirable solution, the board of education should do all within its power to raise the educational expectation level of the citizens through some form of participatory action such as the citizens school survey discussed in Chapter 4. The guides listed below describe a few essential features of a sound long-range building program.

Is based on fact and sound professional judgments.   A good long-range plan of action should stem from conclusions derived from facts and professional judgments, not hearsay, unsubstantiated opinions, personal biases, and superficial explanations. Facts, together with common sense and practicality, are likely to produce a plan that is financially prudent, educationally defensible, and logically justifiable to the public.

Makes the most effective use of serviceable facilities.   Present school buildings represent a substantial amount of capital outlay and should not be cast away lightly. Obviously, any building that is hopelessly obsolete should not be continued in operation, but every bit of useful life should be extracted from a school even though it may mean that some compromises must be made temporarily. Furthermore, no school should be abandoned simply because it is old, if it is still structurally and educationally sound.

Does not freeze the action of future boards of education.   Any building program that commits future boards to a single plan is not desirable. A "one-way" street feature of a long-range plan ignores the unforseeable changes that may take place in the future and may prevent future boards from making choices that may be advantageous to the pupils and the school district at a later date. For example, a board of education may decide to add to an existing junior high school instead of constructing the nucleus of a new one on a separate site. Adding to the existing building may well mean that a future board of education is committed to further additions to that school because the amount of space needed might not justify building the nucleus of a new junior high school at a later date. The "one-way street" action is quite insidious, because it has every appearance of an ideal solution at the time it is taken. It is important, therefore, that the board of education be constantly on the alert to recognize the "one-way street" approach and avoid it.

Avoids the "tack-on" policy.   The practice of adding space to a school a little at a time, or of planning a series of small additions to existing buildings, is costly and may provide capacity where it is not needed a few years hence. A sound long-range plan, therefore, can best satisfy the principles of economy and efficiency when construction consists of sizeable units on adequate sites *where schools will be needed in the foreseeable future.*

Specifies the most suitable grade organization.   There may be several solutions regarding grade organization and attendance areas in a school district, depending upon the character of the educational program, distribution of pupil homes, and the capacity, location, and use of existing schools. Any grade organization should be carefully considered in terms of educational, psychological, and operational factors. The fact that a given grade organization works well in one school district is no guarantee that it will work or even be applicable to any other. To some degree, the capacity, location, and type of available facilities will favor one grade organization over another, but the focus should be primarily on the educational soundness of the plan, rather than simply on providing space for pupil desks. The recommended grade organization should help to provide high quality of education and effective utilization of present buildings with a minimum of pupil inconvenience.

Is educationally effective.   A good long-range plan should produce the maximum educational impact upon the students enrolled in the schools by promoting high staff utilization in schools that are designed for efficient instructional practices. Spatial adequacy and suitability are of paramount importance in providing meaningful learning experiences. Thus, the use of school buildings possessing these two characteristics should be maximized.

Is economical.   A good long-range plan is geared to long-term economy in capital outlay, maintenance, and operation. Such a plan provides for maximum space utilization and keeps costs of operation, maintenance, transportation, supervision, and administration to a minimum. Buildings with a high maintenance cost per pupil should be scheduled for abandonment. Schools that are too small to offer a broad program of modern education should not be continued in operation except on an emergency basis.

Is flexible.   Any long-range plan must provide for the forseeable and make allowances for the unforseeable. The plan should be devised so as to leave as many alternatives as possible open to future boards of education. For example, if a board of education has a choice of providing two high school buildings or one, it would be far more advantageous from the standpoint of future planning and community growth to include two high schools in the long-range plan. The flexibility of such a plan is quite clear. Any future board of education could add to one or both schools, or in the event of a large growth in a given area, could simply plan a third unit and still retain a balance in the size of the high schools in the district.

Takes into account the accepted minimum and maximum range in the size of enrollment.   Current educational practice in the United States suggests certain limits in the size of the various types of schools. Table 5.1 indicates the generally accepted minimum and maximum capacities for elementary, junior high, and high schools. Admittedly, there are a few high schools in the nation exceeding the limits stated in Table 5.1, but such large enrollments in a single school are due primarily to circumstances, such as an extremely high pupil population density, which is fairly common only in major cities. It can be demonstrated mathematically that there is no significant economic advantage in increasing the size of secondary school beyond a capacity of about 1,400 pupils. While no validated research findings exist on the relationship between school size and educational effectiveness, advanced educational programs can be found both in schools whose enrollments are within the accepted range and in those exceeding it. It can be concluded, therefore, that size beyond a certain minimum enrollment does not, per se, contribute to improved education. In considering the size of a school, it is also necessary to take into account the added cost of transportation often associated with large schools. Many educators maintain that very large high schools have no significant advantage over schools with a capacity of about 1,200, and that there is an appreciable loss psychologically and instructionally in such schools owing to their size.

TABLE 5.1   Generally accepted range of enrollment of various types of schools

Type of School	Minimum Enrollment	Maximum Enrollment
Elementary	200	600–650
Middle School (7–8 or 7–9)	500–600	900–1,000
High School (9–12 or 10–12)	600–700	1,200–1,500
High School (9–12 or 10–12) using school-within-a-school concept	2,000	5,000–6,000

Takes into account the size of the school site needed.   Table 5.2 indicates minimum standrds for size of school sites. Within the past decade, the trend has been toward acquiring the largest possible school site. Many school districts have acquired large tracts of land only to discover that neither the architect nor school personnel could devise ways of using so much space. Excessively large sites cannot be justified in urban and suburban areas where land costs are exceedingly high. On the other hand, we cannot be satisfied with the "postage-stamp" sites that were prevalent during the depression years. It can be demonstrated through the use of a scaled drawing of the site layout that the size of the sites suggested in Table 5.2 will provide sufficient space for all of the activities and outdoor instructional programs *normally* associated with the respective schools.

Is related to the financial ability of the district.   A long-range building program should be geared to the financial ability of the school district. It should be realistic and practical from the standpoint of public acceptance but should not compromise desirable goals and sound principles. Fortunately, most citizens are willing to support good education if they are fully informed of current needs and the soundness of proposed methods of meeting these needs.

Provides for safety, welfare, and convenience.   Schools should be located so that pupils do not have to cross principal highways when walking to school. Other barriers such as railroads and rivers should be taken into account. Elementary-grade pupils should not have to walk more than three-fourths of a mile to school, and it is preferable that the walking distance from home to school does not exceed one-half mile "as the pupil walks." The use of half-mile radius circles is not realistic in areas such as the Midwest where the grid system is used in laying out streets. It is suggested that a square, three-fourths mile on each side, be used as the unit for the placement of schools in urban or suburban areas where the layout of streets forms a grid pattern.

Provides new facilities in strategic locations.   The long-range building program relates the location of new schools to those that are to be continued in operation indefinitely. Also, the location of new schools should

TABLE 5.2   Reasonable minimum standards for school sites

Type of School	Basic Number Of Acres	Additional Acres Per 100 Pupils
Elementary (K–6)	5	1
Middle School (7–8 or 7–9)	10–15	1
High School (9–12 or 10–12)	15–20	1

take into account the ultimate abandonment of some of the existing build-ins, insofar as possible. This goal is sometimes difficult to attain when school sites are not available at a reasonable cost where they are needed. Nevertheless, every effort should be made to locate new schools so that they can absorb the capacity of schools scheduled for abandonment, with-out causing unnecessary inconveniences or hardships for the pupils in-volved.

THE EDUCATIONAL PROGRAM AND
THE LONG-RANGE PLAN

School buildings are often regarded as educational tools designed to facili-tate, promote, and stimulate the educational program. Actually school buildings sometimes possess physical characteristics that impose severe re-strictions on the educational program. Inadequate or unsuitable instruc-tional facilities can reshape, limit, or modify the school curriculum beyond tolerable limits. Consequently, the school surveyor should clearly envision the complete educational task to be accomplished *before* he makes any attempt to devise a long-range building program. Techniques for making this study and analysis are discussed in a number of publications.[8] For the purpose of the text, it is assumed that the school surveyor has either de-vised a systematic procedure of his own or has employed one of those de-scribed elsewhere for the review, study, and synthesis of the desired edu-cational program. It is further assumed that:

1. The school surveyor has the major characteristics and features of the recommended educational program clearly in mind.
2. The school surveyor has listed all of the program conclusions and recommendations in the survey report affecting the type, loca-tion, or design of school buildings.
3. The school surveyor has established an order of priority for each program conclusion and recommendation related to school fa-cilities.
4. The school surveyor has specified, insofar as possible, the man-ner in which each program recommendation affects the overall or specific planning of school facilities.

[8]Merle R. Sumption and Jack L. Landes, *Planning Functional School Buildings* (New York: Harper and Brothers, 1957), pp. 43–61; Wallace Strevell and Arvid Burke, *Administration of the School Building Program* (New York: McGraw-Hill, 1959), pp. 80–82; John Herrick, Ralph McLeary, Wilfred Clapp, Walter Bogner, *From School Program to School Plant* (New York: Holt and Company, 1956), pp. 35–47; Basil Castaldi, *The Road to Better Schools*, pp. 52–57; Harold L. Hawkins, *Appraisal Guide for School Facilities*, (Midland, Michigan: Pendell Publishing Co. 1976).

Future Uses of Present School Buildings

Before a long-range building program can be developed, the most effective use or uses of existing facilities must be determined. To do this, the school surveyor should review the evaluation of each building discussed in the survey report, study carefully all of the conclusions derived from the basic data, and examine the preliminary estimate of the overall housing needs of the school district. With this knowledge clearly in mind, he is prepared to make an intelligent decision regarding the future use of each building. Any of four fundamental decisions may be made in regard to each school. The use of the building for instructional purposes may be discontinued. It may continue to be used on a temporary or emergency basis. It may be remodeled and used for an indefinite period of time. Or it may be continued in use indefinitely "as is." Also, serviceable buildings may be utilized in the future to house the same or different grade-level groupings. Once the specific future use of an existing school is determined, a capacity should be computed, as described earlier, in terms of its new use and the program to be housed in it.

While citizens seem to take the continued use of existing school buildings almost for granted, the experienced school building surveyor insists that under certain conditions school buildings should not be continued in operation. A few of the conditions are listed below. The continuing use of a school building is considered questionable if:

1. The building is educationally obsolete and cannot be modernized at a reasonable cost.
2. The building is structurally unsound and endangers the safety of its occupants.
3. The building is no longer needed at its present location, and it is financially unwise to transport pupils to it.
4. The building is unsafe from the standpoint of fire hazards and cannot be made safe and sound at a reasonable cost.

Schools to be abandoned.   When a school is no longer suitable or desired for instructional purposes, it can either be relinquished by the school district and utilized for other purposes or disposed of by the board of education according to law. In the event that a building is scheduled for abandonment, the survey should indicate the method of its disposition. It may be advantageous for a school district to sell its obsolete school buildings. Thus, a school district receives a monetary return from the sale of capital items and simultaneously increases the value of the taxable property from which, in turn, the district may derive additional annual income. Sometimes, obsolete school buildings may still be of service to the school district as maintenance, supply, or administrative centers. It may be argued that if a school is inadequate for instructional purposes, it should not be used for other educational activities such as administration. What is erroneously assumed in this viewpoint is that the spatial requirements of, let us say, administrative functions are the same as those demanded by the educational program. A building may be definitely unsuitable for instructional uses, and still be utilized to the advantage of the school district for other purposes. When a building is retained for other purposes, however, the survey report should indicate the manner in which it will be utilized in the long-range plan.

Schools to be continued in use on an emergency basis.   Sometimes it is financially impossible to replace obsolete and inadequate schoolhouses with new facilities. In these instances, such schools should be operated on an emergency basis. The long-range plans should provide for their ultimate and speedy abandonment. As long as they are in service, however, these schools should be kept safe and healthful. No major expenses for capital outlay are warranted for buildings in this category.

Schools to be remodeled and continued in use.   Expansion or remodeling may be justified in some schools because the building has high educational potential or because a change in use is contemplated. Not all schools with educational potential should be remodeled. Several important considerations should be carefully weighed before major remodeling is planned. The urge to remodel is often stronger than the will to rebuild. Consequently, long-range planners should resist the temptation to remodel when rebuilding might represent a wiser expenditure of public funds.

The expansion of existing schools is often more readily accepted by the public than other solutions, but additions are sometimes difficult to justify from the standpoint of economy, pupil convenience, and need for additional capacity in that area. The question of making additions to existing schools should be considered very carefully. The topics of remodeling and expansion of existing buildings are treated in detail in Chapter 16.

Schools to be continued in use "as is."   Except in rare cases, most schools that are less than ten years old fall into this category. In these instances, the buildings would be utilized in the future in the same manner as they have been in the past. Only buildings or parts of buildings that are structurally safe, educationally sound, and operationally efficient should be continued without alteration.

Community Growth and the Location of New Construction

Timing—the key year.   The overall need for school facilities depends on two distinct variables—the educational program and future enrollments. In the preceding section, it was pointed out that before a long-range building program is developed, a well-defined educational program must be specified. While the nature of the educational program strongly influences the type, design, and function of school buildings, a study of community growth and pupil population provides the facts that determine the future number, size, and location of school facilities within the school district.

In formulating a long-range building program, it is desirable to select a key year for planning purposes. In general, the key year is determined by adding two years to the estimated date of completion of the first stage of the recommended building program. For example, if anticipated enrollments indicate that additional facilities for a given capacity are needed by year "X," the planning capacity should be geared to the enrollments expected in year "X + 2." This suggestion stems from practical considerations with respect to public relations. It is advisable to allow about two years to elapse between the time that one building project is completed and the time at which citizens are asked to vote on another school building referendum. Admittedly, this leeway cannot always be provided in school districts where the bonding capacity is not increasing at the same rate as the school enrollment. All too common is the situation in which a new school is overcrowded on the day it opens. Consequently, a two-year leeway between project completion and referendum on a subsequent project should be built into a long-range building program, if possible.

In selecting the key year in the building program, it is important to estimate the time required for planning and construction. About two years should be allowed for the planning and construction of schools having a floor area of less than roughly 50,000 square feet, and about three years for the planning and construction of schools not exceeding about 200,000 square feet in usable floor area. For example, if the survey findings indicate that a 1,000-pupil high school is needed immediately, at least one year would be required for the educational and architectural planning of the school and the passage of a bond referendum. If the planning and construction of this urgently needed school proceeded with dispatch, the building would probably be ready for occupancy at the end of the third year. If two years are to be allowed for leeway purposes, the key year in this instance is five years beyond the time at which the planning process for the proposed school is initiated.

Location and capacity of new construction.   The location and capacity of new school buildings are directly related to the direction and extent of community growth. In school districts where an annual census is taken in fixed geographical units, rather than by school attendance areas, community growth can be predicted with reasonable accuracy using the percent-of-survival technique. Since, as a rule, most school districts do not systematically collect and update census data, the problem of defining the geographical area where a specified capacity is required is somewhat complicated and requires a special technique. See Appendix B.

Relationship of new construction to obsolete schools.   In determining the precise location of new schools, it is extremely important to take into account existing buildings with a limited educational life. New schools should be located so that they can absorb all or some of the load from existing schools that are likely to be abandoned because of obsolescence. The future configuration of school buildings should facilitate the abandonment of schools that are unsafe, unhealthful, or educationally unsound without causing undue hardships or unnecessary inconvenience to the pupils so displaced.

Additions to existing buildings.   The expansion of existing schools often appears to be an attractive solution to the inexperienced long-range planner. Oftentimes, an addition which makes good sense in the short-range view would be a serious mistake in a long-range building program. The urge to expand existing buildings is very strong among citizens, and school planners should not adopt this solution to building needs without careful study.

The following guidelines should be observed in making decisions regarding school additions. An addition to an existing school is financially or educationally questionable if:

1. The school under consideration is no longer needed in its present location.
2. The building has structural defects that cannot be corrected at a reasonable cost.
3. The school is educationally obsolete and cannot be modernized at a reasonable cost.
4. The building is unsafe or unhealthful and cannot be made safe and sound at a reasonable cost.
5. The site is inadequate and cannot be expanded or improved at a reasonable cost.
6. The addition would not be part of *both* a short- and a long-range building program.
7. The cost of adding to the school is unreasonable in relation to the probable useful life of the existing building.

School Sites

The selection of school sites that will be required in the foreseeable future is an important aspect of long-range planning. Ideally, new schools should be located where they provide maximum convenience and safety for the pupils that may be attending them. New schools should be located in areas that are free from excessive noise, obnoxious gases and fumes, and approaches to airports. Simply stated, a school district should provide proper facilities with sufficient capacity at locations where they are needed at the time when they are needed. To achieve these objectives, a well-conceived site acquisition plan should be included in the long-range building program.

The characteristics of school sites depend upon many factors, including the type of school proposed for the site, its initial and projected ultimate enrollment, the breadth of educational program, the cost and availability of sites, the grade levels to be housed, and the aesthetic values possessed by the community. The specific characteristics and general location of the school sites needed in the future should be clearly stated and discussed in the rationale supporting the site program.

For several reasons, school sites should be acquired several years before a building is actually needed at a given location. Cost usually rises when land is converted from farming or general purposes to residential use. The availability of school sites at locations where they will be needed later is substantially reduced if the selection of a site does not precede the population growth in any part of the school district. And finally, the desired acreage for the site may have to be sacrificed if school sites are not acquired very early, sometimes as much as five years before the actual need arises.

School site acquisition may be handled in at least three ways.

1. The desired site may be acquired outright as soon as the future need for it is established.
2. The desired site may be selected, but not purchased immediately. The school district may take an option on a parcel of land.
3. The desired school site may be carefully watched by the board of education. Oftentimes, when it is not known exactly in which direction the population growth in a school district will occur, a board of education may simply "pinpoint" a site or sites and not act until it feels that it would be wise to acquire the needed land.

Finance

No long-range building program would be complete without some discussion of financial matters relating to capital outlay for new construction, remodeling, and modernization. In most states, the bonding potential of a school district is set by a state finance commission. In any case, the school surveyor must ascertain from state sources the maximum bonding capacity of a given school district before he can develop a realistic long-range building program. Where finances are limited, the long-range plan must be organized in stages. As the school district recovers bonding potential, it can construct additional facilities that may be required.

As soon as the total need for additional facilities has been specified, cost estimates can be made to determine the magnitude of the building program required. If the total amount of capital outlay is within the bonding capacity of the school district, the long-range building program can proceed without restriction. On the other hand, if there is a deficiency in bonding capacity, the school surveyor must plan the long-range program as a series of steps based upon priorities of need and upon rate of recovery of bonding capacity.

The impact of the recommended building program on the tax rate is of paramount importance in the minds of taxpayers who are, in most cases, also voters. Once the magnitude of the required capital outlay is determined and a bonding period and repayment plan are established, it is possible to compute the tax rate for the foreseeable future, provided a projection of assessed valuations has been made in the basic finance study of the school survey. It would not be realistic, in a growing community, to base future tax rates on present assessed valuations. On the other hand, future assessed valuations can fluctuate within wide limits, depending upon assessment procedures and policies. The rate of increase of assessed valuation due to new construction in the school district is also subject to considerable fluctuation. Nevertheless, it is desirable to make a conservative estimate of future increases in assessed valuation in order to give voters as true a picture of the future as possible.

Multi-Stage Planning

The long-range building program is often organized in sequential phases. Each stage of the plan is determined largely by the rate of increase of needed capacity or by financial limitations. In school districts where the rate of growth of pupil population is not rapid, the various stages of the long-range building program are influenced primarily by the rate at which additional capacity is needed.

In rapidly growing school districts, however, financial ability often lags behind the demand for additional capacity. In these districts the solution to the building problem must be ingeniously contrived in order to extract the maximum capacity and educational return per dollar of capital expended. Each stage in the building program will be determined literally by dollars and cents, and the facilities provided under these circumstances require buildings that are designed with extraordinary educational vision. They must possess design features that will satisfy temporary needs without requiring costly remodeling later when their ultimate purposes are to be fulfilled.

THE LONG-RANGE BUILDING PROGRAM—A PLAN OF ACTION

A well-conceived long-range plan contains several essential elements. In the preceding paragraphs, it was suggested that the long-range school planner assemble facts, conclusions, and inferences from conclusions. He was urged to initiate the task of long-range planning only after all the salient facts were written down or carefully noted in his mind. In the process of formulating the recommended long-range building program, it might be helpful to view the entire school facility problem, first in relation to its component parts and then as a unified solution to the problem as a whole. The long-range plan may include the acquisition of school sites, construction of new facilities, abandonment of existing schools, the remodeling and expansion of present buildings, a multi-stage plan of action based upon priority of need or financial limitation, financial implications of the recommended plan, and a rationale supporting the proposed long-range plan. It is realized, of course, that not all of these elements are necessarily included in all long-range building programs, but certainly each of them should be seriously considered in the formulation of any sound long-range building program.

Rationale for the Long-Range Building Program

Every long-range plan should contain a detailed rationale supporting the recommendations. It is unrealistic to expect the public or board of education to accept a plan without a clear understanding of the reasoning that underlies it. The rationale should convince the reader that the recommended plan possesses most of the characteristics described in the following paragraphs.

1. *The rationale should demonstrate that the recommended plan is logical.* The rationale should deal at length with each major recommendation, tracing its evolution from facts through well-reasoned conclusions. Clichés should be avoided insofar as possible, and the voice of authorities should be used sparingly. Facts, professional judgments, reasoning, and common sense are often more convincing to citizens than opinions uttered by some national authority.

2. *The rationale should emphasize the flexibility of the recommended plan.* Boards of education are often quite impressed by the variety of possibilities that the recommended plan offers to their successors, the future boards of education. It is worthwhile, therefore, to accentuate all characteristics of the plan that make provision for unforeseeable developments.

3. *The rationale should stress the educational soundness of the recommended plan.* Citizens, by and large, desire the best educational

program that their school district can provide. School districts that are recognized statewide or nationally for excellence of educational program are known to generate a deep sense of civic pride among citizens. Every effort should be made in preparing the rationale to point out exactly how the various recommendations contribute to high-quality education for the school district.

4. *The rationale should clearly explain the economic and financial advantages of the recommended plan.* People seek the assurance that they are getting a high return for their money. A sound and well-conceived building program is usually designed for maximum financial efficiency, and its economic advantages should be stressed. Citizens are usually more willing to support education when they are convinced of receiving reasonably good value for their tax dollars.

5. *The rationale should emphasize any part of the recommended plan that reflects the feelings and attitudes of the people in the school district.* Any recommendation or any part of the long-range plan that is in harmony with the thinking and attitudes of the community should be highlighted in the rationale, because citizens are more likely to accept a plan that they feel was designed "with them in mind."

6. *The rationale should stress that the recommended plan is advanced in character but conservative in action.* People are interested in the new and yet often loyal to the old. The rationale should assure the citizens that the recommended plan is solidly based on the best practices of the past, but firmly oriented toward the promising instructional patterns of the future. It might also be desirable to explain the evolutionary nature of the plan and to indicate the manner in which a series of gradual changes provides a smooth transition from the good practices of today to the improved teaching techniques of tomorrow. The rationale should convince the citizens that a well-reasoned and properly controlled dynamism for educational improvement is incorporated in the recommended long-range building program.

CHAPTER 6

The Prerequisites of Architectural Planning

The preparation of educational specifications, the selection of a site, and the organization of people for action must precede the architectural design of any school plant. Indeed, school planning may be conceived as a coordinated concentration of human effort. Educational specifications that grow out of the planning process should reflect the best ideas and suggestions from every source, including faculty, consultants, state departments of education, industry, and colleges and universities. This chapter is devoted primarily to the planning activities associated with the organization of people, selection of school sites, and preparation of educational specifications for use by the architect.

THE EDUCATIONAL PROGRAM

The educational program should strongly influence the design of any school building. No educational facility that imposes unwanted restrictions upon the educational program is well planned. Faulty design or overcrowding adversely affects the function of a school. Overcrowding is sometimes unavoidable because of limited financial resources or unexpectedly rapid population growth in the school district. In designing educationally effective school buildings, it is essential that the curriculum be clearly defined before architectural planning is initiated.

Statement of the Educational Program

No architect can design a functional school building for a given educational need without a lucid description of the educational program. The term "educational program" is often used loosely to signify curriculum and vice versa. It is not enough to inform an architect that history, physics, and music are parts of the program. What the architect must know is exactly what the students do in a physics laboratory or in a music room. He must know what equipment is needed and how much space the educators feel a student needs to perform each type of educational experience.

Curriculum development. Considerable time should be spent by the faculty in developing the curriculum before an architect is asked to put a single line on paper. If possible, the architect should be invited to attend some of the meetings devoted to curriculum development, particularly during the last stages of this activity.

While it is not within the scope of this book to discuss effective practices and procedures in curriculum development, as suggested earlier, the group process should be employed in working out clearly specified educational goals and the means of attaining them. These means can then be translated into a logical and pedagogically sound series of student experiences.

As noted above, the architect must be familiar with each different student activity, the number of students participating in it, and the nature of the activity itself. For example, he must know that senior English is taught to groups of 250 students who may subdivide into smaller groups of 10 or 15, or work individually or in pairs part of the time. The architect should be informed that students are also involved in individual and group conferences with the teacher, and that they may use learning devices for the purpose of program enrichment about 10 percent of the time. It is essential that the school designer be aware of the use of special equipment, such as centrally stored tapes from which audio signals may be transmitted to booths located in strategic points within the school. Briefly, every type of student experience should be described for the architect, including the space and equipment required as well as the approximate proportion of time devoted to a given type of activity. This latter information may become quite important if compromises in a school must be made because of circumstances beyond the control of school planners, especially when it is either impossible or impractical to provide for every type of pupil experience in a school building.

Curriculum development is a crucial aspect of school plant planning. Without it, an architect is deprived of the basic knowledge he needs to design an educational facility that meets the need of his client, the school district. Lacking such information, he must look elsewhere for information about the basic educational concepts and student experiences that should underlie the design of the building. This lack of educational information places an unfair burden upon the school architect that may well result in the design of a school that is inappropriate and ill attuned to the specific needs of a school district or institution of higher learning. The development of the desired curriculum, therefore, is one of the first orders of business in the planning of a new school. In all fairness, it must be acknowledged that many educators who want to devote at least six months (a minimum amount of time) to curriculum development are often pressured by architects and members of boards of education to get the building in blueprint form before the curriculum is developed. And there is often a dire need to erect a new school building without delay. Under such circumstances, both the architect and the board of education are acting expediently and in good faith. But the fact remains that a functional school building meeting the needs of a given educational program cannot be planned until such needs are clearly identified through the process of curriculum development. School buildings have a useful life exceeding half a century, and, therefore, they should be planned to meet both immediate and long-range needs.

Promising educational practices.   In developing the curriculum, faculty members should explore the possibility of introducing new practices that seem to hold promise for educational advancement. Certainly, the faculty should strive to improve the educational practices in their school system. Faculty members can learn about other developments by attending conferences and national conventions.

A propitious time to consider incorporation of new educational practices into the curriculum is during the planning of a new school building. At this time architectural changes can be made with ease and often without additional cost.

PRINCIPLES UNDERLYING EDUCATIONAL PLANNING OF A SCHOOL

Educational planning is focused primarily upon the achievement of desired educational goals by means of a logical and well-defined series of learning experiences. In relating educational goals to student experiences, the principles of balance, economy, need, and gradualism should be considered.

The principle of balance.   Educational planners should view each educational goal of the institution in proper perspective. The curriculum should reflect a well-balanced array of student learning experiences that further the basic purposes of the institution. There should be balance among the courses offered and in the depth of penetration required in each course. There should be balanced emphasis on different types of student experiences. Not all courses should receive equal emphasis, but at the same time, emphasis in one area of learning should not be accomplished at the exclusion or expense of another area that is equally important in the attainment of the goals of the school. For example, school planners should guard against overemphasizing the physical sciences at the expense of the humanities or emphasizing the gymnasium and competitive athletics at the expense of the library.

School planners should test the proposed curriculum for balance before translating it into building specifications. They might ask: Is there a direct relationship between the emphasis to be given a learning experience and the goal it is intended to achieve? If the goals of an institution are well balanced, then this test leads to a balanced curriculum.

The principle of educational efficiency.   Curriculum planners are deeply concerned with the type, sequence, and effectiveness of the multitude of learning experiences necessary to achieve educational goals. In selecting the experiences that should be included in the curriculum, first priority should be given to those that are more likely to produce effective, high-quality learning. The type, organization, and sequence of the learning experiences, therefore, should be educationally efficient, i.e., they should produce maximum learning for the minimum expenditure of energy, time, and money. Admittedly, it is extremely difficult, if not impossible, to measure educational return with any degree of accuracy. In this application of the principle of educational efficiency, however, it is intended that the educational planner simply recognize the objectives underlying the concept without becoming too concerned about its mathematical implications.

At some point in the process of developing the curriculum, educational planners should test the various learning experiences under consideration against the principle of educational efficiency. In applying this concept, they should select those learning experiences and educational practices that are likely to yield more effective and desirable educational results and reject those that tend to produce limited or questionable educational outcomes.

The principle of gradualism.   School buildings at all levels of learning must not inhibit curriculum changes, nor should they impose curriculum changes upon the administrators, staff, and students before they are ready for them. For example, if a new building were designed for large- and small-group instruction it would have to be instituted as soon as the school was occupied simply because the building could not house the traditional program. No period of transition to the new system could be provided for teachers or pupils, regardless of whether they were prepared for it or not. In this instance, obviously, the psychological principle of readiness would have been violated.

On the other hand, the principle of gradualism does not suggest that desired innovations should be limited in any way. It simply provides that the curriculum and the building be so conceived that all changes can be introduced gradually and in parts. Thus, the dynamics of the changing curriculum would be planned so that a smooth and gradual transition could be made from the old to the new. Furthermore, changes could be made rapidly in one part of the curriculum and slowly in another, if necessary.

PLANNING FOR COMMUNITY USES

Public school facilities belong to the people of the school district. They are provided primarily for the education of the children, youth, and adults of the school district. Unfortunately, these facilities are often used for this purpose less than 50 percent of the available time during the week and less than 60 percent during the year. Many school districts use school facilities for continuing education programs for adults, evenings and weekends, and offer summer courses for the children and youth of the district. Obviously, this supplementary use of public school facilities improves their utilization to some extent, but much more could be done to better serve the community that supports the public schools. Due consideration should be given to the use of school facilities for recreational and cultural community functions. It is therefore important for school planners to actively explore a wide variety of community uses for possible inclusion in the design of educational facilities.

Consequently, every effort should be made to design school facilities for existing and anticipated community uses. Such uses can be identified through some form of citizen participation. Often, with only minor changes in the plans, play fields, gymnasiums, swimming pools, and large-group spaces can be functionally designed for numerous community activities. The benefits to be derived from such community uses are quite diverse. The pool, gymnasium, and play fields could contribute to better health. The auditorium can serve to enrich the cultural activities of the school district. The cafeteria can be utilized for civic activities designed to improve the community through collective action. The learning resources center is ideal for taxpayers interested in individual self-improvement. And the classrooms can be utilized as meeting places for small groups engaged in constructive community activities. It is important, therefore, that school plant planners consider all of the supplementary community uses of a proposed school facility when it is in the "educational specification" stage of the planning. The architect should know as early as possible what special needs the building is to house and what specific features should be incorporated in the design of the building.

Educational facilities planned for community use are often viewed by taxpayers as a school building with a plus feature. This positive public attitude may have an important bearing on the outcome of a school bond issue. Planning school facilities for community use is, per se, a sound and wise investment of public funds, regardless of other considerations. But when it is coupled with the positive impact that such planning may have on the passage of a bond issue, the case for planning school buildings for wide community use is significantly strengthened. Two excellent publications deal in depth with the planning and function of educational facilities for community uses. The *Community Education Journal*[1] and the Educational Facilities Laboratories[2] in New York have published exhaustive and authentic information on the use and operation of school facilities for community purposes.

If school buildings are to be used for educational and community-oriented functions, they should be planned specifically for this dual purpose. School plant planners should also take into account whether or not the community will use the building while classes are in session. At the present time, for example, there is an ever-increasing demand by community groups to establish daytime child-care centers in school buildings. With more and more mothers joining the work force, this trend will increase dramatically in the near future.

A crucial consideration in school plant planning is the potential conflict between the educational function and the community use. When school facilities are used during the school day for day care centers, programs for the elderly, and for special community health services, there may be conflict with the educational function. Community-oriented school facilities are also used by the public after school hours during the academic year and/or during the summer months. The need for this use is quite pronounced and will grow substantially in the future as working hours are shortened and recreational time is increased.

Under these conditions, school plant planners are presented with a real challenge in designing dual purpose educational facilities. Ideally, there should be no interference whatsoever between school and community uses of a school building. There should be no noise pollution attributable to community functions conducted in a school building. Such public use should not pose any safety hazards to the students in the building or on the school site. The community use of the school building should not restrict nor impede the normal flow of student traffic within the building.

There are other design characteristics that must be given high priority in the planning of school-community centers. School plant planners should provide effective solutions to several questions.

Does the design of the building provide adequate safeguards against vandalism or pilferage when the facility is used after school or during the summer? Are spaces designed for community use self-contained from the standpoint of exits, zoned heating, toilet facilities, and storage spaces needed for each public use? Are the spaces planned for community

[1]*Community Education Journal*, Volume VII, Number 2, National Community Education Association, Washington, D.C. January, 1980.

[2]*Community School Centers*, Education Facilities Laboratories, New York, N.Y. Series of 6 booklets, October, 1978 through February, 1979.

use judiciously clustered in one segment of the school building in order to facilitate control over areas open to the public? Does the plan of the building minimize conflicts between public and school use and does the layout promote harmonious school-community relations? Is the site plan designed for the safety of both students and members of the community who are authorized to use the facility? Is public access to educational spaces effectively restricted by appropriate barriers?

PLANNING FOR SPECIAL EDUCATIONAL NEEDS

There is currently an ever-increasing emphasis on the individual needs of students. The public is demanding a higher level of performance in the basic skills. The massive influx of non-English-speaking students into the public school systems has accelerated the need for transitional bilingual education (TBE). And the widespread focus on individuals with educational and physical handicaps has placed additional demands on the design of modern school facilities.

One of the most comprehensive and well-researched studies on meeting the school facility needs of exceptional students is entitled *Facilities for Special Education Services*.[3] This publication should be read from cover to cover by all educational facility planners, including school architects, and local school officials engaged in the planning of new or modernized school facilities.

Implications for Planning School Facilities for Supplementary Programs in the Basic Skills

In order to satisfy the public clamor for improved student performance in the basic skills of reading, mathematics, and language, school officials have responded by providing supplementary instruction for students who are extremely deficient in these skills. Many of these programs have been established in existing buildings that were not planned for supplementary instruction. Consequently, small groups of three to five students are often found working with special teachers in small unventilated book storage rooms, on an auditorium stage where groups are separated only by movable storage or vision barriers, in corridors where partial partitions are installed, and in libraries where no barriers are used. It is not surprising that teachers and students often report that these spaces hinder the educational program for supplementary instruction.

It is suggested that the well designed school facility make adequate provision for supplementary instruction. The number of clusters of special-

[3] Allen C. Abend, Michael J. Bednar, Vera J. Froehlinger, Yale Stenzler, *Facilities for Special Education Services*, The Council for Exceptional Children, Reston, Virginia, 1979.

ized spaces for this purpose depends upon the size of the enrollment in supplementary instruction in the basic skills. There should be one cluster of related spaces for each team of one special education teacher and one or two teacher aides. This cluster should contain one mini-teaching room having an area ranging between three hundred and four hundred square feet for testing and teaching individual students or small group of five or six students for each teacher-teacher aide team in the program. A space containing approximately six hundred square feet should be provided as a resource center for each skill area included in the program. All mini-teaching rooms should be clustered around the resource center with direct access to this central resource room. Thus, if a school district is providing supplementary instruction in reading, mathematics, and language arts simultaneously, three related groups of spaces should be included in the school facility. Conceivably, these spaces would consist of a cluster of one or more mini-teaching rooms for each skill area, one or more teacher planning rooms with an area of about three hundred square feet each surrounding a common resource room whose size should range from a minimum area of six hundred square feet for single-skill programs to about fifteen hundred square feet when three or more basic skills are involved. If funds are available, it is strongly recommended that an office having an area of about one hundred and fifty square feet be provided for the principal teachers in each area of supplementary instruction. These offices are invaluable in providing such teachers with a space for conferences with students and teacher aides and for individualized testing and instruction of students whenever the need arises.

Implications for Planning Facilities for Bilingual Programs

The space needs of bilingual education are similar to those mentioned above in connection with supplemental instruction but are less demanding in relation to mini-teaching rooms. Students enrolled in the full service or intensive bilingual programs generally utilize regular classrooms for their education in their native tongue. In addition, they are enrolled in "English as a Second Language" classes (ESL) where they are taught to communicate in English in a normal class setting. Another group of students, however, is often given "Support Services." Bilingual students in this category have some understanding of the English language but need supplementary instruction under the guidance of bilingual teachers. The school facility needs for this group are the same as those listed above in connection with spaces for supplementary education. For bilingual education, each cluster of spaces (mini-teaching rooms and resource center) is designed to accommodate instruction in one foreign language. If, for example, both Portuguese and Spanish are in the bilingual program, two clusters should be planned.

Implications for Planning School Facilities for Special Education Programs

Within the past few years, tremendous strides have been made in the field of special education. Originally, special education was primarily concerned with students suffering from physical handicaps, such as vision and hearing. But special education is now a comprehensive service that is often mandated by state laws and supported by state and federal agencies. The scope of the service is very broad, ranging from psychological and educational handicaps to physical disabilities.

The spaces required for this extensive program of individualized service are varied and specialized. The actual number of spaces needed for each facility depends upon the number of students enrolled in the program. Every facility should provide at least one sound-proof conference room having an area between three hundred and fifty and four hundred and fifty square feet for the use of the professional team and parents, sometimes known as the core group, which is required by statute in some states to assess the needs of each student. This space should be carpeted and tastefully furnished with drapes and appropriate furniture. One mini-teaching room, similar to the one suggested for supplementary instruction, should be provided for each special education teacher. One or more resource centers having an area between six hundred and seven hundred square feet should be planned for this program. Additionally, there should be specialized spaces to accommodate four or five students at a time for each type of activity prescribed for the students. These special needs may require space for special education students suffering from dyslexia or other reading difficulties, those with hearing and vision problems, those requiring individually prescribed exercises caused by physical handicaps, and those under group therapy. There are numerous additional features related to special education that should be incorporated into the design of a school facility. Since such a detailed discussion is not within the scope of this book, it is strongly suggested that the publication on this subject cited earlier be reviewed for such details. Suffice it to say at this point that the design of the educational facility should facilitate and promote the freedom of movement of all handicapped students and provide for their participation in as many of the regular activities of the school as possible.

The need for planning educational facilities for the physically handicapped is far greater than is normally believed. Literally, millions of children of school age are physically handicapped. Schwartz points out that, "there are well over 5,000,000 handicapped children in the United States."[4] As indicated earlier, physical handicaps appear in different forms ranging from deafness to the lack of mobility. Special features must be

[4] Lita Linzer Schwartz, *Education Psychology*, 2nd Edition (Boston: Holbrook Press, Inc., 1977), p. 277.

built into educational facilities to satisfy the needs of exceptional children, youth, and adults who attend school in the daytime and evenings. In addition to the specialized spaces required for some types of physical handicaps, particular attention should be given to students in wheelchairs. There should be no barriers between the parking lot and every part of the school facility normally occupied by such students.

Types of School Plants and Planned Enrollment

Although the long-range plan describes in general terms the type of facility needed, its approximate size, and the general area in which it should be located, the school survey or campus master plan should be reviewed carefully when the building is actually being planned. There are two reasons for this review. First, if the facts on which the recommendations were based have changed appreciably since the study was completed, corresponding changes would be needed in the original recommendations. And second, the school survey report or campus plan contains vital information that is directly related to the planning of school facilities.

Common types of educational buildings. Educational facilities may be classified in many ways. For the purpose of this discussion, school facilities are classified according to primary function, that is, according to the grade groupings to be housed in them or the level of education they will serve. A few types of school facilities are described below.

1. An elementary school plant is an educational facility that usually accommodates pupils from kindergarten or Grade 1 to Grades 4, 5, or 6. Buildings housing pupils from kindergarten or first grade to Grade 3 are also called primary schools.
2. The middle school is a building that serves pupils from Grades 4, 5 or 6 through Grade 8.
3. The junior high school usually serves pupils in Grades 7 and 8 (the two-year junior high school) or in Grades 7 through 9.
4. The high school houses students in Grades 9 or 10 through 12.
5. The community or junior college offers two years of post-high school education in technical and semiprofessional curricula, and programs that approximate the courses found in the first two years of four-year colleges.
6. A college is a four-year post-high school institution of higher education offering students a bachelor's degree upon the completion of a prescribed course of study. Technological institutes are included in this category.
7. The university is an institution that consists of two or more colleges offering degrees that range from the baccalaurate to the doctorate.

In the lower educational domain, facilities are usually conceived in terms of the grade groupings described above. Some of the smaller school districts may operate junior-senior high schools housing pupils in Grades 7 through 12. Many eloquent arguments have been posed for and against each type of school listed. There is at present no validated research proving that one grade grouping is superior to another. To be sure, there are many opinions on the matter and a sound rationale is often presented to favor one type of school over another. But, unfortunately, there are not tested and proven guides to indicate just what type of school should be planned under any given circumstances. There is, however, a rule of thumb that might be helpful. The type of school selected should be that which provides the greatest educational efficiency in a given school district. Whether or not, for example, the ninth grade is included in the high school or in the junior high school is of little consequence. The important question is, "Under what organization does the ninth-grade pupil receive the highest level of education per tax dollar expended?" In other words, it is not what one *calls* a school that matters. What really counts is *what the pupil gets educationally* when he attends such a school. Altogether too much emphasis has been placed upon peripheral notions about the various types of schools. In a citizens school survey conducted by the writer, several citizens became disturbed when a junior-senior high school was recommended. Some maintained that senior boys would be able to make dates with seventh-grade girls, and that this situation was highly undesirable. The hypothesis posed by the citizens had not been tested. In fact, this particular school district transported pupils at all grade levels in the same bus. The boy-girl relationship had not been a problem in unsupervised buses in the past, but suddenly it assumed great proportions in a junior-senior high school where the supervision was far greater than it was in a school bus. Such are the extraneous arguments that are sometimes posed when innovations are proposed. Again, it should be emphasized that there is no best type of school or grade grouping. The type of school that makes the best sense in terms of educational efficiency is the one that should be selected.

Planned enrollment for a given facility.   What should be the size or capacity of a proposed educational facility? There is a dearth of research on optimum sizes of educational facilities. Obviously, the lower limit is determined by the lowest number of learners needed to justify a broad educational program at a reasonable cost per learner. The upper limit is reached when the facilities required by fields of learning enrolling the lowest number of students can no longer be accommodated in a single teaching station. For example, if a special laboratory is required to house advanced programs in physics and chemistry, and if these two courses have the smallest enrollments, then the total school enrollment at which a second laboratory would be needed for these advanced courses would represent the upper level of the enrollment range. According to this concept, the lower and upper limits of the capacity of a school would depend upon the desired educational programs. For the school planner who is interested in applying this theoretical concept at the secondary school level, the Program Index Approach developed by Marion Conrad[5] is suggested.

The National Council on Schoolhouse Construction has developed a number of criteria for the size of public schools.[6] According to this source, elementary school capacities should range between 300 and 500 pupils. At the secondary level, the minimum size is set at about 300 pupils and the maximum at about 1,200 pupils. These enrollment ranges reflect the views of many educators.

Of course, it is sometimes necessary to deviate from desirable enrollment ranges. At the elementary level, every effort should be made to provide at least one room per grade, and therefore the minimum size for an elementary school (K-6) should be seven classrooms, or six classrooms if a kindergarten program is not provided. In the judgment of the author, elementary schools (K-6) should not exceed three rooms per grade or 21 classrooms (see Table 5.1). At the secondary level, the enrollment should not fall below 500 pupils or about 150 pupils in the freshman class of a four-year high school. The upper limit should not exceed 1,500 pupils (see Table 5.1). Much has been written about the advantages of a large high school, but the position taken by the National Council on Schoolhouse Construction is sensible and defensible.

Contrary to popular opinion, large secondary schools are not less costly to operate nor are they free of duplication. A study of any 4,000-pupil high school quickly reveals not only duplication but the multiplication of similar spaces including those in the library, which is not duplicated in the ordinary sense. It is simply made larger and more complex, and must contain several copies of numerous books because of the great demand for them. Large high schools can be justified only in cities where the population density is very high, such as New York, Chicago, St. Louis, Philadelphia, Los Angeles, and Boston. In other situations, the single large high school simply channels tax dollars into transportation costs which do not directly contribute to the education of the pupils. In a sense, unnecessary transportation costs represent a waste of public funds.

PREPARATION OF EDUCATIONAL SPECIFICATIONS

No architect should be asked to plan a school before a complete set of educational specifications has been developed by the educational planners. It

[5]Marion J. Conrad, *A Manual for Determining the Operating Capacity of Secondary School Buildings* (Columbus, Ohio: Bureau of Educational Research and Service, The Ohio State University, 1954).

[6]National Council on Schoolhouse Construction, *Guide for Planning School Plants* (East Lansing: Michigan State University, 1964), p. 12.

is unfair and unwise to ask an architect to do both the educational and the architectural planning. He is not an educator and does not pretend to be one. While he may have planned many schools already, he should not be forced to produce plans that are carbon copies of buildings designed for other school districts simply because educators have failed to prepare educational specifications for his guide.

Purpose

Educational specifications serve as the link between the educational program and school facilities. They consist of a series of interrelated statements that translate the physical requirements of the educational program into educational facilities.

The basic purpose of educational specifications is to describe clearly and concisely the various learning activities to be housed in the school, their spatial requirements and special features. The statements should not be couched in general terms such as "appropriate size," "sufficiently large," or "properly related." These terms are quite meaningless to an architect. On the other hand, educators should not submit drawings showing dimensions, shape, and relationships to an architect. The primary purpose of preparing educational specifications is to enable the architect to clearly imagine every detail of educational activity to be conducted in a proposed educational facility. From a study of such specifications, he should be able to develop a number of architectural concepts that fit the situation.

Organization of Educational Specification

There is no best way to organize a set of educational specifications. In practice, school planners often find it convenient to develop educational specifications in three distinct sections. The first is usually devoted to matters related to the educational program, including a detailed description of instructional and learning activities. Expressions of educational philosophy are of little consequence to the architect, for they do not tell him much about the form or design that a proposed school building should assume.

The second group of educational specifications deals with the numerical aspects of the architectural problem. How many students must be housed? How many of the various types of instructional spaces are needed for the desired educational program? Approximately how large should each type of space be, and where should it be located in relation to other spaces?

The last section describes in detail all special features that should be incorporated in the school building. These statements deal with matters such as special shape, ceiling heights, temperature and humidity control, acoustical treatment, and unusual lighting requirements.

Content of Educational Specifications

Some of the broad topics included in a set of educational specifications have already been mentioned in the preceding section. A more detailed account of such topics will be presented here.

The greater the detail and clarity of the educational instructions prepared, the greater the likelihood that a school district will acquire the school building it really needs. Architects frequently refer to educational specifications as the "program" or "educational program." They often speak of "programming a building." The architectural expressions for educational specifications are quite proper, but they have not been adopted in educational terminology because the word "program" has a distinct meaning of its own in pedagogy, and the expression "educational program" conveys a meaning to the architect that is completely different from that intended when it is used in educational specifications.

Part I. Description of the educational function.   The architect must fully understand the function of a proposed school before he can design it. Unless a clear description of specific student and teacher activities is provided, he will be forced to design a structure which reflects his own educational concepts rather than those of the school district, college, or university. Broad, general statements should be kept at a minimum, but should be included when they may give the architect valuable background information.

Perhaps the best approach in preparing Part I of the educational specifications is to describe the educational function of each space, activity by activity. For example, what tasks are performed by teachers and pupils in a room used for instruction in physics? How will the lobby be used? What specific equipment will be located or used in a certain space? What are the weight and dimensions of such equipment? How will it be used? The architect must also be given a clear description of each type of teacher and student activity for each space. How large a group of students does what, with which equipment, and for what percent of the time in a semester? At first glance, the amount of time that a particular activity occupies in a semester may seem irrelevant. Actually, at some point in the planning, the architect may find that for some reason he cannot provide for every single activity in a given space. If he must compromise, he will try to eliminate special features for those activities that students undergo for the least amount of time.

The description of the operational and educational function to be housed in every part of the building should be so detailed that the architect will be able to visualize the entire school in operation before he makes a single sketch. For example, if the large group-small group concept is envisioned for the school, the architect should be able to imagine exactly what takes place instructionally under each circumstance and what special features, if any, are involved. For instance, the architect should be told about the processes involved in handling and using materials, tools, and fixed equipment. Details must also be furnished regarding the work of administrators, secretarial personnel, health officials, custodians, and maintenance crews.

Sample: Description of Educational Function

The program to be housed initially in the proposed building will probably be traditional in many respects. Class size will vary between twenty-five and thirty pupils in science, social studies, English, foreign languages, and mathematics. Homemaking and shop class sizes will range between twenty and twenty-four pupils. It is also expected that classes will be instructed more or less conventionally at the time the school building is first occupied after its completion. It is believed, however, that the existing traditional instructional practices will be short-lived. As teachers and administrators become more involved in developing promising teaching techniques, the building will be utilized more effectively as a modern educational tool.

The educational practices envisioned for this building within the next decade are quite different from those that will be housed in it initially. It is postulated that within the next eight to ten years, one teacher will instruct one pupil in his office. He will work with six or eight pupils in a small room. He will meet fifteen pupils in a seminar situation. He will work with a few groups of twenty-five or thirty pupils in a class and he will conduct large classroom instruction in groups of 150 pupils.

Within the next decade it is also anticipated that approximately three-quarters of the total enrollment will spend about 20 percent of its time in groups of 150–300, about 40 percent of its time in groups of 15–20, about 20 percent of its time in seminar sessions, 10 percent in groups of 5–6 and 10 percent on a one-to-one ratio in the teacher's office. The remaining 25 percent of the student body will be taught in classes of twenty-five pupils using current methods. This group will probably include many students in classes devoted to instruction primarily in art, music, homemaking, business, industrial arts, and vocational programs.

Part II. The physical specifics of the desired school facility.   From the standpoint of the architect, the data included in this section are the *sine qua non* of school plant planning.

(a) *Number and types of spaces.* The architect must know exactly how many of the various types of spaces are desired. Such spaces include classrooms, laboratories, offices, storage spaces, libraries, cafeterias, gymnasiums, custodial closets, lobbies, and the like.

(b) *Suggested size of each space.* The architect should not be expected to do the research required to determine the proper size for each type of space. Educators should supply the approximate square footages needed for such spaces. In general, such information can be determined with relative ease by school officials in an ongoing school system. New concepts can be "tried for size" in existing structures and the approximate area needed for each type of space can be specified. If the architect fully understands the educational program, he can often raise a question about sizes that seem to be too large or too small.

(c) *Space relationships*. The efficient operation of an educational institution depends partly upon the proper location of related spaces. Perhaps no one knows more than the school administrator about the relationship that exists between one type of space and another. It is obvious, for example, that a storage room for chemicals should be adjacent to the chemistry laboratory, but it is not quite so apparent that the entrance to the guidance suite should be removed from the entrance to the general office, or that the office of the guidance counselor should be adjacent to those of the principal and school nurse. A few architects, incidentally, have satisfied these relationships quite ingeniously.

Circles or ellipses could be drawn to represent each type of space. The large spaces could be indicated by large circles or ellipses. One, two, or three straight lines could be drawn between them to indicate a weak, strong, or very close relationship, respectively. The use of straight lines to indicate spaces should be avoided whenever possible, because by using them educators would be entering the province of the architect. Furthermore, educational specifications should allow the architect as much freedom in design as possible.

Sample: Statement of Physical Specifics

Teaching Stations Required	Proposed Area of Each Space	Storage Space (Area)	Relationship to Other Teaching Stations
General Art			
Art	3	1,050	150	
General				Near Homemaking
Typing-Bus.	1	900	50	or Shop
Homemaking			
General	1	1,200		
Clothing	1	1,100	150	
Foods	1	1,200	150	
Office	1	150		Near Multipurpose rm.
Multipurpose				Between Foods and
Area	1	400	50	Clothing

Part III. Description of special physical features. In some instances, the educational program demands the incorporation of certain special features in the design of a school plant. These special features may be dictated by the need for special equipment or by the requirements of certain teaching or learning activities.

It is essential that all exceptional or special features of a school building be clearly set forth space by space. Special features are most often concerned with shape, ceiling height, intensity of lighting, acoustical conditioning or insulation from other spaces, humidity and temperature control, orientation, color, ability of the floor to support more than average weight, type of flooring, arrangement of built-in equipment, and utilities.

Sample: Description of Special Features

Art Room

The art spaces should possess the features listed below:

1. Long dowels resting on built-in racks should be provided to hold rolls of paper at least 36″ wide.
2. Two work sinks and work counters should be installed in the art room. Long gooseneck spigots should be provided.
3. If possible, the art room should have a northern exposure with as much natural lighting as possible.
4. About 200 square feet of the art room should be planned for ceramics and a wet area. The floor should be durable and capable of being easily cleaned in this area where water, clay, paints, and abrasive materials are used and will fall on the floor.
5. Electrical power 220 V for kiln should be available in the ceramic art area.
6. Artificial lighting should simulate the daylight spectrum as closely as possible.
7. About 12 linear feet of tackboard from floor to ceiling should be provided in the art room.
8. This room should be capable of being "blacked out" in order that all details can be seen on color slides and films.
9. If the art room has a beautiful vista at a second-floor location window sills should be dropped as close to the floor as possible to facilitate painting of landscapes.
10. The art room should convey the feeling of being an art studio where creative activity is stimulated.

Homemaking Spaces

Clothing Laboratory

1. Provide a three-way mirror in fitting area.
2. Include about 20 linear feet of shelving for reference books in the clothing laboratory.
3. Include cabinets with at least 150 "tote trays" for sewing supplies and equipment.
4. At least two cabinets to be used as wardrobes should be provided. Each cabinet should be about 4 feet in length. Unfinished garments are stored in such cabinets while work is in progress.
5. A work sink and counter should be provided in the clothing laboratory near the grooming center mentioned later.
6. In addition to high-intensity general lighting, provision should be made for local lighting in clothing laboratory.
7. At least twenty-four double electrical outlets should be provided, two for each pupil station, in the clothing laboratory.
8. About four outlets should be located in the demonstration area used by the teacher.
9. At least two ironing boards should be provided in the clothing laboratory. Provision for storage of irons and other small equipment should be made in the storage space specified for the clothing lab.
10. At least two cutting tables, 32 inches and 6 feet long, should be provided in addition to tables holding sewing machines.
11. At least twelve electric sewing machines should be provided in the clothing laboratory.

EDUCATIONAL FACILITIES PLANNERS

Many people participate in the planning of a school building in one capacity or another. The planning process should tap the creative potential of the faculty, professional persons, administrators, nonprofessional personnel, and students. To realize this potential, these people must be organized. Two basic planning groups are needed, one group to serve as the executive planning team, and the other to act in an advisory capacity to the executive planning team.

The Executive Planning Team

The executive planning team assumes the primary responsibility for planning an educational facility. It has full authority to develop plans of a proposed school building, subject to the review and approval of a higher board, such as the board of education or board of trustees in a college or university.

The executive planning team should consist of the chief school administrator, one of his assistants, the architect, the educational consultant, and a faculty member who is also a member of the central advisory committee discussed in the next section.

The executive planning team reviews educational specifications prepared by the educational consultant and works closely with the architect in the development of architectural plans. While the architect has the primary responsibility for designing the building, the team as a whole continually reviews the plans in terms of educational adequacy. The chief school administrator is the representative of the board of higher authority and, therefore, assumes the role of the client in dealing with the architect. In planning school buildings, however, the final approval of plans and specifications generally rests with a board of higher authority, such as the board of education, board of trustees, state building commission, or school building committee.

The Institutional Planning Team

The institutional planning team is not a new concept in school planning, but its role has not been clearly defined, and its unlimited creative potential has not been fully utilized by school planners. The value of planning teams is well known. Properly organized in an administrative climate that is conducive to creative thinking, the institutional planning team can make a major contribution to the planning of educational facilities.

The institutional planning team is usually composed of a cross-sectional representation of faculty and nonprofessional persons employed by the institution. The group may also include one or two students whenever it is felt that their thinking will contribute to imaginative planning.

The team should include about fifteen persons, a group that is large enough to stimulate the creative process but small enough to avoid awkwardness and loss of group cohesion and informality. In large institutions, subgroups may be organized so that everyone in the employ of the school may make a tangible contribution to the planning of a school plant. The subgroups send representatives to the institutional planning team. Provision should be made in the organizational structure of these groups for ideas and feedback to move from the executive planning team through the institutional planning team to the subgroups and vice versa. Perhaps nothing kills initiative and creativity more quickly than the lack of assurance that an idea will be given full consideration. Feedback may be used to provide this needed assurance.

The institutional planning team is essentially the stimulator and clearing-house for all ideas regarding the educational planning of a school building. The group may make studies of educational matters, or recommend that such studies be made. They serve as a coordinating council for the various subgroups developing concepts, innovations, and ideas to be considered in planning the new facility. While the authority to implement or reject ideas, suggestions, or recommendations rests with the executive planning team, the institutional planning team is entitled to a full explanation when ideas are rejected by the executive planning team. Arbitrary action by the executive planning team would destroy the climate that fosters creativity and encourages participation by both the faculty and non-professional personnel. The institutional planning team reviews educational specifications and all architectural plans. It submits reactions and recommendations to the executive planning team, and it serves as a liaison group between the executive planning team and faculty, student, and interested parents.

The Architect

As mentioned earlier, the architect is a key member of the executive planning team. He has the primary responsibility for translating educational concepts and functions into educational facilities that are conducive to effective learning.

Qualifications of the architect.   In most states, minimum qualifications for school architects are prescribed by law. In and of itself, however, the employment of an architect does not automatically assure a board of higher authority that he will design a school to satisfy their institutional needs. The architect should be creative, competent, flexible, understanding, perceptive of educational needs, open-minded, aesthetically oriented but cost-conscious, imaginative, and practical, and cooperative in spirit. He should:

1. Possess a thorough knowledge of building design, economical construction methods, and efficient use of building materials.
2. Be endowed with creative ability and artistic talent. This characteristic can be judged by reviewing his past works, which need not have been school buildings.
3. Work harmoniously with individuals or groups of people.
4. Be open-minded and willing to explore new ideas. He should refrain from imposing his will upon the executive planning team with respect to educational matters or architectural design that may adversely affect the educational program.
5. Be willing and able to follow detailed educational specifications for the design of a school.
6. Be capable of producing final working drawings that are clear and precise.

7. Conduct himself professionally with dignity, integrity, and honesty.
8. Demonstrate his ability to provide for aesthetics in school design without sacrificing function or ignoring cost.

Procedure for selecting an architect.   As soon as funds are available for the employment of an architect, the institutional board of authority should widely publicize its intention to employ an architect for a given project. Architects may learn of the project through the news media and through the local chapter of A.I.A. (American Institute of Architects). The group entrusted with the planning of a school should seek names of architects whom they may wish to consider.

In this age of rapid travel, no special preference should be given to the local architect. He should, indeed, be considered, but he deserves no favored treatment simply because he lives in the community and pays local taxes. The most important considerations in the selection of an architect are his competence, creativity, and willingness to design a school that can accommodate the desired educational program—*not* his place of business. A number of clichés are often used in support of the employment of a local architect, such as "he is easy to contact," "he can supervise the job more thoroughly," "he is more conscious of our problems," and "as a local taxpayer, he will be more eager to save us money." Obviously, these arguments can be nullified one by one. Any architect is as close as the telephone and a jet airliner can make him. As far as supervision is concerned, on large projects, an architectural firm employs a resident architect, and it really does not matter where the office of the principal architect is located. On small projects, most architects can afford to provide only the supervision called for in the contract, perhaps an afternoon per week. Therefore, the location of the architectural firm is of little consequence from the standpoint of supervision. In one case, a local architectural firm in Illinois admitted publicly that the reason for the collapse of an entire ceiling 200 feet long in a school ten months after occupancy was due to the use of improper clips by the contractor during construction. This statement was not an indictment of the architect. Under the usual contract, the architect is not required to supervise the construction on a full construction-time basis. And finally, the argument is frequently voiced that, as a local taxpayer, the architect is more likely to try to save money through efficient design. The local architect does not possess a magic cost formula. All competent architects can design inexpensive buildings if they so desire. Reputable architects differentiate between cheap buildings and inexpensive ones. If the local architect favors the cheap concept, the local board of education can expect just one thing—a cheap building.

The employment of an architect by a board of education, board of trustees, or its equivalent is one of the most important duties performed by such a board in the construction of educational facilities. Steps to be followed in selecting and employing an architect are listed below.

1. Widespread publicity should be given to the board's intention to plan and construct educational facilities.
2. A list of architects should be prepared by the board of higher authority. All available sources of names should be consulted, including other boards who have recently built new schools or colleges.
3. A brochure explaining the project in detail and a questionnaire[7] requesting pertinent information should be mailed to those on the list.
4. Returns should be screened as objectively as possible and then ranked. Some form of rating sheet should be used.
5. The ten highest-ranking architects should then be mailed questionnaires requesting additional information, including names of persons for whom they have worked.
6. The ten remaining architects should be reranked on the basis of data contained in the second questionnaire and information gathered from direct contacts with their former clients. The number of firms under consideration should be reduced to about five at this point.
7. The architects under final consideration should be invited to appear before the board (1) to make presentations of their own choice, (2) to answer specific questions prepared in advance and placed on a rating sheet,[8] and (3) to exchange ideas with members of the board.
8. Visits should be made by board members to some of the buildings designed by the architects, and discussions should be held with other boards for whom each architect worked in the past.
9. A selection can be made after all ratings and scores applying to each architectural firm have been recorded on a rating sheet.

The contract with the architect.   Because school officials frequently have certain misconceptions regarding the responsibilities and duties of an architect, it may be helpful to list what is and is not within the area of responsibility of the architect in a normal contract.

1. The architect *is* responsible for architectural programming. He *is not* responsible for educational specifications.

[7]Forms available from American Institute of Architects, 1735 New York Avenue, N.W., Washington, D.C. 20006.

[8]Basil Castaldi, *The Road to Better Schools* (Cambridge, Mass.: New England School Development Council, 1955), pp. 99–100.

2. He *is* responsible for preplanning studies. He *is not* responsible for making the final choices among the alternatives he may present as possible solutions to the educational problem.

3. He *is* responsible for preliminary plans, large-scale drawings, and final plans and specifications to be approved by school officials. He *is not* responsible for making architectural changes, at his expense, after final working drawings have been approved by the board.

4. He *is* responsible for bidding and contract award. He *is not* responsible for the legality of the contracts as to form or content.

5. He *is* responsible for the periodic supervision of the construction. He *is not* responsible for continuous "on-the-job" supervision, unless it is so specified in the contract.

6. He *is* responsible for all architectural matters related to the acceptance and occupancy of a school.

7. He *is* responsible for overseeing the correction of defects in construction during the warranty period and acts in the interest of the owner.

8. He *is* responsible for the selection and installation of all fixed equipment. He *is not* responsible for the selection and purchase of movable equipment when he is paid only the normal architect's fee.

The Educational Consultant

The educational consultant is another key member of the executive planning team. The services of a qualified educational consultant are invaluable in planning an economical and functional school building. A competent educational consultant can usually offer suggestions that may result in savings amounting to several times his fee, coupled with improvements in educational efficiency that cannot be readily converted into dollars and cents.

Since, unfortunately, there is no state certification or board of registration for educational consultants, school officials must exercise great care in selecting one. Boards of education must be sure that the qualifications of the educational consultant are higher than those of persons already employed by the board. Otherwise money expended for a consultant would be a waste of public funds.

Qualifications.   The educational consultant should be a person of wide and varied experience. He should:

1. Have received an advanced degree in general educational administration (the superintendency), preferably at the doctoral level, from an accredited university.

2. Have received formal training in school plant planning at the graduate level.
3. Have had broad experience. Work over a wide geographical area, including several states, is an indication that he is unhampered by provincial or regional thinking.
4. Have had teaching experience in the public schools and, preferably, also at the college level.
5. Have had experience in at least two levels of educational government, such as local, state, or federal.
6. Present evidence of his competence through reports, studies, and services rendered to other school districts.

The role of the educational consultant.   The educational consultant has the prime responsibility for the educational planning of a proposed school building. As a member of the executive planning team, he is in an excellent position to assist the architect in converting educational concepts into school facilities.

The consultant can be of assistance to school officials in a number of ways. He can:

1. Advise school officials in the selection of an architect.
2. Be of assistance in the selection of a school site.
3. Review any existing long-range educational plan and make recommendations in the light of new developments.
4. Prepare educational specifications that reflect the thinking of the institutional planning team and the concepts expressed by school officials and the board of higher authority.
5. Review architectural plans and judge them in terms of their ability to satisfy educational needs.
6. Evaluate all ideas submitted by the institutional planning team and make recommendations regarding the disposition of each suggestion.

Selection of an educational consultant.   Since the supply of competent educational consultants is very limited, boards of education would be well advised to ask the school building authority in the state for suggestions. Schools of education sometimes have competent school plant consultants. Care should be exercised, however, not to confuse the prestige of the school with which a person is associated with his professional competence. Only those professors of education who have had training in school plant planning and educational administration and who possess the qualifications listed in the previous section should be considered.

Persons who have had university or state department of education experience in school plant planning and are engaged in private practice are often highly competent and reliable. Even in this case, however, the hiring board should make certain that the educational consultant meets the qualifications listed earlier.

School Officials as Members of the Executive Planning Team

The remainder of the executive planning team consists of a legal advisor and school officials. Most institutions employ a legal counselor on a full- or part-time basis. As a member of the school planning team, he makes certain that all actions, contracts, and procedures comply with the law. He assists in the bonding and business aspects of school plant planning.

The role of the superintendent of schools or college president is crucial. As the chief school officer, he is the status leader of the school district or institution of higher learning. The chief school officer represents his board and is the client whom the architect serves. The final decision in the executive planning team rests with the chief school officer. He has the power to reject or veto any idea or concept proposed by the executive planning team or any member thereof, or by the institutional planning team. As a practical matter, however, the chief school officer should consider each rejection carefully before exercising his veto power. On the other hand, he should not hesitate to reject any suggestion that he feels would be detrimental to the institution, and should explain the reason for his action to the individual or group submitting it.

THE SITE

The school site is, of course, an essential part of any educational plant. In addition to providing the space and setting for the school building, the site must include space for a large number of essential educational functions and supporting services.

Size of School Site

The rule-of-thumb approach.   Several approaches may be used to determine the required size of a school site. The simplest method, by far, is to apply one of the many rules of thumb that are in vogue. Applicable rules of thumb (Table 5.2) are presented for each type of school plant under the various chapters dealing with elementary, and secondary institutions. (Chapters 13, and 14.)

The functional approach.   The functional approach of determining the desired size of a school site is based on a estimate of the amount of area required for each type of outdoor function demanded by modern educational facilities and contemporary educational programs. The sum of the individual areas needed plus 10 percent for unforseeable needs represents the total size of the required site. A number of the functions served by the site are listed below.

The school site must contain:

1. Space for the proposed educational building. A high school building for 1,000 pupils, for example, requires about three acres of land. An elementary school serving 600 students occupies about 1½ acres of land.
2. Space for future additions to the building and for increases in the other functions of the site listed below.
3. Space for main drives and walks.
4. Space for lawn, trees, and landscaping.
5. Space for parking of automobiles (300 sq. ft. per vehicle).
6. Space for service drives and unloading zones.
7. Space for bus loading and unloading, including covered areas and turnaround drives.
8. Space for secondary access to the school site or central campus.
9. Space for practice fields in organized athletics, such as football and baseball.
10. Space for hard-surfaced areas for tennis, volleyball, handball, and the like.
11. Space for informal games.
12. Space for gardens and other instructional areas.
13. Space for social activities and large-group programs, perhaps an outdoor amphitheater.
14. Space for bus garages, and physical plant equipment.
15. Space for landscaping accents, such as pools, fountains, and shrubbery.
16. Space for football bleachers and athletics.
17. Space for public and student picnic areas.

Other Requirements of a School or Campus Site

Location. The general location of an educational facility is usually set forth in the long-range plan (Chapter 5). Before a specific educational building can be planned, however, it is necessary that a definite site be selected for it. For facilities at the pre-college level, the school site should be properly related to future school buildings and to those to be abandoned in the foreseeable future. A well-selected school site, therefore, can conveniently absorb the remaining load of schools scheduled for abandonment. The school or campus site should also be located in an area that is free from air pollution and noxious gases, and far from sources of noise or danger, such as heavily traveled highways, airports, and heavy industry.

Topography and soil conditions.   A good site possesses several physical characteristics. Its topography should be slightly convex and its level somewhat higher than the area immediately surrounding it. It is not necessary that the entire area be flat, provided there is sufficient space in which play areas may be developed at a reasonable cost for grading. In fact, buildings are sometimes "built into" the natural topography of the site in ingenious ways. Borings must be taken in prospective school or campus sites to determine the adequacy of the drainage and bearing of the soil. The presence of ledge cropping through the surface at a few isolated spots should not eliminate an otherwise desirable site from consideration. Modern buildings are generally constructed without basements, and therefore ledge does not generally constitute a major problem.

Aesthetics.   Aesthetic considerations should be stressed in the selection of a site. The building and the site upon which it is located should provide an environment that is conducive to effective learning. Trees, brooks, parks, or golf courses, on or near a potential school site, do much to beautify the area surrounding an educational facility. Such natural features can be used to produce dramatic results by an imaginative landscape architect.

Safety.   Finally, it is imperative that matters related to safety be given high priority in the selection of a school or campus site. If possible, it should not border a heavily traveled highway, railroad, or high-tension electric wires. Drives and walks approaching the buildings should be designed so as to keep the crossing of pedestrians and vehicular traffic to a minimum. Special care should be exercised in the design of a bus-loading area. Driveways should not be located between the unloading zone and an educational facility. Neither should it be necessary for buses to travel in reverse in order to turn around on a school site or college campus.

Placement of the building or buildings on the site.   Educational facilities should be located about 160 feet from any well-traveled thoroughfare in order to minimize the interference from traffic noise. Instructional facilities should be strategically situated on the site with respect to convenience and function. The gymnasium, for example, should be located near the play fields and away from quiet areas, such as the library and classrooms. On the other hand, the auditorium and recreational facilities should be convenient to the parking areas. Aesthetic considerations should also figure in determining placement and orientation of each building on the school site, but not at the expense of function.

The development of the school site.   It is strongly suggested that a landscape architect be engaged to prepare a master plan of the site development. All too frequently, the area immediately surrounding school buildings is carefully planned and developed while the development of the remainder of the site is left to chance. When school planners recommend school and campus sites of the size mentioned in this text, they envision a site that is carefully developed and laid out to accommodate the outdoor functions associated with a modern educational program.

The layout of a school site should be geared both to safety and function. Driveways, for example, should not encircle a building. Such a plan endangers any student using the building. Walks should be located along *natural* paths. One school district delayed the installation of sidewalks until after the school had been occupied for a few months. Sidewalks were then placed where foot paths had been made by students attending the school. While this is a practical approach to sidewalk location, aesthetics should also considered in laying out sidewalks.

Landscaping is an extremely important part of site development. Trees, shrubs, flower beds, and the general arrangement of walks and drives contribute to the general environment of a school building. The design of the building and the layout and development of the site are the important ingredients in the creation of an atmosphere that is educationally stimulating. The building should blend pleasingly into the terrain, and the site should accentuate the beauty of the structure.

CHAPTER 7

Leeway for Change

Education reflects the world in which we are living. Our civilization is in the midst of a technological and scientific revolution. The world has shrunk as the time needed to traverse the globe has dwindled. The boundaries of our world itself are rapidly expanding into the outer limits of earth space. We are engaged in the conquest of the universe and in the discovery of the secrets of life itself. As part of this wave of change, it is natural to anticipate changes in thought, in attitude, in modes of living, in occupations, and in education, and thus the plans of any educational facility on the drawing board must provide for the instructional practices of today as well as for those that will be conceived by and for generations yet unborn.

PREPARING FOR THE UNFORESEEABLE

Planning a school building for educational practices that are still unknown seems to be an impossible assignment. Of all the aspects of school plant planning, the task of designing a school for not yet apparent instructional needs requires the highest level of thought from planners. Use of the "brainstorming technique" might be quite fruitful in achieving this objective.

Projection of Present Trends

Obviously, we cannot plan for the future in a vacuum. We must grasp certain clues that enable us to imagine concepts and practices that may or may not be adopted in education. It should be remembered in designing for the unforseeable that the ridiculous notion of today may be the accepted and desired practice of tomorrow. The objective of planning for the unforseeable has been accomplished if school planners can answer the questions, "How can this seemingly fantastic innovation be accommodated in this building in the event that the citizens fifty years hence desire it?" A word of caution is in order, however. Cost limits the extent to which a building can be planned for the unforseeable. Obviously, in planning for the unforeseeable, design features that do not add substantially to the cost of a school plant should be incorporated in the building, but those that require appreciable additional capital outlay should be adopted only after careful study.

School planners can prepare themselves for the task of planning for the unforeseeable by carefully analyzing present trends in educational innovations, their types, and objectives. For example, do current trends seem to indicate greater or less attention to the individual learner? Do they seem to give greater emphasis to program enrichment? To self-instruction? To supervised study? To reorganization of learning experiences? To new forms of administrative and instructional organization? To increased student services? To a greater use of automated aids to education? To increased or decreased student participation in learning experiences? These are only a few of the questions that might be raised in a faculty "brainstorming" session. Indeed, school planners should consider both national and international developments in their review of existing educational trends.

Once the trends have been identified and clearly stated, school planners should try to project the existing trends. As a bonus, this aspect of the planning will tend to bring to light many clearly forseeable practices which can be incorporated into the plans of a building. It is important, however, that the thinking of the planning team should not stop at this point. It must proceed farther, much farther into the future, into the realm of the unknown. Clues that may be gleaned from a study of the present trends should be amplified and imaginatively projected, so that the school building of today can be designed with special features that will facilitate the incorporation of unforseeable educational practices some time in the distant future.

Clearly, as mentioned earlier, it makes no sense to plan for ideas or concepts that are unlikely to be realized during the life of the proposed school building. On the other hand, there are numerous design features that can simplify modifications to a school building in the future. The revision of plans of conventional buildings to accommodate future innovations is a matter for considerable study in terms of long-range economy. As noted previously, the type and magnitude of such revisions depend upon the nature of the future practices inferred or suggested by a systematic study of current trends. For example, if private tutoring were envisioned for the future, present classrooms could be planned for easy conversion to teacher-offices by introducing a system of bolt-type prefabricated partitions into the plans. It is realized, of course, that new and improved construction materials and methods will appear on the market in the years to come. But it must also be remembered that while new products will be developed in the future, the building constructed today will not change substantially in material or products incorporated in it for at least half a century. Consequently, the architect must ingeniously utilize the building materials of today in meeting the educational needs of tomorrow.

Preparing for Unforeseeable Enrollment Growth

Increases in enrollment are not always predictable in an urban or suburban center. The problem in a large community is complicated by changes in population density. For example, the change of zoning in an area from single- to multiple-dwelling units may mean a substantial increase in pupil enrollment in an area once thought to be stable.

In view of the unpredictability of enrollment growth, it would be prudent and reasonable to assume that any school should be designed with a potential increase in capacity of about 25 percent in mind. The planning for this hypothetical growth can be accomplished very easily when plans are in the pencil stage. Buildings can be designed so that a given space can be changed from one function to another without difficulty and without the expenditure of unreasonable amounts of money. It is realized, of course, that the principle of expansibility is not new or revolutionary. In fact, it has been foremost in the minds of architects and educators for many decades in planning functional school buildings. Until recently, however, the full potential of this concept had not been explored. It is now generally accepted that the principle of expansibility can be employed in planning for both the foreseeable and the unforseeable aspects of educational change.

Leeway for unforeseeable enrollment growth can be gained by incorporating in the initial plans of a school building those features that tend to facilitate expansion of the structure at a later date. In planning for this eventuality, it is important to make certain that the area of the school site is sufficient and that utilities and other services possess the potential for expansion and accommodate the additional student load. If these conditions cannot be met even for a hypothetical increase in enrollment of 25 percent, then school planners might well reconsider their choice of the school site. Obviously, there are sometimes circumstances under which these conditions cannot be met, but such circumstances should be compelling before the planning team accepts a school site that cannot accommodate even a modest hypothetical increase of 25 percent in enrollment.

Assuming that the site can accommodate such an increase in student load, it would be ideal if the exact nature of the hypothetical addition to the building were known, but such is not often the case. Ideally, educators would assess all educational trends and extrapolate their implications for the future. But it is not practical to expect this of superintendents of schools, college presidents, and their staffs, who, generally speaking, are already overworked in the day-to-day operation of schools. They have neither the time nor the funds, except in rare situations, to divert human resources for the research necessary to discover trends that may suggest the school of the future. In time, the various state departments of education might perform this type of research service. From a practical standpoint, educators must assume that the current fundamental areas of learning will persist for the next decade or two. It is realized that the methodology of instruction may change quite drastically, but, from the point of view of the school administrator, any attempt to predict the individual instructional experiences that students will undergo in our schools within the next two decades would be highly speculative. A sound approach to planning for the unforeseeable might be to concentrate upon the major areas of learning rather than on specific student experiences or techniques that might be used to impart skills and knowledge to the students of the future. Thus, planning for possible enrollment growth can be reduced to the simple task of making certain that a load of about 25 percent could be sensibly added to a proposed school building on a space-by-space basis. For example, if four science rooms are required now, how could one or two more such spaces be added to the building in the future if they were needed? Would the two additional spaces be functionally related to the existing spaces? How could spaces for fine and applied arts be expanded by 25 percent? The answer to these questions should be more detailed than, "We have the space along this corridor or at the end of this wing." Under the technique suggested above, the number of each type of space is simply increased by 25 percent to satisfy a hypothetical situation. The figure of 25 percent was selected arbitrarily. Any other percent that seems to be more appropriate in a given situation can be used. In some instances the figure could be zero if it were almost a certainty that no expansion could occur.

In planning schools for enrollment growth, it is imperative that proper functional space relationships be preserved in the expanded school building. The importance of maintaining good space relationships is well recognized among educators and school plant planners. It should be emphasized that a building is not necessarily planned for educational expansion simply because it is designed with numerous open-ended corridors. The ultimate circulation pattern is a vital concern in planning the expansion of a school building. A school facility that is well designed for potential enrollment growth must also preserve the integrity of spatial relationships. The architect should be able to demonstrate both the physical expansion and the operational relationships of spaces serving related functions in any plan designed for future expansion. For example, it is not enough for an architect to show that a wing can be expanded to accommodate a given number of rooms. He should also be able to show a board of education or board of trustees that the unified clustering of the science spaces, shops, art rooms, and the like can be maintained in the expanded building. He should prepare a single line drawing of the expanded school for the appraisal of the respective boards and school officials.

Preparing for Unforeseeable Enrollment Decline

School enrollments are subject to a large number of sociological and economic forces. There are periods of large increases in school enrollments in certain school districts followed by periods of decline. Some communities mature while others age. Some are created and some are on the wane. In the preceeding section of this chapter, the focus was on unforeseeable enrollment increases. But it is equally important to make provision for possible enrollment decreases.

School plant planners would be well advised to ask themselves the question, "How could the proposed building be utilized fully if the enrollment were to drop by fifty percent?" For many school districts, this question is no longer hypothetical. It has become a reality. And, unfortunately, the school buildings of the past were never designed for this eventuality.

During the design stages, school officials should make every effort to identify as many noneducational uses as possible for a proposed school facility. With these possibilities in mind, both school officials and the architect should incorporate into the building design special features that would facilitate noneducational uses of the building, such as clustering of related spaces, isolation of one part of the building from the other, separation of utility lines so that heat, light, and power distribution can be controlled for certain segments of the building.

Educational facilities that are not used to capacity for their originally planned grade groupings may sometimes be utilized by students assigned to different grade levels. For example, a middle school designed for grades six, seven, and eight could also accommodate students in grades two through five, if such a facility has been designed with this possibility in mind. Oftentimes, when school enrollments in a school district drop drastically, it may be possible to abandon obsolete school buildings and transfer students from these schools to those that are more functional. This practice is widespread and well justified. But the school facility to which students are transferred is not always properly planned for these students. For example, if first grade students are transferred to a relatively new middle school, the chalk trays may be too high, the locker combination locks difficult for these children to operate, and the urinals too high from the floor. All of these items could have been easily designed for the use of students in all grade levels if this potential use had been envisioned when the middle school mentioned above was in the design stages.

Preparing for Unforeseeable Educational Practices

At times it seems almost hopeless—and yet it is fascinating—to try to design a structure for functions that are yet unknown. Our buildings will far outlast most of the present educational practices and must, therefore, be designed with this fact in mind.

School plant planners should design buildings that are easily adaptable to future practices. This concept is not new, by any means, but it needs to be taken more seriously by school designers. To be sure, a small number of outstanding school architects are already designing truly adaptable school buildings. Unfortunately, a larger number are still planning traditionally oriented school buildings, in accordance with the dictates of boards of education who encourage them to produce a more or less conventional type of school building. The desire of boards of education to avoid antagonizing or arousing citizens by introducing radical changes in school design is, of course, understandable. But it is equally important for such boards to realize that adhering strictly to conventional design can lead only to mediocrity. Designing adaptable school buildings requires boldness, imagination, and an adventurous spirit on the part of all concerned. This spirit is contagious, and it can be transmitted from the board of education to the electorate through a good-community relations program.

A few general design characteristics that promote modifiability in school buildings are discussed in this section. Concrete examples of the application of this principle are presented in the latter part of this chapter. School facilities designed for unknown educational practices should possess the following general features:

1. All instructional spaces should be capable of being altered in size and shape at a reasonable cost.
2. All utilities should be easily accessible to all parts of a school building.
3. Mechanical and electrical elements should be installed so as not to impede the relocation of interior partitions.
4. Ceilings should be designed so as to facilitate changes within a school building.
5. The type of luminaries employed should not restrict the placement of interior walls within the building to any major extent.
6. The design of the building should facilitate the installation of electronic devices in all parts of the structure.

Economic Considerations in Preparing for the Unforeseeable

As mentioned earlier, preparing for unpredictable instructional practices should be done judiciously. Obviously, when design features that provide for the unforeseeable do not add appreciably to the cost of a school building, they should be incorporated in its design. On the other hand, if inclusion of all features promoting flexibility increases the cost of the school by more than 10 percent, the individual features should be studied and evaluated very carefully and reintroduced into the plans one at a time. Oftentimes, the original capital outlay for items involving flexibility and adaptability can be significantly reduced by simply making the *provision* for

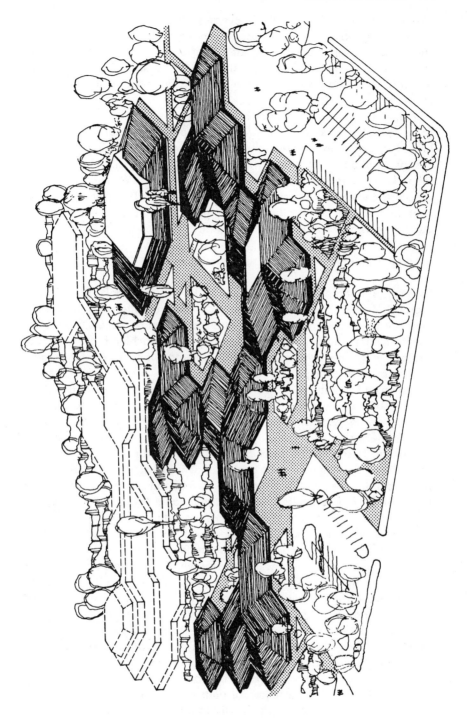

FIGURE 7.1 Preparing for the Unforeseeable Future.

later construction of a conceivable change that may occur in the future. In general, whenever it is less costly to make a given provision for future change during construction than at a later date, it should be made when the school is being built, provided the sum of the costs of all provisions for the unforeseeable do not increase the construction cost of the school by more than 10 percent.

It is not known whether or not the 10 percent figure for investment in features that provide for the unknown is proper. It is reasonable to assume, however, that an investment for this purpose greater than 10 percent of the cost of a building might be difficult to justify. It is possible to incorporate many features that promote both adaptability and flexibility without appreciably increasing the cost of a school building. Therefore, the 10-percent figure suggested for the purpose of anticipating unforeseeable innovations seems reasonable and sufficient.

Leeway in Relation to Fads versus Function

Fads can oftentimes impede leeway for change. A school administrator or a group of faculty members can impose certain features on the architectural design of a school that make it difficult to make sensible changes in the curriculum later. Fads come and go, but the teaching function will persist for a long time. Whenever the planning team is confronted by a fad endorsed by the principal or faculty committee—a technique or student grouping whose value is not validated or widely recognized—the planning group should analyze the educational needs on a functional basis and design the school accordingly. It is not sound planning to design a building around the wishes of an individual or of a group of individuals unless their wishes are based upon educationally functional concepts.

In one case involving the design of a middle school in a New England school district, the junior high school principal had grouped students in four rooms under four teachers for instruction in language arts, social sciences, mathematics, and science. The students moved from room to room and attended centrally located classes for physical education, music, art, and shop or homemaking. In designing the middle school, the principal simply grouped the basic four rooms in a cluster with two clusters on the first floor and two on the second. When it was pointed out that all of his science rooms were decentralized, thus necessitating a quadrupling of equipment, he simply shrugged his shoulders and insisted that the group of four rooms be kept together at all cost. The science teachers were consulted in this matter and they objected to the decentralization on a least three scores. They pointed out that the demonstraton concept was quite important at the seventh- and eighth-grade level. They stated that it was not likely that the school district would purchase four units of every piece of science equipment, even though the principal insisted that it was theoretically possible to do so. And they felt that the inconvenience of moving equipment up and down stairs was great enough to deter the use of a single piece of equipment in all science rooms. The teachers, in this case, were not allowed to plead their case before the planning team, and so the principal succeeded in locating two science rooms on the first floor, two on the second and, incidentally, a fifth science room at the opposite end of the building. The short-sightedness of this kind of planning is clear. Long after the principal retires, the building will remain functionally restricted for the teaching of science.

PRACTICAL CONSIDERATIONS PREPARING FOR THE UNFORESEEABLE

It would be almost impossible to list, even in elementary fashion, the many ways in which it is possible to provide for the unforeseeable in planning a school. A few examples of flexibility and adaptability of school buildings are presented in the hope that they may generate many others.

Sumption and Landes[1] properly refer to "modifiability" in the planning of school buildings. They discuss the principles of adaptability, flexibility, expansibility, and contractibility. Schools designed with these features in mind can provide amply for unforeseeable changes in methodology, student grouping, course offerings, type of instructional machinery and equipment, teaching aids and materials, size of enrollment, and the like. It can be seen, therefore, that planning for the unforeseeable could involve much more than the ability to change the size and shapes of spaces within the exterior walls of the structure and to expand it in one or more directions.

Ideally, a school building should be capable of modifications in many forms. It should be planned for both horizontal and vertical expansion. It should contain internal partitions and supporting columns that facilitate the reshaping and resizing of interior spaces without functional limitations. It should be designed so that electrical power, utilities, communication cables, electromagnetic wave guides, optical systems for lasers and masers, and other technological devices yet to be invented can be brought to or utilized in any part of the building. Obviously, it would probably be far more expensive to attain this ideal then to adopt a more realistic approach to the problem. A few general approaches will be treated in later sections of this chapter.

Expansion

The continued trend toward urbanization, with its rapid increase in population densities in metropolitan areas means that land will be at a premium

[1]Merle R. Sumption and Jack W. Landes, *Planning Functional School Buildings* (New York: Harper and Brothers, 1957), p. 201.

in the future. As a result, school buildings should be conceived for vertical expansion in order to conserve expensive urban land. The structure and footings of a single-story building in an urban or suburban area should be designed so that additional supports could be incorporated in the structure in the future for the addition of a second or third floor to the school.

Horizontal expansibility has long been recognized as a desirable feature in a school building. When the function of the expanded building has been determined, the architect customarily plans the ultimate structure and then cuts it back to the spaces needed for the first stage of construction. When the future need has not been determined, the building should still be planned for expansion but in a more general fashion. Circulation areas should be designed so as not to hinder future expansion. Utility lines should be designed with future expansion in mind. The planning team should always ask itself the question, "Where and what would we be likely to add to this building if we were asked to increase its capacity by 25 percent?" even though the likelihood of such expansion appears to be quite remote at the time the school is being planned.

Attention should be focused on the general layout and circulation pattern of a building as well as on specific design features. Ideally, a school building should be designed so that it is capable of being expanded sensibly and functionally in five directions—on four sides and upward. Speaking more realistically, school plant planners should strive to design school buildings so that they can be expanded sensibly in at least three directions.

Contraction

Until recently, contractibility was not considered essential in the planning of educational facilities. With school enrollments growing from year to year, the emphasis was primarily on expansibility. This principle was discussed in the preceding section. The enrollment trend has now changed. In many school districts, enrollments have dropped substantially over the past few years. Many school officials and boards of education have been caught unprepared. They have had to face the difficult and sensitive decisions of what to do with superfluous and unneeded classrooms or entire school buildings.

Planning for an unforeseeable decline in school enrollment was discussed earlier in this chapter. It is much more difficult than planning a school building for expansibility. School plant planners can provide for substantial decreases in school enrollment in the long range plan in two ways. The simplest solution is to devise a long range plan so that obsolete buildings can be phased out easily if school enrollments drop. In this connection, the location of new facilities would be a major consideration in planning for unforeseeable decreases in enrollment. This approach is particularly adaptable in older school districts where the age of some of the school facilities exceeds fifty or sixty years. In a relatively young school district, however, planning for contractability is much more complicated. If all of the existing school buildings are relatively modern and highly functional, the need for less space cannot be solved easily by simply closing out excellent buildings. A more realistic approach would be to continue using a school facility for educational purposes but allow part of it to be used for noneducational activities. However, this solution is not always practical or feasible because the building was not designed with contractability in mind. The section in this chapter entitled "Preparing for Unforeseeable Enrollment Decline" describes a number of possible solutions that utilize the principle of contraction.

Adaptability

Adaptability refers primarily to the ease with which spaces designed for a given function can be transformed to accommodate changes in methodology, student grouping, teaching aids, and the like. For example, by installing uniformly spaced standards on the walls of a classroom, it is possible to convert a regular classroom with chalkboards and tackboards on two walls to a general physical science room with peripheral counters and wall storage simply by hanging counters, shelves, storage cabinets, sinks, and other needed accessories on the standards. Rubber hoses could be used to connect the hung science sinks to the various utilities. Such a room is highly adaptable. Generally speaking, the concept of adaptability is confined to the conversion of existing spaces to new functions by modifying them internally. School planners also refer to the adaptability of a school building as a whole. In this sense, the term is related to the ability to utilize a building designed for a specific purpose for another purpose. For example, can a given junior high school be readily converted to a middle school? If it can, then the building is said to be adaptable.

In a broad sense, the concept discussed above is closely associated with multipurpose spaces. Any instructional area that can be used for many functions possesses a high degree of adaptability. Elementary school cafeterias, play areas, high school general science rooms, college student union buildings, and multipurpose lobbies are examples of highly adaptable spaces.

In planning for the unforeseeable, every effort should be made to include features that facilitate internal changes in all instructional areas. Special attention should be given to the multipurpose use of all walls, to the ease of locating power and utilities in various parts of the room, to the possibility that equipment may be hung from the ceiling, to the control of internal lighting within a given instructional area, and to the quick and simple rearrangement of furniture and equipment on the floor. How far this concept is pursued depends upon the amount of funds that the planning team feels it should invest for the unforeseeable.

Flexibility

The term flexibility is closely related to adaptability but is somewhat broader in scope. Flexibility is conceived as a feature of a school building that facilitates extensive changes in the sizes and shapes of teaching areas without endangering the structural system of the building. Adaptability makes it possible to accommodate new functions in given spaces, while flexibility makes it possible to redesign old spaces to satisfy new needs.

The basic ingredient of flexibility is fluidity.   Accordingly, all walls of a school building, with the exception, perhaps, of the outside envelope, should be conceived as temporary space dividers. Ideally, it should be possible, in a flexibly designed school, to relocate all internal partitions without jeopardizing the structural system of the building. No conduits, pipes, ducts, or other service elements of the building should be located in the walls. Also, no interior walls should be load bearing. Heating, cooling, and lighting systems should be concentrated in the floors and ceilings. It is not usually financially justifiable to provide all of these features throughout an entire school building. Furthermore, many of the walls in a school may never be moved simply because no change of position is desired or required by the educational program. Consequently, good school planning calls for the judicious application of the principle of flexibility. If movable walls are desired, it is imperative that supporting columns be strategically placed so as not to interfere with sight lines when the position of the internal partitions is changed to meet the demands of a changing curriculum.

The principle of flexibility should be applied to the equipment as well as to the building. The design of a school should facilitate the relocation of instructional equipment. For example, flat floors, rather than risers, are preferable in instructional areas because they permit flexibility of seating arrangements. Many colleges and universities still adhere to the traditional rise-type classroom, which destroys flexibility in the placement and arrangement of furniture and equipment.

Practical Features of Modifiable School Plants

A few suggestions related to the planning of a school building are presented in this seciton. These suggestions are focused upon those elements of school planning that will promote expansibility, adaptability, and flexibility.

1. *Placement of a building on the site.* First and foremost, it is essential that school planners select a site of adequate size in accordance with the standards suggested earlier. Assuming that the area of the school site is great enough, the building should be placed so that additions can be made to it on all four sides if possible. If not, additions should be possible on three sides of the school.

2. *The traffic pattern and location of corridors.* Corridors, stairways, and exits should be located so that the traffic pattern may flow naturally into any space added to the original structure. Also, the initial design of a school building should be aimed at keeping the costs of expansion at a minimum through the proper placement of corridors and stairways.

3. *The central utility core concept.* The establishment of a service core in the central part of a building is one method of providing for the unforeseeable. Wires, pipes, ducts, and cables can be easily extended to pay part of the building from a centrally located service core.

4. *Anticipation of new instructional aids.* The imaginative school plant planning team endeavors to anticipate technological advances in instructional aids. There are currently a number of promising technological developments that should be taken into account in planning a school building. Open- and closed-circuit television are now quite commonplace in school design. The use of teaching devices is spreading at all levels of learning. Self-instructional devices, including automated, centralized tape recordings involving the use of scores of listening booths throughout a school building, are beginning to appear. Computerized teaching devices using at least three branching stages are in the experimental stage. A single computer can give individual personalized instruction to several hundred students at a time, and the PLATO project at the University of Illinois indicates that this type of mass-individualized instruction is not too far in the future.

5. *Destructible partitions.* Destructible partitions are often used in lieu of movable partitions where the need for removing a partition is not immediate. The destructible partition is preferable to other types of walls from the standpoint of capital outlay when a movable or operable partition is not clearly required. A destructible partition is designed so that it can be destroyed without affecting the structure of the building and without the problems of relocating pipes, ducts, wires, or cables that are often imbedded in ordinary partitions.

The destructible partition has an important place in school design. Operable partitions that are only rarely operated are costly and unnecessary. Conventionally designed permanent partitions that enclose ducts, wiring, and plumbing are very costly to eliminate and may even become a formidable barrier to change. The destructible partition, on the other hand, can provide an excellent acoustical barrier at a reasonable cost, one that can be easily removed at a later date without difficulty or expense. Thus, the inclusion of a large number of destructible partitions in the design of a school building provides additional insurance that the building can cope with the unforeseeable.

6. *The movable partition.* The movable partition serves fundamentally the same purpose as the destructible partition, but the movable partition is salvageable, and it can be relocated without much difficulty. Several types are currently available. One types utilizes a nut-and-bolt as-

sembly system which enables two men to move a 35-foot partition from one location to another in about eight hours. Another type of movable partition is quite ingenious in design. It utilizes a pneumatic rubber boot along the top. A section of the partition, with the boot deflated, can be moved easily by two men. When the new position is reached, the boot is simply inflated and the panel is automatically sealed at both top and bottom. From the standpoint of cost, the nut-and-bolt system still has an economic advantage over other types. The pneumatic type of partition, however, holds much promise for the future.

7. *Suspended ceilings.* The introduction of suspended ceilings in the design of a school building provides a great flexibility at a very reasonable cost. In certain circumstances, suspended ceilings using tile may actually be less costly than some of the common nonsuspended types. The advantage of the suspended ceiling in relation to flexibility is quite obvious and needs no further elaboration.

8. *Ideas that look toward the future.* Planning for the unforeseeable must focus on those design features that facilitate and encourage both minor and major changes in an educational facility. To conceive and create a design that readily lends itself to change, school planners must ask themselves, "What provisions in the design of the school should be made now so that certain changes can be made later at a reasonable cost?" "What special features should be incorporated in the plans at this time?" More specifically, they might ask themselves what they would do:

(a) If the heating capacity were to be increased by 50 percent?
(b) If air-conditioning were to be installed?
(c) If utilities were needed in any part of the school where they are now lacking?
(d) If electrical power of various voltages were required in any part of the school?
(e) If computer consoles were to be installed in selected classrooms?
(f) If radio wave guides were to be installed in the science and engineering areas?
(g) If self-instructional teaching devices with a centralized control point were to be installed in any part of the building?
(h) If carrels were to be provided for students in the ratio of one per two students? One for each student?
(i) If offices were to be provided for all secondary school teachers?
(j) If effective germicidal lamps were to be installed in instructional areas?
(k) If luminescent chalkboards using ultraviolet light were to be introduced in all classrooms?
(l) If the building were required to have instructional spaces for tutoring (teacher with one student), for groups of 3, for groups of 6, for groups of 15, for groups of 30, for groups of 90, for groups of 150, for groups of 300, for groups of 450 in the same building?

(m) If instructional spaces for over fifty students were to require the installation of automated feedback instructional equipment?

(n) If 25 percent of the instructional materials were to be produced by a staff of artists at the school?

(o) If 20 percent of the instructional staff were composed of trained teacher aides who need offices, equipment, and space for in-service training?

(p) If the school were to be expanded vertically?

(q) If instructional programs could originate thousands of miles away from the school and be conveyed to the students in any classroom via picturetelephone?

(r) If the library and communications center of the school were, at the request of the student, to send audio and visual information automatically to the student's home at any time during the day or night? (This idea is now economically feasible.)

(s) If the school were to provide its own air pollution filtering plant?

(t) If a systematic plan whereby students were to learn from their peers were to be instituted?

This list purposely contains a number of suggestions that would seem revolutionary to the conservative and even somewhat advanced for the liberal, but it is hoped these thoughts indicate that character of the ideas that should emanate from the planning team when it endeavors to cope with the problem of planning for the unforeseeable.

CHAPTER   8

Adequacy, Efficiency, and Economy

Adequacy, efficiency, and economy are three related fundamental concepts in the planning of educational facilities. The adequacy of a school plant is measured by the degree to which it satisfies the quantitative and qualitative requirements of the educational program. Efficiency is related to the functional characteristics incorporated in the design of the facility. And economy is calculated by an estimate of the potential educational return per dollar expended for school facilities, although, of course, one cannot measure the absolute educational return per dollar expended. At any rate, there is greater economy in school plant planning when the expenditure of funds is more likely to produce increased educational returns or greater utilization of space and materials over a long period of time.

ADEQUACY AND SUITABILITY OF SCHOOL SPACES

The concept of adequacy is primarily concerned with the number, size, shape, and quality of educational spaces. Adequacy alone does not ensure a well-planned school facility. Suitability of instructional spaces with respect to function and operation of a school is a correlated consideration. In more specific terms, spaces for learning should be suitable from the standpoint of environmental controllability, shape, atmosphere, location, ease of maintenance, long-range economy, and the like.

Adequacy of Number

Educational specifications should state the number of the various types of spaces estimated to be both necessary and sufficient for the desired educational program. Any reduction in the number of proposed spaces from the number appearing in the specifications results in a corresponding cutback in the educational program.

In addition to the proper number of instructional spaces, a certain number of supporting spaces must be included in any educational facility. Such noninstructional spaces include storage areas, preparation rooms, faculty offices, research areas, washrooms, locker spaces, toilets, lounges, and the like. The number of such spaces planned depends primarily upon the type and size of the school planned and upon the scope of the educational program to be housed in it. These needs will be discussed in detail in later chapters. Suffice it to say at this point, that a necessary and sufficient number of both instructional and supplementary spaces should be provided in any school building. The terms "necessary and sufficient" suggest that spaces in excess of the number called for by the educational program should not be included.

Adequacy of Size

The size of an instructional space directly influences its proper functioning, particularly if the number of square feet provided for a given space falls below the minimum needed for the function to be accommodated in it. Suggested sizes for selected educational spaces are presented later for each type of school plan. These figures are based on accepted practices.

The functional analysis technique may also be employed. The space required for each activity should be determined by actual measurement, under experimental conditions, if necessary. It is surprising that the functional analysis technique, despite its relative simplicity, is not universally adopted. For example, it may be necessary to determine the space required for ten student carrels. It is quite easy to compute the space needed for a table 3 feet wide and 2 feet deep. The dimensions required for a chair and circulation space can be estimated as 3 feet long and 3 feet wide. The total square footage per carrel and circulation space then becomes 15 square feet. For ten carrels, at least 150 square feet would be needed. If we add an estimated 50 square feet for circulation, the size of a room for ten student carrels would be approximately 200 square feet. This procedure can be applied to any instructional space, provided the number of students involved and the estimated space requirement of each type of learning activity are known. In situations where new experiences are being introduced in the curriculum, experimental situations may be set up to determine the approximate amount of space needed. The author has found this technique to be quite fruitful. In some instances, the use of this method has revealed that spaces smaller than those suggested by "rules of thumb" were adequate for the function under consideration.

Adequacy of Environmental Controls

Adequacy of environmental controllability is vital to effective learning and to healthfulness. Thermal, acoustical, and visual controls are directly related to the needs of the human body. Instructional spaces should be designed with ample thermal capacity, including controls for both heating and cooling. In addition, they must have illumination and acoustical characteristics.

Details regarding the specific requirements associated with environmental control will be discussed in subsequent chapters. It is intended, at this point, simply to make note of the need for adequate heating, cooling, humidity, lighting, and acoustics. Environmental controls are a vital part of plans of educational facilities.

Suitability of Shape

The shape of an instructional space should be suited to the function it is designed to serve. In general, rectangular, almost square classrooms are quite suitable for classes of about thirty students engaged in non-laboratory-type instruction. Shape may be critical in some instructional spaces. For example, a combination lecture room-laboratory, where peripheral laboratory tables are desired, should be almost square. A music room should not be long and narrow. Elementary-grade classrooms can be supervised more effectively if the space is "squarish." On the other hand, a storage room should be long and narrow to make the most efficient use of floor space. In fact, a width of about 7 feet is preferable from the standpoint of economy. Characteristics of the various spaces are discussed in the chapters pertaining to the planning of elementary school, secondary school, and college buildings.

Suitability of Atmosphere

The environment created by an architect in the design of a school building should be psychologically stimulating to the students. Color, proportions, shape, lighting, fenestration, texture of interior surfaces, and furniture and furnishings all contribute to the atmosphere produced within an instructional space. Obviously, the total effect should both please and stimulate the student. He must sense that he is an integral part of the space and that he is welcome in it. Instructional spaces should possess warmth, coziness, and attractiveness.

In this connection, color can be used most effectively to help create a proper psychological environment. Birren has spent a lifetime studying color and its effect on human beings. He has written an informative and well-documented treatise[1] on the subject. Color psychology is a topic of major concern to school planners as they seek to create an environment that is suitable for learning.

[1]Faber Birren, New Horizons in Color (New York: Reinhold Publishing Co., 1955).

Adequacy of Space Relationships

A school building should be designed so that it functions as a single organism. All of its parts should be located in proper relationship to each other in order that the activities in the building can be conducted efficiently, conveniently, economically, healthfully, and safely.

Clustering of functionally related spaces.   From the standpoint of economy, efficiency, and ease of communication between faculty and staff, it is highly desirable that spaces housing similar or closely related instructional activities be clustered together. For example, all science spaces, such as those for biology, chemistry, physics, and general science, could be located in a single cluster in a high school building. In a college or university, for example, a chemistry building, a physics building and a biology building, could be clustered, perhaps, around a science library. In general, it is recommended that an educational facility be conceived and designed as a series of clusters of related spaces. The relationship of one cluster to another and other matters will be treated in chapters dealing with the planning of each type of school.

Separation of incompatible and unrelated spaces.   Incompatible spaces should be well separated. For acoustical reasons, for example, it is necessary to separate spaces planned for noisy activities from those whose activities are quiet, e.g., shop areas should not be near the library. For psychological reasons, it is highly desirable to separate the entrance to the guidance office from that of the principal's office, but for functional reasons, the interior areas of the guidance suite should be adjacent to those of the principal. For aesthetic reasons, large masses may be separated somewhat. For reasons of economy, air-conditioned spaces would be separated from the power plant or boiler room. From the standpoint of natural lighting, it might be necessary to separate adjoining wings by substantial distances, if natural lighting were to be the primary source of illumination. The principle of separation should be applied judiciously in school plant planning, for example, by spacing the clusters or related spaces properly rather than isolating an individual space from the cluster to which it is closely related. The time necessary for students to travel from one space to another should be taken into account too. If distances between classroom buildings become too great, it may be necessary to increase the time allowed between periods, and, perhaps, lengthen the school day.

Location in relation to safety and health.   In placing each function within the building or on the school site, planners should pay careful heed to the safety and health of the students and staff. For example, the location of storage space in lofts in shop areas presents a serious safety hazard. Spaces requiring service drives should be laid out with great care to insure the safety of students and school personnel. Unloading zones should be properly situated in relationship to both sidewalks and main driveways. Students should not be required to cross driveways in traveling from the bus unloading area to the building or in walking from the play areas to the gymnasium. On a college campus, it is desirable simply to eliminate all vehicles from the central core of each group of buildings.

THE EFFICIENCY OF A SCHOOL BUILDING

From a practical standpoint, it is difficult, if not impossible, to draw a distinct line between efficiency and economy. For the purpose of this discussion, efficiency refers to architectural design that is likely to improve the instructional effectiveness or operational characteristics of the building. Economy, on the other hand, has reference to actual savings in capital outlay that can be effected through architectural design. In a broad sense, therefore, efficiency is related to greater functional return per dollar expended, while economy is associated with the attainment of a given educational result at the lowest possible cost. For all practical purposes, efficiency and economy are almost indistinguishable in matters pertaining to the cost of operation, maintenance, and replacement.

Greater educational return can be achieved in a host of ways through the creative design of a school building. School planners and faculty should keep efficiency of instruction in mind as they consider and discuss various proposals. The question that one should ask himself in relation to efficiency is, "Is this particular solution to the problem likely to yield the greatest educational return?" To arrive at a proper answer, one should further ask such questions as, "Does the solution promote the convenience of both teacher and students?" "Will most teachers find it simple to implement?" "Can the proposed solution be adapted to most of the situations that are likely to be encountered?" "Will the solution facilitate instructional or learning activities?" "Is the proposed solution too complex or elaborate in terms of the foreseeable need?"

Efficiency of Function

All school planners want to design a building that is tailor-made for the educational function of the school. It is paramount that the functional aspects of a proposed school building be stated and described so clearly in the educational specifications that the architect has no difficulty or uncertainty in preparing sketches that are reasonably close to the desired design in terms of function.

As mentioned earlier, it is not possible to list functional features that apply to all educational facilities. A creative planning team and an imaginative faculty can supply the architect with hundreds of functional suggestions. In fact, it is not unusual to gather several hundred promising ideas from a faculty of fifty teachers, when the techniques of group dynamics are employed.

In planning for functional efficiency, school planners must also take into account the type of teaching materials and instructional equipment that are to be employed by the faculty, for functional efficiency demands that both the building and its equipment be conceived as a single, unified educational tool.

Many ideas related to functional efficiency will evolve, as the faculty works with the planning team. One idea in a group suggests another. It might be helpful to describe one or two situations in which this approach was used. After a group of teachers had become thoroughly acquainted with the concept of functional flexibility, it was suggested that faculty offices and classrooms be supplied with uniformly spaced vertical standards such as those used for bookshelves, so that chalkboards, shelves, cabinets, or coat hangers, could be hung on the walls of such spaces. A faculty member could prepare charts and graphs on a small unit chalkboard hung in his office. He might then unhook it and carry it to the lecture room where he could hang it on the standards for instructional use. In designing a gymnasium-natatorium, a faculty member posed the idea of locating the pool about 50 feet away from the gymnasium floor and parallel to it. The intervening space above the lockers and showers could contain folding bleachers that could face either the pool or the gymnasium. When the pool was being used for swimming meets, the bleachers could seat spectators in the natatorium. When the bleachers were reversed, spectators could face the gymnasium play area during basketball games. When the bleachers were folded, the space between the two facilities could be used for instruction in physical education. The first example was submitted by faculty members who were planning a junior high school, and the second originated in a group of professors who were planning a college physical education facility. These examples illustrate to some extent the variety of ideas that may be offered by the school planning team and the faculty and staff associated with it.

Efficiency in Maintenance and Operation of a Building

School plants should be planned and designed to keep the cost of maintenance and operation at a minimum. Operational costs are directly related to the cost of services, fuels, expendable supplies, utilities, and the like. Maintenance costs refer primarily to the expenditure required to maintain the building and its equipment in its original state of utility.

Operational efficiency.   School planners should give a penetrating look to all matters related to the operation of a school. Services represent relatively large operational cost. Consequently, the building should be designed, the materials chosen, and the equipment selected on the basis of maximum human efficiency. For example, easily and quickly cleaned surfaces should be chosen over those that involve a lower initial cost but are more costly to maintain. Features that save the time of employees who operate or occupy the structure are important. For example, the placement of doors and the location of service spaces with respect to entrances, driveways, unloading zones, and each other should be carefully studied to minimize unnecessary loss of time or motion. Fuels and utilities should be conserved as much as possible. Heat losses and gains must be taken into account not only for purposes of providing sufficient heating or cooling capacity but also for achieving economies in the operation of the system. Additional insulation or low-conductivity windowpanes mean greater initial costs, but the savings in operational costs over the life of the building will generally more than compensate for them. The design of the building should reduce waste of electrical power, gas, and water as much as possible. For example, the use of low-voltage light controls would permit the custodian to control all of the lights in a building from a single panel. By pressing a few buttons in the custodial area after a given hour, he could activate relays that extinguish some or all of the lights in a building, or the lights could be controlled automatically by use of a time clock. Water conservation is also desirable, but not at the expense of function. The use of spring faucets is a case in point. In order to wash one's hands at a public lavatory hygienically, it is necessary to use tempered running water. Spring faucets, one carrying hot and the other cold water, simply cannot be operated hygienically. On the other hand, a knee- or foot-operated single-spigot faucet having tempered water is an excellent solution, because it both achieves economy and meets sanitary requirements. The initial cost may be somewhat higher, but the operation is both functional and economical.

Efficiency related to maintenance.   Efficiency of maintenance is concerned with durability and cost of upkeep. Materials that are relatively maintenance-free should be given preference over less costly materials requiring greater care. The life expectancy of both materials and equipment is a basic consideration in the selection of such items. Those which have the lowest depreciation cost per year should be given first consideration, unless such choices adversely affect the educational function.

Efficiency in Storage and Handling of Materials

All materials should be stored as close as possible to the place where they are used. Storage rooms, therefore, should be strategically placed in a building with reference to *delivery*, *distribution*, and *utilization*. Sound business practice demands that storage spaces be controlled. Consequently, storage rooms should be designed and situated so that control is facilitated. It is also necessary to plan storage spaces to prevent spoilage or damage to materials stored in them. Unfortunately, architectural engineers often utilize storage rooms for ducts, transformers, distribution boxes, and the like. Besides reducing the effective size of storage spaces, the secondary use of these spaces may damage the supplies or materials placed in storage.

Efficiency in the Design of Circulation Patterns Within a School

The architectural design of student circulation space has a pronounced influence on the educational function of a school building. Circulation patterns must allow student traffic to flow rapidly from one part of the building to the other; however, extreme care must be exercised to insure that the space provided for circulation is both necessary and sufficient. Excessive circulation space is wasteful from the standpoint of both initial investment and operation. There seems to be a slight tendency among a few school planners to overdesign circulation spaces. In one instance, for example, there was a single loaded corridor 10 feet wide surrounding three sides of a large cafeteria-dining area. In another plant, two corridors were provided to serve three rows of classrooms. In both of these cases the excess corridor space added somewhat to student convenience, but in neither case did the circulation pattern indicate an efficient use of space.

Secondary corridors and lobbies should be carefully studied in any school facility plan. Circulation space should be completely adequate, but in planning the size of lobbies, corridors, and other circulation spaces in a school building, it should be remembered that efficiency in circulation space yields two bonuses—savings in initial capital outlay and reductions in operational costs.

ECONOMY

Every effort should be made by school planners to achieve maximum economy in both capital outlay and operation of a proposed school building. Economy, however, should be differentiated from cheapness. A building should be economical but not cheap. Economy, as used in this text, is not the acquisition of a school facility for a given enrollment at the lowest possible cost. Rather, it is defined as the achievement of maximum educational and utilitarian value per dollar expended. According to this concept, the lowest-cost building is not necessarily the most economical. For example, a school district in northern Illinois constructed a brick and masonry school at a phenomenally low cost per square foot. When it was viewed by the author after it was barely five years old, the mortar had crumbled so badly that a pencil could be pushed through an outside wall. The building had settled so badly that light could be seen through the walls of one of the toilet rooms. And water damage had caused the window frames to rot, permitting cold air to enter the building. The superintendent of school conceded that the school district had a serious problem on its hands, because the building was too new to abandon and yet too costly to continue in operation.

How Much Economy Can Be Achieved by Educational Boards?

Conscientious members of boards of education or boards of trustees spend months poring over plans and specifications in an effort to achieve real economies in school buildings. Their worthy efforts are concentrated on items of construction that represent only a small percent of the total cost of the project.

Human Effort and Potential Savings.   Let us demonstrate the low potential savings that may be effected by educational boards in selecting less costly materials for walls, flooring, hardware, ceiling, lighting, acoustics, and the like. On the average, the total cost of a building is distributed as follows:

  20 percent for fees, furniture, furnishings and equipment, and site development.
  80 percent for construction, of which 26 percent is attributable to heating, ventilating, electrical, and mechanical equipment.

If we subtract 26 percent from the construction cost for heating, mechanicals, and the like, the remainder is 54 percent of the total cost. Assuming further that labor represents about one-half the cost of construction, and also that a board of education or trustees has practically no control over it, the cost of all remaining construction materials in a school plant is thus reduced to about 27 percent of the total cost. Lets us assume further that about one-half of the materials cost is predetermined by the physical requirements, such as steel beams for framework, slabs of concrete, and the like. Consequently, a board is left with about 14 percent of the cost of building materials over which it has some choice. If we also assume that it will cost at least one-half of the 14 percent to acquire basic materials over which the board has a choice, the maximum possible saving that could be effected by a board of education or trustees appears to be 7 percent of the total cost of the school. Since most members of boards of education or trustees are not professional engineers or architects, it is reasonable to assume that, at best, a saving of 2 or 3 percent in the total cost of a building might be effected at a personal cost to the board members in time and effort that is inordinately high in relation to such savings.

In view of the foregoing discussion, it can be seen that the time invested in discussions, research, and study to effect economies is not always commensurate with the savings that are realized. All boards must review plans and specifications in terms of function, efficiency, and economy. It is suggested, however, that economy not be belabored by educational boards because after initial corrections have been made the return is disappointingly small when compared with the additional effort that must be expended. More substantial economies are possible through creative building design, long-range planning, use of new concepts, and the like, which are discussed subsequently.

True and false economies.   School planners must differentiate clearly between real and false economies. A true economy must meet the following two tests:

1. The reduced cost in capital outlay does not adversely affect the curriculum or educational efficiency of the school.
2. The reduced initial cost does not result in *increased* maintenance and operational costs.

The first test deals with intangible educational outcomes that are somewhat difficult to evaluate. Nevertheless, school planners should be fully convinced that an economy does not hinder or restrict the desired educational program before incorporating it in the plans of a school building. The second test, on the other hand, is quite objective and relatively simple to apply. For example, Pierce[2] concludes that "the flourescent system (of school lighting) will probably cost slightly more initially, but the annual cleaning, relamping and operating costs will more than offset this slight difference in less than a year's time." While Pierce's conclusion may seem startling to the proponents of incandescent lighting, it was supported by a study conducted by a school district in the Boston area on the comparative cost of purchase, installation, and operation of both types of lighting under controlled conditions. It was found that the initial higher cost of the fluorescent fixtures was compensated for in less than seven years because of their lower cost of operation and maintenance. Since the average life of a school building is over half a century, the fluorescent fixtures were actually producing income for the school district after the initial difference in cost between the two types of fixtures was equalized.

While this illustration is quite striking, many others could be included which are not so dramatic nor so obvious. For example, the use of costly glazed tile on the lower part of corridor walls and in toilet rooms is a real economy. The installation of expensive ceramic tile on toilet room floors represents another real economy. The plastering of both sides of light-

[2]David A. Pierce, *Saving Dollars in Building Schools* (New York: Reinhold Publishing Co., 1959), p. 88.

weight concrete blocks on walls between two classrooms is a real economy, because it significantly decreases noise interference between two
adjoining instructional spaces. The installation of suspended acoustical
ceilings on a mechanical track system is another real economy from the
standpoint of maintenance, replacement of tile, and adaptability of the
space as a learning laboratory. The installation of wall-to-wall carpeting in
certain areas of a school building also represents a real economy from the
standpoint of money saved and improved educational function.

Economy Related to the Design of a School Building

The design of a building strongly influences its cost. In discussing cost reduction by educational boards, it was assumed that the design of the building was approved and fixed before board members sought to effect economies by selecting less costly equipment, furniture, and interior surfaces.
Not only does the design of the building have a profound influence on the
initial cost of a school plant but it also affects its cost of operation.

The compact design.   The School Planning Laboratory[3] has found a
close relationship between "compactness of a school building and both
subsequent maintenance and operation expense," in elementary and secondary schools. There was also a strong negative correlation between initial cost of a building and compactness. In these studies the index of compactness was obtained by dividing the perimeter footage by the square
footage within the walls. The compactness effect was more pronounced in
the larger buildings than in the smaller structures, as might well be expected. In designing economical buildings, therefore, it is desirable to
keep the linear feet of perimeter per square foot of enclosure as small as
possible. The architectural profession has applied this principle of economy to school design for many years. Many architects have turned to the
cube, the circle, and more recently to the sphere as exemplified by the introduction of the geodesic dome by R. Buckminster Fuller, in their efforts to
achieve maximum compactness.

In designing educational facilities, however, school planners should
bear in mind that the primary purpose of a school building is to educate
pupils. No predetermined design should be adopted unless it satisfies the
requirements of the desired educational program. If the compact plan satisfied the educational need just as well as the rambling type of school
building, then the principle of economy would dicate that the compact design be selected. On the other hand, there may be circumstances, particularly in the design of elementary schools, where the rambling single-story,
finger plan is particularly suitable. The author believes that school planners should give a strong preference to the compact plan but should not in-

[3]School Planning Laboratory Research, Repts. 3 and 4. (Stanford, Calif.: Educational Facilities Laboratories, Inc., Stanford University), 1961.

sist upon it in all situations. It is also felt that a rambling school cannot be justified in terms of economy unless its design meets a specific educational need.

The compact design does not mean that the entire school must be designed as a single large cube or hemisphere. Indeed, architects have utilized this principle in many ingenious ways. They have used a series of cubes varying in size. They have planned circular school buildings. They have employed combinations of spheres, cubes, and cylinders. Of course, the influence of compactness on economy of school construction is less pronounced in school buildings having areas under 15,000 square feet. For secondary schools containing less than 50,000 square feet, the correlation between cost of construction and compactness[4] was −0.78, while schools with areas in excess of 100,000 square feet yielded a coefficient of correlation of −0.90. A similar research project was conducted at the School Planning Laboratory[5] using data related to elementary schools, which are generally substantially smaller in area than secondary schools. Even in these cases, the economy due to compactness was quite pronounced. The coefficient of correlation between compactness and the cost of elementary schools was −0.41.

The principle of compactness suggests that greater economy of initial capital outlay and operational cost with respect to heating and cooling is obtained when the perimeter of a building is kept as short as possible. For this reason, jogs should be avoided whenever possible. Long, narrow wings are less desirable from the standpoint of economy than structures in which wings are combined to form a more compact building. For example, arranging classrooms so that the narrow end faces the corridor tends to promote compactness and economy. The geodesic plan is another illustration of compact design in school plant planning.

Planned Economy for Capital Outlay Programs

Economy can be the result of educational planning that takes place long before a building is conceived or proposed. In fact, economy is an important aspect of long-range planning. The strategic location of new buildings, the judicious rehabilitation of facilities with educational potential, and the abandonment of obsolete school buildings contribute to educational economy.

A few highlights of economy related to long-range educational planning are reviewed. A more detailed account appears in Chapter 5, where many elements of long-range planning are discussed. Economy in long-range planning is promoted by acquiring school sites in advance of the time when they are needed. It is not always necessary to purchase the site early. On the other hand, an educational board should obtain an option on

[4]*Ibid.*
[5]*Ibid.*

property that may be required for the expansion of an educational institution as many as five years prior to the anticipated need, if possible. New schools should be located properly in relation to the area of future population growth of the school district and to existing buildings that are likely to be abandoned in the foreseeable future. Economy may be improved through the development of a long-range financial plan that is designed to keep the credit rating of the school district as high as possible. It can provide for the timing of financial transactions that are advantageous to the school district. Economy can be achieved by selecting the proper type of grade organization in terms of the educational program to be offered and in relation to existing school buildings with educational potential for future use. And finally, economy is substantially improved when new facilities are designed for real, as contrasted with pseudo-, expansion. In the experience of the writer, there has rarely been an occasion when an architect was unable to show that provision was made for future expansion of the school. In fact, he would often draw a few dotted lines showing exactly where such expansion could occur in the building, but there was little or no consideration, in most cases, as to exactly what educational functions would be housed within the space enclosed by the dotted lines or how they would be related to existing functions. All that the architect was doing, in such cases, was to point out that there was sufficient land for the building to be expanded at the end of a corridor. Educators must help the architect to envision specific educational uses for the space contained within the dotted lines. Such planning fosters economy.

Another aspect of economy that precedes the planning of a building is the employment of an architect who can prepare a proper set of final working drawings and specifications. Economy is substantially improved if the architect prepares plans and specifications that are complete, detailed, and easy to understand. A board of trustees or board of education may never really know how many additional dollars a contractor adds to his bid simply because he wants to be "on the safe side" in translating ambiguous specifications into the cost of labor and materials. Also, drawings and specifications that lack sufficient detail may lead to change orders and misunderstanding during construction, both of which are costly.

Suggestions for Improving Economy in School Plant Planning

It would be a monumental, if not impossible, task to list every conceivable method of achieving economy in planning school buildings. A few suggestions are presented here with the expectation that many other money-saving ideas will evolve during the planning process.

1. Economy is improved when instructional spaces can be designed to serve several functions. In such cases, the room utilization factor is likely to be increased and, under certain conditions, fewer spaces may be needed.

2. Classroom ceilings can be lowered to nine feet or nine feet six inches without any harm to the educational program. Such a change would result in savings of both initial capital outlay and in heating and cooling costs.

3. A reduction in the amount of glass in a school building decreases the cost of both maintenance and operation. The use of fixed glass is more economical than the installation of movable window sash.

4. The quantity of ventilation should be kept as low as possible but consistent with minimum needs, about 10 cubic feet of fresh air per student per minute or less in some states.

5. Construction materials should be selected on the basis of ease of maintenace and durability. As mentioned earlier, substituting materials that reduce the cost of initial capital outlay does not necessarily achieve economy.

6. Stock plans should be avoided since they do not save educational institutions money in the long run. According to Pierce, ". . . the cost of a project can be reduced by using stock plans only when the school is willing to settle for inadequate and incomplete planning; and, therefore, willing to settle for less than the most appropriate functional provisions in the building."[6]

Where stock plans have been used, the results have been less than encouraging. The amount that can be saved is insignificant. For example, if the architect's fee is 6 percent, one-quarter of the fee or 1½ percent is reserved for supervision. Consequently, a school district can effect savings on only the remaining 4½ percent of construction cost. Since sites and soil conditions vary greatly, some revision will be required in the structural aspects of stock plans. If we assume that it would cost a school district about 1 percent for the adaptation of stock plans to a given site and orientation, then the school district would have a potential saving of 3½ percent, providing its school program is exactly the same as the one for which the original stock plans were designed. Changes in stock plans will probably be needed because the educational needs in a given district are likely to differ from those served by the stock plans. Perhaps another 2 percent of construction cost would be needed to employ an architect to modify the stock plans to satisfy the educational needs of the school district. At this point, it would appear at first that a school district can save about 1½ percent of the construction cost of the proposed school after all changes are made. However, stock plans must be designed and continuously kept up-to-date at the standard cost of architectual services. This cost must be shared and borne by the school districts using such stock plans. Consequently, potential savings of about 2 percent are virtually wiped out by charges made to the state or school districts for the original stock plans. When it is realized further that the modifications required to meet local needs represent at best a se-

[6]Pierce, *Saving Dollars in Building Schools*, p. 32.

ries of compromises between the changes that need to be made and those that can be made because of the necessity of adhering to the basic concepts of design in the original stock plans, the appeal of stock plans almost disappears.

7. A rather impressive case for prefabrication can be made on the basis of the potential savings possible through mass production of major sections of a school building if we can ignore the differences in educational function, site conditions, and community needs that exist from district to district. Prefabrication has a great deal of appeal when the construction cost of a school is compared with that of custom-built facilities. Savings attributable to prefabrication techniques rapidly evaporate when the cost of construction of prefabricated school buildings is contrasted with that of buildings incorporating the principles of modular design. Conventional construction utilizing the modular design concept enjoys many of the advantages and savings associated with mass production methods without the disadvantages that generally accompany prefabricated buildings.

It is often not realized that even conventionally planned buildings are prefabricated to a large extent. The major difference between the so-called prefabricated buildings and those of modular design lies in the extent to which the parts of a building are preassembled at the factory prior to delivery on the site. Under prefabrication procedures, relatively large sections of walls and ceiling structures are preassembled. In both conventional and prefabricated buildings, practically all of the component parts are prefabricated. For example, bricks, steel framing, doors, window sash tiles of various types, etc., are prefabricated in any type of construction. Consequently, the potential savings that are often claimed for the prefabricated type of building become relatively insignificant compared with the cost of construction of buildings of modular design which take advantage of both prefabrication and preassembly.

The major disadvantages of prefabricated schools are quite similar to those associated with the use of stock plans. In the first place, the cost in time and money of changing previously designed buildings to meet special educational and site needs can be so great that compromise educational solutions are likely to be accepted. Certain changes might require revisions in the location of the central utility core, for example. Under the prefabrication process, the consequences of such a change might be quite costly. Jigs must be changed. Entire sections must be redesigned. Original fixtures and equipment for the school may no longer be sufficient or adequate. In view of the consequences of some such changes, the natural tendency would be to adjust the educational program to the building. Also, when prefabricated buildings are erected, obsolete or nonfunctional features of a building are not likely to be changed from building to building, because of the size of the investment in the original design of the school and the tools and jigs for the efficient production of such structures. When modular design is used, on the other hand, all changes in plans to meet specific needs can be made by the stroke of an architect's pencil at no extra cost in planning and design.

In all fairness, it should be stated that the process of prefabrication possesses at least three important advantages over other types of construction. First, large parts of a structure can be assembled in a shop under ideal conditions. Second, a minimum amount of labor is needed on the site. Third, the time required to erect a prefabricated structure on the site is dramatically reduced by over 50 percent using mass-producing technique. It should be restated, however, that prefabricated schools have much appeal if the school district is willing to shape its educational program around the building instead of designing the building to fit the desired educational program. Prefabricated school buildings merit serious consideration when the need for educational space is so pressing that there is no time to acquire a conventional school building.

OPERATIONAL ECONOMY

The rapidly increasing costs of labor, materials, and energy over the past two decades have placed a high premium on certain aspects of school plant planning. Formerly, these matters were inconsequential. Labor was so cheap that a school building could tolerate a number of items that were low in initial cost but relatively costly to maintain. School plant planners were able to overlook possible savings in heat, light, and power because the cost of energy was insignificant in relation to the operational costs of a school building. Today, the situation is quite different. The high cost of labor and the dwindling availability of energy places an extremely high value on the cost of maintenance and on the selection of energy-saving equipment. There is also a greater emphasis on the ways and means of conserving energy losses. See Chapter 9 for energy saving measures.

Planning for Minimal Expenditures for Maintenance

The design of school buildings that are not costly to maintain entails much more than selecting materials that are easy to clean. To be sure the choice of such materials is an important consideration, but that is just the beginning. There are many other important aspects of planning that can produce dramatic savings in the cost of maintaining a school facility.

Let us look, for a moment, at the placement of equipment, lighting, plumbing, shrubbery, or lawns. With high labor costs, time represents money. School planners would be richly rewarded in the form of substantial savings in maintenance costs if the architect were required to design a building in which each item requiring routine maintenance is installed so that the time required to maintain it is at a minimum. There are hundreds of such items in a school building, including light fixtures located in the high ceilings of an auditorium, boiler tubes in a confined heating plant, and shrubs that hinder lawn mowing. These undesirable design elements consume hours of valuable time. Every effort should be made to eliminate all design features that increase the time required for maintaining the facility or the equipment associated with it.

It is not practical in this publication to describe the many ways by which savings in maintenance cost can be achieved. If the principle stated above is kept in mind in designing a school building, the appropriate solutions will evolve naturally in the course of the planning. The application undoubtedly suggested by the above principle—i.e., design features that promote efficiency—reduces the time required for maintenance and bolsters the operational economy of the educational facility.

The Principle of Least Probable Maintenance

It often pays high dividends to determine the potential cost of maintenance over a long period of time. Indeed, the practice of selecting materials that are durable in quality and economical in maintenance is an application of this principle. But the potential savings or losses over the life of the building are not always known. For example, many materials that are enduring and easily preserved are also more costly in initial capital outlay. The added initial cost, however, should be balanced against the estimated savings in cost of maintenance over a period of at least twenty to thirty years. Once these two figures are determined, the answer becomes self-evident.

Until recently, very little thought was given to the potential cost of maintaining building equipment, such as boilers, circulators, pumps, electronic controls, plumbing control devices, and electrical relays. The functional specifications of such equipment were prepared by the architect, and the contractor was obligated to conform to the specifications. Accordingly, the contractor simply selected the specified equipment that was the lowest in cost. Potential maintenance cost was of little or no concern to the contractor. In the interest of greater long-range economy, it is suggested that all persons involved in planning educational facilities consider the overall maintenance cost of equipment. It might be quite profitable for a school district to include some statement concerning the "frequency-of-repair" characteristics of potential maintenance costs, in addition to the usual functional specifications of all equipment to be installed in a school building. This practice may encourage some manufacturers to include long-term maintenance guarantees on their equipment. Thus, in selecting the equipment for a school facility, the contractor would be responsible for selecting equipment that is both low in maintenance and functional in design. In general, the cost of maintaining equipment is directly related to the level of sophistication of the equipment. The more complicated the equipment, both mechanically and electronically, the more important it is to determine the potential cost of maintaining such equipment in accordance with the principle of least probable maintenance.

CHAPTER   9

Planning for Energy Conservation

Prior to the Middle East embargo on oil shipments to the United States in 1973, architects, educational facility planners, and school officials were not fully aware of the impending depletion of world sources of energy derived from fossil fuels. At that time, energy was of no particular concern to the public or school officials. There was an overabundance of fuel and the cost was relatively low. Accordingly, there was no reason for anyone to become apprehensive about energy consumption. Under these conditions, architects and school plant planners were only concerned with the form of energy that would be supplied to a proposed school building—coal, oil, gas, or electricity. Boards of education often asked architects and utility companies to make studies in depth in order to determine the cost-effectiveness of each form of energy for a particular school facility in a given location. In this connection, it is interesting to note that the electric companies were very aggressive and often successful in promoting "all electric" school facilities. They spared no effort and were ingenious in their attempts to convince local school officials that electricity was the clean, cost-effective heating energy of the future at a time when the cost of electricity per British Thermal Unit (BTU) of energy was about 1.5 times that for oil heat.

Since 1973, however, the future outlook on energy has changed completely. The recognition by the public and leaders of the world that the supply of fossil fuels is finite has been shocking. The dwindling supply of energy from fossil fuels, such as coal, oil, or gas has become a major concern of the industrialized nations of the world. A few farsighted scientists issued warnings of an impending depletion of fossil fuels on the earth about a half century ago. But no one seemed to have taken these warnings too seriously. These scientists predicted that there would be a serious energy shortage before the year 2000 and that the world supplies of fossil fuels would be completely exhausted about the middle of the twenty-first century, assuming that the demand for energy continues to grow in the future at the same rate it has increased in the past. And still, no one believed them! And why should they? After all, more and more oil reserves were being discovered. The supply of oil far outstripped the demand and fuel prices were quite low. Automobile makers were producing high powered vehicles with very low efficiency. It was not until the beginning of the 1980s that the world began to realize that the supply of fossil fuel energy stored in the crust of the earth was very limited and finite, and that it was being depleted at an alarmingly high rate. The predictions of when the present known reserves of coal, oil, and gas will be completely depleted varies from the beginning of the twenty-first century to about the year 2060. These predictions are based on the increased demand for energy caused by the growth in world population and by the foreseeable industrialization of underdeveloped countries. Under these circumstances the energy outlook for the future is bleak.

Solar energy, bio-mass energy, wind energy, geo-thermal energy, and energy from the sea are all viable alternatives for the future. But there has not yet been a major scientific breakthrough in any of these potential approaches. For this reason, the world needs more time for scientists to solve the world energy crisis. If the industrialized nations of the world are to avoid reverting to the level of the economy and the way of life that was prevalent two or three centuries ago, energy conservation is the most viable alternative for the next two or three decades. For school districts, however, energy conservation is much more than planning for the future. For them, energy conservation is imperative, if they are to cope successfully with the skyrocketing price of fuels.

In concluding this introductory narrative on energy consumption and conservation, it might be enlightening to take a brief look at the unbelievable rate at which energy is consumed compared to the time required to produce it. A real situation will be cited to illustrate this point. A family in New England is using an efficient, airtight Fisher wood stove to heat a Cape Cod-style house with an area of about 1000 square feet on the first floor and 600 square feet of space developed in the attic. The total floor area of the house is about 1600 square feet. During the coldest part of the winter, this wood stove maintains the temperature of the house at about 70° Fahrenheit and consumes one cord of hard wood in four weeks. Foresters have found that it takes an average of five trees between 35 and 40 feet high to produce one cord of fire wood. The time required for an oak seedling to become a tree of this size is between 15 and 20 years depending upon soil conditions. For the purpose of this discussion, let us assume that the growing time for such a tree is about 17 years or 200 months. Thus, it takes 200 months to produce five trees that will heat one average size house in New England for one month! In this case, energy is consumed 200 times as fast as nature can produce it through the process of photosynthesis.

Hopefully, the energy picture of the future will be brighter. For the present, conservation is the best insurance against economic disruption and an unsatisfying way of life. For school officials and boards of education, conservation of energy has both external and internal implications. Conserving energy contributes to the well-being of the industrial nations throughout the world. But, internally, conservation of energy becomes an absolute necessity in terms of fiscal considerations. The dramatic increases in energy prices make energy conservation an unconditional imperative of modern educational management.

THE ESSENCE OF ENERGY

A few short years ago, the word "energy" was primarily restricted to the routine vocabulary of the scientist and the engineer. Today, "energy" has become a household word for something that is of vital concern to everyone in the industrialized nations of the world. "Energy" is something whose cost has doubled and redoubled over a very short period of time. Energy is also that elusive something that appears and disappears at the whim of circumstances beyond our control. And it is becoming more and more evident that energy, whatever meanings and forms it may take, is something that is seriously threatening the way of life of everyone living in the industrialized nations of the world.

Scientifically, "Energy is that which is capable of doing work." But, to boards of education, school officials and school plant planners, energy is coal, oil, gas, electricity, and solar power. It is also lighting, heating, cooling, and power for communications devices and mechanical equipment. Few people realize that our own sun is and has been the only primary source of energy for our earth ever since the world was formed millions of years ago. The sun is a nuclear furnace that continually radiates a substantial amount of energy in the form of light and heat onto the surface of the earth. It must be remembered that the supplies of fossil fuels found in the crust of the earth in the form of coal, oil, or gas are the products of solar energy which took thousands and thousands of years to accumulate. And it is frightening to face the stark reality that, at the anticipated rate of energy consumption, all of these accumulated reserves will be exhausted before the end of the twenty-first century. The exact time at which our fossil fuels will be fully consumed is still open to question. But there is absolutely no question that the time will soon be at hand when there is no more coal, no more gas, and no more oil that can be economically extracted from the crust of the earth.

While the energy outlook of the world is not particularly bright at this time, there is every reason for looking toward the future with optimism and renewed hope. We still have the nuclear furnace on the sun that is producing energy at an enormous rate. The world is indeed blessed by the abundance of energy that the sun continually showers upon its surface every day. In fact, the sun is daily supplying the earth with an amount of energy that is many more times the amount of energy that the world is likely to need in the foreseeable future. This energy arrives in the form of light and heat, and some of it reappears in the form of vegetation, wind, weather, ocean waves, ocean currents, and temperature differentials both in the oceans and in the atmosphere. With these forms of energy in mind, the future is really exciting and challenging. There is indeed an abundant source of energy—the sun. In due time, human creativity and ingenuity will discover the ways and means of converting this vast source of energy into forms that can best serve the inhabitants of the earth.

ENERGY NEEDS IN SCHOOL FACILITIES

In order to conserve energy intelligently in any educational facility, it is helpful to identify and locate all fixtures, appliances, and equipment that consume energy, including all types of teaching aids that need power. In general, the items that use energy fall into two major catgories. Most of the energy supplied to a school building is associated with the health and comfort of the occupants. This group includes energy for heating, cooling, ventilation, and lighting. The second category consists of a multitude of items that are used in conjunction with the teaching process. Since the amount of energy consumed by each teaching aid is often relatively small, the total amount of energy required by such items is frequently underestimated. But when it is realized that instructional equipment includes power tools, shop machinery, kitchen ranges, clothes dryers, sophisticated computers, and other electronic systems, the amount of energy consumed by such equipment is no longer negligible. It must be taken into account in any plan which is designed to control energy.

Uses of Energy for Health and Comfort

As indicated above, the major portion of the energy required for an educational facility is devoted to the health and comfort of the occupants of a school building. The energy is used for heating, cooling, ventilation, lighting, and for various types of automated control mechanisms (see Chapters 11 and 12).

Energy for heating.   Throughout the United States, a considerable portion of the energy budget is allocated to heating, which includes space heating, water heating, and heat for food preparation. Ordinarily, this energy is derived from coal, gas, oil, or electricity or from various combinations of these sources of energy. In addition to the energy required to produce heat, power is required to distribute the heat to various parts of the building wherever it is needed. This ancillary equipment consists of fans and various types of pumps and automatic valves. Power for these items is almost always in the form of electricity which activates motors of one sort or another. And finally, controls, such as thermostats, automatic valves, internal and external photoelectric devices, and various types of gas detecting systems, consume electricity even when they are on a "standby-mode."

Energy for ventilating.   Ventilating systems generally consume energy in two ways. Heat must be provided to all incoming fresh air so that cold drafts are avoided. Some designers are using a number of clever ways of recovering heat from air that is being exhausted from the building. This approach will be discussed in more detail in this chapter under the section entitled, "Planning Energy Efficient Facilities." The second major use of energy in a ventilation system is to maintain a supply of fresh air in all the classrooms and other parts of the building, such as the gymnasium and auditorium. A substantial amount of energy is consumed by scores of electric fans that move air from one point to another at predetermined rates of flow. All air movement is not by fan, however. In some of the older school buildings, gravity systems are still in operation for providing the necessary ventilation in classrooms. Regardless of the functional merits of this system, it cannot be denied that it is energy efficient. Perhaps it should be resurrected and included in the design of future schools.

Energy for artificial lighting.   An enormous amount of electrical energy must be supplied to hundreds of lighting fixtures in school buildings. A visual environment is extremely important from the standpoint of health and educational function, and adequate levels of illumination should be maintained despite the energy cost involved. Until recently, the upward trend in the use of energy for artificial lighting has persisted. Only a few years ago, architects were designing school buildings with very little fenestration in order to keep the cost of air conditioning at a minimum. In so doing, the amount of energy devoted to artificial lighting increased substantially.

Artificial lighting is found almost everywhere in a school building. It appears in closets, in storage rooms, in crawl spaces, and pipe trenches. It is seen in attics, in the corridors, above the stairways, inside of walk-in safes, and hidden behind panels for the indirect lighting of walls. Artificial lighting is also widely used for local illumination on various articles of furniture or equipment found in schools, such as sewing machines, shop tools, kitchen ranges, table and floor lamps, microscopes, and art and drafting tables. But the list of uses of artificial lighting does not stop with these few illustrations. There are also many special applications of artificial lighting. Athletic fields are highly illuminated for night games. The auditorium is supplied with thousands of watts of artificial lighting. And all of the spaces occupied by students and teachers during the learning process are well illuminated by artificial lighting. This partial list of the more common applications of artificial lighting in a school building clearly indicates that the use of artificial illumination is widespread throughout an educational facility and represents a substantial portion of the total energy that is supplied to the building.

Energy for cooling.   In certain parts of the United States, the amount of energy used for cooling school buildings during the warm seasons of the year accounts for a relatively large part of the energy budget. To be sure, the designers of air-conditioned school buildings have been cognizant of the high energy consumption of cooling equipment. In an effort to reduce the cost of cooling, they have decreased the amount of fenestration and have specified the installation of insulating glass. Unfortunately, architects rarely insisted that all exterior walls and roofs be heavily lined with thermal insulation in the planning of educational facilities.

In fairness to the architects, however, it should be pointed out that they were deeply concerned about the high energy consumption of cooling equipment long before it became an expensive and precious commodity. Consequently, architects and engineers devised several ingenious methods of reducing the cost of cooling. Among them was the use of heat for cooling. This paradox was accomplished through the application of the diffusion principle using high pressure steam. On a more conventional note, engineers developed heat pumps to transport heat out of the building in the summer for cooling. During cold weather, the same pumps can be used to heat the building by simply reversing the cycle and transporting heat from the outside winter air or from the ground into the building where it is desired.

Energy for Instructional Uses

Some of the instructional uses of energy have already been mentioned in connection with artificial lighting. But, illumination is only part of the energy requirement of the teaching equipment. To be sure, many types of electronic teaching devices consume relatively small amounts of power. But the aggregate of all these low users of power becomes quite important particularly in a fairly large secondary school enrolling over 1500 students. For example, one television set may use as little as 200 watts of power, but 100 such units in various parts of a school would consume 20,000 watts or 20 kilowatts of electricity per hour. One electric iron in the homemaking laboratory uses about one kilowatt of electricity, but 30 of them would consume 30 kilowatts of power per hour. The same reasoning applies to tape recorders, slide and film projectors, electric typewriters, business machines, electronic equipment in the science laboratories, kilns in the arts and crafts room, and special equipment for reading. Sophisticated computers and automated devices for large group instruction also consume an appreciable amount of energy. But perhaps one area of a secondary school where large amounts of power are used for instructional uses is that devoted to vocational education and industrial arts. Relatively large machines and numerous power tools are found in these areas. And finally, the amount of energy required by the homemaking areas for instructional purposes is probably second to that expended by industrial shop areas. Ranges and clothes dryers consume thousands of watts of electricity per hour. Fortunately the number of clothes dryers, ranges, dishwashers, and clothes washers provided in these spaces is relatively small. But, the cost of energy required to operate them over the course of a year can easily reach several hundred dollars. The auto-tutorial teaching aids associated with the so-called "wet carrels" in the learning resources center also need energy for their normal operation. Each of these teaching devices is transistorized and consumes only small amounts of energy. But, taken as a whole, the amount of energy that they use annually is not negligible.

From the standpoint of energy conservation, the primary purpose of calling attention to the wide variety of instructional equipment, teaching aids, and learning devices that consume energy in a modern school facility is to alert school officials to the hundreds of energy outlets that must be monitored and controlled in effecting energy saving measures. The object of energy conservation is not to reduce the number of teaching aids but rather to make certain that power is not expended uselessly.

Other Uses of Energy in School Buildings

In addition to the major uses of energy in a school facility mentioned earlier, there are a few less obvious energy needs that are worthy of note. In most states, elevators are required for the physically handicapped. These vertical conveyances require energy whenever they are in use. The custodial workshop is often equipped with various types of power tools. The physical education area may have equipment for washing and drying towels as well as electrically powered whirlpool baths and other related equipment. The entire school facility may be serviced by a public address system that consumes power. Signaling devices such as bells, chimes, fire and smoke alarms are all users of energy, albeit the amount of power consumed by these signalling devices is quite small.

Although the transportation of students is not considered part of a school facility, the amount of energy consumed by this school service is enormous indeed. Except for the New England states, most school districts in the country own and operate their own school buses. It is not within the scope of this book to discuss this educational service. Suffice it to say, however, that school officials and boards of education can save a substantial amount of energy by streamlining bus routes, reducing the number of bus stops, improving bus maintenance, and operating each vehicle at optimum speed and capacity.

A STEP BY STEP APPROACH TO ENERGY CONSERVATION

Energy conservation will not just happen. It must be planned as a series of sequentially related steps. The techniques for conserving energy range from measures that are simple and inexpensive to those that are more extensive, more costly, and more technical. Unfortunately, the specific measures or changes that lead to energy conservation are not always obvious. Consequently, some kind of systematic examination of a given school facility is required in order to determine the exact nature of the changes that promise to conserve energy. Such a study would also include a cost analysis of such changes and what affect they are likely to have on the educational function. The questions that must be raised before any energy conservation action is taken are: "Does the proposed action interfere with the educational process in any way?" "Does the proposed action create an atmosphere that is not conducive to learning?" "Is the proposed action really energy-effective?" "Is the proposed action cost-effective?" A "no" answer to one or more of the preceding questions denotes that the proposed energy-saving action may not be in the best interest of the school district from the standpoint of economic efficiency, educational impact, or the well-being of students and teachers. Energy conservation should not outweigh educational function or the healthfulness of a school building. Let us cite a typical situation to show the need for balance between energy conservation and healthfulness. In order to save energy in an elementary school built in 1912, the board of education proposed that the temperature in each of the eight classrooms be reduced from 75° Farenheit to 68° Farenheit. An examination of the building revealed that all of the window sashes were loose and there was high infiltration of air through the wooden sheathing on the lower walls. The rooms were noticeably drafty on cold wintry days, and when the wind was blowing, it was almost impossible to maintain a uniform temperature throughout the classroom. While the obvious saving in energy looked very attractive, the consequences of changing the thermostat setting from 75° Farenheit to 68° Farenheit were not entirely positive. Realistically, this change could threaten the health of some of the students occupying the classroom. It could induce a level of discomfort that would reduce the efficiency of learning and decrease the effectiveness of the teacher. Consequently, although the proposed change described in the above example would appear to be cost-effective, it would not satisfy the basic requirements of healthfulness and educational soundness.

A step by step approach to energy conservation is outlined in this chapter. A detailed description of each step, together with numerous forms and checklists can be found in the *Energy Sourcebook for Educational Facilities*[1] published by the Council of Educational Facility Planners. This

---

[1]*Energy Sourcebook for Educational Facilities*, Council of Educational Facilty Planners, International, 29 Woodruff Avenue, Columbus, Ohio 43210, 1977.

publication is one of the most comprehensive and authentic sources of information about energy conservation in school facilities that currently exists in the United States. It is well organized, lucidly written, practical in design, and extensive in coverage. For the convenience of the reader, the sequence of steps presented in this book for developing an energy conservation plan of action follows the same order as that which appears in the *Energy Sourcebook* mentioned above.

In most situations, the plan of action for energy conservation consists of four sequentially interlocking parts ranging from the simple to the more complex. The first step is a preliminary energy conservation survey which is conducted by local school maintenance and operation personnel. This study deals with energy conservation matters that are relatively uncomplicated in nature and that can be put into effect by the local staff without further technical training. The second step is a little more technical. Local personnel assemble all of the physical data about a given building and send them to a computer center. These data are then fed into a computer that is programmed to yield various types of energy information through the use of a model building similar to the actual school building from which the data were obtained. In this step, energy gains and losses are quantified and energy costs are determined. The third step calls for a two or three hour inspection of a school building by various types of engineers and architects. The suggested energy saving measures that are recommended by this team of experts may be quite sophisticated and quite technical in nature. There is very little quantification of cost data and energy savings by this team. In a sense, it is somewhat similar to the preliminary energy survey, except that it is conducted by a team of experts. The fourth step is conducted by a team of experts over an extended period of time. A large amount of technical data is assembled and many types of calculations are made to support a wide variety of recommendations. Each of these four steps is discussed in detail in the following sections.

Step One—The Preliminary Energy Survey

A team of local school staff is organized to conduct a preliminary survey of a given school building. This team is usually made up of a representative from the administrative office, such as the director of building maintenance and operation, or equivalent, and the maintenance and custodial staff of the building that is being surveyed. Similar groups are established to survey each school building in the district. The organization and structure of the energy survey teams for each school are designed to facilitate the implementation of desirable energy conservation measures. These teams accumulate a wide variety of practical information about energy conservation. They become highly knowledgeable groups who can provide the basic data for some of the more technical energy audits that may be conducted at a later date for every school building in the school district. The primary responsibility of each school team, however, is to recommend and implement energy saving measures that are relatively simple to execute. These measures often require little or no capital outlay funds. And finally, since each school team has been involved in the energy conservation program from the time of the program's initiation, they are well informed about the various techniques associated with energy conservation. Furthermore, they will be in a better position to implement energy saving measures that are more complex and comprehensive in nature than those introduced in Step One, if and when a more sophisticated energy audit is made by experts at a later date. In completing Step One, it is suggested that the team use the comprehensive checklist for conducting a preliminary energy survey found in the *Energy Sourcebook for Educational Facilities.*

Step Two—Computer Simulation Analysis

For a nominal fee, the energy characteristics of a real school building can be analyzed by a computer under simulated conditions. The principle underlying this technique is not particularly mysterious or complicated. The characteristics of a real building are compared with the known characteristics of a model building that are programmed into the computer. Several models have been developed by the Educational Facilities Laboratory in California. These models simulate buildings that were constructed during specified periods of time, such as those built before World War II and after 1945. Within the groupings, the computer models are further classified as to shape, construction, and mechanical systems. The models are also categorized as to whether they are elementary schools or secondary schools. This technique is also called "PSECS (Public Schools Energy Conservation Service)—Computer Simulated Model." The address is available in the *Energy Sourcebook.*

The characteristics of the real building are entered into the computer which, in turn, compares the real situation with that of the appropriate model which is programmed into the computer. The computer print out does not list individual energy-saving measures nor does it specify any saving that would result from each measure. It does, however, state potential energy savings that could be expected in the real building as a percent of current costs. For example, the computer printout would *not* show that if all of the single-pane glass in a school building were replaced by insulating glass the saving would be a certain number of dollars. It would indicate that it would be possible to save a certain percentage of the cost currently expended for energy in the real building if an energy audit of the building were made and the energy conservation measures were implemented. These limitations apply only to the PSECS analysis mentioned as a second step in approaching the energy saving problem. Stated differently, for a nominal fee, the PSECS method would indicate how close to the ideal model the real building is performing with respect to energy conservation. If the real building has been ideally retrofitted, for example, the PSECS report would simply show that the expected savings in that particular building were negligible. In practice, however, PSECS would not be applied to a retrofitted building. Rather, it would be employed as a second step in the energy conservation program. To be sure, the results of the PSECS could be instrumental in the ultimate retrofitting of a given school facility if additional studies show that retrofitting is warranted.

There are other applications of the "Computer Simulated Model" in making an energy analysis of a real school building, however. The data for this more sophisticated analysis are quite technical and complex. It is usually provided by several professional engineers and an architect who make studies in depth of school facilities that are scheduled for retrofitting. In this application, the computer provides specific information regarding expected energy savings, cost of retrofitting and pay-back periods. This approach will be discussed in Step 4 under the "Maxi-audit." Suffice it to say, at this point, that the PSECS report is intended to show potential overall savings in energy, if any, through the use of energy conservation measures. It is *not* designed to provide any kind of detailed analysis of specific needs. The PSECS report can be invaluable to school officials because it can indicate whether or not further study and analysis of a given building is warranted, from the standpoint of energy conservation.

Step Three—The Mini-audit

Let us review what has been accomplished in Steps One and Two. In the first step, a team of local staff members, knowledgeable in the maintenance and operation of school buildings, has attended workshops sponsored by the appropriate state and local agencies on energy conservation · Each team has acquired as much knowledge as possible on immediate steps that could be taken in order to conserve energy. Each team surveyed a school facility and made recommendations to school officials of the local school district on how energy could be conserved. Some, if not all, of these recommendations have been implemented for each school surveyed. Secondly, this knowledgeable team has assembled accurate and detailed information that has been recorded on the appropriate forms and submitted to the Educational Facilities Laboratories, under the PSECS program. A report has been received by the local school district that additional energy savings are possible in certain school buildings in the district. The potential magnitude of these savings has also been included in these reports. On the basis of this information, local school officials have selected a few school buildings where substantial savings in energy could still be made. These officials have also made a study of whether or not these selected school buildings are part of the long range school facility needs of the district. As a result of a comprehensive study by school officials and the board of education, a decision has been made to take additional steps to conserve energy in certain school buildings. The local maintenance and operational staff has taken every conservation measure within its level of expertise and budgetary limitations. There is computer-generated information to indicate that sizeable potential savings in energy and in tax dollars can be made in certain school buildings in the school district. Thus, the board of education has authorized school officials to study the matter further and return to it with recommendations. They have approved a "mini-audit" of selected school facilities in the school district.

The "mini-audit" is a sound and well-conceived third step in meeting the urgent and pressing need of saving energy as well as public funds. The mini-audit is conducted by a small number of highly trained professionals over a short period of time. This team of professionals usually consists of a structural engineer, a heating and ventilating engineer, an architect, and a representative from the utility company. This group, together with one or two school administrators walk through a given school building over a period of two or three hours. This group of professionals concentrates primarily on two aspects of energy conservation. They focus on measures that can be accomplished quickly and on those that are not costly, such as operational practices, eliminating unnecessary energy consuming equipment, and reduction of light intensities in certain areas. This team also searches for ways and means of reducing energy consumption that can be accomplished easily and with relatively small amounts of capital outlay. For example, the hot water supply system may be separated from the main boiler, so that the school boilers could be shut down earlier in the school year and be "fired-up" at a later time. This recommendation would involve some expenditure of funds, but it would save a considerable amount of costly energy during the late spring, summer (if the building is used during this period), and the early fall.

There are several reasons underlying the use of a mini-audit. First, the overall cost is reasonable and has the potential of being highly cost-effective. Secondly, the team consists of experts that are not readily available in most school districts. Thirdly, this audit is an extension of the one conducted in Step One by local school personnel. In the mini-audit, the survey includes high level technical expertise that was not available in Step One. In both instances, however, energy saving measures that are feasible and not too costly are recommended. It seems natural, systematic and logical that the process related to energy conservation should be a continuum that ranges from the simple to the more complex and from the least expensive measures to those of greater magnitude and cost.

Step Four—The Maxi-audit

The maxi-audit is the *sine qua non* of retrofitting an existing school building in cases where substantial amounts of capital outlay funds are required. Relatively inexpensive retrofitting measures such as adding insulation, caulking doors and windows frames, and installing clock-controlled thermostats may be taken at any time. Extensive retrofitting may be partial or comprehensive.

In either instance such action should be the direct result of a maxi-audit. The maxi-audit is generally conducted by a competent and experienced engineering and architectural firm, which has a team of experts in the fields of architecture, structural engineering, heating, cooling and ventilating engineering, electrical engineering, and solar energy engineering. Care should be exercised in selecting a consulting firm to make a "maxi-audit." It is extremely important that the qualifications of each chief professional person whose expertise is required for the audit be thoroughly scrutinized. It should be emphasized in this connection, that not every architectural or engineering firm is capable of conducting a maxi-audit of a school facility. The cost of making this type of energy audit is relatively high and a school district would be well advised to consider several firms for making this audit. It is suggested that the same procedure described in Chapter 6 for the selection of an architect for the planning of a school facility be employed in choosing a consultant firm to conduct a maxi-audit for the school district.

The maxi-audit is a comprehensive, methodical, expert investigation of the energy characteristics of an educational facility. This in-depth energy study of a given school facility is extensive; detailed and cost estimates are geared to the cost of labor and materials that are prevalent where the school building is located. Besides the building, the maxi-audit includes a close examination of the educational uses of energy, such as audiovisual equipment, auto-tutorial aids, shop machinery, homemaking appliances, typewriters, business machines, and kilns. The pattern of power usage in the entire school facility is examined very closely from the standpoint of energy conservation. Also, the possibility of using a piece of equipment more efficiently and at maximum capacity is explored in every instance, such as operating dishwashers with a partial load. These are only a few glimpses of the type of investigation that is required by the consulting firm that conducts a maxi-audit for a school district.

The maxi-audit differs enormously from any of the approaches to energy conservation mentioned thus far in one major respect. It is an accurately *quantified*, scientific investigation of the energy characteristics of an educational facility, including every type of energy use found in the building, on the school site, and off the school site in the transportation of students to and from school. The quantification of energy savings is an invaluable piece of information for school officials and the board of education in assessing energy conservation measures. This detailed information enables them to make intelligent decisions regarding the expenditure of capital funds for retrofitting a school building. One of the most important end products of the maxi-audit is a cost analysis of the pay-back period required to retrieve the cost of capital outlay and interest through the savings in energy brought about by a recommended capital outlay expenditure.

The energy consultant provides a wide variety of data. It includes a description of the existing pattern of energy consumption and current unit

costs for each major energy use within the building. The consultant prepares and submits a considerable number of energy conserving recommendations. Each recommendation has a price tag attached to it together
with a realistic financial analysis of each aspect of the recommendation.
The information submitted with each energy saving recommendation includes the anticipated annual reduction in energy consumption, cost savings per year, cost of capital outlay required to implement the recommendation, length of the pay-back period, and the priority of a given recommendation among the other items recommended.

The cost of a maxi-audit is not modest. It represents a substantial initial investment that has the potential of returning savings that are many
times the initial cost over the remaining life of a school building. Despite
the cost, there is really no other way of obtaining the information required
for retrofitting an existing building. The cost of a maxi-audit is fully justified, however. First of all, the audit must be conducted by highly trained,
competent, and experienced architects and engineers. Secondly, the work
required by these experts is often greater than that which would be required if this same team were asked to design a new building of the same
size and shape of the existing facility. In designing a new building, the
team makes all of the required computations for achieving maximum energy efficiency of the proposed new structure. These computations involve
all forms of energy to be consumed in the building, such as lighting, heating, cooling, mechanical equipment, appliances, and electronic devices
for various and sundry types. In conducting a maxi-audit, these same computations and studies must be performed for an existing building. This aspect of the maxi-audit addresses itself to the question, "How much energy,
of the various types, would be required to operate the existing structure
under optimum conditions?" Obtaining the answer to this question is time-
consuming and relatively complicated. But, in a maxi-audit, the answer to
the above question is only the beginning point. Phase two of the maxi-
audit represents another segment of the study that involves a high level of
creativity and expertise and requires a great deal of time on the part of the
team experts. The question to be answered in phase two is, "In what ways
can the existing building, equipment, and pattern of energy use be modified in order to conserve energy?" This phase demands a concentrated
study of the use and operation of the building and calls for an extended
period of observation by the team of experts. As can well be imagined,
phase two takes considerable time. It is time that would not be spent on the
planning of a new building. The maxi-audit includes phase three which
develops the data obtained in phase two and compares the information
with the corresponding information prepared under phase one. The question to be answered in phase three is, "What energy saving measures are
feasible, how much will it cost to implement them, and what is the pay-
back period for each one of them?" The response to this question is highly
technical, fiscally oriented, and broadly based. More specifically, the consultants must look at all alternatives for each recommended mea-

sure and select the one which seems most appropriate. They must make detailed cost studies of capital outlay funds and interest needed to effect the recommended changes. And they must compute the anticipated amount of energy saved by each recommendation, convert these energy savings into dollar savings and estimate the number of years needed to compensate the school district for the funds expended to implement the proposed energy-saving measure. All of this work takes time and costs money for the services of the team of experts. In view of the extensive nature of the maxi-audit, it can be seen that it could be an expensive venture on the part of a school district. But, it can also be one of the most rewarding investments that a school district has ever made. If the savings in the cost of energy to the school district are quite substantial, the pay-back period for the cost of the maxi-audit can be very short, indeed. But, the school district will really never know this for sure until a maxi-audit is completed!

ENERGY CONSERVATION THROUGH RETROFITTING

The word "retrofitting" has been recently added to the English language. Perhaps, the best way to describe it in relation to energy conservation is the act of modifying an existing structure in a manner that would result in the saving of energy. From another point of view, retrofitting could be envisioned as changing an existing building that consumes energy liberally and wastefully to one that makes optimal use of energy and conserves it as much as possible. Perhaps, the term retrofitting could be further clarified by asking a question. "What cost-effective changes can be made to an existing building and its equipment today that will conserve energy for the remaining useful life of the building?"

Retrofitting is often a costly and highly technical undertaking. It is strongly recommended that a maxi-audit be completed before any funds are committed to a retrofitting program. The board of education and school officials should know in advance what the pay-back period is for each measure. A ten year pay-back period is generally considered to be a good investment of public funds. Longer pay-back periods are also justifiable if the savings in cost of energy is relatively high. For example, if it costs $100,000, including interests, to replace all the windows and doors with insulating glass and if the savings in the cost of energy are $10,000 per year, the pay-back period is ten years. This hundred thousand dollar capital outlay expenditure would be an excellent investment on the part of the school district. After ten years, the $10,000 saving would continue to accrue to the school district if the cost of energy did not change. On the other hand, if the annual energy savings were only $5,000, the pay-back period would be twenty years. In this case, the economic benefits would not be as attractive as the ten year pay-back period, but the national goal of conserving energy would still make such retrofitting quite desirable.

Retrofitting a school building should be done on a priority basis. A maxi-audit will recommend an order of priority. Usually, those measures that have the shortest pay-back periods are given the highest priority. In some instances, measures that require a large expenditure of capital outlay funds initially may have the shortest pay-back periods. For this reason, initial costs should not automatically override other considerations. Retrofitting should be done with the same thoroughness that is exercised in the construction of a new school building. The project should be clearly defined. The architect and engineers should be selected with care. Specifications should be prepared by the architect and his engineers and the project should be bid in accordance with procedures discussed in Chapter 15.

Retrofitting varies greatly from school building to school building. For this reason it is felt that a maximum-audit is absolutely necessary if a school district is to expend public funds wisely in retrofitting a school facility. No attempt will be made to describe the multitude of forms that retrofitting may assume. It is suggested, however, that the *Energy Sourcebook*[2] be reviewed in this connection. It contains several examples of school buildings that have been retrofitted. It also mentions many individual modifications that can be made to a school building in order to conserve energy. In some of the examples described in the *Energy Sourcebook*, not only was energy saved through system and building modification, but energy was also gained by including passive solar energy features in the retrofitting project.

Common Elements in the Art of Retrofitting

A wide variety of energy conservation techniques are employed in retrofitting school buildings. They range from simple and inexpensive measures to those that are more complex and costly. They differ from situation to situation. They vary from engineer to engineer. And they are different from one climatic regime to another. Despite these differences, however, there are also similarities in the art of retrofitting that tend to simplify the task of coping with energy conservation measures. These common elements include the selection of energy-efficient equipment, the reduction of energy losses or heat gains through the exterior surfaces of the structure, the recovery of energy that would otherwise be lost to the atmosphere, and the prevention of energy waste due to lack of proper controls and monitoring procedures.

These common elements are mentioned briefly in this section. They are, however, described and discussed in greater detail later in this chapter under the section entitled, "Planning Energy Efficient School Buildings." Since the primary goal of retrofitting is to make existing buildings more energy efficient, it follows that any technique or action that promotes

[2]*Ibid.*

energy conservation in new facilities is equally beneficial in retrofitting existing school buildings.

Heating, cooling, and ventilation.   The efficiency of heating, cooling, and ventilating equipment is a major consideration in any retrofitting program. Each unit must be capable of extracting the maximum amount of utility, usefulness, and serviceability for each unit of energy that is supplied to the unit. Thus, every effort should be made to select heating, cooling, and ventilating equipment that is highly efficient from the standpoint of energy consumption.

Artificial lighting.   During the process of retrofitting, artificial lighting provides fertile ground for conserving energy in school buildings. Fixtures should be selected on the basis of minimum energy consumption per lumen of light produced. Also the intensity of light falling on the task of students engaged in learning activities should be kept at a reasonably high minimum. The light intensities provided in recently constructed schools is far above that which is needed for good seeing conditions.

Air infiltration.   The elimination of the infiltration of air from the outside to the inside of a school building is of paramount importance with respect to energy conservation. In some of the older buildings, not only does air infiltrate around windows and doors, but also through the walls themselves, particularly around the loose mortar between the bricks.

Energy distribution and its control.   Generally, two forms of energy are widely distributed throughout a school building. They are heat and electricity. Electric power is available everywhere in the building. Heat is also supplied to all parts of the building occupied by teachers and students and to a lesser amount in spaces where temperatures must be maintained a little above 32° Fahrenheit so that water pipes will not freeze.

In many of the more recently constructed school buildings, the distribution of heat among the various parts of the building is fairly well controlled on a room by room basis. Some areas are still overheated due to the proximity of these spaces to major pipe lines. In the older buildings that are more likely to be retrofitted, such controlled distribution of heat is either nonexistent or not very effective. Consequently, a considerable amount of heat energy is wasted when these buildings are in use or because heat cannot be properly controlled throughout the building. There is also a waste of heat in these buildings when they are not in use because certain spaces receive heat regardless of the need for it.

The distribution of electrical energy throughout a building presents no problem but its control from a central point leaves much to be desired, particularly in the older school buildings. In many cases, it is almost impossible for the custodian to make certain that all outlets are not consuming energy uselessly without disconnecting power from major parts of the building. The obvious solution to this problem lies in the installation of low voltage switching devices which readily lend themselves to centralized control. Under this system a panel of signal lights would indicate where electric power is being supplied in all parts of the school building at any given time.

PLANNING ENERGY EFFICIENT SCHOOL BUILDINGS

As mentioned earlier, the world faces the inevitable depletion of its fossil energy reserves. Conservation is needed not only to extend our present supply of energy but also to soften the economic impact that the increasing cost of energy is having on school budgets throughout the United States. In attempting to conserve energy, however, care must be exercised to make certain that all conservation measures really save energy. Some of them may appear to be very attractive and appealing at first glance. But, upon further study and consideration, they may actually waste more energy than they purportedly save. On the other hand, there are many energy saving measures that are sound and stand the test of scientific analysis. Both false and real energy conservation measures are discussed in this section.

Questionable Energy Conservation Practices

1. *Reducing the weekly use of a school building.* Various plans have been advanced by boards of education and school officials to reduce energy consumption in school buildings by rescheduling the use of educational facilities. Under one plan, schools would be closed entirely for a four or five week period during the coldest part of the winter and the school year would be extended into the summer for an equal length of time. Another proposal would operate the schools four days per week and extend the time for each of the four days to compensate for the lost day. In this plan, school buildngs would be closed from the end of the school day on Thursday until the following Monday morning. To be sure, the cost of energy consumed in a school building can be subtantially reduced by these measures, but does it really conserve energy within the boundaries of the school district. There is reason to believe that the closing of school buildings may actually waste energy in some situations. If the net gain or loss in energy consumption is measured *within the boundaries of the school district* rather than within the boundaries of the school site, the conclusion may be quite surprising.[3]

A hypothetical case will be cited to illustrate the questionable nature of the four-day school week from the standpoint of energy conservation. Let us assume that a school district has an enrollment of 2000 students and

[3]Carsie K. Denning and Edmond A. LeBlanc, "Community Education and the Energy Problems," CEFP, *Council of Educational Facility Planners Journal*, January, 1980.

that the board of education has introduced a four-day school week and increased the length of each of the four days to compensate for the time lost on Friday. Under this plan, all of the school buildings could be set on "low heat" from Thursday evening to Monday morning. Beyond any doubt, the amount of energy saved *on the school site* would be substantial and measurable. This represents an impressive plus for the school budget. Let us now look at the negative side of this alleged energy saving measure. What happens to the 2000 students who are not in school on Friday? It can be assumed that most of them will be home on these cold days. Many students will be at home watching television, cooking snacks, and consuming energy. Some of them will be in their room with the thermostat raised a little, the lights turned on and consuming energy. And some of the high school students will be driving their automobiles and consuming fuel. When the additional consumption of energy by these 2000 students on their Friday holiday is compared to the amount of energy saved in the school buildings, studies reported by Denning and LeBlanc[4] suggest that, on the whole, it is highly probable that the total increase in energy consumption within the boundaries of the school district due to the Friday holiday will exceed the amount of energy saved on the school site. This would represent an *energy loss* within the boundaries of the school district as a result of the Friday holiday. The burden of the cost of energy for the Friday holiday is simply shifted from the school to the parents of the 2000 students enrolled in the school. No useful purpose would be accomplished by this kind of "energy saving" measure.

On the other hand, real savings could be effected if a school facility were planned initially for maximum energy conservation. Educational services could be maintained at optimum levels and the cost of supplying energy to a school building could be held at a minimum. This approach is realistic in function, promising in concept, and effective in economic efficiency.

2. *Reduction in educational services.* Some school districts have seriously considered closing the school building promptly at the end of the school day during the cold winter months. In these instances, students would be deprived of extra help from teachers and the use of library and other school facilities. Some students might not be able to participate in extracurricular and athletic activities.

Under close scrutiny, it is questionable whether or not this practice would result in any noticeable savings in the energy budget at the end of the year. And even if some savings were effected, would the amount of money saved compensate for the loss of educational opportunities suffered by the students? This energy-saving measure and others like it should be carefully examined relative to educational values lost and the number of dollars gained, if any.

[4]*Ibid.*

Sound Energy Conservation Practices

There are several effective and well-founded techniques for keeping the amount of energy consumed in a school facility to a minimum. Each one is presented from the standpoint of energy conservation. It is realized, of course, that it may not be possible to implement all of them in all cases. It is hoped, however, that this list of techniques will serve to stimulate the creative thinking of educational facility planners in designing school buildings that are both educationally effective and energy efficient.

1. *Shaping the building.* Heat loss or gain is directly proportional to the total area of the walls, floors and ceilings of a structure. Theoretically, the external surface area should be kept at a minimum. A sphere meets this requirement. It contains maximum volume with minimum exterior surface. For obvious reasons, a spherical school building, though possible, is not too practical. The most practical shape that provides maximum volume with a minimum of exterior surface is the cube.

In view of the foregoing considerations, the ideal shape of a school building from the standpoint of energy conservation is one consisting of a large cube or a combination of cubes of varying sizes joined together to form a single, contiguous structure. Consequently, the long and narrow, single-storied buildings of yesteryear should be avoided. The high rise tower building is not consistent with the principle described above. Neither is it desirable to design a building with jogs or indentations. Not only is this practice wasteful in energy but it also is not economical to construct. A building constructed in the shape of a hemisphere could be considered if there were some ingenious way of utilizing the odd-shaped spaces along the curved walls. Perhaps, some creative architect may find a practical solution to this problem and design a structure that is efficient both in space utilization and in the conservation of energy.

2. *Orienting the building.* For maximum absorption of passive heating from the sun, one side of the building should face east and the other side should face the west. The south wall should also be exposed to the sun. Care should be taken to control heat gain in the summer and permit maximum energy gain from the sun in the winter.

Whenever possible, passive solar heating features should be designed into the building. These characteristics are discussed later in this chapter, but the orientation of the building should be such that passive solar heating can become an important part of the heating system of the school building.

3. *Insulating the building.* It is a well-known principle of physics that the conductivity of heat varies from substance to substance. From the standpoint of energy conservation, the transmission of heat from one side of a wall or window to the other should be held to a minimum. The transfer of heat from within the building to its exterior through roofs, basements, and basement walls should be kept as low as possible.

Our present perceptions of brick and concrete should be reexamined. Indeed, from the standpoint of maintenance and durability these materials are economical, functional, and desirable. But in terms of thermal efficiency, looks are deceiving. Visually, it would appear that brick, mortar, and concrete are good insulators of heat. Quite the opposite is true. In fact, heat travels through concrete nine times as fast as it does through an equal thickness and area of wood. And stone conducts heat about twenty times as fast as wood. In other words, a wooden board one inch thick is thermally equivalent to concrete nine inches thick and to a stone wall twenty inches thick. It is not suggested that the use of stone and concrete be abolished in the construction of school buildings. The intent of these comments is to simply point out that these materials are not good heat insulators despite their massive appearance. When these materials are used, they should be lined with highly insulating substances, such as fiberglass and insulating panels. Wood, on the other hand, is a good insulator and may have a wider application in school construction, particularly in areas where wood is plentiful. The penalty for using wood, however, is its relatively high cost of maintenance. The architect is in an excellent position to advise school officials as to the best balance between the use of wood and concrete.

Materials of construction should be chosen so that heat losses from the building to the atmosphere in the winter and heat gains from the atmosphere into the building in the summer are kept at a minimum. Exterior walls and ceilings exposed to cold attics should be heavily insulated. The amount of glass on the north side of the building should be reduced as much as possible but not below that required for good seeing conditions through the use of natural light. Basements should be designed so that the heat transfer between the building and the earth is as low as possible.

4. *Selecting and installing windows and doors properly.* The loss or gain of energy within a school building is greatly affected by the design, construction and method of installation of windows, doors, and ventilation units. Unless special precautions are taken in the selection and proper installation of doors, windows and ventilation units, the transfer of heat through these openings by conduction and by the infiltration of air could result in substantial losses of costly energy.

Conduction of heat energy through windows and doors.   Windows and doors should be designed to severely impede the flow of heat from one side to the other. Since windows must be constructed of transparent substances such as glass or special plastics, the choice of materials is quite limited. However, great strides have been made by the glass industry in restricting the flow of heat through windows by providing alternate layers of glass and air in a sandwich-like panel of glass or plastic sheets. Ideally, a vacuum between two sheets of glass separated by one centimeter (about one-half inch) would effectively impede the flow of heat through the window by conduction. Technologically, it is impractical to construct such a window panel due to the tremendous force of the atmospheric pressure on both sides of the panel tending to shatter the glass into the evacuated space between each sheet. Thus, the glass industry has created an acceptable substitute that is relatively easy to produce but which is not as thermally efficient as the ideal situation described above. Insulating glass, as it is called, consists of two sheets of glass separated by about one centimeter of moisture-free air or nitrogen and is sealed along the edges. Such glass panels are also produced with two layers of gas separated by three sheets of glass. In this case, the window panel would consist of an outer sheet of glass followed by a layer of dried air or dried nitrogen, then another sheet of glass, followed by a second layer of gas and covered on the other side by another sheet of glass. This combination of alternate layers of glass and gas effectively impedes the flow of heat through the panel and conserves energy.

The construction of insulated doors is much simpler than that described above for windows from the standpoint of heat transmission. First of all, doors need not necessarily be transparent. Thus, the choice of materials of construction is less restrictive. Weight and thickness of doors is somewhat less stringent than that for windows. Consequently, the door industry has produced a wide variety of insulating doors from light, hollow, doors filled with insulating materials, to the more massive solid doors which are fabricated from highly insulating substances. If a door requires that a person should be able to see through it for safety reasons, small panels of insulating glass can be installed at the proper height to meet this specification. Thus, from the standpoint of energy conservation, all exterior doors in a school building should have the capacity of severely impeding the flow of heat from one side to the other.

Infiltration of air around windows and doors and ventilation units.   In any building, substantial amounts of heat are transmitted through the infiltration of air around the perimeter of windows, doors, and ventilation units. In general, there are two major sources of infiltration of air around these openings. One of them is around the window sash, the door, or the cover of ventilation units; that is, the element that opens and closes. This source can be effectively corrected by a special design of the edges of the windows, doors, and covers and by the use of weather-stripping. The other source of infiltration is also located around the perimeter of windows, doors, and covers and by the use of weather-stripping. The other source of infiltration is also located around the perimeter of windows, doors, and ventilation units, but it occurs at the interfacing of the frame within which the window, door, or cover is mounted, and the building itself. This source of infiltration of air can often be remedied by properly installing the frames that are specially designed to keep the infiltration of air at a minimum, and by caulking the edges where the frames interface with the building. The caulking material should be vermin-proof, long-lasting, weather-resistant, and capable of withstanding a fairly wide range of temperature changes without cracking or crumbling.

5. *Selecting efficient heating, cooling, and ventilating equipment.* The heating and cooling of school buildings is accomplished by converting one form of energy to another through the use of an appropriate contrivance. Fuel is one form of energy that can be burned on the site to produce heating and cooling for the building. Or, energy that is produced off-site in the form of electricity, can be transported to the school building and then be transformed into heating and cooling. The contrivance commonly used to convert fuel directly into heat is the boiler or furnace. Electricity, on the other hand, can be transformed into heat by the resistance method (heating coils) or by a heat pump. Cooling is usually produced either by a diffusion process utilizing high pressure steam or by a heat pump which is powered by electricity.

For the purpose of this discussion, however, it is important to understand that some type of specially designed contrivance is necessary to convert fuel or energy from one form to another. While the heating and cooling industry is experimenting with a number of more sophisticated contrivances designed to conserve energy, the boiler and the heat pump are still the major practical contrivances for generating heat or infrigidation. Thus, in designing a heating and cooling system for energy conservation, special care should be exercised to specify the contrivance that has the highest energy output for a given input of energy. The more efficient the contrivance, the less fuel or electricity consumed to produce a given result and the more energy conserved in the process. The continued improvement of heat pumps holds much promise for the future with respect to energy conservation. The contrivance itself is simply a machine that moves heat from one location to another. The electricity consumed by this machine is not directly converted into heating or cooling. It simply powers the pump which moves heat from the ground or atmosphere into the building during cold weather or transports heat from within the building to the ground or atmosphere during warm weather. Consequently, the efficiency of the heat pump can be far greater than that resulting from other means of converting energy into heating or cooling.

Ventilation is another important aspect of energy conservation. The amount of fresh air required per student per hour in the past can be substantially reduced in most instances. In some states the amount of fresh air required per student is modest, realistic, and economically justifiable. These states specify 10 cubic feet per minute per occupant when the outside temperature is above 35° Fahrenheit, and no fresh air is required for temperatures below 35° Fahrenheit. In these instances, the lower volume of air required per student reduces the amount of energy needed for ventilation.

The efficiency of heating, cooling, and ventilating equipment is a major consideration in energy conservation. Ideally, the maximum amount of useable energy should be extracted from the amount of available energy supplied to a given school facility. Hence, when the source of energy is intended to heat the building, all of it should be utilized for that purpose. Electrical heating most closely approaches this ideal. When resistance electrical heating is used, all of the energy purchased provides heat for the building, except when the transformers and meters are placed outside of the building. When various fuels are used for heating, the efficiency of the boiler and heat distribution systems can greatly affect the amount of heat that actually reaches the spaces where such heat is required. This reduction stems from two causes. A certain amount of heat is lost through the stack in the combustion process, and cold air from the outside is needed to support the combustion. During this necessary and essential chemical action, the outside air tends to cool the heating equipment. And finally, when heat is transmitted from the boiler room to the classrooms, for example, some of it is lost en route where it is not needed or wanted. Cooling, heating, and ventilating equipment does not always use energy efficiently. For this reason, care should be exercised in selecting equipment that possesses a high energy efficiency rating.

6. *Utilizing electric power efficiently.* The major part of the electrical energy consumed within a school building for purposes other than heating or cooling is attributable to artificial lighting and to the operation of mechanical equipment associated with the heating and cooling of the school building.

The proper design of an artificial lighting system provides fertile ground for conserving energy in a school building. First of all, the number of foot-candles of light intensity striking the task of students engaged in learning activities in school has been raised continually, since the end of World War II. When energy was inexpensive, the increase of intensity of light in classrooms from 30 foot-candles to 70 or 80 foot-candles was not a major cause for concern. The research conducted by various groups of lighting engineers was well done, in most cases, but the nature of the tasks for which the various light intensities were applied, tended to be focused on specialized activities that occupied only a small part of the curriculum of the student. And, as long as energy was still quite inexpensive, increases in the overall intensity of light in a classroom presented no real problem. Today, the situation is quite different. The question that is posed for educators and school boards due to circumstances beyond their control is, "What is the minimum intensity of classroom illumination that is healthful and provides a good visual environment for the tasks normally performed in the teaching-learning process?" With this objective in mind, it can be seen that the intensity of high quality light at the task level of the student could be reduced to 30 foot-candles in regular classrooms. It is well known that the acuity of elementary and secondary age level students is very high. Hence, high light intensities are not needed for such students. To be sure, if the same spaces are to be used for educating the elderly, a higher intensity of light is needed. However, in view of the energy crisis, it might be well to plan certain spaces for use by both young people and adults and to design others for young people only. In spaces, for both young and old, additional lighting could be "switched-on" when adults are occupying the space. Otherwise, the 30 foot-candle intensity could be maintained when the regular school was in session.

7. *Controlling energy distribution effectively.* Both electrical and heat energy should be readily available in sufficient quantity at any location in a school building where it is needed at a given time. Conversely, energy should not be supplied and consumed in any part of the building where it is not required. These two considerations suggest that a sophisticated system of control in the distribution of electricity and heat (also cooling) be made an integral part in the design of the building. Such controls can be provided at a relatively small additional cost through the use of remote relays and controls activated by a low voltage wiring network or by a low powered radio transmitter within the building. The controls can be activated by the custodian from a central location, perhaps near the boiler room. Also, clock mechanisms can be employed to control energy availability at various points in the school. There is one drawback in the use of clock controls, however. Power outages also stop clock movements that are not battery operated. This, in turn, changes the real time at which such clocks turn the energy "on" and "off." Consequently, these clocks need constant monitoring by school personnel who may find it necessary to reset them from time to time.

Control over the temperature of hot water is another way of saving energy. Rather than allowing the individual mixing of hot water with cold water at every point of usage, it might be advantageous to supply hot water to each faucet at a temperature that requires little or no mixing with cold water. In widespread, strung out buildings, this arrangement may be somewhat more difficult to achieve, but special consideration should be given to devise ways and means of conserving energy by controlling potential waste of hot water. Such wastes often occur when the temperature of the water at the mixing faucet is higher than needed or when the hot water faucet is left partially open. Even in large buildings, it might be possible to bring relatively long hot water lines close to a point of usage and mixing hot and cold water centrally at that point, so that water flowing from the hot water spigots, in toilet rooms, for example, is at the proper temperature for hand washing.

8. *Recovering normally wasted energy.* School plant planners should always be on the alert for ways and means of recapturing heat that may be lost to the atmosphere or ground. For example, a certain amount of fresh air is required to ventilate classrooms. Normally, warm air inside of the building would be exhausted in order to provide space for the fresh air. Some architects exhaust the warm air through spaces above the ceiling in order to minimize the loss of heat from the classroom through the ceiling. If a plenum chamber is used to distribute air throughout the building, the

heat from the exhausted air could be exchanged with the fresh cold air being drawn into the building. In this way, the heat from the exhausted air could be recovered and transferred back to the classroom while the so-called stale air could be exhausted—minus heat.

There are often spaces within a school building that are unavoidably hot, such as boiler rooms, kitchens, pipe trenches for heating pipes, and foods laboratories. This excess heat is ultimately dissipated through the walls and by natural infiltration. It might be worthwhile to design a school facility so that this excess heat could be redistributed to other parts of the building. This feature would make it possible to reduce the temperature to comfortable levels in areas where excess heat is generated or accumulated and transfer this excess energy to other parts of the building where it is needed. Thus, energy that is normally wasted would be recovered.

9. *Exploiting humidity control to save energy.* Humidity control has been widely used to promote comfort within homes, schools, and other types of shelters. Humidification has not been used very extensively for the purpose of energy conservation. It is well known that human comfort within an enclosure is a function of both temperature and humidity. Discomfort occurs when both temperature and humidity are high. It is also recognized that the human body controls its comfort level and temperature through the process of perspiration. Discomfort sets in when the body cannot cool itself by the evaporation of perspiration due to high humidity.

The school plant planners of the future should utilize the effect of humidity on human comfort in an effort to save costly energy. During the heating season, the room temperature can be dropped and the level of humidity can be increased to the level of comfort for the occupants of the building. It is realized, of course, that the level of the humidity should be kept within limits so that furniture, doors, and equipment are not affected in any way. But even a temperature drop of three or four degrees Fahrenheit could produce substantial savings in the cost of energy in a school building over the heating season. The same principle could be applied to cooling. It might be possible to use dehumidifiers instead of air conditioners in certain areas and save the cost of energy to operate high capacity condensers that are found in air-conditioning equipment.

PLANNING SCHOOL BUILDINGS FOR SOLAR ENERGY

The energy from the sun is free, but collecting it and puttng it into practical use still costs a considerable amount of money. The outlook for solar energy is promising and very optimistic. The solar energy industry is making rapid strides in the development of more efficient and less costly solar energy systems. For this reason, all new school facilities should be designed and oriented so that solar energy systems can be incorporated into them at a later date.

A Brief Look at Solar Energy

It is indeed difficult to imagine the enormous amount of solar energy that reaches the surface of the earth every day. To be sure, the intensity of the solar energy is not uniform the world over. It varies from place to place, from day to day, and from hour to hour. But, the accumulated amount of solar energy falling on one square foot of horizontal surface per day, even in February in the northern hemisphere, is surprisingly high in many parts of the world.

Looks are sometimes deceiving as we feel the pleasant and soothing warmth from the sun in a sheltered area even in the middle of the cold season. Under these circumstances, the sunshine looks gentle, pervasive and innocuous. Actually, the light and heat produced by the nuclear furnace on the sun is very intense. in fact, it is so intense that the retina of the human eye can be burned and permanently damaged if one stares directly at the sun for any length of time.

Without getting deeply involved in the technical aspects of solar energy, it might be helpful to the reader to describe the active collecting of solar energy in more meaningful terms. Let us place one gallon of water in an insulated wooden box whose interior is painted black and is covered by a sheet of glass having an area of one square foot. Let us further assume that the box is level, has been exposed to the sun for a full day in February, has not lost any of its heat to the atmosphere and is located out-of-doors in Boston, northern United States, or northern California. If the initial temperature of the one gallon of water from a faucet was 40° Fahrenheit, the temperature of the water would have risen to 150° Fahrenheit at the end of a clear day! This idealized but realistic situation clearly shows that the amount of energy available from the sun annually is enormous. In extracting energy from the sun, however, allowances should be made for a variety of heat losses. In practice, the temperature of the gallon of water in our example would have lost a considerable amount of heat directly from the box to the atmosphere. An additional amount of heat would have been lost in transit while pumping the water from the box to the inside of the building, where it could be put to practical use. In this hypothetical situation the temperature of the water reaching the inside of the building at the end of the day could conceivably have dropped to 78° Fahrenheit, which is still sufficiently high to heat a building.

Realistically, the efficiency of commercially produced solar energy systems is surprisingly high but it varies with the ambient temperature of the atmosphere. Consequently, panel-type solar energy collectors are more efficient during periods of warm weather than they are in the winter months. But it must be remembered that no matter how well solar energy systems are designed and engineered for efficiency, they cannot develop more energy than was available at our hypothetical box described above. But, solar energy engineers have been very ingenious in capturing the energy from the sun. A few of the more advanced manufacturers of solar energy collectors have virtually created "solar energy traps." Once the energy enters the collector, very little escapes. The transfer of energy from the collector to some storage device within a building is accomplished with as little energy loss as possible. Sophisticated temperature devices control the rate of flow of water or air through the collector unit so that the temperature of the water or air returning to the building is as high as possible. The total area of the collectors is determined by the geographical location of the system. The area of the solar collectors may range from several hundred square feet for heating water to several thousand square feet for space heating. Although the technology underlying solar heating and cooling is well developed and scientifically sound, cost is still a formidable barrier to the widespread use of active solar energy systems. These systems are discussed in detail in the following section.

The Core Features of an Active Solar Energy System

Any active solar energy system must perform three basic functions. It must be capable of collecting the energy of the sun efficiently and transforming that energy into a form that can be easily transported from one place to another. The system must be able to move the energy from the collector to the interior of a building. And the system must provide some means of storing the energy, once it has been conveyed from the collector to the interior of the building. Each function is discussed briefly in the following sections.

Solar energy collectors.   There are basically two types of solar energy collectors on the market. One of them concentrates the solar energy at a point or along a straight line through the use of lenses or reflectors. The other type is simply a flat, box-like structure that entraps the energy that enters the box. The concentration type collector is complex and must always be aimed directly at the sun, while the flat solar panel is relatively simple to construct and functions well in a fixed position. For this reason, solar panels are more practical for heating purposes in school buildings.

There is a wide variety of solar panels on the market. Some are very sophisticated and highly efficient. Some trap the solar energy inside of evacuated glass cylinders that resemble fluorescent tubes. Others consist of copper tubing soldered onto a sheet of copper that is placed inside of a box whose sides are about 6 inches high. The bottom and sides of the box are covered with insulation. The copper sheet, with the pipes facing the top of the box, is laid on the insulation. The pipes and copper sheet are sprayed with a special type of heat absorbing black paint. And the top of the box is sealed and covered entirely with glass or sheets of plastic. In simpler terms, the box resembles a miniature greenhouse.

The working medium in a collector is either water or air. The heat is removed from the box by passing cold or cool water through the copper tubing which is soldered to copper base. There are many variations of the arrangement described above on the market but the principle is always the same. Black, heat absorbing pipes or plates are sealed in a well-insulated, glass covered box. The collected heat is removed from the enclosure by passing air or water through the box. The heated air or water is then brought into the building. For those who are interested in obtaining more detailed information about the many types of solar panels that are available on the market, it is suggested that brochures be obtained from the various manufacturers of solar energy equipment. The Department of Energy distributes lists of solar energy suppliers. Incidentally, these brochures offer a rich source of information on solar energy. Not only is the reading exciting for the solar energy enthusiast but it clearly demonstrates the creativity and ingenuity of the manufacturers of solar energy equipment in a free enterprise system. In addition to brochures, there are a number of good books on the subject written by experienced authorities in the field, such as Halacy[5] and Daniels.[6]

Transference of solar energy.   After solar energy is collected, it must be moved from the collector to the inside of the building where it can be stored or used as desired. The medium for conveying solar energy from the collector into the building is usually air or water. When air is selected as the medium, fans are used to circulate the air from the building to the collector and back to the building through a closed system of ducts. These ducts are well insulated in order to minimize the loss of heat during the process. Water, however, is more commonly used as the medium for transporting solar energy from the collector to the building. Water is pumped through the sun-heated collector and is returned to the inside of the building after absorbing heat from the solar panel. The pipes connecting the building storage unit to the collector are heavily insulated in order to keep heat losses from the water in transit at a minimum. Antifreeze is usually mixed with the water in order to prevent freezing during cold weather.

In both water and air systems, the designers of the systems have incorporated temperature control devices that prevent the transfer of heat from the building to the collector. When the temperature of the medium in the collector is close to that in the building, the fans and pumps become inoperative. In some water systems, there are controls that drain the water from the pipes when the temperature of the water in the collector approaches the freezing point. In some systems, there is also a computer controlled flow valve that keeps the amount of water or air flowing through the collector at an optimum volume at all times.

[5]D. S. Halacy, Jr., *The Coming of Solar Age* (New York: Harper and Row, 1973).
[6]Farrington Daniels, *Direct Use of the Sun's Energy* (New York: Ballantine Books, 1977).

Storage of solar energy.   Since solar energy is available only during daylight hours, it is necessary to store some of the collected energy for use at times when solar energy is not available or insufficient in quantity. This situation may arise when the sun is not shining brightly, during the night, or when the outside temperature is so low that the amount of energy collected is not sufficient to maintain the proper temperature within the building.

Solar energy is commonly stored in water or in stones. There are also physical-chemical methods of storing energy but the problems associated with these methods are still plaguing those who experiment with them. Consequently, large tanks of water (ranging from 10,000 to 15,000 gallons) are used for storing solar energy for space heating if water is chosen as the transporting medium. When air is the transporting medium, several tons of loosely piled stones in or adjoining the basement of the building are used to store the solar energy. Warm air from the collectors is filtered through the stones which absorb the heat.

The retrieval of the stored heat is a relatively simple process. The hot water it pumped to other parts of the building where the heat is required. Or, air from the building is circulated over the warm stones and returned to other parts of the building where additional heat is needed.

Practical Considerations Related to Active Solar Energy Systems in School Buildings

Theoretically, solar energy is ideal. It is free. It is nonpolluting. It is constant and renewable. It is abundant. It can be used for both heating and cooling. It reduces our dependence on fossil fuels. And, ultimately, solar energy will greatly improve the quality of the air we breathe, when its use becomes widespread.

There are, however, practical limits to the extent that solar energy can be utilized in school buildings at this time. The major drawback is cost. The cost of solar panels, pumps, controls, and storage systems is still very high. To be sure, the federal government and some states are paying part of the cost, but the full purchase price for a total solar energy heating and cooling system for a school building is still beyond the budgetary reach of many school districts. But the future prospects look very promising. With the advent of more efficient equipment and improved design, the cost of solar energy systems should drop considerably and become more affordable for more and more school districts in the nation.

On the other hand, the possibility of utilizing solar energy at this time must not be overlooked. It should, however, be limited primarily to hot water heating. This application of solar energy is economically justifiable and very practical for a number of reasons. First of all, no special storage system is needed. The existing water tank also serves as the heat storage tank, assuming, of course, that the water tank is not less than 500 gallons. Secondly, the cost of purchasing the limited number of solar panels that are needed to supply energy for hot water purposes is cost-effective. And thirdly, the heat transfer system can be very simple, uncomplicated, and relatively inexpensive.

Solar energy for space heating need not be ruled out entirely, however. If space heating is planned for a school building, it should be done judiciously. It is suggested that a conventional backup heating system supplement the solar energy system. By so doing, the size of the solar energy system can be scaled down to one that is economically efficient. In this instance, a considerable amount of money can be saved by eliminating almost all of the solar energy storage. Under these circumstances the solar energy panels can supply solar heat to the building during daylight hours in varying quantities. Any deficiency in heat is automatically compensated for by the standby system. Under this arrangement, whatever energy is collected from the sun represents a saving in the cost of energy for the building. On the other hand, the cost of purchasing the number of solar panels and ancillary equipment required to heat the building on a 24-hour basis employing extensive storage and distribution facilities would not be economically efficient until the manufacturers of solar energy equipment can find ways of reducing the cost per British Thermal Unit of heat delivered to the point of need within a school building.

Planning School Buildings for PASSIVE Solar Energy Heating

Thus far, the major focus has been on active solar energy systems. In these instances, as mentioned earlier, solar energy is collected at some location outside of the building. It is then transported into the building and is stored in water or stone for distribution within the building wherever it is needed at a later time. Passive solar energy heating, on the other hand, is primarily a function of building design and requires no special equipment.

Under the concept of passive solar heating, no effort is made to pump solar energy from the outside of the building to its interior. However, through ingenious building design solar energy is allowed to enter the building naturally and is trapped within it by various methods. A number of typical methods for capturing solar energy at little or no extra cost are listed below. Passive solar energy is achieved primarily by building orientation and design.

1. *The south window wall.* The admission of heat through the south walls warms objects and surfaces within the building when the sun is shining. The heat is trapped within the enclosure by the so-called greenhouse effect. In classrooms, special care should be exercised to keep the glare away from student desks through the use of venetian blinds or their equivalent. Also, reflecting shades should be closed at night to keep the heat within the building.

The architect should design the proper overhang along the south facing windows so that sunlight will not enter the building during the summer months when the sun is high in the sky. The dimensions of the overhang will depend upon the location of the building on the earth with respect to the solar plane. Solar angle tables should be consulted in determining the proper angle of the shadow line for winter and summer.

2. *Using a roof reservoir for sun heating.* Flat roofs can be made into shallow water reservoirs by forming a watertight glass or plastic covered box two or three inches deep over part of the roof area. The box would be filled with water. Since the roof is already coated with black asphalt which absorbs heat, the temperature of the water would rise and store solar energy.

The specific application of this concept depends upon the climate where a given building is located. An insulated and reflective cover could slide over the box at night, during which period the accumulated heat in the water would be radiated into the building. This application assumes that outside temperatures do not fall below freezing. In colder climates, however, it may be necessary to add antifreeze to the water. If covering the reservoir with reflective material at night is not feasible, the sun-heated water would still reduce the amount of heat that would be conducted through the roof during daylight hours when outside temperatures are low.

3. *Air heat collectors.* An air heat collector could be located on the roof of the building consisting of a simple box about 4 feet wide, 8 feet long, and 12 inches deep, insulated on the inside. Its interior surfaces would be painted black and the top would be sealed with a glass or plastic transparent covering. This box would be tilted to the proper angle depending upon the latitude of its location. Two ducts would be attached to the box. The inlet duct would receive cool air from within the building while the exhaust duct would force air warmed by the sun into the building. No fan would be needed since the air would be moved by natural convection.

4. *Skylight solar heating.* Solar energy could be admitted and stored at various points within the building through the expedient use of skylights. Ideally, the solar energy should fall on massive stone or masonry walls or on floors that are painted in dark energy absorbing colors. During the daylight hours, heat from sunlight entering through the skylight would be absorbed by the floors, walls, and other materials. At night the stored solar energy would be released into the building.

5. *Collecting solar energy in containers of water.* Several 55-gallon drums of water could be stacked inside of the building along a window wall facing south. These barrels would be painted black on all sides. At night insulating doors covering all of the windows could be closed. The warm water would then radiate heat within the building and keep it warm. Aesthetics would be a matter of concern in this approach to passive solar heating. However, any imaginative architect would find no difficulty in creating a pleasant aesthetic atmosphere in utilizing this approach to passive solar energy.

6. *Going partially underground.* It is well known that the temperature of the soil a few feet below the surface rarely falls below freezing in

most of the United States. It is also a recognized principle of physics that the flow of heat through a wall, floor, or ceiling is directly proportional to the temperature difference between the two sides of the surface. For example, if the temperature were 70° Fahrenheit inside a building, and 0° Fahrenheit outside, the amount of heat lost to the atmosphere per square foot of surface is approximately twice as much as that lost to the ground five or six feet below the surface. Consequently, the more of the building that is underground, the less will be the loss of heat from the building during cold weather.

It is not suggested, however, that school buildings be entirely underground. Two important considerations should be borne in mind when school plant planners are thinking about underground school facilities. As more and more of the building is constructed below the surface, more and more energy will be required for artificial lighting. On the other hand, as more and more of the building is constructed below the surface of the ground, less and less heat is lost from the building in cold climates. At some point, there is a balance between heat energy saved and electrical energy consumed for lighting purposes.

The concept of building at least part of the structure underground has merit from several points of view. Some heat energy will be saved for reasons mentioned earlier. Passive solar energy features can be incorporated into the facility because part of it is still above the topographical grade. In fact, light wells extending below the surface of the ground can be designed so that they may become effective solar energy traps.

It may be of interest to mention that there have been a number of proponents for school facilities built completely underground in the recent past. Their reasons for underground school buildings have considerable merit. Underground schools are ideal as civil defense shelters, not only for the students but also for the residents of the community. Underground schools conserve land use, particularly for parking. Underground schools are free from noise pollution. And underground schools are purportedly less expensive to build and maintain. In warm climates, the supporters of underground schools contend that the added cost of energy for artificial lighting is more than compensated for by savings in the cost of energy for air conditioning aboveground buildings.

3

Planning an Educational Facility

CHAPTER 10

A Practical Plan

The purpose of this chapter is to suggest a systematic sequential plan of action for identifying school plant needs, exploring alternative solutions, and developing suitable options. The process starts at a point when there is an intuitive feeling on the part of someone associated with the schools that some kind of school facility is needed, and culminates in the fulfillment of that need if such need is justified. This discussion is primarily concerned with process. From time to time, the procedures presented in this chapter reflect many of the fundamental principles described earlier in this text. When appropriate, these principles will be summarized for the convenience of the reader. It is suggested, however, that the reader review those sections of the book which discuss these principles and theory in greater detail.

TASK ONE: DEVELOPING A LONG-RANGE PLAN

No substantial capital outlay funds should be expended by a school district unless such expenditures are a part of a valid long-range plan. This rule should apply to funds used for major maintenance, remodeling or expanding existing school buildings, or for new construction. Before a sizable amount of money is committed for a given project, it is in the best financial interest of the school district to assure itself that such monies are not used for vaguely conceived purposes.

Step One: Make an Enrollment Projection

There are currently several standard methods of projecting future pupil enrollments. Perhaps the simplest method is the percentage of survival techniques that was discussed in Chapter 4. Avoid using the absolute number of pupils gained or lost from grade to grade each year. This seemingly logical approach leads to gross errors in making estimates of future enroll-ments. Always use ratios. Once the average grade-by-grade ratios are computed, it is necessary to refine these ratios by applying reasoned pro-fessional judgment. The validity of this enrollment projection depends greatly upon the wise adjustment of such computed ratios. In this connec-tion, it might be advantageous for a school district to employ an experi-enced educational consultant to make an enrollment projection. If sufficient funds for this purpose are not available, a consultant might be re-tained on a per diem basis (one or two days) to refine the ratios and com-plete an enrollment projection that was partly prepared by the school dis-trict.

In a large school district, it is necessary to make an enrollment projec-tion for each residential area. Such residential areas should be established approximately along elementary-school attendance areas. Once fixed, such residential areas should not be changed, even though pupils living in such areas may be assigned to schools located in other residential areas. The reason for retaining residential lines over a number of years is to accumulate sufficient data to establish a growth or loss pattern for each residential area. Information related to residential tracts is extremely use-ful in selecting sites for new school buildings and in determining future cost of pupil transportation.

Step Two: Conduct a School Building Survey

Chapter 5 contains the basic information for conducting a school building survey. The nature and degree of precision of the desired data are also specified. It is suggested that the various methods of conducting school sur-veys discussed in Chapter 4 be reviewed and that one of those methods or their equivalent be selected. If time is of the essence, the professional sur-vey is perhaps the best approach. If "selling a solution to the public" is seen as a problem, the citizens school survey is undoubtedly the best choice under such circumstances.

Step Three: Adopt a Long-Range Building Plan

Educators and boards of education are frequently placed on the defensive during a campaign to support the passage of a school referendum simply because they lack a well-defined long-range plan. Opponents of educa-tional referenda often use this technique to discredit school officials and school boards and, in so doing, succeed in defeating a school bond issue.

Aside from the public relations aspect, however, the adoption of a sound long-range plan is simply good business. A proposed action con-cerning educational facilities should be an integral part of a well-con-ceived long-range school building plan for the school district. This ap-proach assures the school district that each proposed action within the plan moves the school closer to the achievement of the educational goals set forth in the long-range plan. As mentioned in Chapter 5, any long-range plan should be flexible. It serves as a tool for the school district, not as its master. Thus, as circumstances and situations change in a school district, the long-range plan should be modified to reflect these changes. On the other hand, the long-range plan should not be so provisional or contingent that it loses its meaning. At any given time, a school district should have a clear, well-stated, defensible long-range plan within which it is operating. When the need for changes in the long-range plan arises, such modification should produce another long-range plan that is as precise and as justifiable as the original.

The principles underlying the formulation of a sound long-range plan are discussed in depth in Chapter 5. It is suggested that any long-range plan considered for adoption be tested against the thirteen criteria listed in Chapter 5. If the proposed plan violates three or more of the criteria stated there, a serious question would exist as to whether or not the long-range plan should be adopted as proposed.

In essence, the adopted long-range plan is the blueprint that charts the future course of the school district. Not only does the adopted plan specify the nature of this action but it also assigns a priority to each element within it.

Step Four: Board of Education Takes Official Action

After the long-range plan has been adopted, school officials and the board of education would normally begin to implement the plan in accordance with the order of priorities specified in it. Since there may be a lapse of time between the adoption of the long-range plan and the implementation of individual elements contained in it, the board of education should always review the proposed action called for in the long-range plan in relation to the circumstances existing at the time when the action is contemplated. Unless the time lapse mentioned above is extremely long (over two years), it is more than likely that the actions stated in the long-range plan are still valid.

On the other hand, if the situation in the school district is substantially different from what it was when the long-range plan was prepared, no further action should be taken on any other element of the long-range plan. Under these conditions, it is strongly recommended that Steps Two and Three be repeated and a new long-range plan be adopted by the board of education. However, if the proposed action is still part of a sound long-range plan, the board of education should take positive action to move the proposal forward.

Step Five: Enlisting Citizen Participation

The advantages of enlisting citizen participation have already been discussed in Chapter 4. Many boards of education involve lay citizens in matters requiring a school referendum or a town meeting vote. In all but the New England states, boards of education are responsible for providing educational facilities. Thus they have a choice as to whether or not citizens should be involved in the planning of school facilities. In New England, however, school committees are not authorized to construct school facilities. In these six states, it is required that a school building committee be appointed to plan and construct school buildings, except in certain cities that operate under special charters. Consequently, school building committees rather than school boards determine whether or not to use citizen groups.

In arriving at a decision as to whether to enlist citizen participation in the planning of a school building, the board of education, except in New England, may wish to consider the attitude of the citizens with respect to education in general and the construction of school buildings in particular. If the climate appears to be favorable to the action proposed by the board of education, the involvement of lay citizens is strictly optional depending upon the philosphy of the members of the board in this regard. On the other hand, if the citizen attitude is neutral and even a bit negative toward the proposal, citizen participation should be encouraged by school officials and the board of education. Specific details and suggestions concerning citizen participation in educational matters are presented in Chapter 4.

TASK TWO: PLANNING A SCHOOL BUILDING

Step Six: Obtaining Planning Funds

In general, boards of education include planning funds in their budget in anticipation of future expenditure related to capital outlay. It is often difficult to determine how much money should be earmarked for planning purposes. There is a wide variety of practices among school districts in this regard. Some school districts set aside $5000 to $10,000 to be used for preliminary planning purposes. This amount allows them to engage an architect and an educational consultant to explore several alternatives, one or more of which may be presented to the electorate for its consideration. Under this procedure, the proposals submitted to the public contain very few details other than the estimated cost and the general nature of the proposal. The major advantage of this approach is that if the proposal or proposals are rejected by the citizens, the school district has lost only a nominal amount of money in such an aborted venture.

There are also a few disadvantages associated with this approach. Under this plan, many of the best architects would not be attracted to the speculative nature of such a proposition. A second deterrent on the part of architects and consultants is that they both would be required to provide more services than the funds could reasonably purchase. Thus, their normal and legitimate fees could be realized only if the proposal materialized. Consequently, under normal economic conditions, such a school district could not easily attract the best professional services when token funds are appropriated initially. Only those not employed at the time could afford to apply.

A second approach is, by far, the most defensible of the three that will be discussed in this section. Under this plan, the school district would earmark for planning purposes an amount equivalent to 1–1.5 percent of the estimated total cost of a potential project. A rough idea of the possible cost of a given proposal can usually be obtained from the school facilities division of the state department of education. With this estimate in hand, the board of education can begin planning intelligently. Let us illustrate how such an estimate could be used. If the total cost of a proposed high school were estimated at $5,000,000, the school district would be well advised to earmark about $60,000 for the preliminary plans and associated fees. Under this plan, the educational consultant and the architect, together with the school officials and the board of education, could complete all work up to the "design development" stage of the proposed high school.

The advantages of this approach are many. In contrast with the first method, the school district can attract the best available professional services because it has the funds to pay legitimate fees in full. Secondly, the proposal presented to the electorate can be described in precise terms and in considerable detail. Thirdly, the plans of the proposed building are developed to the point where the architect can make a fairly accurate cost estimate of the project. And finally, school officials and members of the board of education are in a better position to defend the proposal on the strength of its educational merits, which are clearly reflected in the detailed plans of the proposed school building. The major disadvantage of this procedure is, of course, that a larger amount of money is at stake in the event that the proposal is rejected by the electorate.

A few school districts move confidently ahead in planning for a needed school facility by setting aside sufficient funds for the complete planning process including the cost of going to bid. This method, of course, enjoys all of the advantages of the second approach discussed above. It does, however, have one colossal advantage and one conspicuous disadvantage over either of the other two procedures discussed earlier. The major advantage of this method over the others is that the taxpayers of the school district will know exactly what the construction cost of the building is before they are asked to vote any capital outlay funds for the project, since the bidding process is completed. The obvious disadvantage of this procedure is that a very substantial amount of district funds would be lost if the project were to be turned down by the voters.

In states where school building committees are required, it is suggested that the school committee, in preparing an article for the town warrant creating a school building committee, also request that an amount of money be appropriated for the use of the committee equivalent to about 1 percent of the estimated total cost of the project. If this request is approved by the voters, the appointed building committee may, at its discretion, follow the first or second procedure described earlier. In fact, it has the option of following the third procedure by asking the voters to appropriate sufficient additional planning funds to carry the work of the committee through the bidding stage at a subsequent town meeting.

Step Seven: Securing Professional Services

Once funds are available for planning purposes, the board of education should engage a capable and skillful architect. Chapter 6 contains a detailed procedure for the selection of an architect. One of the most important decisions falling upon a board of education in the planning of a school building is the selection of a highly competent architect. Every board member should clearly understand that the architect strongly affects both the function and the cost of a school building. The author has had firsthand experience in which two architects have been given identical educational specifications in the same school district only to find that there was a significant difference between them of approximately 12 percent in the cost per student.

An analysis of the plans clearly disclosed the reason for this difference. In one instance the architect kept circulation space at a minimum by the ingenious grouping of rooms and the careful placement of doors, and designed the building in a delightful combination of cubical spaces in order to keep the volume of the building low. The second architect favored a more open concept, spacious glass-walled peripheral corridors, open lobbies, and a generous amount of circulation space. He also introduced two-storied glassed-in courts for both natural light and architectural effect. In this particular school district, the additional cost amounted to almost a million dollars. It is not intended to discuss the merits of one plan over another. Both schools adequately satisfied the educational requirements. Both schools were pleasant and educationally stimulating. And both schools had a distinct architectural character of their own. The point being made, however, is that the basic philosophy of the architect can greatly influence the design of a school building and thus control the cost and sometimes the function of the building. Before making the final selection of an architect, a board of education would be well advised to visit some of the schools designed by the architects under consideration and talk to the school officials with whom each worked.

If cost is of prime concern, the board should ask the state department of education what the average cost per student was at the time when the bids were awarded for a school designed by each architect, and then compare the cost per student of each architect with the state average, taking into account changes in construction cost for differences in time of construction. This information could be quite revealing. In fairness to the architects, however, the superintendent should review the educational specifications for each of the buildings compared. If the educational requirements are comparable, and the cost per student is high, the architect was generous in providing noneducational space. If the educational specifications are generous and the cost per student is high, the architect cannot be held solely responsible for the high cost. On the other hand, a low cost per student does not, per se, mean that the architect above was responsible for the result without analyzing the educational specifications. If low cost is coupled with austere educational specifications, then part of the responsibility for the low cost is attributable to the frugal allocation of educational space and part of it to ingenious architectural design. And finally, if the educational specifications call for a generous allocation of space, and the cost per student is low, the architect has accomplished an extremely rare feat.

If the school district is in the process of planning a middle school or high school building, it is strongly recommended that an educational consultant be employed to prepare educational specifications and review the development of architectural drawings as the plans progress from one stage to another. Chapter 6 describes the selection procedure and qualifications of an educational consultant. The employment of an educational consultant in planning an elementary school is optional. Such facilities are not as sophisticated as those for the upper grades, and one of the local school administrators can often work with the architect, from time to time, as an educational advisor. This person is often the principal-designee of a proposed new elementary school building, or the principal of an existing elementary school.

Step Eight: Selecting the School Site

The selection of a school site is one of the major responsibilities of the board of education. It is an involved, complicated, and time-consuming endeavor. For this reason, the school board should seek the advice of a number of professional persons in making its final determination. These persons should include the superintendent of schools, his chief administrator, and other members of the professional staff. The architect and the educational consultant should also make their recommendations to the school board. If the location of the school site becomes controversial, as it sometimes does, it might be helpful for the school board to establish a citizens advisory committee to assist it in this task.

The nature and function of a school site are discussed in Chapters 5 and 6. It is suggested that this list be used as the starting point. Some of the items included in the list may be deleted if they are not applicable and others should be added in order to satisfy certain local needs not reflected in the initial list. Once the set of criteria has been established, the task of pinpointing a number of potential school sites becomes a matter of evaluating a number of possible sites in terms of these criteria. Some site evaluators find it helpful to use a score sheet listing all of the criteria. As each site is considered, a number ranging from 0 to 10 is placed beside each item—0 for poor and 10 for superior. The sum of the individual scores then becomes the total score for a given site. If more than one person scores all of the sites, the average score for each site is used in ranking the potential school sites.

Step Nine: Preparing A Comprehensive Set of Educational Specifications

A good set of educational specifications is the *sine qua non* of planning functional school buildings. This task is the responsibility of the superintendent of schools or his designee in the absence of an educational consultant. When a consultant is employed, it becomes his responsibility to receive a wide variety of input from many sources, including school administrators, teachers, students, classified personnel, and citizens. He submits the completed set of educational specifications to the superintendent of schools, who receives reactions to them from all concerned persons or groups. The consultant will then modify the specifications to reflect these reactions insofar as possible. At this point, the educational specifications are submitted to the board of education for its final review and approval.

As soon as the educational specifications are approved by the board of education, they are transmitted to the architect, who will follow them in designing the building. It should be mentioned at this time, however, that the architect should also be given an opportunity for input at the time when the consultant is preparing the educational specifications. Thus, when he receives an approved copy from the board, they should come as no surprise since he was involved earlier in their development.

In the event that the school board chooses not to employ an educational consultant, it is suggested that the person assigned this task review Chapter 6. It is further suggested that he become very familiar with Chapters 13 and 14. These chapters contain specific requirements that should be included in the specifications. It might also be helpful if he would scan the table of contents for any topics or features that should become a part of the specifications. For example, Chapter 3, which is quite theoretical in content, might offer or suggest a number of ideas that should be incorporated in the specifications.

Step Ten: Stage I—Preliminary Drawings—Schematic Design Phase

The most crucial time in the planning of a school building that is functional, outstanding, and distinctive occurs during the schematic design phase of the architectural drawings. It is at this time that the educational consultant can make his greatest impact on the function of the building. It is the time when teachers and school administrators can get positive responses to changes from the architect. The reason is obvious. At this point the proposed school building is no more than lines on a piece of paper. The architect can easily accommodate most of the changes requested by his clients, because the plans at this stage do not represent a large investment by the architect on the structural and mechanical design of the building.

In Chapter 8, it is clearly demonstrated that boards of education or school building committees soon reach the point of insignificant savings in their discussion of changes in materials or surfaces specified in the architectural specifications. The facts presented in that section quickly disclose that, in spite of good intentions on the part of all persons involved in the planning, such a time-consuming exercise can, at best, result in a saving of 2 or 3 percent in the total cost of a school building under the best conditions with respect to the timing, bidding, and economic situation when the bids are advertised. The point being made is that the savings are so miniscule that other factors beyond the control of the committee can easily wipe them out. Such an effort to save money in the construction cost of a building by substituting less expensive materials is highly commendable, but it is made at the wrong time and on items that are not likely to result in significant savings.

On the other hand, boards of education, school officials, and school building committees would find it far more profitable to start their economy studies when it can make a substantial difference in the ultimate cost of a building—at the schematic design phase. It is not suggested that the choice of materials described in the architectural specifications be overlooked, but rather, that the time spent on this activity be kept to a reasonable amount, since the law of diminishing savings per hour of discussion time expended soon reaches the point of insignificant returns. On the other hand, the design of a school building, which becomes fixed after the schematic design phase of the planning, does have an *enormous* effect on the cost of the building and on its efficiency as an educational tool.

It is suggested that the principles discussed in Chapters 3 and 8 be reviewed. It is further suggested that additional items of economy of design generated by those involved in the planning be considered and reflected in the design of the building whenever possible. It can be stated categorically that the amount of time spent by all concerned at this stage will be quite rewarding from the standpoint of significantly reduced costs and substantially increased educational function.

Step Eleven: Stage II—Progress Prints—Design Development Plan

At this point in the planning of a school building, the outside perimeter of the proposed building becomes more or less fixed. The functional design features of the school are beginning to display their ultimate form, and the major economy measures influenced by the design of the school have been taken. During this phase, most of the changes occur within the perimeter of the building and are concentrated primarily on the functional aspects of the building. The nature of the changes, at this time, appear as refinements in the overall educational configuration of the school building developed during the first phase of the planning. The consultant, school officials, and teachers can still make suggestions during this phase, provided they are submitted within a week or two of the onset of this phase and provided that the changes can be accommodated within the perimeter of the building approved by the board of education at the completion of the first phase.

In fairness to the architect, there is a practical reason for the restrictive conditions imposed on the extent of changes that can be made in Stage II. These limitations have nothing whatsoever to do with the attitude, philosophy, or personal feelings of the architect. They reflect the stark reality of architectural planning. It is imperative that the planning of a building move forward in a systematic and orderly fashion if the architect is to meet the deadlines imposed upon him by the school district. Also, the architect must employ, at considerable cost to him, a battery of highly trained persons such as designers, structural engineers, heating engineers, electrical engineers, communication and electronic engineers, plus a host of consultants in specialized fields such as acoustics, food services, auditorium lighting and controls, and the installation of specialized teaching equipment and devices. These individuals are brought into the planning in a predetermined sequence and at the proper time.

At the end of Phase I, the person primarily involved in the planning is the design architect. To be sure, he consults from time to time with each of the specialists when suggestions and ideas are submitted to him. He reacts to suggestions, oftentimes, upon the advice rendered by such persons who are primarily concerned with the feasibility of the suggestion. Outside of this kind of dialogue between the design architect and the specialist, no substantial investment in time or work has been made on the plans by these experts in Stage I. It is clear, therefore, that the architect is understandably more receptive to a wide variety of changes in the drawings in the schematic design phase of the planning.

During Phase II, the various engineers and consultants begin working on the project in a tangible way. They begin to make studies, calculations, and drawings that supplement the architectural planning. Their work assumes that the approved schematic design is final with respect to perimeter, total area, total volume, and stated functions appearing in the educational specifications. As mentioned earlier, if a few outstanding suggestions are presented to the architect in the *early phases* of this stage, they might still be incorporated in the plans, provided the various experts have not progressed beyond the point at which the change can be made without redoing the plans. Very soon in the design development phase, however, the engineers and consultants have invested a substantial amount of time, energy, and effort on the project. Thus, it is quite likely that certain changes suggested at this point could result in the scrapping of whatever work has been done by these engineers and starting all over again. Under these conditions, the forward momentum of the planning is retarded and may even retrogress. In addition to being unnecessarily costly, a number of such changes could seriously affect the deadlines and delay the occupancy of the proposed school building.

While requests for changes should be discouraged after a certain time suggested by the architect for the reason stated above, there may be a few situations when changes can be justified at any stage—sometimes even after construction has started. Any glaring error that deleteriously affects the educational functions of the building should be corrected at any time and at all costs. Hopefully, the team of educational and architectural planners would have corrected any oversight during the early stages of the planning. In spite of the best of intentions on the part of all concerned, any rule allowing no changes after a given date should be broken wisely and with demonstrated cause.

Step Twelve: Stage III—Final Working Drawings and Specifications

Stage III is the final phase in the architectural design of a school building. At this point about 95 percent of the educational planning is completed. During this phase of the planning, the architect is deeply involved in a multitude of client-oriented details such as the choice of surface materials, the selection of doors, the development of an integrated lock system, the selection of appropriate fixed educational equipment in the laboratories and learning resources center, and the choice of communication systems.

It is during this phase of the planning that the architect will ask the client for his preferences. These questions may be concerned with floor surfaces in various parts of the school, such as carpeting, terrazzo, sealed concrete, exposed aggregate, and tile. They may be focused upon certain aspects of the interior decoration of the building. They may include a discussion of various types of wall and ceiling surfaces in certain spaces within the building. They may relate to the nature and extent of the site development around the building. These are only a few examples of questions that may arise during this stage of the planning. Behind the scenes, however, the engineers and consultants are hard at work putting the final touches on the working drawings and preparing a comprehensive set of specifications that clearly define the materials, installation, and functional performance of all equipment and the nature of the workmanship expected from the builders of the proposed school building.

Step Thirteen: Procedures After the Approval of Drawings and Specifications

After the board of education has approved the final working drawings and specifications, these documents are made available in sufficient quantities to all contractors wishing to submit bids for the construction of the school. Chapter 15 contains a detailed discussion of post-planning procedure. For the most part, the architect is responsible for all of the technical work associated with bidding and the awarding of bids to the lowest responsible bidder as required by law for the construction of buildings financed by public funds.

TASK THREE: GENERATING PUBLIC SUPPORT

The best-developed plans of a much-needed school building are useless unless the public or its elected representatives provide the necessary funds for its construction, furnishings, and equipment. There seems to be a natural tendency among many school officials and boards of education to postpone informing the public until the plans and specifications are completed. There is, indeed, some basis for this approach. Educators and members of boards of education may feel that the public is not interested in partial information. The question is often raised, "Why bother taxpayers until we have something to show them?" This position is justifiable in some situations. If the electorate has always exhibited a generous and supportive attitude in the past toward education, this approach could result in the passage of the school referendum for the acquisition of additional facilities. Attitudes change rapidly. Past history may no longer be a reliable indicator of public support. More and more taxpayers are offering increasingly greater resistance to school referenda. Thus, it is important that serious consideration be given to the public attitude toward education very early in the planning of school facilities.

Step Fourteen: Assessing Public Attitude

As soon as the board of education has adopted the long-range plan (Step Four), it should make an assessment of public attitude. This task need not be time-consuming or complicated in most cases. It can take the form of an open discussion called by the board of education with parents, teachers, school administrators, students, and classified staff. While no specific plans could be discussed at such a time, it would be possible for the board of education to get a "sense" of the feeling of the group. For example, if the proposed action called for the construction of an elementary school at a possible cost of a million dollars, the questions that might be asked of the group could be:

1. "How do you think the people whom you know living in the school district would react to an expenditure of this magnitude if it meant 'X' dollars on the tax rate?"
2. "How would they feel about locating it in the south side of the district?"

3. "What arguments do you think opponents of the proposal would raise against it?"
4. "What arguments could be used to counteract those of the opposition?"

In a relatively small and cohesive school district, the technique described above might suffice.

In a larger school district, it might be more productive to use a well-designed questionnaire prepared by a professional group with expertise in polls. In this case, some form of sampling technique should be adopted. It might be more economical for a school district to make a small investment in a scientific survey of public attitude before spending large sums of money for architectural plans that may never be used by the school district due to repeated rejections by the citizens.

Step Fifteen: Developing a Strategy for Gaining Public Support

There are a number of techniques that are likely to improve public support on a school bond issue. Each will be described briefly. The list is by no means complete. Other approaches should be explored by school officials and the board of education. Each community has its own character and cultural makeup. Thus, a technique that is effective in one school district may be a disappointment in another. For this reason, some of the techniques listed below may not be applicable to all school districts. In some situations local school officials may well find that it will be necessary to modify these suggested approaches or develop new ones. Regardless of the techniques used, however, there are two basic considerations to bear in mind in connection with public support. First, it is important to know the level of public support for a potential bond referendum. And secondly, it is equally important to select a technique that is motivating rather than coercive, and one that is in harmony with public sentiment. It might be helpful to study the suggestions listed below with those thoughts in mind and choose the approach that best fits the situation.

1. *Establish a citizens advisory committee.* This technique has already been discussed under Step Five earlier in this chapter. Specific information regarding the creation and organization of the citizens committee is presented in Chapter 4. Properly staffed and well organized, a citizens study committee provides the opportunity for many lay members of the community to become involved in educational matters. This technique can build mutual trust and understanding between school officials and board members on the one hand, and citizens groups on the other. This positive attitude, if it can be achieved in a school district through this process, could provide substantial support for the passage of a bond referendum.

2. *Consider the use of the installment plan.* In some school districts, the economic climate may not be conducive to the passage of a bond referendum for the entire foreseeable school needs. Under the circum-

stances, it might be possible to consider completing the project "by parts." At first glance, this approach may seem fragmentary and impractical, but, with careful planning, it can be used effectively in many instances. A study should be made to determine the feasibility of this approach. After all of the facts related to the economic status of the school district are assembled, an assessment of how much the school district can afford to spend on capital outlay expenditures must be made. In a few cases, the determination may not be what the school district *can* afford to spend, but rather, how much it is *willing* to spend for public schools. In either case, it is necessary to determine what that figure is. The next step in this technique is to make a study of all the options that could be considered within that expenditure level. If, after a careful study, it is found that the adoption of the "installment plan" concept is not feasible, the board of education can simply discontinue any further consideration of this approach.

On the other hand, if the proposed school can be built in two or three planned stages, consistent with the bonding capacity of the school district, the architect should fully explore these alternatives during the schematic design phase of the planning. The installment plan approach can also be developed as an option and be held in abeyance in the event that citizens reject the entire project. The board of education should make an assessment of the public attitude just prior to the date of the bonding referendum. At that time, it may decide on one of three options. The board may wish to ask the electorate to vote on the entire facility; it may choose to present only the first installment of the proposed school; or it may give the citizens an opportunity to vote on either proposal.

3. *Start the public information program early.* The public information program should start as early as Step Six. The superintendent of schools or his designee should be assigned the responsibility for public information in the local newspapers, on the radio, and on television. Additionally, information should also be transmitted by word of mouth as much as possible. A speakers bureau should be established, consisting of administrators, teachers, students, interested and supportive citizens, and members of the board of education. Such speakers should be available to present the school story and specific details on the status of the project at meetings of local groups whenever such groups request such reports.

4. *Organize coffee groups.* One of the most effective methods of word-of-mouth transmission of information takes place in a small neighborhood group meeting in the home of one of the neighborhood residents. Groups of ten to fifteen people are assembled in one home and a member of the "speakers bureau" mentioned above can act as a resource person.

It should be reemphasized that this activity should start early. Many school administrators view this approach as proper during the "hard-sell" phase of the campaign. Actually, it is far more effective if it is started at the time a building is still a gleam in the eyes of school officials and members of the board of education. To be sure, meetings of this nature in various parts of the district will not be too frequent in the early stages of the planning. The first meeting should be held no later than Step Six and the second may take place immediately after Step Nine. A series of meetings in different places of the district at these times could produce an enormous amount of feedback that would be valuable to the planners of the school building.

5. *Develop a greater awareness of public opinion.* While it is true that most elected officials are very sensitive to the pressures and demands of their constituents, they are not always conscious of the less apparent and subtle feelings that exist just below the surface. School officials and members of the board of education should make a conscious effort to "keep their fingers on the pulse" of public opinion. This informal and incidental source of information often provides hints and clues that can be followed up through the more formal lines of communication. By "keeping their ears close to the ground," school planners can take positive and constructive action in developing a supportive attitude toward the public schools on the part of the voters of the district.

6. *Become thoroughly familiar with every detail on the proposed building, why it is the best answer and why it is being located at the proposed site.* Every school official and each member of the board of education (and the school building committee, where one exists) should become intimately familiar with every aspect of a school facility proposal. One of the major weapons wielded by the opposition is that of discrediting the persons identified with the proposal. It takes only one incorrect or partially correct statement by anyone of the official family to seriously damage the credibility of the proponents of a project. Once such misstatements are made, opponents of a project take the offensive and the entire proposal is placed in jeopardy. When this happens, it is best to "stop, look, and listen."

Care must be exercised in responding to the opponent on matters affecting the credibility of the official family. The persons on the defensive are at a distinct disadvantage. Under these unfortunate circumstances, it is suggested that the person making the incorrect statement *not* answer the charge. The group, as a whole, should determine the best strategy to follow, and some other official, preferably the superintendent of schools or the chairman of the board, should serve as the spokesman. If one of these persons was involved, the other should act. If both are inadvertently involved in voicing incorrect or vague statements, some member of the board should assume the role of clarifier.

Another common practice utilized by the opponents of school referenda is attacking the logic or reasoning underlying the need for the proposal as a whole, or any part of it. For example, opponents may agree, on the surface at least, that the project is needed, but may "zero in" on what they unilaterally label as costly frills. Such frills could be almost anything in the building that can be called "too big," "too costly," "too luxurious." Or the proposal may be attacked because it is inadequate, too little, or an un-wise expenditure of public funds. Regardless of the attacks, the objective is identical—to kill the proposal.

The only countermeasure for such attacks is to make certain that all persons associated with a proposal are familiar with every detail of the reasons underlying all aspects of the project. Obviously, it is unrealistic for every member of the official family to know everything about the entire project. It is important, however, that someone in that group be an expert on any question that may be raised about the project. It is also prudent for members of the group who are less familiar with a given question or issue to defer to someone else in the group who is the expert. It is better not to answer a question at all than to give an answer that may turn out to be incorrect or partly correct. This is especially true when questions are di-rected at certain details of the project. Everyone in the official group, how-ever, should be well versed in the reasoning and logic underlying the pro-posal itself. All should be able to defend its location, its capacity, and its function.

Everyone should be able to justify the major activities planned for the building. For example, why is a swimming pool needed in the building? Why are not more provisions made for vocational education? Do we need such a large auditorium? Why can't we use the cafeteria as an auditorium by locating a stage on one end of it and eliminate the auditorium? Again, if any member of the official group does not have the answer to such ques-tions, it is best not to answer them but to refer persons raising such ques-tions to the expert on the board or on the staff.

7. *Know the real issue underlying the opposition points of view.* There are always two categories of reasons associated with the opponents of school referenda. The expressed arguments reflect the overt reasons for opposing a proposal. These are important, of course. But it is even more crucial to know the covert reasons for opposing the referendum. The pro-ponents of a school issue can play the same game on the opponents as the opponents play on the proponents. The major thrust of the proponents of a school facility should be aimed at neutralizing the *covert* reasons. Thus, every attempt should be made to differentiate between the stated reasons for opposing a bond issue and the real ones. Once the real reasons are identified, they should be kept clearly in view as the public information and citizen participation programs are developed.

There are, to be sure, a thousand and one reasons why citizens op-pose school bond issues. Some of these stated reasons, of course, are real. Others are perhaps just as effective but do not reveal the true motivating force of the opponents. For example, a citizen may privately feel that taxes are already too high in a school district. He is opposed to anything that will increase his tax bill regardless of the nature of the expenditure. This con-viction, on his part, is the real reason for his opposition to a school bond issue. Publicly, however, he may not wish to take a position opposing education by arguing against a bond issue. Thus, he may use subtle approaches in opposing the school bond referendum, without revealing his unwillingness to support additional taxes for school purposes.

A study made by the writer of the reasons most often expressed publicly in opposition to school bond issues can be divided into three distinct groups. The first category would include reasons related to the argument that "we can't afford it." The common element among these reasons is cost. Whatever it is that is being questioned, it costs too much. These reasons could encompass the entire project or parts of it. For example, we can't afford this frill or that space. The second group of reasons overtly offered by opponents of school bond issues is related to the argument that "we don't need it." These reasons are all too familiar, such as "we don't need a new school," "we don't need the field house," "we don't need the swimming pool," and "we don't need an auditorium." And finally, the third category of expressed reasons for opposing a school bond issue assumes a more conciliatory attitude but one that is equally devastating to the passage of a bond referendum. These reasons are related to the argument that "we need something, but not that."

This is an interesting approach in that citizens offering reasons that fit into this third category are not questioning the need. They are openly opposed to the solution, but they are nonetheless not opposed to the project. There is little solace to be gained from this type of opposition, however. The objective is the same—*defeat the bond issue.* If the reasons offered by this group of citizens are genuine, and this may not always be true, it might be possible to gain some support from this group in the next attempt to pass a bond issue, if the first fails to pass. Some of these citizens could be asked to serve on a citizens committee to revise the solution that was defeated and to develop one that still meets the educational needs of the school district and is more acceptable to the public than the original proposal.

In view of the foregoing discussion, it can be seen that it is very important to look beyond what appears on the surface. It is vital to the success of a bond issue to identify the true nature of the public resistance, which is often at variance with the reasons stated publicly by such opponents. In a few cases, very little can be done to counteract these unrevealed arguments. For the most part, however, a knowledge and understanding of these underlying reasons can be extremely helpful in developing an effective campaign for the passage of a bond issue.

CHAPTER 11

Safety, Health, and Comfort

The safety of those occupying a school building is of prime concern to the architect, educators, and boards of education. Safety hazards in school plants may be due to building design, site planning, selection of floor materials, and the location of obstacles, such as fire extinguishers, water fountains, electrical floor stubs, and protruding pipes. No school planner or architect can justify the introduction of safety hazards in a school building on the basis of architectural design or aesthetic unity. Although safety cannot always be completely assured, every effort must be made to achieve as high a safety level as possible. For example, a service driveway must be located near a school building even though it introduces a safety hazard. It is difficult, if not impossible, to plan the crossings of walks and drives at grade level so that they are absolutely safe. The site planner should take every conceivable precaution in laying out both the drives and the walks to increase the safety of those using the educational facility.

HAZARDS ASSOCIATED WITH THE
MOVEMENT OF PEOPLE

A few areas of concern regarding safety of people moving from one part of the school plant to the other are discussed in the following paragraphs.

Ramps

Ramps, like stairways, are a nonmechanical means by which people change their elevations from one level to another. They are an integral part of the circulation system within and outside of a school building.

 The use of ramps in schools is receiving increased attention from both architects and educational planners, especially as a means of meeting the needs of physically handicapped students, particularly on college campuses where students must travel from building to building. Ramps should be designed for wheelchair use and should be covered with nonslip materials. The slope of a ramp should not exceed 10 percent, which is equivalent to a rise of not more than one foot for a horizontal run 10 feet in length. Within a building, elevators are preferred for the use of physically handicapped persons. However, where the change in elevation within a building is less than three risers, a ramp is preferable to stairs from the standpoint of safety for all students traveling from one level to another.

Architects and school planners should give additional thought to the problem of handicapped students who travel from place to place by means of wheelchairs. While elevators adequately meet the needs of such students within the building itself, ramps should be provided wherever necessary, so that they can reach the elevators from out-of-doors. Furthermore, sidewalks and outside areas should be planned with the handicapped student in mind. It should be possible for such a student to travel by wheelchair from the bus-unloading zone on the campus to any other point within and outside of buildings where students are normally required to report for instructional purposes.

Stairways

Stairways can be dangerous, so certain precautions should be taken in their design. Stair runs should not exceed sixteen risers nor should they be less than three. The riser height on all principal stairways should not exceed 6½ inches and treads should not be less than 10½ inches deep, exclusive of nosing or overhang. Experiments conducted in one of the major department stores in Boston revealed conclusively that accidents on stairways were reduced when the riser heights in a stair run did not vary by more than ⅛ inch. The engineer conducting the experiment was convinced that uniformity in riser height was fully as important as the riser height itself. Stairways should insure a rapid and safe egress from a building when emergencies arise. Speedy evacuation from a school is imperative in the event of fire, the escape of noxious fumes, or other dangers. Stairways, therefore, should be specifically designed for such emergencies.

Multistory buildings should have at least two main stairways located well apart from each other. At least two independent and smoke-free paths to safety should be provided from any point in a school building where students work. For example, some state codes require that a door be located in every partition between classrooms adjacent to the wall opposite the corridor. In the event that hot gases filled the corridor, students could travel from room to room until they reached a smoke-free stairway in multistory buildings. Two stairways terminating on the same landing should be considered as a single stairway. Stairways should run at right angles to main corridors and should be enclosed in fire-resistant stairwells. Handrails may be composed of combustible materials. It is also important that main stairways be open to egress and that they lead to an exit on the ground floor.

Stairways should be at least two lanes in width, with 44 inches between handrails. Handrails should be installed between 26 and 30 inches above the nosing on the stair tread. Where pupils of many ages attend a school two handrails, one at the normal height and one at a lower position, should be provided for the safety of both younger and older children.

Corridors

The mass movement of students from one point to another on the same floor level in a school building usually takes place through a corridor. Corridors should be wide enough to accommodate the traffic and they should be free of obstructions and bottlenecks. It is generally accepted among school planners that main corridors should be at least 8½ feet wide. In schools with enrollments exceeding 200 pupils, they should be wider. The width of secondary corridors, on the other hand, is governed by the number of classrooms served by each corridor, and by its length. In any case, secondary corridors should not be less than 7 feet wide in the clear.

There should be no projection into the corridor greater than 8 inches beyond the face of the corridor wall. Doors should be installed so that they do not project into the corridor by more than 8 inches. In addition to being a safety hazard, doors opening farther into a corridor create a bottleneck and thus appreciably reduce the effective width of the corridor. Also, radiators, fountains, fire extinguishers, and the like should be completely recessed in corridor walls.

"Dead-end" corridors are very dangerous and should always be avoided in planning. Corridors should always terminate at an exit or at a stairway leading to an egress. Doors that open onto a stairway or tend to block passageways create safety hazards and should, therefore, be avoided.

HAZARDS DUE TO NOXIOUS GASES, CHEMICAL AGENTS, OR RADIOACTIVITY

The danger from commercially produced heating gas in school buildings is well recognized, but the hazards resulting from inhalation of fumes produced by some cleaning agents, insect sprays, and paint thinners are not quite so obvious. Every effort must be made to minimize the hazard from noxious fumes. Admittedly, it is often difficult to cope with the problem of poisonous vapors because it is not always possible to determine the type, origin, or location of the source of such fumes.

The presence of detectable amounts of heating gas in the atmosphere creates a potentially explosive situation, particularly in the case of propane gas. Since bottled gases are heavier than air, they "spill over" onto the floor and are, therefore, difficult to detect through the sense of smell until the accumulation has reached dangerous proportions. Regardless of the type of heating gas used, however, the selection of the equipment, the installation of the distribution system, and the attachment of equipment and appliances to the outlets supplying such fuel should be performed with the utmost care by competent craftsmen.

The problem of noxious fumes in schools is elusive. Architects have worked diligently to minimize the health and fire hazards from noxious or combustible vapors, particularly in areas where the need for special precautions is obvious, such as bus garages and paint-spraying shops. There are, however, a number of other spaces in an educational facility where the problem of harmful vapors is present. While hoods are provided in chemistry laboratories, special provision for the escape of noxious gases is not always made in the preparation rooms. Nor is special attention always given to the exhaust of fumes from cleaning agents and chemicals used in the physics and biology laboratories. The custodian is often required to refinish furniture in his shop, but rarely does one find a well-ventilated custodial workshop. Maintenance personnel often clean parts of light fixtures and rugs using agents that emit noxious fumes, but one does not often find a properly designed space for this function. All of the places where noxious gases should be exhausted in a school building cannot be listed. It is hoped, however, that school planners will make a mental note of the areas that might require additional ventilation because of the possible production of noxious fumes. Electronic sensors should be provided.

The wide use of radioactive materials for experimental purposes in high schools and colleges has introduced another element of danger in educational structures. Radioactive materials are now available in a variety of forms. Nuclear research laboratories are an integral part of many comprehensive institutions of higher learning. The commercial producers of nuclear equipment have taken every precaution to protect students from possible harm through design and proper use of shielding materials.

The proper storage of radioactive materials vitally concerns school planners. While industry can cope with matters related to radioactive safety through the design of the equipment, educational planners and architects are responsible for the safe storage of radioactive materials. It is imperative that the planning provide for stringent control of access to radioactive storage areas. No student should be able to accidentally find himself in an area where radioactive materials are stored. It is also necessary that special attention be given to the radioactive shielding surrounding such areas. The Atomic Energy Commission has published a considerable amount of information to guide architects in designing hazard-free spaces where radioactive materials may be used.

HAZARDS ASSOCIATED WITH NORMAL
SCHOOL ACTIVITIES

Hazards are associated with many activities normally conducted in a school building. While such potential sources of danger cannot always be completely removed, they can and should be minimized or controlled as much as possible. School planners may wish to prepare a comprehensive checklist of specific dangers to be avoided in the design of school buildings in relation to students, faculty, clerical staff, and custodians.

Students

In reviewing plans of school buildings, each detail should be checked with the safety of the student in mind. A few questions will be raised in order to suggest major areas of concern. If hot gases in the corridors block student egress from an instructional area, is there another means of escape? Are doors designed so that they cannot be accidentally slammed into the faces of students? Are floors slippery in the corridors, wet shower areas, main entrances, and classrooms? Are there dangerous projections or protrusions in the corridors, classrooms, and other areas where students congregate? Are electrical circuit boxes and other controls properly shielded and located away from student access? Has every safety precaution been taken in normally hazardous areas such as shops, gymnasiums, laboratories, playgrounds, and stairways? Has adequate provision for first aid been made in the chemical laboratories? Is lighting in the various shops and laboratories adequate for the learning tasks to be performed? Is supplementary local lighting provided on power machines in the shops? Are electrical floor stubs avoided in teaching areas? Are catwalks, balconies, and other elevated areas fully protected? Can large expanses of glass be easily shattered by direct bodily contact by students? Are walks and drives planned for maximum safety, with a minimum of crossing of foot and vehicular traffic? Do driveways separate the building from play areas, thus causing a safety hazard?

Faculty and Staff

Many of the hazards listed above apply also to the faculty and staff. For the most part, schools are still designed without the work of the custodian in mind. Oftentimes, lights in auditoriums and gymnasiums are difficult to change and require the use of extra-long ladders. Pipes are seldom color-coded. Without such coding, custodians may receive serious burns from hot steam lines. Pipe trenches may be unlighted and studded with dangerous projections. Electrical equipment is not always completely free from shock hazards. Boiler controls and equipment are not always located for maximum safety. In multistory buildings, elevators are not always provided for the conveyance of heavy equipment from one floor level to another. These are but a few of the hazards confronting the custodial personnel in a school. The health dangers produced by the use of cleaning agents in certain parts of the school are also of major concern to school plant planners.

PLANNING FOR COMFORT AND CONVENIENCE

Functional school planning has long been considered a fundamental concept of school design. However, it is also important to include the dimensions of comfort and convenience in planning educational facilities.

It is generally agreed among educators that human comfort is conducive to effectual learning. Consequently, a school should feature comfortable lighting, humidity and temperatures, seating, colors, ventilation, and acoustical environment. It is also believed that a well-planned school should be functional and also provide for the convenience of its occupants whenever possible. Convenience is important in location of rest rooms, design of traffic patterns, layout of equipment, location of storage and shelving, and grouping areas of related activity. The cause of convenience deserves careful consideration, especially during the period when thoughts related to the functional aspects of the school are being crystallized. For example, while the functional aspects of the heating system are being discussed, it would be wise also to consider the safety and convenience of the custodian and engineer who will eventually operate the equipment. It is hoped, of course, that school planners will evolve a plan that is aesthetic, efficient, and convenient.

Architect Louis Sullivan believed that *form follows function*. The wisdom of this axiom cannot be overstated. Aesthetic integrity deserves careful consideration in the design of any educational facility, but if there is an unresolvable conflict between aesthetics and function, aesthetics must inevitably yield to function.

SANITARY FACILITIES

School planners are concerned with both the physical and the mental hygiene of those for whom schools are planned. Consequently, architects and engineers work as a team to create conditions that provide for the physical well-being of the occupants of a school building. By and large, the healthfulness of a building is determined by the design and function of the heating, cooling, and ventilating systems, and by its visual and acoustical environment. Healthfulness is also promoted by the selection of easily cleaned interior surface materials whose design reduces the accumulation of dust and air polluters. A building designed with the health of its users in mind also provides for emergency situations involving illness or injuries.

Plumbing Requirements

Plumbing requirements are often reduced to a simple formula with respect to the size and number of facilities, lengths of pipe runs, proper pipe pitch, and dollars and cents. Admittedly, all of these considerations are of prime importance, but the so-called "slide rule" approach to school planning often falls short of insuring healthful conditions in a school.

Nationally recognized standards call for the following allocation of plumbing fixtures as specified in Table 11.1.[1] The minimum quantity of plumbing fixtures in buildings serving adults, such as office buildings, factories, colleges, and universities, varies with the number of persons housed in the building. According to the New York State Labor Code, the minimum plumbing fixture requirements for buildings in which large numbers of persons are engaged in gainful pursuits are given in Table 11.2.

Toilet Facilities

A toilet room should be easy to clean, attractive, well ventilated, properly equipped, and uncongested. Every effort should be made to select fixtures, wall materials, and flooring that can be kept spotlessly clean with ease. The choice of colors in a toilet room is also quite important. The more attractive the space, the less likely it is to be defaced.

Congestion may be a problem in poorly designed toilet rooms. For example, the location of mirrors over lavatories contributes to congestion. It might be better to locate mirrors elsewhere in the toilet room. A shelf could be installed under the mirrors where girls might temporarily place their purses. In addition to distributing students within a toilet room, relocating the mirrors reduces maintenance of lavatory drains in the girls' rooms because fewer bobby pins will be dropped in the lavatory. Then too, there is a significant increase in the potential utilization of the lavatory. One student can be engaged in washing, while another is combing his or her hair at a location removed from the lavatory fixture.

Cleanliness and ease of maintenance must be kept in mind in planning toilet rooms. Good lighting and attractiveness are desirable even in toilet rooms. School maintenance personnel affirm that attractive and well-illuminated toilet rooms are usually cleaner than those that are drab

TABLE 11.1 Ratio of students per unit plumbing fixture

Type of School	Water Closets Girls	Water Closets Boys	Urinals Boys	Unit Lavatories	Drinking Fountains
Elementary School	35	60	30	50	75
High School	45	100	30	50	75

[1]National Council on Schoolhouse Construction, *Guide for Planning School Plans* (the Council, 1964), pp. 78 ff.

TABLE 11.2 Required number of plumbing fixtures in public buildings

No. of Men	Toilets	Urinals	No. of Women	Toilets	No. of Men or Women	Lavatories
221–270	6	5	191–240	8	201–225	10
281–300	7	6	271–300	10	251–275	12
341–360	8	7	331–360	12	301–325	14
361–390	9	7	391–420	14	351–375	16
401–450	10	8	451–480	16	401–425	18
461–480	11	9	511–540	18	455–475	20
521–540	12	10	571–600	20	501–525	22
631–640	15	11	Above 600	1 additional toilet per 30 women	551–571	24
701–720	16	13			Above 600	1 additional lavatory per 25 persons
721–750	17	13				
761–810	18	14				
821–840	19	15				
881–900	20	16				
900 and above	1 additional toilet per 60 men	1 additional urinal per 50 men				

and dark. The use of interior surfaces that are easy to clean tends to improve the healthfulness of toilet rooms. The installation of floor drains and hose-outlets in such spaces also promotes cleanliness because it permits custodial personnel to wash the floors with ease. Floor surfaces should be impervious to moisture and acid resistant, particularly in areas surrounding urinals.

The type of toilet fixtures selected may have an important bearing upon the healthfulness of toilet rooms. Although floor-type urinals possess many advantages, they present one serious drawback. Because of the difference between the coefficient of linear expansion of the china and the flooring material into which the unit is imbedded, a small crack eventually develops at the juncture between floor material and urinal. In time, body wastes collect in the crack and sometimes seep under the floor surface, producing an unpleasant odor, which can be removed only by tearing out the floor covering or tile. With wall-hung urinals this problem is avoided, and in addition they are less costly to purchase and install. Also, it is easier to clean the areas near the urinals. Wall-hung toilet seats are also desirable, because they permit the custodian to keep the toilet area clean more easily than do ordinary pedestal-type toilet fixtures. Wall-hung toilet fixtures are somewhat more costly than other types of such fixtures, and economy may dictate the use of the pedestal-type fixture.

Ventilation is a vital aspect of healthfulness in toilet rooms. A mechanical ventilating system that is capable of producing about twenty complete air changes per hour in the room is essential. Natural ventilation of toilets through open windows would appear to be acceptable, but the lower portions must be kept closed for reasons of privacy, especially in single-story buildings, and the upper sections, which are controlled manually, are not always open enough to provide the necessary ventilation. Mechanical ventilation, on the other hand, is effective and automatic.

Toilet seats and flush mechanisms should provide for maximum sanitation. Toilet seats of the open-front variety are highly desirable. Flush valves should be of the foot-operated type. Such flushing devices have been in operation in some institutions for almost a quarter of a century without presenting any unusual maintenance problem.

The location of toilet spaces deserves careful thought from the standpoint of their relationship to the educational function, public or school utilization of such areas, nature of the users of certain toilet rooms, and convenience. The accepted location of all gang toilets in most of the schools constructed before World War I was in the basement of the building—the boys' area on one side of the basement and the girls' toilets on the other. After World War I, gang toilets were removed from the basement areas and distributed, in stack formation, on each floor. Generally, there was one set of gang toilets for each sex on every floor level. And, in most cases, such toilet facilities were placed adjacent to each other for reasons of economy. After World War II, however, toilets became more widely distributed throughout school buildings and the use of single watercloset toilet rooms became quite common. Moving toilets from the basement to more convenient locations throughout the building has been an improvement, but it has not gone quite far enough. The convenience of the faculty has been all but ignored in the planning of schools, although many teachers' rooms or lounges have been provided with toilets. But, in many situations, the toilets in the teachers' room are the only ones designated for faculty members. In large high schools or colleges, the teachers' lounge may be located far from many of the classrooms where teachers spend most of the school day. It would be highly desirable, therefore, to locate a simple toilet and lavatory space for men and one for women faculty members adjacent to each gang toilet provided for students. Such an arrangement would satisfy both the distribution and convenience requirements of such a facility.

Lavatories

Most lavatory fixtures found in educational institutions are not designed for both healthfulness and economy. While a few installations do satisfy the need for sanitation, they do not provide for economy of water consumption. A few installations reduce the waste of water, but ignore requirements of sanitation. The standard two-spigot faucets, one for cold water and the other for hot water, produce the most unsanitary conditions under normal school use. In this case, the student must plug the drain and fill the lavatory to a given height with a mixture of hot and cold water at the desired temperature, just as he would at home. A lavatory used in this fashion in a school, however, soon accumulates dirt, since students do not ordinarily clean the lavatory after use. The spring-type or delayed closing faucets, on the other hand, save water but do not permit students to wash their hands under sanitary conditions. When two spigots of this type are employed, the student can leave the drain plug open when he washes his hands, but he cannot control the temperature of the water flowing from either spigot. Therefore, unless the hot water supply is tempered, he must wash with cold water. His other alternative, of course, is to close the drain and fill the lavatory bowl as described above. This procedure creates the same unsanitary conditions mentioned earlier.

What is desired in a hand-washing lavatory is an installation that saves water and promotes healthfulness. In public toilets, no student should have to wash his hands in water collected in a basin that is not thoroughly clean before he uses it. Consequently, the use of a drain plug in a wash basin is ruled out. If economy of water consumption is not a major concern, an ordinary mixing faucet with a single spigot is an excellent solution to the handwashing problem. Experience in many schools using this type of installation has proven that students do not habitually leave faucets running after use. In discussing the operational aspects of such installations with school principals and custodians, the author found that in no case was there a feeling that water was wasted excessively. Another possible solution would involve the use of a temperature-controlled hot-water system in which each lavatory would possess a single delayed-closing spigot. In this situation, the student would depress the handle and wash his hands while the water continued to flow for a few seconds. Where such units have been used, there has been an almost constant problem of readjusting the mechanism controlling the length of time the water continues to flow. Often the flow of water stops too quickly. The best solution to this problem is one in which a foot-operated mechanism controls the flow of water. Under this method, water ceases to flow when the foot is removed from the pedal. Either a single-spigot mixing faucet or a controlled water temperature system can be used with the foot pedal.

Certain other handwashing needs merit attention. Soap may be provided in one form or another at locations convenient to lavatories. Liquid soap systems facilitate the distribution of soap, but added maintenance is required to keep the system from becoming clogged. The recent development of soap pads for school use holds much promise and would seem to have some advantage over either bar, powdered, or liquid soaps. Some provision should also be made for hand drying in toilet rooms. Ordinarily, students use cloth rollers, paper towels, or electric hand dryers to dry their hands. Towels generally create a maintenance problem. The cloth roller must be laundered when it is completely soiled. Paper towels may be scattered over the floor or stuffed into lavatories and toilets. In either situation, however, the maintenance problem is not intolerable. Electric hand dryers are functional and satisfactory, provided they are furnished in sufficient numbers. Electric dryers are noisy and require more time for hand drying than other methods. Therefore they usually create some congestion, but maintenance is low and littering is avoided. The initial cost of such units is eventually offset because there is no expense for paper towels or laundering cloth rollers.

Drinking Fountains

Water fountains should be readily accessible in areas where strenuous physical activity is carried on, such as playgrounds, gymnasiums, and playrooms. They should also be distributed throughout a school in convenient locations where water is already available.

The choice and installation of drinking fountains are of utmost importance in maintaining healthfulness in school buildings. They should be constructed of impervious materials and be designed so as to minimize the chance of contamination. Orifices should be located so that students' mouths do not come in contact with them and so that waste water does not fall upon the nozzle. The installation of water bubblers on the periphery of work sinks is not recommended, because students washing hands or equipment are apt to contaminate the bubblers during the washing process.

Nozzle heights are very critical, particularly in elementary schools, where there is a wide range in the age and development of pupils. Acceptable heights for water fountains are as follows:

    a. Twenty-four inches above the floor for kindergarten and primary grades.
    b. Twenty-eight inches for upper elementary-grade pupils.
    c. Thirty-two inches for junior high schools.
    d. Thirty-six inches for senior high schools and colleges.

Water Supply

Unless the water supply system is part of a municipal system, it should be planned by a competent engineer. Where wells are used, a minimum supply of 25 gallons of water per day is required for each student for normal needs. Additional capacity of adequate storage is needed for firefighting equipment and special educational uses, such as laboratories, homemaking areas, and shops.

For obvious health reasons, drinking water should be free from nitrogenous or undesirable mineral content and harmful bacteria. It is of extreme importance that the plumbing system be designed so as to prevent back-siphoning from toilet fixtures, swimming pools, and the like.

Sewage Disposal

Unless it is part of a municipal sewer system, the sewage disposal system at any school should be designed by a competent sanitary engineer. Sewage disposal fields on school property can become a serious health hazard unless the system is properly designed. Soil percolation and terrain are critical factors in the design of a sewage disposal system. Only a well-qualified sanitary engineer can interpret the results of soil tests and drainage characteristics of the site in designing a healthful sanitary system.

THE THERMAL ENVIRONMENT

The effectiveness of the teaching-learning situation and the efficiency of school personnel are greatly influenced by the climate produced within the school building. The thermal environment should be designed to provide for the health and comfort of the individual. Comfort is determined primarily by the rate of exchange of heat between the individual and his environment. Thermal control of the environment simply regulates the net body heat loss or gain for given conditions. Contrary to popular belief, comfort is not necessarily a function of the air temperature alone. The temperature of the walls and other interior surfaces is more directly related to comfort than is the temperature of the air itself. For example, on very cold days, the exterior walls are relatively cool. Hence, the body radiates more heat to them than it receives from the outside walls of the building. The body, therefore, experiences an uncomfortable cooling effect even though the temperature in the room is about 72 degrees Fahrenheit. Clothing insulates the body and reduces the radiational loss of heat, thus producing a feeling of comfort on cold days. Discomfort, on the other hand, may be produced when the heat gained exceeds the heat lost. There is a considerable variation among individuals with respect to thermal comfort in any given set of conditions. This variation is due primarily to differences in basal metabolism that are dependent upon sex, age, activity, and individual characteristics.

Comfort and health of an individual are related, as noted above, to the equilibrium of heat exchange between him and his environment. The exchange is affected mostly by convection and radiation, and to some extent by conduction when the individual is sitting or lying down. Consequently, the temperature of the air and that of large surfaces become the major contributors to comfort. When walls are cool, air temperatures must be kept at a level that is considerably higher than normal if comfort is to be maintained. When wall and ceiling temperatures can be held close to that of the atmosphere within the room, an air temperature of 65°–68° Fahrenheit at shoulder height for kindergarten and primary-grade students, and of 68°– 70° Fahrenheit for older students, is both healthful and comfortable. Convection causes air temperatures to vary with height in any given space. The difference in temperature between the floor and the five-foot level should not vary by more than 3° Fahrenheit.

The relative humidity in a space for learning strongly influences the comfort of the individual. The comfort index varies both with respect to temperature and humidity. At temperatures of about 72° Fahrenheit, a relative humidity of 60 percent is quite acceptable. As air temperatures rise, however, the relative humidity should increase if comfort is to be maintained. The human body utilizes the principle of evaporation in order to achieve a comfortable equilibrium. Since evaporation is much more accelerated when the humidity is low, spaces in school buildings requiring higher temperatures, such as drying rooms and special science laboratories, should be dehumidified, if necessry, to keep the humidity in the vicinity of 40 percent.

Ventilation Requirements

Until recently, schools in many areas have been overventilated. The old rule of thumb specifying that every classroom provide 30 cubic feet of fresh air per minute for each student is now being replaced by fresh-air requirements that are more reasonable. Where state codes govern the ventilation capacities of mechanical systems in public schools, as in Massachusetts and New York, the ventilation requirement in schools has been substantially reduced, because it is generally accepted among school planners that the 30 cubic foot per student requirement is excessive and unnecessary in the ordinary school classroom.

The purpose of ventilation in schools is twofold. It is well recognized of course, that a major function of ventilation systems in schools is the removal of body odors from classrooms and obnoxious odors from toilets, laboratories, and kitchens. It is not as generally recognized, however, that cooling is really one of the most important functions of a ventilating system. When it is realized that human beings generate about 250 Btu (British Thermal Units) per hour, the need to remove heat from classrooms assumes new proportions. For example, the amount of heat generated by 300 persons occupying a multipurpose room can be as high as 75,000 Btu per hour, which equals the heating capacity of many home furnaces. Once a given instructional space in a school is heated to the desired temperature, ventilation for cooling must be provided unless the heat loss of the room exceeds the amount of heat generated by its occupants. In some spaces in a school building, such as shower rooms, drying rooms, and basement storage areas, it is necessary to provide ventilation to remove excessive moisture, as well as heat.

It is fairly well agreed among school planners and designers that a ventilation system providing between 10 and 15 cubic feet of fresh air per student per minute is adequate for the dilution and removal of obnoxious substances from the air in classrooms.

Heating, Cooling, and Ventilation Systems

It is not within the scope of this book to discuss the engineering aspects of the various mechanical systems commonly installed in school or college buildings, but a certain amount of descriptive information regarding these systems may be helpful to educational planners. As a rule, heating, cooling, and ventilating are conceived as a single system rather than three isolated and independent systems. Each of these three types of mechanical equipment could operate quite satisfactorily as an independent unit from the standpoint of engineering design, but it would not be economical for it to do so, since many parts of an integrated system can be designed for dual or triple use. Basically, the mechanical system consists of a source of heat, a device for cooling, a method for ventilating (window, fans, closed systems), and a means of conveying heat from one point to another.

The design of mechanical equipment has reached a high level in terms of efficiency and automation. The choice of mechanical equipment is no longer as simple to make as it was only a quarter of a century ago. Closely tied to the selection of the equipment is the choice of a fuel for heating purposes. While wood and coal were the only common fuels not too long ago, today heat energy can be derived from oil, gas, electricity, the earth's surface, and the earth's atmosphere. And there is a strong likelihood that solar and nuclear energy will become available for heating purposes in the not-too-distant future. The debate regarding the best source of heat continues. The greatest competition for the heating dollar has been between gas and oil and, to a lesser extent, coal. Electricity is beginning to challenge oil and gas as a heat source, just as oil and gas made inroads on coal as a fuel in the past. The choice of fuel is primarily a matter of economics involving both the cost of the fuel and the operation of the equipment which converts the energy into heat. For example, while the cost of electricity per Btu of heat developed is generally higher than it is for other fuels, the system does not require the employment of a stationary engineer in a school, nor does it require the construction of a boiler room. It is the total cost over a period of time that should have a strong bearing on the selection of a fuel or form of energy. Again, the heating engineer can make an important contribution in this selection (See Chapter 9).

Heating.   There are at least five basic types of heating systems, ranging from the heat pump to forced hot air. Each system has features that are
best suited to a particular situation. For college campuses, a high-pressure
steam system is most likely to produce the best results, particularly when a
central power plant is provided. For high schools having a capacity of 1,000
or more pupils, both low-pressure steam or a hot-water system can be used
advantageously. In smaller educational facilities, it is possible to install
forced hot-air, hot-water, or low-pressure steam systems.

The two less commonly used heating systems are heat pumps and resistance-type electrical heating units. The heat pump basically operates on
the same principle as does a refrigerator. Heat is taken from one temperature zone and moved to another through the use of a compressor and a
special fluid. During the winter, for example, heat is taken from coils
placed in the ground or in the air and conveyed to the interior of a building. During the summer, the cycle is reversed. Heat is taken from the interior and conveyed to the coils. Thus, a heat pump serves as an air-conditioning unit in the summer and as a heater in the winter. Another promising type of heating system consists of individual resistance-type, electrically heated baseboard convectors. In some instances, electrically heated
coils are used to heat water contained in a radiator-type heat exchanger.
This method provides so-called "wet-type heat" electrically.

Radiant-heat systems merit serious consideration for use in educational facilities. The system consists of a network of piping that is usually
embedded in the floor or ceiling of the space being heated. When hot
water is pumped through the pipes, the entire floor or ceiling is heated.
Radiant-heated floors are ideal in kindergarten rooms where children
often sit on the floor. The major advantage in radiant heating is comfort.
Heat radiated from a large surface does not depend upon the intervening
air medium for its effectiveness. Thus, it is conceivable that persons occupying spaces heated by radiant panels may be quite comfortable when the
air temperature is several degrees below the usual 68° Fahrenheit.

Cooling.   General air-conditioning is receiving much attention in the
planning of educational facilities. The prospect that school and college
buildings may soon be used year-round strongly accentuates the need for
cooling as well as heating. For this reason, general air-conditioning is commonplace in modern college buildings. The central air-conditioning system
using ducts, which is found in home air-conditioning, is not very economical when entire sections of large buildings are involved. The most common method of cooling such buildings involves the use of chilled water. A
three-pipe system with air handlers and traps to collect the condensate
from the moisture in the air seems to be one of the most effective and economical methods of providing cooling in the various spaces in a school
building. The additional cost of the third pipe and provision for trapping
the condensate is nominal. If funds are not available to purchase cooling
equipment during construction, it might be prudent to plan for future air-

conditioning by installing the third pipe and specially designed air blowers at the time of construction. The cooling unit may be installed later.

The cooling unit is usually located on the roof of the building to be air-conditioned. Two basic types are currently available. The compressor type, which is mechanically driven, is quite common in both home and industrial units. A second type is a diffusion method that uses heat to produce cooling. In this instance, the same steam boilers are used to produce space heating in the winter and space cooling in the summer.

Ventilation methods. Many ingenious methods of ventilating buildings have been devised. In one instance, warm room air was drawn through the space between the top of the suspended ceiling and the bottom of the roof. Thus, the exhausted air provides a warm buffer between the ceiling and the roof. Another method simply exhausts the air through the corridors and ultimately out of the building.

Whenever air is exhausted, there is a corresponding intake of fresh air. In general, fresh air is preheated before it enters the classroom. The fresh air is often mixed with a certain proportion of recirculated air before it is introduced into the spaces to be ventilated. One frequently used method of providing a mixture of tempered fresh air and recirculated air is the unit ventilator. These units are generally installed along the outside wall of a building with a direct intake of fresh air from the outside. The unit can be adjusted to mix predetermined proportions of fresh and recirculated air. When unit ventilators are employed for air cooling, they can be set for the recirculation of air only. It should be pointed out, however, that a certain amount of fresh air is desirable even when the system is in the cooling cycle.

Special attention should be given to the ventilation of certain areas in school and college facilities. The gymnasium and natatorium are two facilities that merit special design considerations. The obvious problem in the natatorium, reduction of moisture, can be handled through an exhaust system which simply forces moisture outside of the building, or through a dehumidifier whose condensate can be fed back into the pool. Locker and shower areas also deserve special consideration with respect to ventilation. Air is sometimes exhausted through the locker so that odors from soiled clothing are exhausted to the outside. Excessive moisture is also a problem in these spaces. Kitchen areas require ventilation primarily for cooling but also to prevent food odors from permeating the school building. And finally, special ventilation is required in spaces where noxious fumes are likely to be present, such as a paint room, chemistry laboratory, biology laboratory, and the like.

Control of humidity. Although architects are currently not paying special attention to general humidity control in school buildings, both comfort and learning can be appreciably improved if *complete* air-conditioning is provided.

CHAPTER 12

Acoustical and Visual Environments

By and large, architects and engineers have given much thought to the comfort, health, and safety of school personnel and students, but their convenience and psychological needs have not always received the attention they merit. For example, one junior high school in central Illinois was designed so that on a cold wintry morning it took the custodian about 45 minutes to open dampers, close valves, and turn on switches located in different parts of the 1,500-pupil school. It would have been much more efficient if at least some of the equipment could have been operated by remote control and if the valves could have been located to permit more efficient use of the custodian's time.

The psychological well-being of faculty, staff, and students is also an important aspect of school planning. Architects have, to be sure, made a conscious effort to produce structures that are psychologically stimulating to the learner. However, much more can be done to plan schools that reflect the psychological needs of school personnel. School planners should also take into consideration design features that can reduce environmental causes of fatigue, such as background noises, glare, structural vibration due to mechanical equipment, and the like.

THE ACOUSTICAL ENVIRONMENT

A significant portion of the instructional function depends upon good hearing conditions. Consequently, it is just as imperative to design a school building with excellent hearing conditions as it is to plan instructional spaces with a first-rate visual environment.

Sound control in school buildings deals with two distinct types of acoustical problems. One is concerned with sound-conditioning within a given space, while the other is focused upon sound transmission from one space to another. Contrary to popular belief, sound-conditioning does not necessarily solve the sound transmission problem. The principles under-lying the solutions to one type of problem are quite different from those re-lated to the other.

Sound-Conditioning

Sound-conditioning refers to the treatment of interior surfaces of a given space to attain the desired reverberation time for the type of activity to be housed in the space. The persistence of sound within an enclosure after the source is shut off is called reverberation. Reverberation time, in the strictly technical sense, is defined as the time required for any given sound to de-crease in intensity to one-millionth of its initial value. Optimal reverbera-tion time is the recommended reverberation time for a specific space that is consistent with its volume and purpose. Table 12.1 contains a list of

TABLE 12.1   Optimal reverberation times for selected educational spaces[1]

Type of Space	Volume in Cu. Ft.	Optimal Reverberation Time for Schools in Sec.	Estimated Number of Additional Sabins Required for Each Space
Kindergarten	13,200	0.60	847
Elementary school classrooms	9,900	0.63	556
Secondary school classrooms	9,240	0.63	509
Science laboratories	13,320	0.57	835
Homemaking	12,936	0.67	727
Business machines rooms or laboratories	9,240	0.63	528
Art rooms	12,320	0.65	698
Music rooms	12,150	1.09	260
Library reading room	19,800	0.59	1,220
Auditoriums (for schools)	95,160	1.13	1,412
Gymnasiums	145,920	0.84	6,427
Cafeteria	55,000	0.76	2,202
Conference room	5,500	0.66	
Shops and corridors	Maximum treatment within practical limits		

[1]Basil Castaldi, "Sound Control in School Buildings," Ph.D. dissertation, Teachers College, Columbia University, 1952, pp. 72, 75.

spaces commonly found in schools, together with their optimum reverbera-tion times. Volume is a critical factor in dealing with reverberation times. The figures appearing in Column 3 should be adjusted in situations where the volume of the space in question differs from that appearing in Column 2. The correction for volume is made as follows:

(a) For volumes greater than those appearing in Column 2, *increase* the reverbation time in Column 3 by 0.0015 second for each 1,000 *cubic feet* of volume in excess of figures given in Column 2. (Round off figures to the closest 1,000 cubic feet in all computa-tions.)

(b) For spaces having volumes less than those shown is Column 2, decrease the reverberation time in Column 3 by 0.0015 second for each 1,000 *cubic feet* of volume of difference beween the space in question and the figure given in Column 2.

Amount of Acoustical Treatment Required

Column 4 in Table 12.1 contains the number of additional Sabins of absorp-tion that would be required in educational spaces of the type and volume indicated in Columns 1 and 2, respectively. The number of square feet of accoustical material needed is determined by dividing the number given in Column 4 by the noise reduction coefficient of the material to be used. The figures appearing in Table 12.1, Column 3, were computed by the Sabin formula in which the optimal reverberation times appearing in Column 2, Table 12.1 were substituted. In determining the additional absorption re-quired in each space, it was also necessary to estimate the number of Sa-bins of absorption present in a room before accoustical treatment. The amount of additional acoustical treatment required in any space should be computed by an acoustics expert. Good hearing conditions in classrooms are not guaranteed by the common rule of thumb used by architects—treating the entire ceiling. Acoustical treatment should be computed on a room-by-room basis, depending upon its use, its size, and its shape. For this reason, educators should insist that competent acoustical consultants participate in the planning of a school in the same manner as the heating consultant, the lighting consultant, and the structural consultant.

Distribution of Acoustical Materials Within an Enclosure

A number of studies[2] have clearly demonstrated that acoustical materials are not as effective when applied over an entire ceiling as when they are applied in other locations. In some classrooms in which the entire ceiling is treated, the amount of sound absorption is excessive, and the quality of hearing conditions is substantially reduced. In order to produce good hear-ing conditions, it is necessary to:

[2]*Ibid.*, pp. 102–109.

(a) Add sufficient sound-absorption materials to obtain optimum reverberation times within an enclosure, consistent with its function.

(b) Retain the sound-reflective properties of the ceiling to improve the transmission of sound from one end of the room to the other.

Only sufficient and necessary amounts of acoustical materials should be used, and they should be located at points of maximum sound pressure within a room. Applying such materials where sound pressure is at a minimum reduces the effectiveness of the materials and wastes money. For example, sometimes acoustical materials are installed in the concave depressions in corridor ceilings, using pan-type concrete construction. Acoustical improvement is insignificant under such an arrangement because very little of the noise generated in the corridor strikes the acoustical surface. Another example of inefficient use of acoustical materials is found in high gymnasiums where ceilings over 22 feet above the floor are fully treated with acoustical materials. Again, the acoustical results are quite disappointing. It would have been far better, in this case, to treat the upper walls of the gymnasium instead of the entire ceiling.

Acoustical materials should be located where the sound pressures are at a maximum, whenever, possible. Theoretically, high sound pressures from noises generated within a room exist in areas where large surfaces intersect at angles less than 180°. In conventional classrooms where the intersecting angles of large surfaces approximate 90°, the sound pressure is very high at such intersections. When sound strikes in the vicinity of the intersection of two walls in a room, it usually undergoes two reflections before returning to the interior of the room where it can reach a listener again. Thus, if two adjacent walls are treated, the intensity of the sound ultimately reflected back into the enclosure after at least two corner reflections is substantially weakened.

For the most effective distribution of acoustical materials and for improved hearing conditions, it is suggested that:

1. Acoustical materials be used at the edges of larger surfaces, where two surfaces meet, and at the corners.
2. No sound-absorbing materials be installed on the central areas of ceilings in classrooms or lecture rooms.
3. The edges of ceilings and upper edges of walls in classrooms be treated with acoustical materials.
4. Acoustical treatment *not* be massed on one wall or ceiling of an instructional space.
5. Sound materials be installed in panels or vertical strips about two feet wide in large rooms. Acoustical patches, uniformly but not symmetrically distributed, may also be used quite effectively in larger instructional spaces.

Noise Control in School Buildings

Thus far, we have been concerned with the judicious use of sound-absorbing materials to enhance a wanted sound produced in a room. The intelligibility of wanted sounds can also be significantly improved by the reduction of noise interference originating outside of the room.

Unwanted sounds may be controlled by:

1. Selecting a school site that is removed from sources of unwanted sounds.
2. Suppressing them at the source.
3. Isolating noisy areas from quiet ones.
4. *Acoustically* (not necessarily physically) isolating noisy equipment from the rest of the structure.
5. Designing partitions possessing the proper sound transmission loss.

In planning a school for sound control, it is also helpful to bear the following principles in mind.

1. It is uneconomical to reduce the intensity of a sound entering a room to a level much below the existing or normal noise level within the room.
2. For maximum economy, all sound paths into or out of a room should be insulated to about the same level against penetration of unwanted noises. For example, it is not justifiable to install a movable partition having a transmission loss of 40 decibels when the ceiling and duct work provide for, let us say, a 25-decibel transmission loss.
3. It is not economical to reduce the duct noises to a level much below that existing in the ordinary classroom environment.

The transmission of noise in any building is either air-borne or structure-borne. Sounds normally produced in a classroom or lecture hall are air-borne. Speech, music, and audiovisual equipment originate sounds that reach the listener through the intervening air. The containment of this type of sound within the enclosure where it originates is relatively simple. The introduction of massive, nonporous partitions and heavy acoustically stripped doors with double-glazed windows usually solves this problem. In most situations, it is not necessary to take all of these precautions to control air-borne noises. Oftentimes, a well-designed, massive, air-tight partition between two adjoining instructional spaces suffices.

The isolation of structure-borne noises, on the other hand, is a problem that is not easily solved once the building is constructed. Unless structure-borne noises are handled properly by the design of the building, noise control measures may be costly and only mildly effective. An excellent example of structure-borne sound in a school is that made by the impact of hard heels on concrete. Such sounds carry over long distances, without much attenuation through the structure of the building. Another source of structure-borne noises is the mechanical equipment in the building, such as fans, pumps, transformers, air-conditioners, steam pipes, and water systems. Isolation of noise sources from the structure is one of the best methods of coping with such structure-borne noises. Acoustical discontinuities in the structural design of a school also help to control structure-borne noises. Resilient platforms should be provided for noisy equipment, such as pianos, record players, drums, and other instruments resting on the floor. Stages, for example, are designed as resilient platforms in order to minimize structure-borne noises.

Noise from Ventilating Systems

A common source of unwanted noise is the ventilating system, which may give rise to motor noises, turbulent air at grille openings and within ducts, and "cross-talk." None of these sources of noise presents a technological problem. The science of ventilation is so advanced that none of these acoustical deficiencies need be tolerated in a well-designed school. "Crosstalk" refers to the transmission of sounds from one space to another through the ventilating ducts. This shortcoming can be readily corrected by installing a sufficient amount of duct liner inside ducts.

Acoustical Partitions

Walls separating one instructional space from another should be acoustically designed so that noise generated in one space does not interfere with the activities in the adjoining instructional spaces. With the advent of many types of movable partitions, it becomes of paramount importance that the partition selected possess at least the minimum required acoustical properties. It is also essential that permanent or destructible partitions be designed with sufficient acoustical transmission loss to satisfy the conditions under which they are to be utilized.

The following rule of thumb may be helpful in the design or selection of a partition separating instructional spaces: "The transmission loss in decibels of any partition should be equal to ten plus the difference between the outside noise level and the acceptable background noise for the space in question."[3] Stated in mathematical terms,

[3]*Ibid.*, p. 113.

$$T.L. = 10 + (O_{db} - B_{db})$$

where $T.L.$ = minimum transmission loss of the desired partition
         O = noise level in decibels on the outside of the partition
         B = noise level in decibels of background noises within the
         space to be enclosed

The application of this formula, however, should be made by an acoustical consultant.

Table 12.2 may be of some assistance in guiding educational planners in the choice of partitions to be used between various types of instructional spaces.[4] In applying these figures, care should be taken that other paths of sound transmission have transmission losses equal to or greater than the figures given in the table. Other paths include ceilings, ducts, windows, and doors.

Construction of partitions possessing transmission losses of about 60 decibels is costly. Such walls can usually be avoided in the planning of school buildings simply by removing the exceptionally noisy spaces from

TABLE 12.2   Minimum sound transmission losses (in decibels) between several types of instructional spaces

	Auditorium	Music Teaching Room	Office	Study Area	Classroom or Lecture Hall
Classroom or lecture room	45–55	45–55	35–45	35–45	35–45
Study hall	X	45–55	35–45	35–45	35–45
Office	X	45–55	35–45	35–45	35–45
Vocal music teaching room	X	50–65	35–45	45–55	45–55
Corridors	35–45	35–45	X	X	25–35
Shop	45–60	45–60	X	X	35–50
Gymnasium	45–60	45–60	X	X	35–50
Cafeteria	45–60	45–60	X	X	35–50
Toilet	45–55	45–55	X	X	35–45
Mechanical equipment room	45–55	45–55	X	X	35–45
Business machines room or laboratory	X	X	35–50	X	X
Band room	50–65	50–65	X	X	40–55

[4]Ibid., p. 132.

the quiet zones. Only in very rare cases, therefore, will it become necessary to resort to the design of partitions having transmission losses in excess
of 45 decibels.

Table 12.3 contains the transmission loss range for various types of
wall construction.[5]

Carpeting as a Substitute for Other Acoustical Materials

The use of carpeting as an acoustical material in school buildings is receiving increased attention by both educators and architects. At the present
time, the major deterrent to the widespread acceptance of carpeting in
school buildings is the luxury image associated with in the past. Resistance
to the use of carpeting in school has all but disappeared. Following World
War II manufacturers of carpeting and the Educational Facilities Laboratories in New York made a number of studies showing that due to lower
maintenance the payback period for carpeting was less than twelve years.
The case for carpeting based upon the initial cost is no longer crucial due to

TABLE 12.3   Sound transmission loss of selected types of wall construction

Type of Construction	Average Transmission Loss in Decibels
A. 4″ hollow pumice cement block, no plaster on faces	12
B. Single sheet ¼″ plywood	22
C. Single sheet ½″ fiberboard	22
D. Single sheet ⅛″ glass	28
E. Double wall, ¼″ fiberboard faces on 2×2-inch wood studs	28
F. Heavy wooden door, 2½″ thick; rubber gaskets, felt strip at bottom	28
G. Single sheet ¼″ plate glass	33
H. Same as "A" above with ½″ of gypsum plaster on one side only	33
I. Same as "A" with ½″ gypsum plaster on both sides	38
J. ¾″ plaster board on one side of 2×4-inch studs	38
K. 4″ structural clay tile core of 4″ hollow cinder block with ⅝″ plaster on both sides	42
L. 2×4 wood studs, ½″ gypsum plaster faces on ⅜″ gypsum lath, special nailing or resilient clip on plaster lath	42
M. 4″ reinforced concrete wall	48
N. 8″ brick walls, ½″ gypsum plaster faces	52

[5]Ibid., pp. 133–134.

new methods of carpet installation that make it possible to replace finished wood or tile flooring with carpeting. Furthermore, with the everchanging cost of materials, cost predictions become meaningless. The advice offered in the *Guide for Planning Educational Facilities* regarding carpeting is timely and sound. The guide suggests a logical approach, " . . . carpeting should be evaluated on the same basis as other floor coverings—initial cost, upkeep, and ability to do the job."[6]

The use of carpeting in spaces such as classrooms, seminar rooms, corridors, and libraries involves several considerations related to function,[7] such as the need to:

1. Eliminate cold floors and conserve energy.
2. Reduce the severity of injuries due to falls.
3. Eliminate floor generated noises due to the movement of chairs, desks, and the like.
4. Absorb noises and improve the accoustical environment.
5. Create an atmosphere that is quiet, a esthetically pleasing, and conductive to effective learning.

THE VISUAL ENVIRONMENT

In the past, any discussion of visual conditions in school buildings was confined for the most part to artificial and natural lighting. In fact, until recently, natural lighting has been considered the primary source of illumination in school buildings. For this reason, the maximum width of classrooms has been limited to about 22 feet. Since the light reaching the innermost part of a room enters through the upper portions of the windows, the width of classrooms has been determined to a large extent by the height of classroom ceilings. The old rule of thumb held that the width of a classroom should not exceed twice the distance from the floor to the top of the glass portion of a window plus one foot. Recently, the emphasis has shifted from natural to artificial illumination, which no longer fixes the width of any space in which adequate lighting is desired.

Visual environment is a much broader concept than school lighting, however. School planners must be concerned with natural and artificial lighting, with brightness differences, reflection coefficients, fenestration, and interior decoration. All of these factors affect the visual characteristics of a given space and the quality of the seeing conditions in school buildings. Every instructional area in school building should posses an environment that promotes the visual health of its occupants.

[6]*Guide for Planning Educational Facilities* (Columbus, Ohio: Council of Educational Facility Planners, 1969), p. 125.
[7]*Guide for Planning Facilities* (Columbus, Ohio: Council of Educational Facility Planners, 1976), pp. 8–9.

Illumination Levels in Educational Spaces

The intensity of the illumination in any classroom is crucial to good seeing conditions, and the distribution of the light within the enclosure should be uniform and free from glare. The intensity of illumination required in school buildings depends upon the function of each type of teaching area and can vary widely from one to the other.

There is still no optimum value of light intensity that can be recommended for each space. The foot-candle values given below refer to minimum required levels of illumination. The unit foot-candle is defined as the intensity of light striking a surface at a distance of one foot from a standard candle. During the early part of this century, it was believed that because the human eye is so extremely adaptable, light intensities ranging from 15 to 20 foot-candles were acceptable levels of illumination. In modern school design, however, the illumination levels have increased substantially. The accepted ranges of reasonable levels of illumination are shown in Table 12.4. When energy was abundant and inexpensive, there was a gradual trend toward raising the levels of intensity of illumination by substantial amounts. Research is still inconclusive regarding the absolute value of the level of illumination that should be maintained in various instructional spaces. Blackwell's work at the University of Michigan provided new insights on the problem of light intensity.[8]

In his research, Blackwell analyzed thirty-one samples of handwriting taken from a sixth grade class in Toronto, Canada. In order to obtain a 90 percent visual efficiency, the intensity of illumination was varied from one foot-candle to over eighty foot-candles, depending on the writing samples. The study did not establish whether or not high intensities were

TABLE 12.4 Ranges of illumination recommended for various educational areas.

Type of Space	Foot-Candles of Illumination Required
Classrooms, study halls, libraries, offices, art rooms, shops, and laboratories	30–40
Special education rooms, drafting rooms, typing rooms, and sewing rooms	50–70
Physical education, reception rooms	20–25
General service rooms, such as auditoriums, cafeterias, locker rooms, rest rooms, and stairways	15–25
Open corridors and storerooms	10–20

[8]Richard H. Blackwell, "Development and Use of Quantitative Method for Specifications of Interior Illumination Levels on the Basis of Performance Data," *Illuminating Engineer*, 54 (June 1959), p. 317.

absolutely necessary to protect the visual health of the students. It did, however, show that visual efficiency dropped below the 90 percent level for more than 40 percent of the class when the average intensity was reduced to below sixty-three foot-candles. It is not unreasonable to assume that pupils would not be asked to perform tasks as difficult as those included in the experiment for more than fifteen minutes per day at the elementary school level. In view of the need to conserve energy (See Chapter 9), it is difficult to justify raising the intensity of illumination to the sixty foot-candle level in all instructional spaces for the relatively small gain in visual effectiveness.

Brightness ratios.   Acceptable visual environments depend upon the intensity of the illumination and upon the brightness differences existing in any given space. An intolerable visual environment may be created in a room that possesses a high intensity of illumination, unless brightness ratios are maintained within acceptable limits. Brightness ratios are determined by comparing the brightness of the visual task with that of the surrounding field of vision. On the basis of the brightness goals adopted by the National Council on Schoolhouse Construction[9] for a total environment where critical seeing is necessary, the following criteria are suggested:

(a) The foot lambert brightness of any surface viewed from any normal standing or sitting position in the schoolroom should not exceed ten times the foot lambert brightness of the poorest-lighted task in the room.

(b) The foot lambert brightness of any surface viewed from any standing or sitting position in the schoolroom should not be less than one-third the foot lambert brightness of the poorest-lighted task in the room.

(c) The foot lambert brightness of any surface immediately adjacent to the task should not exceed the brightness of the task and should be at least one-third its brightness.

(d) The brightness difference between adjoining surfaces should be reduced to a minimum.

(e) The brightness goals stated above assume a lighting system that provides from 30 to 50 foot-candles on the poorest-lighted task. As foot-candle levels are increased, sources of high brightness should be controlled to approach more nearly the brightness of the task. The extent of the area of the surface producing the brightness has a measurable effect upon visual comfort. Generally, small areas of either extremes of brightness are less noticeable than are large areas of the same brightness.

[9]National Council on Schoolhouse Construction, *Guide for Planning School Plants* (East Lansing: Michigan State University, 1964), p. 130.

(f) Light distribution from any source should be such that direct and specular glare are eliminated for the observer to the greatest possible degree.

(g) These objectives or goals should be achieved without the loss of a cheerful, friendly, and aesthetically pleasant classroom environment or of a balanced and acceptable thermal and auditory environment.

In planning school buildings these goals are achieved through the proper selection of surface textures and color, though a wise choice of luminaries, and through the design of the building itself. Simply stated, these goals demand that normally dark areas be made brighter and that sources of high brightness be reduced or controlled. More specifically:

1. Floors should be as light in color as possible. Floor surfaces should possess light reflection coefficients ranging between 30 and 40 percent.

2. Walls, including the wainscoting, should be quite reflective. The light reflection coefficient of walls should be greater than 60 percent.

3. Ceilings should diffuse as much light as possible. Reflection factors of over 90 percent are suggested for soffits and ceilings.

4. Chalkboards should be as light in color as possible. Since large areas of black chalkboards absorb a considerable amount of light, green or beige chalkboards are preferred. When perfected, whiteboards are ideal.

5. Furniture surfaces, such as desk tops and chairs, should posses a light-reflecting factor of about 40 percent.

6. Adjoining surfaces should be finished in colors that create a minimum brightness difference. For example, dark trim around windows violates criterion (d) because it presents too great a contrast to the brightness of the light entering through the window. Another violation of this principle is committed when door trims are painted or stained in dark colors in rooms with pastel-colored walls.

7. High brightness should be controlled electronically, mechanically, or architecturally. The common sources of high brightness are glare from the sky or snow cover, direct or reflected sunlight, and artificial light from incandescent bulbs or fluorescent tubes. Lighting engineers and architects have developed many very effective solutions to the problem of glare. Educators and school plant planners should insist that the architect and the lighting engineer design the building with lighting fixtures and light controls that will satisfy both the specific requirements of illumination in a given space and the lighting goals described in the preceding paragraph. It is not within the scope of this book to discuss luminaries and the light distribution and glare characteristics of the various fixtures. Suffice it to say, however, that luminous ceilings merit serious consideration where high-quality general illumination for instructional spaces is required. Suspended light fixtures of both the fluorescent and incandescent type are also quite satisfactory, provided they illuminate both the ceilings and the floors, and

provided that they are properly spaced and installed at a sufficient distance below the ceiling. There are instances where concentric ring-type incandescent fixtures, for example, have been installed so close to the ceiling that they create a series of light and dark spots on the ceiling surface. The same undesirable condition results when certain fluorescent fixtures are attached directly to the ceiling.

Fluorescent lighting.   In the past, there has been some controversy over whether or not to install fluorescent-type fixtures in school buildings. Questions were often raised concerning possible health hazards associated with fluorescent-type illumination. It has been fairly well established, however, that the light source, whether it be sunlight, incandescent light, or fluorescent light, has no deleterious effect on the eyes of human beings, provided it satisfies the light goals described earlier. The choice of type of illumination, therefore, cannot be made on the basis of student health. From the standpoint of long-range economy, fluorescent lighting is demonstrably cheaper than incandescent fixtures. While the initial cost of fluorescent fixtures is substantially higher than that of incandescent lighting, the amount of light produced per kilowatt of power is almost 50 percent greater for fluorescent-type fixtures. One school district in the Boston area made careful cost studies of the two fixtures and found that within seven years the savings in the cost of power compensated for the initial cost and maintenance of fluorescent fixtures. As energy costs increase, the payback period decreases accordingly.

Control of natural light.   Bothersome natural light appears in the guise of snow glare, sky glare, and direct sunlight. Oftentimes, windows in instructional spaces facing north have not been equipped with light controls on the assumption that direct sunlight does not enter from this direction. True, it does not, but the visual environment in such a space leaves much to be desired. The light reaching the occupants of such a space from the sky is bright enough to cause headaches.

Natural light can be controlled in many instances by the appropriate design of the building itself. Overhangs, horizontal or vertical louvres, and externally mounted slats or venetian blinds help to control natural light. Also, natural light can be controlled effectively by the judicious use of fenestration. Vision strips along the exterior walls of a building require a minimum of internal light control and satisfy the psychological needs of the pupils with respect to an environment that is conducive to learning.

The control of natural light within an instructional space may be achieved through the use of some type of window covering designed to shield the students from glare or direct sunlight. The most common device for controlling natural light is the translucent shade on spring-loaded rollers. In this case, separate opaque shades with special side channels are drawn over the translucent shades to insure complete darkening of teaching spaces when motion picture projectors are used. With the increased use of the rear projection screen and television, the traditional "blackout" is no longer necessary. "Brownouts" are preferred because students can take notes during audiovisual presentations. Venetian blinds are considered the best devices for internally controlling light in a classroom. They are, however, considerably more difficult to maintain than drapes, curtains, or reticulated light screens.

Types of Natural Lighting

The window wall. Natural light may be introduced into an educational space in various ways. The most common method, of course, is the ordinary window. Architects have employed a wide variety of window arrangements in bringing natural light into the classroom. They have designed instructional spaces with window walls containing panes which extend from floor to ceiling over most of an outside wall. Their primary objective in this case is to create the pleasant and desirable feeling of transplanting part of the out-of-doors into the classroom.

The windowless wall. In contrast is the windowless wall which permits no outside light to enter an instructional area. The major argument favoring the use of windowless classrooms stems from the need to reduce the amount of heat gain within an enclosure and hence to reduce the load associated with air cooling on hot days. Some architects have suggested that windowless walls tend to reduce student distractions caused by the outside world. On the other hand, many educators argue that students should not be isolated from the rest of the world while in school. They also maintain that it is psychologically desirable for the learner to be distracted once in a while during the learning process. The argument has also been posed that students should be able to look at distant objects from time to time in order to relax the muscles controlling the focusing mechanism of the eye. This eye accommodation cannot be made in a windowless classroom of limited dimensions. And finally, the opponents of the windowless classroom argue that a person does not feel comfortable if he is confined to a windowless area for long periods of time. Obviously, proof is still needed to substantiate the psychological arguments posed both for and against the windowless classroom. Suffice it to say at this point that tradition and persistence of habit would dictate that visual contact with the outside world be maintained as part of the visual environment of the modern classroom.

The limited window wall. There are several window arrangements that lie somewhere between the window wall and the windowless classroom. The most promising, at this time, seems to be the vision strip along most of the outside wall of a classroom. The height of the window sill, in this case, would be about 6 inches below the eye level of seated pupils and the top of the vision strip would be located about 6 inches above the eye level of the teacher in standing position. Another scheme for admitting a limited amount of natural light into the classroom involves the use of floor-to-ceiling slits. These slits may be located near each end of the room. The surface between the two groups of slits is usually a large opaque wall. This pattern of fenestration allows the occupants to have some visual contact with the weather and the outside world. The primary purpose of this window design is to keep the amount of heat gain within the classroom at a minimum. Another less important but significant advantage of the slit pattern is the ease with which an instructional space can be "browned out" for audiovisual presentations.

Sky domes.   The unhappy experiences associated with skylights in the past have strongly prejudiced members of boards of education and boards of trustees against the introduction of top lighting in educational facilities. It is true, of course, that skylights installed in the past presented a serious problem because of water leakage, maintenance difficulties, and cold air entering directly below them.

Modern sky domes present an entirely different and exciting picture. The problem of leakage has been solved completely. If sky domes are installed according to the manufacturer's instructions, no water leakage whatever should occur. Sky domes are generally constructed of clear or frosted plastic. Modern sky domes are so advanced in design that condensation flows through weep holes that conduct the condensate away from the dome where it will evaporate harmlessly into the room. There is also an electrical heating element attached to the underside of the sky dome that prevents the downdraft of cold air into the classroom.

The visual and psychological effect of the sky dome is dramatic. Natural light floods the educational spaces and creates a feeling of psychological warmth and visual comfort. There is a sense of being outside, particularly when clear plastic domes are employed. On the other hand, unless frosted plastic is used to diffuse the incoming sunlight, glare can be quite annoying and uncomfortable. Fortunately, there are a number of devices that effectively control the sky dome glare and also make it possible to darken the room completely for audiovisual purposes (see Chapter 9).

CHAPTER 13

Planning Elementary and Middle Schools

It is becoming increasingly difficult to classify schools, particularly at the elementary level. At one time, there were basically two types of common schools, the grammar school, Grades 1 through 8, and the high school, Grades 9 through 12. Then, after World War I, the junior high school, serving Grades 7 through 9, emerged as an answer to the educational needs of the 1920s. As a result, three types of schools came into being. The school serving pupils from kindergarten or Grade 1 to Grade 6 became known as the elementary school. The school attended by pupils in Grades 7 through 9 became the junior high school. And the school housing Grades 10 through 12 became the senior high school. These grade-level organizations are by no means universal. In many parts of the United States, the so-called 8–4 (eight-grade grammar school and four-year high school) organization still persists. In Illinois, there are even separate elementary (1–8) and high school (four-year) districts in operation in the same geographical area. In recent years, another type of school has appeared—the middle school, which usually serves Grades 5 through 8. Where a middle school is adopted, former elementary schools become neighborhood units that serve kindergarten through Grade 4, and the high school houses pupils in Grades 9 through 12. The case has yet to be made as to which grade organization is best. It does not matter what one calls a school. What really counts is the quality of education the pupil receives there.

The author has seen both superior and mediocre instruction in all the types of schools listed above. An excellent educational program can be provided under any of the organizations mentioned. The organization for a given school district should be one in which the existing usable school facilities can best serve the physical requirements of the desired educational program. Educators may honestly favor one type of organization over another on the basis of experience, personal preference, or conviction. There is to date, however, no documented evidence that strongly favors one type of grade organization over another. Fundamentally, it is believed that instructional effectiveness depends far more on the interaction between pupils and teachers than it does upon the number of grade levels housed in a given building. Until the educational psychologists can uncover evidence demonstrating that a higher quality of learning occurs under a given grade organization, school plant planners should feel free to recommend the grade organization that best suits the needs of the desired educational program of a school district from the standpoint of cost, economy, pupil convenience, and safety.

For the purposes of this discussion, elementary schools refer to school buildings that are designed to house pupils under the age of 13, regardless of the grade organization. Under this definition, the elementary school building must provide for pupils at various stages of physical and mental development. School planners should be aware of these variations when they plan elementary school buildings. Table 13.1 indicates the magnitude of the differences among pupils that are likely to attend elementary schools. From Table 13.1 it is clear that the elementary school must be quite versatile if it is to satisfy the diverse needs of its occupants. In height, children will range from about 46 inches to almost 6 feet. In weight, they will range from a scant 27 pounds in kindergarten to a hefty 150 pounds in Grade 6. Most seat heights in kindergarten will be 10, 11, or 12 inches above the floor, while seat heights in Grade 6 will be in the 13-, 14-, 15-, and 16-inch range. These differences in physical characteristics are accompanied by different levels of intellectual and social development among the pupils. The range of differences among individual pupils does not seem to present any problems where the self-contained classroom is used,

TABLE 13.1   Range of physical differences between pupils in selected grades

Characteristic	Kindergarten	Grade 3	Grade 6
Weight in pounds	46.1	68	156
Height (with shoes) in inches	45	53	70
Eye height standing—above floor (inches)	35	49	65
Shoulder height standing—above floor	30.6	42.5	58
Seat height (inches) above floor	9.8	14.0	18.8
Eye height seated—above floor (inches)	26.6	31.3	49.6
Elbow height seated (above floor)	13.5	18.6	29.6

Source: *Children's Body Measurements* (U.S. Department of Health, Education and Welfare).

that is, where a group of pupils of a given age or intellectual level are taught in a single room by one teacher.

Until recently, the self-contained classroom was considered quite adequate for instruction at the elementary level, but educators are beginning to doubt the sanctity of this concept. The elementary school program is undergoing an orderly and systematic transformation. For this reason, school planners should give greater emphasis to the likely shape of the elementary school of tomorrow than to the pseudo-stable instructional practices of today.

THE CONTEMPORARY ELEMENTARY SCHOOL

A number of emerging concepts, which are discussed in the next section, are altering the conventional pattern of elementary schools. In some situations, the administrative organization seems to have changed but the traditional practices still prevail. For example, a school district recently constructed a middle school. Actually, it was a middle school in name only. Grades 5 and 6 were still being taught in the same manner as they were in the former sixth-grade elementary school, and pupils in Grades 7 and 8 in the new middle school were being treated as they were in the junior high school with almost complete departmentalization. The lower grades, under this arrangement, did not reap many of the benefits claimed for the middle school, and the upper grades experienced none of the significant educational changes predicted by the proponents of the middle school during the referendum that authorized construction of the school.

PRACTICES AND CONCEPTS

The Multipurpose Self-Contained Classroom

Under the traditional concept of elementary school education, between twenty-five and thirty pupils in one grade are assigned to a single room and a single teacher for all of the experiences they will undergo at that grade level. In some of the more advanced schools, supervisors of science, mathematics, and social sciences regularly meet with the teachers in order to assist them with their work. More often the regular teacher in the self-contained classroom receives assistance and advice in the areas of music and art. Generally, pupils assigned to single classrooms in a conventional school use a common multipurpose room for physical education and indoor recreation.

Groupings within the regular classroom.   Even in the traditional self-contained classroom, there is provision for grouping. First of all, if there are two or more classrooms per grade, some school districts assign pupils of high learning ability to one room, average pupils to another, and, possibly, slow learners to a third, if three sections per grade are needed.

Once the pupils are grouped in classrooms, the teacher in each classroom subdivides the pupils into two or three other groups. Two methods are generally employed. The teacher may organize three permanent groups according to ability, in which case each group stays together regardless of the subject being taught. Or the teacher may organize three levels of instruction for each major area of teaching and assign pupils to each level according to their ability in that area. For example, a pupil could be a member of the top group in reading, the middle level in science, and the lowest group in arithmetic. This provides more effectively for individual pupil differences than the first method. Both groupings, however, are aimed at meeting the individual needs of the pupils.

Functional aspects of the self-contained classroom. Under the aforementioned pupil grouping, the teacher works very closely with about ten pupils at a time. When a group of about ten pupils is being instructed by the teacher, the other twenty or so are studying, reading, drawing, or doing independent work.

Many activities take place within the conventional elementary classroom. Individual or group pupil projects are conducted in science, social studies, or language in one part of the room. Report preparation and small-group work may be taking place in another. Construction of simple instructional projects is one part of the learning experience of the pupil. These projects may involve making plaster of paris topographical maps, use of simple machines and levers, cutting mathematical shapes out of cardboard to demonstrate the concepts of area and volume, using water to show the relationship of the volume of cubes and spheres, and work with musical strings.

To summarize, the self-contained classroom must be highly versatile and easily adaptable to a multitude of purposes. And it must accommodate several activities simultaneously without excessive interference between them.

Application of Promising Concepts

Elementary school education is approaching the threshold of a golden era. New concepts are challenging time-honored traditional practices. Multipurpose teaching aids are making a significant impact upon the quality of modern education through the enrichment of pupil experiences in the classroom. Newly developed techniques aimed at large-group instruction, effective use of electronic teaching aids, and cooperative instructional practices among groups of teachers are being tested. A more sympathetic attitude toward democratic administration on the part of principals and supervisors is also changing the character of the elementary school. Several promising concepts and practices were discussed in Chapter 3. A few of them are particularly suitable for elementary schools. When the administration and staff are receptive to new ideas, the discussion of innovative practices can prove to be quite stimulating for many of the participants. Such discussions often produce dramatic improvements in the school curriculum. Where this adventurous spirit exists among the school staff, the administrators, and generally in the community, the introduction of new concepts that are studied carefully and implemented wisely and intelligently often generates a deep sense of pride within the community.

It is suggested that the concepts and practices described in Chapter 3 be reviewed and seriously considered in the planning of an elementary school. Special attention should be given to team teaching, the nongraded school, variable class size, and the epideikic (inquiry-demonstration) concept. The planners of elementary schools that are futuristic in concept should also review and consider other potentially sound and promising practices and concepts that may be in the developmental or emergent stage when an elementary school facility is being planned.

PLANNING CONTEMPORARY ELEMENTARY SCHOOLS

At some point in the planning of a school facility, architects and school planners must become concerned with the physical requirements, such as how many spaces are needed, how large they should be, and where they should be located in relation to each other. This type of information is contained in this section. Also, review Chapter 9 for energy conservation measures.

The school discussed in this section is based upon the self-contained classroom concept, which is currently popular throughout the United States. The conventional elementary school is a proven concept which should not be viewed as obsolete or inferior in any way. The self-contained classroom has had a long history of success and, it might be added, many of the leaders of today are either the product of the self-contained classroom or the one-room school which is a single classroom housing eight grades under the guidance of one teacher. It should be pointed out that the promise of the concepts discussed in the preceding section has yet to be validated through research findings. These new concepts have much in their favor and may become universally accepted in the not-too-distant future. For this reason, whenever a traditional school is being planned, it should be designed with the new concepts clearly in mind so that changes in the building can be made at a reasonable cost.

The Site

The minimum size of an elementary school site should be at least 5 acres plus one acre per 100 pupils of *ultimate* (includes future additions to the school) enrollment. In growing urban and suburban areas, the board of education should pinpoint the location of future school sites so that sufficient acreage is available when and where it is needed.

Building Height

A single-story building is preferred at the elementary school level. Some of the more advanced elementary schools, for example, have direct access from the classroom to the out-of-doors where an outside classroom is available to the pupils during good weather. Also, the outside classroom, separated from other outside classrooms by shrubbery, serves as a laboratory in the study of plants, solar heat, and weather. From the standpoint of building cost, there is no significant difference in cost per square foot of usable area between the single- and multiple-story school.

In cases where land is at a premium, a two-story building is preferable. Furthermore, it is desirable to locate the first floor about 10 or 12 feet above the ground when the site is small. In this case, the building would be supported by columns and the pupils would have a large covered area under the building for recreational purposes. "The school on stilts," so to speak, makes it possible for pupils to utilize almost the entire area of a small school site.

Maximum Size of School

There is, to date, no research that specifies a maximum or optimum size for an elementary school. It is generally accepted, however, that an elementary school of optimum size is one with about fifteen teachers. The maximum size is considered to be about three rooms per grade, including kindergarten, or approximately twenty or twenty-one teachers. In cities, where the density of pupils is extremely high, the maximum size of an elementary school will necessarily be considerably higher than twenty-one teachers. In these situations however, it is strongly suggested that two or three schools within the same school be planned. For example, if a school of fifty classrooms is needed in a given area, three separate and distinct administrative units should be provided. When such a school is being designed, space should be provided for three principals, three secretaries, three teachers' rooms, etc.

Required Spaces

Table 13.2 includes specific information about spaces commonly found in elementary schools.

TABLE 13.2   Types, number, and sizes of spaces in an elementary school

Type of Space	Number Needed	Normal Class Size	Suggested Net Area in Sq. Ft.
Kindergarten	1 per 20 pupils	20	1,000–1,200
Kindergarten storage, wardrobe, toilets	1 per room		300–350
Classrooms	1 per 25 pupils	25	850–900
Library	1 per 15 or fewer teachers		900–1,000
Remedial room	1 per 5 teachers	6–10	350–450
Special class-rooms (retarded, gifted)	as needed	12–15	900–1,000
Storage for special classroom	1 per special class-room		150–200
Auditorium	a. 1 separate unit for schools with more than 21 teachers. Capacity: 50% enrollment b. Combined with cafeteria in schools having 15–21 teachers c. Multipurpose rooms in schools having fewer than 15 teachers		8 sq. ft. per person
Stage			600–800
Physical education	1 full-time use unit per 15 teachers		2,400–2,800
Storage for physical education	1 per P.E. unit		400–450
Cafeteria (1) Dining	a. one unit having capacity of ⅓ enroll-ment b. Combined with auditorium in schools of 15–21 teachers		10–12 per diner

(CONTINUED)

TABLE 13.2 (CONTINUED)

Type of Space	Number Needed	Normal Class Size	Suggested Net Area in Sq. Ft.
	c. For smaller schools, combined also with physical education and assembly hall		
(2) Kitchen	1 per cafeteria dining		1½ per meal
(3) Food storage	1 per cafeteria dining		½ per meal
(4) Serving area	2 per dining area		0.8 per diner
Principal's office	1 per 21 or fewer teachers		200–250
Outer-office clerk additional clerk	1 per school		250–300
	1 for schools between 15–21 teachers		100–150
Health suite	1 per school		500–550
Teachers' workroom and lounge	1 per school for 15 or fewer teachers		500–600
Custodial office-work-shop	1 per school		500–550
Storage of outdoor maintenance equipment and instructional equipment	1 per school		300–350
Central storage of instructional materials	1 or 2 per school		0.8–1 per pupil
Book storage near classrooms	1 per wing and/or floor		80–100
Receiving rooms—incinerator	1 per school		150–200

Space Relationships

In the elementary school, with its self-contained classrooms and common spaces for indoor recreation, assembly, and hot lunch, the problem of space relationships is not over-complicated. Figure 13.1 suggests a desirable arrangement of spaces in an elementary school. The degree of relationship is indicated by the number of lines between any two spaces. No lines between them signifies that no close relationship exists. The architect, in this case, may locate the space or cluster of spaces where they best fit into the plan. One line between two spaces denotes a weak relationship. The two spaces, for example, could be located on the same floor or wing. Two lines between any two spaces or groups of spaces means that there is a close relationship and that such spaces could be located across the corridor from each other. Three lines between two spaces denotes a close relationship, in which case they should be contiguous.

Special Design Features

A school planning committee routinely explores many special ideas in planning an elementary school. A few of these special features are suggested in this selection.

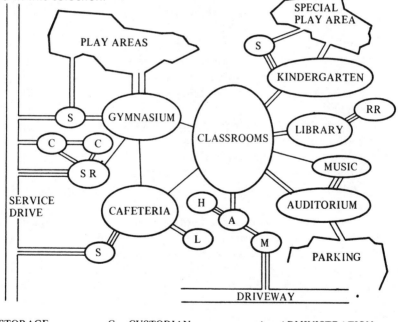

S – STORAGE	C – CUSTODIAN	A – ADMINISTRATION
S R – STORAGE AND	L – TEACHERS' LOUNGE	M – MAIN ENTRANCE
RECEIVING	H – HEALTH	RR – REMEDIAL READING

FIGURE 13.1   Schematic Diagram Showing Desirable Space Relationships In Elementary Schools.

1. *Television reception.* Today every classroom and the multipurpose room as well should be equipped to receive a good television signal. In schools located near broadcasting stations, the problem is relatively simple to solve if the building does not have a steel framework. The use of "rabbit ear" antennae is adequate. In the majority of schools, however, the television signal is relatively weak and a master antenna system is required. It is suggested that the master antenna receiving system be installed with plugs in each classroom and in other spaces appropriate for the reception of open-circuit television broadcasts when the school is constructed. The excuse that "we have the conduit" is not valid when, for an additional cost of just a few dollars per room, the entire reception system could be installed at the time of construction.

2. *Acoustical environment.* The topic of acoustics has been covered in detail in Chapter 12. Suffice it to say, at this point, that a suspended acoustical ceiling should be considered in the planning of elementary schools. The space above the tiles can be used for many purposes, such as exhausting warm air from the room, so that a blanket of warm air covers the classroom ceiling in winter. Above a suspended ceiling there is also adequate space for installing pipes, cables, and wires at a later date. Furthermore, such a ceiling is not very costly. It provides a well-controlled acoustical environment for classrooms where pupils may learn with fewer acoustical distractions and where teachers may teach with less fatigue.

3. *Visual surroundings.* The proper use of color is essential in any elementary school. Color can be employed to stimulate learning in the classroom, and its psychological effect upon the learners should be explored in planning the interior decoration of elementary schools. Age of the pupils, orientation of the classroom, and its purpose are all important in this regard.

4. *Health room.* The health room is frequently located near the administrative offices without much regard to its function. In small elementary schools where a nurse is not on duty even part-time, the health room should be adjacent to the office of the principal so that either the principal or a staff member can help or supervise a sick child simply by opening an intervening door.

The first-aid function should not be ignored. A general-use lavatory is not adequate for this purpose. It is suggested that a deep sink with gooseneck be installed in the health room area. Ordinary lavatories may be included in the toilet rooms, which should be adjacent to the health room. A small room, separate but adjoining the examination room in the health suite, should be provided for children who become ill during the school day.

5. *The elementary school library.* A library that is not staffed is really nothing more than a book storage room. As such, it does not serve the purpose of a library. Libraries should be provided in elementary school buildings and they should be staffed by competent persons on at least a half-

time basis. In surveying school districts, the writer has often been somewhat disillusioned when the superintendent of schools had to unlock the library room before it could be entered while school was in session. A library is essential in an elementary school, and groups of pupils should be allowed to use it under the guidance of the librarian. A rotating collection of library materials can be furnished to the classrooms through the use of properly designed library displays on casters. Such carts are loaded in the library and rolled into the classrooms where they may remain for a few days before being replaced by the librarian with another set of materials.

6. *Storage of pupil wraps.* Two methods are in general use for storing pupils' outer clothing and overshoes during the school day in elementary schools. The most common method, particularly in the lower elementary grades, is to provide a cloakroom accessible directly from the classroom. This arrangement is quite adequate from the standpoint of supervision of pupils and pupil belongings, but it entails the loss of a wall for use as a chalkboard. Even when an interlinked system of horizontally swinging doors is used, it is difficult to keep exhibits attached to the doors. On the other hand, if a long counterbalanced panel that slides up and down is used, the wall space of doors enclosing the cloak closets becomes usable.

The second method involves the use of corridor lockers for the storage of pupil wraps. The corridor location for lockers is not as widespread at the elementary level as are wardrobes installed within the classrooms. There are three drawbacks to the use of corridor lockers in elementary schools. It is more difficult for the teachers to supervise pupils in the corridor. The pupils, particularly in the lower grade levels, often forget combinations or lose locker keys. And, unless rubber bumpers are provided on the doors, lockers are a source of undesirable noise. On the other hand, corridor lockers utilize space already available in the corridors, and their use increases the amount of usable wall space in the classroom.

7. *The so-called multipurpose room.* The multipurpose room is sometimes called the "triple-threat" room, because it seems to be a threat to the three activities normally conducted in it. For example, the flat floor provides poor sight lines to the stage when this space is used for assembly. The chairs and tables must be removed before this space can be converted from a cafeteria to a play area, and vice versa when the room is transformed from a play area to a cafeteria. The use of in-wall tables facilitates the conversion, but they are expensive and not particularly suited to a good social situation during meals.

A serious objection to the multipurpose room is that it gives the appearance and assurance that all of the extra-classroom needs of an elementary school can be met by that single room. It is easy to assume that the single "triple-threat" room can meet certain extra-classroom needs. In reality, of course, such is not the case. In general, one multipurpose room can meet the needs for assembly, indoor recreation for all pupils for two periods per week, and dining for a school of about twelve classrooms. Beyond this point, a second large space is needed for a school not exceeding twenty or twenty-one classrooms. In this instance, two of the three functions would be combined in one space. In the interest of operational efficiency, the assembly and dining functions could be combined in one room, and a separate space provided for indoor recreation. There are several advantages to this arrangement. The tables and chairs can remain in the room when the space is used for assembly. When more assembly capacity is needed, the tables may be replaced by chairs. The "cafetorium" may also be used as a large-group instructional space without removing tables and chairs. And finally, during inclement weather, the recreation room can be used by pupils who finish eating early.

8. *Classrooms.* It should be borne in mind that all pupil experiences, with the exception of physical education and perhaps music, take place within the self-contained classroom. Consequently, the room must be designed for instruction in art, science, language, social sciences, arithmetic, and music, if these activities are not conducted elsewhere. The room should be furnished with a work sink and work counters on both sides of it, primarily for experiments in science and art. There should be an alcove where pupils may construct paper, cardboard, and wooden models of various types for science, art, arithmetic, and social sciences.

The classroom should be spacious and functional. It should, if possible, approach the shape of a square to simplify supervision. It should be designed to include two or three well-defined locations, such as a science and art area, a project area, a reading area, and perhaps an alcove where helping teachers may assist the teacher in working with small groups.

Fenestration has also received much attention in recent years. Emphasis has ranged from one extreme to the other—from the complete window wall to the windowless classroom. Architects have argued that it is easier and more economical to control the environment in a windowless classroom. Architecturally, this may be a valid argument, but the opinion among educators is quite mixed on this point. Some argue that it is not desirable to remove the pupil from the world in which he lives for the sake of easy temperature control. A few maintain that the pupil is subjected to fewer distractions in a windowless school than in a conventional building, while some counter this argument by pointing out that an inspiring teacher can hold the class's interest anywhere, even in a classroom where pupils may look out of the window. The thinking on this matter is quite confused. Perhaps a compromise solution is in order. If artificial light is the primary source of illumination in a classroom, it might be desirable to provide a simple vision strip across the outside wall of a classroom. In this case, the window sill should be about 6 inches below the eye level of the seated pupil and top of the vision strips should be approximately 6 inches above the eye level of a teacher standing in the classroom.

Again, it should be emphasized that a proper brightness balance must be maintained within a classroom in accordance with standards discussed in Chapter 12. Brightness balance should apply to the furniture and equipment as well as to the room itself. Color, acoustics, and brightness balance are all matters of major concern in planning classrooms that are conducive to effective learning.

9. *Site development.* In some instances, site development is left to chance or to "if funds are available," but site development is an integral part of a well-planned school plant. It seems ridiculous to acquire a site of, let us say, eight acres without developing a major portion of it for pupil recreation, parking, and educational purposes. In fact, the school site could also be planned for use by the public for Little League baseball, outings, and other recreational purposes when it is not being used for school purposes. Summer recreational programs could also be accommodated on a well-developed school site.

The natural assets of a school site, such as trees or brooks, should be preserved whenever possible. Brooks can lend beauty and interest to a school site, but too many school planners regard them as a liability that must be eliminated. A few imaginative architects and school planners have converted a liability to a beautiful asset by preserving, widening, or deepening a brook.

THE MATURING MIDDLE SCHOOL

The middle school is a relatively new educational concept in the United States. Neither an elementary school nor a secondary school, it is a new-born institution specifically aimed at the educational and psychological needs of pupils in the 10- to 14-year age group. As a rule, middle school facilities are designed for pupils in Grades 5 through 8. A few middle schools are planned for pupils in Grades 6 through 8 or 9. These grade groupings may suggest that the middle school is a substitute for the upper elementary and lower junior high school level. It is not. The new institution is not a substitute for anything. It is a middle school.

THE EDUCATIONAL VIABILITY OF THE MIDDLE SCHOOL

The Concept of the Middle School

The middle school is not a new fad in grade grouping or a novel building replete with new gadgets and electronic equipment. It is not a thing at all. It is simply an exciting idea that opens an entirely new vista in the education of pre- and neoadolescents. For many years educators have strongly felt the need for some type of transitional program between the conventional elementary school where pupils are mothered by a single teacher and the high school where they are treated more as adults. The junior high school, as currently conceived, does not seem to satisfy the psychological needs of the neoadolescent. As its name suggests, the junior high school has become a junior version of the more prestigious high school. It is true, of course, that the subject matter in the junior high school is taught at a lower level of sophistication than the corresponding courses in the high school, but the basic administrative organization and methodology employed in the junior high school are quite similar to those of the senior high school. It is self-evident that the special needs of the learner determine the specific nature of the educational institution serving them. Also, of course, the psychological and educational needs of the 12-year-old pupil in junior high school are quite different from those of his 17-year-old brother in high school. It follows, therefore, that the school required for the younger brother must be significantly different in character from that attended by the older brother. That new and different school is called the "middle school."

At the present time, the middle school has no precise definition or pattern. In practice it seems to be anything that the local school district wants it to be. Unfortunately, it is sometimes nothing more than the last two years of a conventional elementary school and the first two years of a traditional junior high school clumped in a single building and labeled a "middle school." It can be an ungraded school for pupils from 10 to 14 years of age organized for team-teaching, large- and small-group instruction, and variable-length class periods. It can be the traditional elementary-junior high school program with greater emphasis on the specialized areas, such as music, science, art, practical arts, and physical education for pupils in Grades 5 and 6. And it can be a school in which there is a gradual and meaningful transition from the self-contained classrooms in Grade 4 to the completely departmentalized organization in Grade 9. The middle school is still a pliable concept which is focused not so much on a building as it is upon the special needs of the pre- and neoadolescent. Theoretically, at least, the middle school concept can be housed in any flexible building.

The word that best characterizes the middle school at the moment is "fluidity." It is in the process of becoming. Its shape, design, and function are limited only by the creativity of the human mind. It possesses an elasticity that encourages the introduction of a large variety of exciting instructional innovations. It has no tradition, no set pattern, and no preconceived educational characteristics to hinder its full development. The only fixed notion of the middle school at this time is its purpose—to satisfy the educational needs of preadolescent and neoadolescent pupils from the time they leave Grade 5 or 6 until they enter Grade 9.

The Strengths of the Middle School

The development and growth of the middle school can be justified psychologically, educationally, sociologically, and logistically. The emergence of the middle school is a direct outgrowth of a long-felt need for such an educational institution in the United States.

Psychological need.   For a number of years, educators have been concerned about the lack of a transitional period between elementary and junior high school. They have felt that preadolescent pupils change very adruptly from the sheltered and highly directed life in a self-contained classroom with a single teacher to the semidirected routine in junior high school under the informal guidance of several teachers. Under the middle school concept, pupils in Grades 5 through 8 pass through the period of transition in a systematic fashion. The middle school makes it possible for pupils in Grade 5, for example, to spend 75 percent of their time under one teacher and the remaining 25 percent under the guidance of two others. During the sixth and seventh grades, pupils may spend as much as 50 percent of their time under one teacher and the remaining time under a departmentalized organization. And, at the eighth-grade level, a pupil may spend about two periods per day under one teacher and the remainder of his time in departmentalized work. Thus, the psychological need for a period of transition between the elementary school and the high school can be satisfied by interposing the middle school between them.

The middle school is so adaptable that it can be conceived, planned, organized, and shaped to satisfy many of the psychological needs of pre- and neoadolescent pupils. Activities and instruction can be organized to give pupils a feeling of security and belongingness. Through the use of small-group instruction each pupil can experience a feeling of accomplishment, self-confidence, and group acceptance. To be sure, these psychological objectives could theoretically be achieved in existing schools under certain conditions. Unfortunately, neither elementary nor junior high schools possess the required spatial flexibility or instructional versatility to accomplish these goals. The middle school is currently so pliable that any needed characteristic can be incorporated in it.

Educational need.   Lack of time for teaching is a matter of great concern to modern educators. There simply is not enough time to teach the desired subjects to pupils within the present academic schedules. Our public schools seem to be constantly adding subjects to the educational program without curtailing any of those already being offered. The time will soon arrive when this procedure can no longer be sustained without drastic changes in the length of the school day, week, or year.

The middle school can be designed to increase the effectiveness and efficiency of the learning process. Some of the materials being taught in the high schools can be introduced in the middle school. New methods of teaching must be developed and perfected to meet this need for more concentrated learning in a shorter time. No longer, for example, can we afford the luxury of offering general science courses in the seventh, eighth, and ninth grades; oftentimes, one science course is no more than a rehash of the previous course at a more advanced level. Perhaps, it would be more efficient to introduce a basic science program earlier, so that in, say, Grade 5 pupils could conduct simple experiments using laboratory equipment instead of waiting until Grades 8 or 9 to engage in purposeful experimentation. It may also be necessary to revise the course content and to reprogram the sequence of learning experiences for more efficient use of pupil time. The middle school is an excellent starting point for such changes. It is just taking form. It is still flexible and, hence, responsive to the needs of modern education. For creative educators and school planners, the middle school is both a challenge and an opportunity.

The middle school may be of value also in meeting the problems of dropouts, who have become a major national concern of both educators and government officials. Sometimes pupils who drop out of school are called "force-outs." They feel forced out because the school failed to offer them challenging and meaningful experiences. Even though these pupils may not drop out until they are in high school, their decision to do so can sometimes be traced to a lack of interest which they first experienced in the lower grades. The middle school is so versatile that it can offer a wide variety of diverse experiences to a large number of pupils. Consequently, the middle school offers a ray of hope regarding the potential force-out who may choose to remain in schools and thus become a greater asset to society.

Sociological needs. The middle school offers some relief with regard to the problem of racial imbalance in the United States. If the middle school were planned for about 1,000 pupils, its attendance area usually would extend over a relatively large area. It is frequently possible to achieve racial balance in a school of this size by locating it strategically.

The middle school is sometimes an integral part of a school park where an elementary, middle, and high school may be located on one large multipurpose site. The school park plan is another attempt to break through the barriers that hamper attainment of racial balance within a school district.

Logistical needs. In many school districts, the adoption of the middle school is the ideal answer to the housing and transportation problems. By planning an intermediate grade school serving Grades 5 through 8, it is frequently possible to convert present junior high schools to four-year high schools and to accommodate the increasing number of pupils in kindergarten though Grade 4 in existing elementary schools. As four-year schools ascend in popularity and elementary schools assume the role of neighborhood schools, the ideal link between the two increasingly appears to be the middle school. Under these conditions, the middle school solves the problem of logistics and often improves the sociological posture of the school district.

PLANNING A MIDDLE SCHOOL

A long step may be taken in the direction of the middle school concept without seriously alarming teachers, pupils, or parents in a stable, conservative community. After public acceptance of the middle school concept has been achieved, the board of education and superintendent of schools should develop policies governing the reorganization or redefining of the attendance areas for the respective schools.

The Special Characteristics of an Effective Middle School

The transition from the conventional elementary-junior high school concept to the middle school should be careful and evolutionary. The changes in instructional pattern may occur gradually at a pace that is comfortable for teachers and pupils. The middle school seems somewhat different but in reality is closely related to the traditional patterns in many ways.

Grade grouping.   A gradual transition from the existing 6-3-3 or 6-2-4 to the 4-4-4 organization can be planned. It would not be surprising, therefore, to find that a middle school planned initially for Grades 6 through 9 would later house pupils in Grades 5 through 8.

Student separation   Most of the modern middle schools are planned so that the lower two grades are assigned to one side of the building and the upper two grades to the other. While this practice has some merit, it should not be carried to such an extreme that specialized rooms, such as shops, homemaking suites, and science laboratories are decentralized for the sole purpose of preventing a fifth-grade pupil from crossing the path of a seventh-grade pupil on his hurried trip to and from the specialized space. In passing, it may be noted however, that parents who often protest against intermingling pupils of various age groups in school where they are highly supervised, rarely seem to question the practices of transporting pupils of all ages in school buses where practically no supervision is provided.

Team teaching.   Some provision is included in the modern middle school for the beginning of a team-teaching program. Seminar rooms are usually provided for the group activity of the team teachers, and a workroom having an area of about 400 square feet is often located in the vicinity of the teachers lounge. It is furnished with work tables and chairs and equipped with copiers, mimeographs, duplicating machines, a drawing table, artist's and draftsman's supplies, and photographic devices. The teaching team would thus be able to produce some of its own instructional materials. In the beginning, at least, most of the team teaching would be focused upon the upper two grades, but in time all of the pupils in the school could be exposed to some form of team teaching.

Variable group size   The effective middle school can include provision for a limited amount of instruction in larger groups of about 60–80 pupils. In general, this is accomplished simply by including a few movable partitions between pairs of regular classrooms. A space about 78 feet long and 23 feet wide could be provided for teaching a group larger than the conventional twenty-five or thirty pupils simply by opening a partition. Provision for teaching in larger groups could also be made in the cafeteria and auditorium spaces. The expansible spaces may not seem to be very exciting or extraordinary at first glance, but in the hands of creative teachers and administrators, their potential for educational improvement is greatly enhanced, provided their widths approximate 30 feet.

Number of instructional spaces for the effective middle school.   In planning a middle school, some regular, self-contained classrooms are usually retained in their conventional form while others are given a specialized orientation. The distribution of regular and specialized classrooms, of course, depends upon the desired middle school program. In the middle school, it can be assumed that (1) pupils in Grade 5 will spend 25 percent of their time in specialized rooms and the remainder under a single teacher; (2) pupils in Grades 6 and 7 will spend half of their time in regular classrooms and the remainder in specialized spaces; and (3) pupils in Grades 8 will spend two periods (about 25 percent) of their time under one teacher and the remainder with several others. Under these conditions, the approximate distribution of instructional space would be as follows:

> Fifth Grade: *Three units* of regular classrooms to *one unit* of specialized space.
> Sixth and seventh grades: *One unit* of regular classroom to *one unit* of specialized space.
> Eighth Grade: According to programs—using formula below.

1. *Number of teaching periods needed.* The following formula may be used to determine the number of faculty periods per week required for each course:

$$Pwk = \frac{En}{C}$$

where: Pwk = Number of periods per week required to staff a given course
E = Number of pupils enrolled in the course
C = Desired class size
n = Number of class meetings per week for the respective course

2. *Teaching stations needed.* To convert *Pwk* into the number of teaching stations required, simply divide the sum of the *Pwk* for each subject by the number of instructional periods each classroom is available per week multiplied by 1.20. The computed number of teaching stations incorporates a surplus of 20 percent in order to provide sufficient leeway for scheduling difficulties and unavoidable variations from the desired class size.

To illustrate the application of the formula above, let us assume that the desired educational program for pupils in Grade 5 is as follows:

Number of pupils to be served:	120
Total number of periods in the school week:	45
Desirable class size for all courses:	30
Number of periods per week each pupil attends physical education classes:	2
Periods per week per pupil for assembly, conferences, etc.:	3
Number of academic instructional periods per week:	40
Periods per week per pupil under a single teacher:	30 (in regular classroom)
Periods per week per pupil in a specialized *science* room:	5
Periods per week per pupil in specialized *art* room:	2.5
Periods per week per pupil in specialized *music* room:	2.5

(The science, art, and music values of 5, 2.5, and 2.5 are braced together as 10.)

The number of spaces required to house the program and enrollment in the example set forth above is as follows:

$$\text{Regular Classrooms—periods} = \frac{120}{30} \times 30 = 120 \text{ periods per week}$$

$$\text{Science—periods} = \frac{120}{30} \times 5 = 20 \text{ periods per week}$$

$$\text{Art—periods} = \frac{120}{30} \times 2.5 \times 10 \text{ periods per week}$$

$$\text{Music—periods} = \frac{120}{30} \times 2.5 = 10 \text{ periods per week}$$

To convert these period requirements to classrooms, divide each result by 40 and multiply by 1.2. Thus, the spaces needed for 120 pupils in Grade 5 are:

Regular classrooms $\qquad = \dfrac{120}{40}\ (1.2) = 3.6$ teaching stations

Science rooms $\qquad = \dfrac{20}{40} \times 1.2 = 0.6$ teaching station

Art rooms $\qquad = \dfrac{10}{40} \times 1.2 = 0.3$ teaching station

Music rooms $\qquad = \dfrac{10}{40} \times 1.2 = 0.3$ teaching station

CHAPTER 14

Planning Secondary School Buildings

Because of the current state of flux in grade organization, it is not always clear what grade levels are included in the secondary school grouping. For the purpose of this discussion, secondary schools are facilities designed to house pupils from thirteen to eighteen years of age. Students in this age grouping may attend middle schools, junior high schools, high schools, or senior high schools. The term used to designate a school is of little or no consequence in planning, but educational function and physical needs of pupils in this age group play an important role in the design, size, location, orientation, and interior treatment of school buildings.

In the absence of validated research regarding the design of secondary school buildings, the rationale underlying the various topics discussed in this chapter is based primarily on generally accepted practices in secondary school planning. Admittedly, it would be far better to rely on research findings, but they are not available. Recently, the Educational Facilities Laboratories in New York sponsored important projects in schoolbuilding research which are making a significant impact on the design of educational facilities in the United States and Canada. Nevertheless, the quantity of validated research on school buildings from the standpoint of educational function is still disappointing. For this reason, it is necessary to rely primarily on professional judgments and opinions which may or may not be based on research findings. School plant planners confronted with the problem of planning school buildings for the thousands of pupils who need school facilities today, or perhaps even yesterday, cannot afford the luxury of waiting until research findings are available.

CONTEMPORARY EDUCATIONAL PRACTICES COMMON TO SECONDARY SCHOOLS

In planning secondary school facilities, it should be borne in mind that secondary school programs vary from district to district and sometimes even from school to school within the same school district. For this reason, there is no common or typical secondary school facility that can be described in definitive terms. Within these different facilities, however, there are a number of educational practices that are similar in most of them. The degree to which these practices are employed in each situation will vary somewhat from school to school, but they will generally appear in one form or another. The most prevalent version of each practice is described in the following paragraphs.

Complete departmentalization. Under prevailing practice, the secondary school is fully departmentalized by subject-matter area. A department head is usually given the responsibility of determining the course content, selecting textbooks, and choosing the type of instructional materials to be used in a given area of learning. He is the instructional leader and supervises the teaching and methods followed in his department. If he is imaginative, forward-looking, and sensitive to good human relations, the instruction may be of a superior character. On the other hand, if his appointment was not made strictly on the basis of competence, the instructional effectiveness of the department may be disappointing, the methods may be obsolete, and teacher morale low. By and large, the department structure has operated at an acceptable level of efficiency for at least a half-century. Conscientious department heads have made the system work from an administrative point of view. Psychologists, on the other hand, might question the wisdom of compartmentalizing learning.[1]

The teaching of classes. In most situations, teachers instruct pupils in groups called classes. The usual class includes between twenty-five and thirty-two pupils for most courses. With good reason, teachers and administrators much prefer class sizes as close as possible to twenty-five. The size of the group also depends upon the subject being taught. As a rule, most of the group sizes lie within the aforementioned limits, with the exception of classes in advanced sciences, art, and homemaking where the maximum may fall well below twenty-five. The class size in music may vary over a wide range. In some secondary schools, the group size for music instruction may range from 25 to 250, depending upon the type of musical activity. Industrial arts classes are often officially restricted to twenty, but many actually reach twenty-five pupils. Physical education may be taught well, according to prevailing practice, in groups of forty to forty-five pupils, while typewriting may be taught effectively to groups of about thirty-five pupils under the guidance of a single teacher.

The teacher instructs a given class for a period ranging from 45 to 60 minutes four or five times per week for a total of about 250 contact minutes per week per class. Each teacher usually offers instruction four or five

[1]See Chapter 2.

periods a day for a total of about 1,250 minutes per week. The time spent by pupils in formal classes of various types ranges from 1,200 to 1,500 minutes per week at the upper secondary level of instruction. At the lower secondary level, it is customary to reduce the length of class period and to increase the number of periods the pupil must attend each week. For example, a thirteen-year-old pupil in Grade 7 might enroll in seven courses for a total of thirty-five instructional periods per week. In this case, the length of the class period is usually reduced to about 40 minutes. A pupil in Grade 12, on the other hand, may be assigned to only twenty 60-minute periods of formal instruction per week for a total of about 1,200 minutes in supervised classes.

Pupil movement.   In the contemporary school, teachers are usually assigned to a given classroom where pupils come to them period after period for instruction during the school day. Under this system, the pupils move from one room to another where the different courses are offered. At the end of each period, a complete reshuffle of pupils occurs within the school. This situation creates a real problem in the circulation of pupils within a secondary school. Pupils move not only from class to class, but also from classroom to library, to cafeteria, to gymnasium, to auditorium, to study halls, and to other supplementary spaces.

Grouping.   In the secondary school, pupils are grouped either homo-geneously, according to some predetermined criteria, or heterogeneously in random fashion. Oftentimes, they are grouped according to reading ability, aptitude, generally intelligence, curricula, and the like. When two or more sections of the same course are taught, homogeneous grouping is often employed to reduce the range of differences in learning ability among the pupils in the class. There is still much controversy regarding the value of homogeneous grouping over heterogeneous grouping. Both groupings are found in secondary schools, depending upon the philosophy of the administration and the board of education.

Once the group is formed, it remains intact during the entire semester or year. It is generally not combined with any other similar group. The teacher simply treats it as a class, introducing learning experiences appro-priate to the group and subject matter being taught.

Teaching aids.   The instructional tools of the prevalent secondary school consist primarily of books, chalkboard, and paper. Demonstrations are restricted primarily to the physical sciences, home economics, art, and industrial education. Motion pictures are available for classroom use on a limited basis. Overhead projectors are used in a few classrooms. Some teachers introduce slides into the curriculum at some point. Record players and tape recorders are usually available at the audiovisual center, but the teacher does not, as a rule, avail himself of such aids very frequently, preferring to use the book and chalkboard as his major instructional tools. While electronic teaching aids such as television, computer instruction, and feedback systems could be effectively utilized in all schools, the orientation of the secondary school does not place a very high value on such aids or assign them a very important role in the educational program.

Large-group activity.   In the contemporary secondary school, the major large-group activity is the "school assembly." Secondary school principals often insist on facilities that can accommodate the entire student body at a single sitting for assemblies which may be called as often as once a week or as infrequently as ten times a year.

Secondary school principals can make a very strong case for the inclusion of an auditorium that can seat a minimum of the largest single class—usually freshman—plus about 50 percent of that class enrollment. Often an auditorium that can seat one-half the student body is adequate. Under the contemporary concept of a secondary school, when the total enrollment exceeds 1,000 pupils, it is difficult to justify an auditorium capable of seating the total student body simultaneously for assembly and dramatics alone.

THE RELATIONSHIP OF EDUCATIONAL FUNCTION TO SECONDARY SCHOOL FACILITIES

A vital responsibility of educators involved in planning a school building is the translation of teaching and learning activities into the physical features of a building. The accent at this point is on activities, actions, and direct experiences of both pupils and teachers. We are more concerned at this juncture with the curriculum than with the broad educational program, although both ultimately play a crucial part in the planning of a secondary school.

The architect is not expected to be familiar with the curriculum of a given secondary school, until he is given a clear picture of it by school officials. He should be presented with a document that translates curriculum into suggested space requirements. This document is commonly called educational specifications by educators and simply "a program" by architects. In any event, the architect is entitled to a fairly detailed set of educational specifications. They should be free from ambiguities and restrict the architect's work as little as possible. It should be borne in mind that the creative talents of the architect cannot be released if educators insist on making quasi-architectural sketches of the various spaces in a proposed school. It is far better to inform the architect about the activities and functions to be housed in a given space and to give him an estimate of the number of square feet required. Sometimes special features such as orientation, ceiling height, or length of a space are necessary to accommodate unusual equipment or instructional practice. In these instances, the architect would welcome specific information, but generally educational specifications should be prepared so as to give the architect as much freedom as possible.

METHODS AND FUNCTIONS ASSOCIATED WITH SECONDARY SCHOOLS

One or more of the methods listed below is employed in teaching both small and large groups of pupils. Some of them are easily recognized, and others are not.

Presentation. The most common method of instruction is one in which the teacher presents ideas to a group of pupils. The student receives the instructional stimuli via sight and hearing. The learner, in this situation, is quite passive. The teacher transmits ideas to students by a number of means. They may involve books, locally prepared materials, the use of a chalkboard, overhead projector, filmstrips, moving pictures, tape recorders, and the like. In all of these situations, however, the process is quite directive in character. The presentation is made by the teacher or by means of a teaching aid.

Demonstration. This method of instruction is somewhat similar to the presentation method. The major difference lies in the manner in which the student receives the stimuli. In demonstrations, sight plays a major part in the transfer of ideas to the pupil. In general, the teacher sets up an experiment to demonstrate a basic principle or phenomenon. Demonstration is a direct experience by the pupil as opposed to the vicarious experiences conveyed by the teacher using the presentation method.

Diagnostic and evaluation function. The diagnostic aspect of the instructional function is frequently overlooked by school plant planners. The testing, evaluation, and analysis of pupil progress is of paramount importance in any educative process. School facilities do not generally lend themselves to testing and diagnosing pupil work. In fact, cheating is made easy in the typical classroom by the proximity of one student to the other. Admittedly, the cost of providing individual cubicles in a room that is scanned by a rotating television camera might be difficult to justify solely on the basis of the need to reduce cheating. On the other hand, it is possible to introduce features that are likely to minimize the temptation for pupils to copy from one another. Flexible seating arrangements and the use of electronic devices that permit immediate feedback from the student to the teacher should be considered in planning a school plant. The function of testing, evaluating, and diagnosing a pupil's work should be borne clearly in mind when schools are being planned.

Reinforcement of learning. In Chapter 2, it was brought out that reinforcement of the initial stimulus is a necessary aspect of effective learning. Obviously, school planners should design secondary schools so that learning can be reinforced in as many ways as possible. Several suggestions were made in Chapter 2 regarding the application of the principle of reinforcement to the planning of secondary schools.

COMMON ELEMENTS OF SECONDARY SCHOOL PLANNING

The Secondary School Site

The requirements of the school site have already been discussed in Chapter 5. The rule of thumb regarding optimum size of a secondary school site varies considerably from source to source, but in practice, a site of 10 acres (junior high school level) or 15 acres (high school) plus one acre for each 100 pupils of ultimate enrollment is generally accepted as a minimum. There appears to be no validated research thus far which indicates the optimum size of a secondary school site with respect to educational return. The increasing cost of land and the accelerated urbanization and suburbanization of the population reduce the availability of desirable land, and prices for school sites are rising rapidly. It is conceivable that the size of school sites may have to be drastically reduced in some areas. In open country, every effort should be made to meet or surpass the practical standard stated above.

Translating Program Requirements into Instructional Spaces

After the educational progam has been fully worked out by the school staff and approved by the board of education, the number of pupils that will probably be enrolled in each course should be estimated. The number of periods per week that each course will be offered to a given number of students should also be noted. Two techniques may be employed in arriving at the required number of spaces.

The Conrad method. Conrad[2] has developed a very accurate technique that indicates either capacity or number of needed teaching stations for a given student enrollment.

The Castaldi nomogram.[3] The nomogram consists of a chart from which the required number of spaces can be read directly for secondary

[2]Marion J. Conrad, "A Technique for Determining Operating Capacity of Secondary School Buildings," doctoral disseration, Ohio State University, 1952.

[3]Basil Castaldi, *The Castaldi Nomogram* (Cambridge Mass: New England School Development Council, 1953).

schools organized on a 25-, 30-, or 35-period week. For other administrative organizations of the school week, the Castaldi Formula underlying the nomogram can be used directly. It is as follows:

$$T.S. = 1.25\frac{E}{C} \cdot \frac{n}{N}$$

Where $T.S.$ = Required number of teaching stations
   E = Number of students enrolled in a given course
   C = Desired class size
   n = Number of periods per week pupil attends a given class
   N = Number of periods in the school week

The formula may be used to answer questions such as: How many rooms are needed if 300 pupils are to be enrolled in art, which meets twice a week? The desired maximum class size is 25 and there are 40 periods in the school week.

$$T.S. = (1.25)\frac{300}{25} \cdot \frac{2}{40} = 0.75$$

In this case, 1.0 art room is needed. The 0.75 teaching station obtained by applying the Castaldi Formula is rounded off to the next highest integer.

Determining the Size of Various Spaces

The functional analysis approach.   The most satisfactory method of determining the size of instructional spaces is to list all of the major activities that are expected to occur in a given space, together with the type of equipment and number of pupils that will be involved in each activity. A layout designating the space needed for the equipment and for each pupil or group of pupils will yield the approximate area needed for the activity in question. The total area included in a teaching space is the sum of the combination of activities carried on simultaneously which requires the greatest floor space. It is presumed that other teaching experiences can be conducted effectively within the given space even though the room is larger than it actually needs to be for the activity under consideration.

The rule-of-thumb approach.   As mentioned earlier, validated research indicating optimum sizes or capacities of various types of instructional spaces is practically nonexistent. Since the need for school facilities is urgent, and the construction of school buildings cannot be postponed until such research findings become available, school planners have resorted to a rule-of-thumb approach. Although there is no proof that the specific figures in the rules of thumb apply to minimum, maximum, optimum conditions or otherwise, there seems to be general agreement that spaces planned according to the rules of thumb function satisfactorily, at least when judged on a subjective basis. In the absence of other more scientifically oriented data, the rule-of-thumb approach would seem to be acceptable, and no apologies should be made for its use now in planning school buildings. It is important that school planners be aware of the subjective origin of the rules applied in the design of school buildings.

PLANNING CONTEMPORARY SECONDARY SCHOOLS

The so-called conventional school planned today often contains many characteristics of the school of the future. But, at the same time, the conventional school tends to be somewhat conservative in character, and its design and functional concept are generally not too far removed from the pattern of the past. Thus, innovations incorporated in such buildings are usually modest. The conventional secondary school should be designed with the potential innovations discussed in Chapter 2 clearly in mind.

SPECIFIC GUIDELINES FOR PLANNING SECONDARY SCHOOLS

Suggested Space Allocations

The specific sizes and comments presented in Tables 14.1 through 14.3, inclusive, are not the product of research nor are they attributable to any one person or group. They reflect the current thinking of both educators and school plant planners. Admittedly, the quantities listed in Tables 14.1–14.3 are likely to change from time to time as research becomes available or as educational practices undergo certain transformations. It is felt, however, that school planners will deviate from the figures presented in Tables 14.1–14.4, of course, when the educational and service functions demand more or less space in certain situations.

It should be reemphasized that the space arrangements shown in Figure 14.1 conform to current accepted practice. For example, it is generally agreed that all science rooms should be clustered together and that locker and shower rooms and play areas should be adjacent to the gymnasium, etc. The degree of relationship is indicated on the diagrams by the number of lines drawn between each element. Three lines denote a very close relationship, in which case one space should adjoin the other. Two lines mean that the two spaces should be in the same general area, perhaps no farther apart than a corridor's width. One line between two spaces or clusters indicates that it is desirable but not essential that the two spaces be located in the same general area. An absence of lines between any two

TABLE 14.1   Specialized instructional spaces in secondary schools

Type of Space	Suggested Max. Class Size	Suggested Area of Each Space	Suggested Area of Adj. Stor. Rm.	Comments
A. Art				
1. General art	25	1,000–1,200	100–150	North orientations not mandatory if adequate lighting is provided.
2. Arts and crafts	25	1,100–1,400	175–225	
B. Commercial Education				
1. Office machines	25	800–900	20–40*	Special attention should be given to sound transmission problems. Electrical outlets should be available at every pupil station and at teacher's desk.
2. Office practice	25	800–900	20–40*	
3. Typing	35	850–950	20–40*	
C. Homemaking				
1. General	24	1,200–1,400	50–75	It would be desirable to design this space so that by opening or closing partitions it could become part of either room adjacent to it.
2. Multipurpose area (living center)	4–8	400–500		
3. Clothing	24	900–1,000	50–75	
4. Foods	24	1,000–1,200	50–75*	
D. Music				
1. Band-orchestra	Varies	1,200–1,600	Cabinets	Music practice rooms should be slightly overacousticized to prevent the blending of sounds. (See Chapter 12, "Acoustical Environment.")
2. Instrument storage space		250–300	Cabinets	
3. Chorus	Varies	1,200–1,400	Cabinets	
4. Practice room	1–6	100–125		
5. Practice room	1–4	75–100		

*Optional.

TABLE 14.1 (Continued)

Type of Space	Suggested Max. Class Size	Suggested Area of Each Space	Suggested Area of Adj. Stor. Rm.	Comments
6. Practice room	1-2	50-75		High-grade stereophonic equipment should be installed in band and chorus room. One amplifier can serve more than one space. One office per instructor needed.
7. Theory	30	700-850		
8. Office		150-200		
9. Listening and recording room and music library	6-10	350-450		
E. Physical Education				
1. Gymnasium (one teaching station for physical education only)	40	3,700-4,400	300-400	The size of the gymnasium varies with bleacher seating capacity. Standard size basketball court requires a gymnasium with an area of approx. 5,600. Add 3 sq. ft. per person for bleacher seating capacity.
2. Gymnasium (two teaching stations with folding partition)	40	5,600-7,000	250-350	Where more than two teaching stations are required, balcony area spaces should be considered for both movable seating and teaching space.
3. Corrective room	20	600-900		Adjoining gymnasium area.
4. Coach office		250-300		
5. Toilets (including public)	The total of areas 3-7 inclusive should be approximately 0.7 to 1.0 × total area of gym. Number of shower heads: Pupils 1 : 4 boys—1 : 3 girls			
6. Showers and locker rooms				
7. Team room		700-900	250-300	In spite of opinions to the contrary, the American girl seems to favor stall showers.
8. Other standard girls gym	40	3,000-4,000	250-300	

TABLE 14.1 (Continued)

9. Auxiliary gym—one teaching station (girls)	40	2,000–2,400	14–16 ft. ceiling	Provision should be made for ticket office, checking, public toilets, and display.
10. Lobby		800–1,000		
11. Visiting team room		500–700		
F. Physical Sciences				
1. Biology	25	900–1,000	150–175	Science rooms should be "squarish" to permit use of peripheral laboratory units. Television jacks should be installed in all science spaces.
2. Chemistry	25	1,000–1,100	200–250	
3. General science	30	900–1,000	125–150	
4. Physics	25	900–1,100	200–250	
5. Growing room		200–300		Need not be exposed to the out-of-doors if controlled fluorescent lighting is provided.
6. Darkroom		60–100		May be related to either the art room or science area.
G. Industrial Arts (nonvocational)				
1. General (Composite) Shop	20	1,500–2,000	150–200	One locker, dressing-washing room per two shops, if possible.
2. Mechanical drawing	25	850–950	50–75	
3. General metals	20	1,700–2,000	150–200	Avoid the use of the loft storage areas in all shops.
4. General woods	20	1,500–1,800	150–200	Provide high ceilings only in metals and woods shop.
5. Electrical shop	20	900–1,200	100–150	
6. Power mechanics	20	1,600–2,200	150–200	
7. Metal shop	20	1,600–2,000	150–200	
8. Wood shop	20	1,400–1,600	150–200	
9. Graphic arts	20	1,000–1,100	150–200	

TABLE 14.1 (CONTINUED)

Type of Space	Suggested Max. Class Size	Suggested Area of Each Space	Suggested Area of Adj. Stor. Rm.	Comments
10. Planning room		400–450		
11. Other finishing room		100–300		
12. General storage space			100–125 per shop	Planned as a single large space
H. Occupational Education				
1. Agriculture shop plus agriculture green house	20	2,400–2,600	500	
2. Auto repair	20	1,400–1,600	500	
3. Auto body shop plus frame straightener	20	5,000–5,400	300	Storage area fire proof.
spray booth		5,000–5,400		
		450–500		
		450–500		
4. Baking	20	2,400–2,600	400	
5. Boat building	20	2,800–3,200	300	
6. Cabinet making	20	3,000–3,400	400	
finishing room		300		Dust-free and well ventilated.
7. Carpentry	20	3,000–3,400	400	
8. Commercial art	20	1,400–1,600	200	
9. Cosmetology	20	1,400–1,600	150	
10. Data processing	15	1,100–1,300		
11. Dental lab	20	1,600–1,800	200	
12. Distributive ed. rm. plus	25	1,000–1,200		
store		500		
13. Drafting	20	1,500–2,000	150	
14. Electronics	20	1,200–1,500	100	

TABLE 14.1   (CONTINUED)

15. Electrical shop plus electrical lab	20	1,800–2,000	150	
—machinery electrical Lab		800	100	Storage for unfinished work.
—appliances	20	500–600	100	Storage for unfinished work.
16. Food trades area plus dining and sales		2,000–2,400	400	
2 dressing rooms		800		
		50 each	20	
17. Machine shop plus inspection room	20	3,000–3,200	400	Storage for specific clothing.
		300–400		
18. Medical assistant	20	1,100–1,300	150	
19. Medical lab	20	1,200–1,400	200	
20. Metal fabrication	20	2,800–3,200	400	
21. Optical tech.	20	1,400–1,600	200	Storage—fire proof.
22. Painting and decorating	20	1,500–1,700	200	
23. Pattern making	20	1,900–2,100	200	
24. Plant maintenance	20	2,800–3,000	250	
25. Plumbing	20	2,000–2,400	300	
26. Practical nursing	20	1,800–2,200	350	
27. Printing	20	3,600–3,800	300	
28. Sheet metal	20	2,000–2,400	300	
29. Upholstery	20	1,500–1,700	200	
30. Welding	20	2,400–2,600	350	
31. Clothing textiles	20	1,600–1,800	200	
32. Consumer economics	20	800–900		
33. Dietician's assistant	20	800–900		
34. Family living	20	800–900		
35. Fashion design and merchandising	20	1,000–1,200		
36. Foods and nutrition	20	1,500–1,800	300	

TABLE 14.1 (CONTINUED)

Type of Space	Suggested Max. Class Size	Suggested Area of Each Space	Suggested Area of Adj. Stor. Rm.	Comments
37. Home aides				
a. Geriatric aides	20	1,000–1,200	300	
b. Pediatric trng.	20	1,000–1,200	300	
38. Nursery school aides	20	1,200–1,400		
39. Kindergarten aides	20	1,000–1,400		
40. Related classrooms	20	800–900		
I. Other Specialized Spaces				
1. Mathematics lab.	25	850–900	100–125	Located near similar rooms.
2. Language arts lab.	30	900–1,000	75–100	Located near similar rooms.
3. Social studies lab.	30	900–1,000	75–100	Located near similar rooms.
4. Other				
J. Nonspecialized Instructional Spaces				
1. Large classrooms	35	800–850	20–40*	About one-third of the nonspecialized classrooms should be grouped in pairs separated by a movable partition having a noise reduction coefficient in excess of 38 decibels. Television reception and origination jacks should be installed in these rooms.
2. Medium classrooms	30	750–800	20–40*	
3. Small classrooms	25	650–700	20–40*	
4. Core curriculum	30	850–900	75–100	
5. Commercial	30	750–800	20–40*	

TABLE 14.2   Supplementary instructional spaces in secondary schools

Type of Space	Suggested Area of Each Space	Comments
A. Auditorium		
1. Stage	1,800–2,200	An auditorium that
2. Audience space	7–8 sq. ft per pupil	seats 350 persons is needed for any
3. Check room	200–300	secondary school.
4. Lobby	1,500–2,000	For larger schools,
5. Public toilets		the absolute mini-
6. Storage space (as near stage as possible)	250–300	mum should be an auditorium that seats the largest single grade plus 50. But it is recommended that the auditorium seat at least one-half the ultimate capacity of the building. Maximum capacity— seating the whole student body at one time, provided its seating capacity is not greater than 1,200–1,500.
B. Audiovisual (related to library)		
1. Work room—preview room	250–300	
2. Storage space	350–450	Adjoining workroom
C. Library (Instructional Material Center)		
1. Reading room (40–75 capacity)	1,200–2,000	Reading space should accommodate about 10 percent of the enrollment, plus car- rels (3–5% of enroll- ment). Minimum capacity —about 40, and maximum about 75 pupils. For larger schools, plan two or more reading rooms.
2. Office (librarian)	125–150	
3. Book processing room	150–200	Space for receiving, re- cording and cata- loguing new books and for repairing worn or damaged books.

TABLE 14.2 (CONTINUED)

Type of Space	Suggested Area of Each Space	Comments
4. Conference room(s)	150–300	One per each 300 pupils of enrollment.
5. Storage space	175–240	
6. Carrels for self-instruction. provide carrels for 3–5% of school enrollment.		Approximate—25 sq. ft. per carrel. Allocate about one square foot per student based on total school enrollment.
D. Cafeteria		
1. Kitchen	2 sq. ft. per meal, minimum	Plan to feed the ultimate anticipated enrollment in not more than three shifts.
2. Dining area	12–15 sq. ft. per diner	The capacity of the dining area of the cafeteria should not be less than ⅓ of the ultimate anticipated enrollment plus 50. Consider continuous feeding, which can add up to 20 percent of the capacity of the cafeteria.
3. Serving space	0.5–0.8 sq. ft. capacity of dining area	For secondary schools whose enrollments are less than 300, plan to seat at least ½ of the ultimate anticipated enrollment. (This allows more time for the use of this area for other activities such as music, study, and assembly.) Locate one or two handwashing areas adjacent to the cafeteria. Plan one serving line for every 200–250 pupils dining in each shift. Kitchen area—allow at least 2 square feet per meal to be served.

TABLE 14.2   (CONTINUED)

Type of Space	Suggested Area of Each Space	Comments
		Dietitian's office—one per cafeteria. Lavatory and dressing room facilities—one per cafeteria.
4. Storage space and can wash area	approx. 0.8 sq. ft. per meal	Easily accessible from service drives.
5. Toilets		
6. Handwashing area		
7. Teachers' dining area	12 sq. ft. per diner	Located near but separate from pupil cafeteria.
E. Remedial Instructional Spaces		
1. Reading	400–500	Remedial rooms may be located in library area and planned for supervision by the librarian through the use of vision strips. Privacy gained by closing draw curtains when needed.
2. Speech	400–500	
3. General	400–500	
F. Student Activity		
1. Activity room	450–600	Size depends upon the nature of its uses.
2. Storage space	80–100	Location within view of main office.
G. Study Hall		
1. Study room	15–20 sq. ft. per pupil	Storage is needed if study hall is used as a multipurpose room.
2. Storage space		

TABLE 14.3 Administrative and related areas

Type of Space	Suggested Area of Each Space	Comments
A. Administration		
1. Principal	200–250	One principal's office per school.
2. Vice-principal	150–200	One assistant principal's office for each 500 pupils in excess of 400.
3. Clerk-waiting area	300–350	
	100 per clerk	One general office per school.
4. Storage (office supplies)	75–100	
a. Vault	50–75	
5. Toilet	40–50	
6. Conference rooms	250–300	
B. Guidance		
1. Guidance counseling office(s)	120–150	
2. Guidance director's office	150–200	This suite should possess a pleasant and informal atmosphere with drapes, carpets and easy chairs.
3. Guidance library and waiting room	200–250	One guidance counselor's office for every 300 pupils of ultimate anticipated enrollment.
4. Space for guidance in small groups	125–150	
5. Space for individual testing	40–50	One guidance counselor library-waiting-browsing room per guidance suite.
6. Storage space	30–40	One testing cubicle for every 3 guidance counselors.
C. Health		
1. Office (nurse)	150–175	Should be located adjacent to guidance suite on the opposite side of administrative suite.
2. Exam room	275–300	
3. Waiting space	100–150	
4. Restrooms (2 cots)	100–125	At least one waiting room per suite.
5. Toilets	30–40	One nurse's room.
		One exam room.
		At least two dressing-rest rooms.
		One dental room, if the community has a school dental program.

TABLE 14.3   (Continued)

Type of Space	Suggested Area of Each Space	Comments
D. Teachers' Rooms		
1. Common lounge	700–800	The size of this space depends upon the number of teachers to be served. The suggested size would be adequate for a faculty of about 30 teachers.
2. Toilets—restrooms (one or more) for each sex)	250–300	At least one teachers' restroom per school for each sex. At least one common teachers' lounge and workroom per school. A small teachers' lavatory related to each gang pupil toilet is desirable.
3. Workrooms	300–350	This function could be housed in the faculty dining room if it is properly designed for a dual function. Simple movable partitions could be used to screen one or two work alcoves.
4. Storage	30–40	
5. Faculty library	450–500	Located within the library complex.
6. Faculty office	100–120	One office for each three teachers.

spaces or groups of elements means that no relationship exists between them. In this case, the architect may locate the space wherever he believes they will best fit into the architectural scheme of the building.

Relationship of clusters of spaces to each other.   Figure 14.1 shows the arrangement of groups of spaces in a traditional secondary school building. Essentially, the groupings are divided between quiet and noisy areas. They are also arranged with regard to the need for proximity to the service drive, outdoor play areas, or main entrance. The art cluster is sometimes related to the stage rather than to the industrial arts or home economics on the premise that the art room is used in relation to the painting of scenery. While this argument has some merit, the functional relationship between art and mechanical drawing, between art and interior decoration, and between art and clothing design is more obvious. In some plans, the fine arts areas are completely divorced from related instructional areas, but such an arrangement is perhaps more a matter of architectural convenience that it is of educational function.

TABLE 14.4 Service areas

Type of Space	Suggested Area of Each Space	Comments
A. Custodian		
1. Office	100–150	Located near the general
a. Storage	50–75	receiving room and
		boiler area. At least
		one office per build-
		ing.
2. Toilet and shower	100–125	
3. Work shop	250–300	At least one workroom.
4. Storage of custodial		Storage space for custo- dial supplies and clean-
supplies	150–200	ing agents.
		Shower and locker facili- ties.
5. Service closets (with slop sinks)	20–25	These closets should be located adjacent to each gang toilet and near each of the large spaces, such as audi- torium, gymnasium, and cafeteria.
6. Receiving room	150–200	Adjoining storage spaces.
7. Storage of out- door equip- ment	100–150	Should be at grade level so that wheeled equip- ment can be driven or pushed into the storage room.
B. Other Service Spaces		
1. Book storage at various loca- tions	40–50	One serving each wing and floor of the build- ing.
2. General storage of instruc- tional supplies	½ sq. ft per pupil in school	One or two per school depending upon the size and plan of the building.
3. Toilets		See Chapter 11.

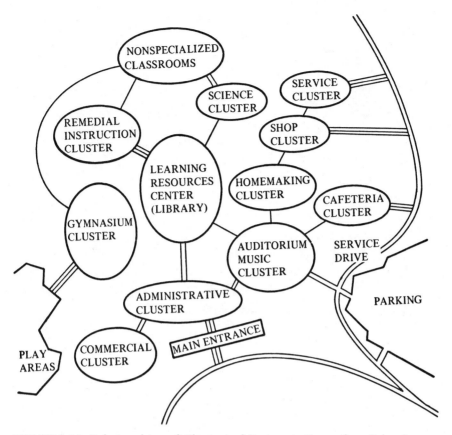

FIGURE 14.1 Relationships of Clusters of Spaces in Secondary Schools

The commercial cluster.   It is desirable, but not essential, to locate the commercial cluster near the general office. Those who advocate relating this cluster (Figure 14.3) to the office do so on the premise that some of the pupils may get actual office experience in the school office. Also, it is argued that where school funds are restricted, some of the office machines in the classroom may also be used by regular office employees. These reasons have merit, but if the architectural scheme does not permit the location of commercial classrooms near the office, no serious educational handicap is likely to result.

The administrative cluster.   The administrative cluster is made up of three distinct but functionally interrelated parts as indicated in Figure 14.2. The location of the guidance suite is crucial in this cluster. It should be between the general office and the health suite. If possible, the pupil entrance to the general office should be completely divorced from the

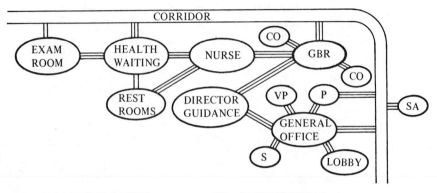

CO – COUNSELING OFFICE   VP – VICE PRINCIPAL
GBR – GUIDANCE BROWSING ROOM   SA – STUDENT ACTIVITY ROOM
P – PRINCIPAL   S – STORAGE

FIGURE 14.2 The Administrative Cluster

entrance to the guidance-browsing-waiting area. It is often possible to locate the entrance to the general office "around the corner" from the entrance to the guidance room. This arrangement keeps the disciplinary function of the principal's office completely dissociated from the guidance function. Internally, however, these two activities are closely related. Records kept in the general office are of basic concern to the guidance counselor. Conversations between the principal and the guidance people are also part of an effective guidance program.

The health and guidance functions are closely related. Many times, guidance counselors find that pupil difficulties arise from health problems. In such instances, the nurse and the guidance counselor work as a team in seeking to help the pupil. The nurse's office and health records should be easily accessible to the guidance counselors, and these two spaces can be closely related externally as well as internally, since the functions involved are psychologically compatible.

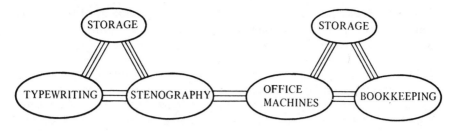

FIGURE 14.3 The Commercial Cluster

The library cluster.   The library itself is surrounded by a large number of spaces occupying a first order of importance. In Figure 14.4 these spaces are connected to the library by three lines. It is essential that these spaces be arranged in the library area so that they can be easily supervised by the librarian. This can sometimes be achieved by installing vision strips in certain spaces and by locating others for direct supervision. Regular classrooms should be located in the general library area if such an arrangement is feasible. Sometimes the library is isolated when it serves both the school and the community.

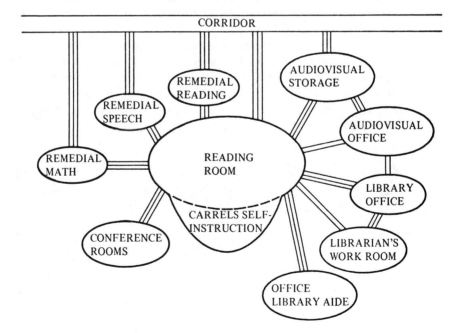

FIGURE 14.4 The Library Cluster.

School planners do not generally view the isolation of the library from nonspecialized classrooms with any degree of alarm, although it would be convenient to place regular classrooms in the library area.

The science cluster.   If the architectural scheme permits it, the science cluster might well adjoin the rooms in which mathematics is taught. While the specific location of the science cluster (Figure 14.5) itself is not critical, the clustering of the individual science rooms in one area is essential, partly to facilitate the movement of costly equipment used for demonstration purposes from one laboratory to another. It is also important that the science teachers be able to work as a team and exchange ideas freely.

The shop cluster.   This group of related instructional areas may be located wherever the architect feels it best fits into his total concept, provided it is at ground level near a service drive and that it is far enough away from quiet instructional areas so as not to disturb them. The progression shown in Figure 14.6 starts with the heavy industrial shops and culminates with arts and crafts shops. Existing shop clusters suffer most from a lack of sufficient storage. The need for storage in shop areas is three-fold. Space is needed for the storage of large tools, for the storage of unfinished pupil projects, and for the storage of materials and supplies. Small tools are often stored in the shop itself in lockable wall cabinets. The storage room for materials and supplies should be easily accessible to the service drive for unloading lumber, steel, and sheet material. It should also be convenient to pupils in the adjoining shops.

Planning rooms, one serving two shops, are essential in shop areas. Some educators feel that it is just as important for pupils to learn how to plan and detail projects on the drawing board as it is to learn how to use tools to construct the project itself. Planning rooms can also be used by the teacher when he gives special instruction to individuals or groups of students working on a given project.

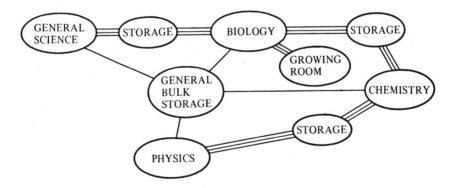

FIGURE 14.5 The Science Cluster

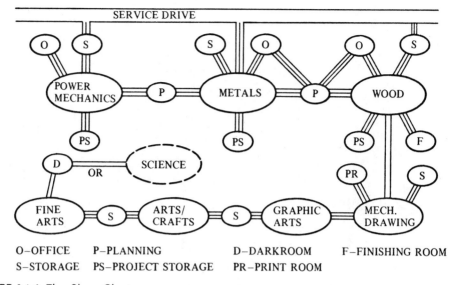

O—OFFICE   P—PLANNING   D—DARKROOM   F—FINISHING ROOM
S—STORAGE   PS—PROJECT STORAGE   PR—PRINT ROOM

FIGURE 14.6 The Shop Cluster

The auditorium-music cluster.   The auditorium and music areas are closely related. Dual-purpose use of dressing rooms is necessary to justify such spaces, for they will be required very few times during the school year. The author has seen a number of dressing rooms near auditorium stages filled with broken chairs, desks, and other school equipment. Instead of being used as a junk storage room when they are not used for dressing, these spaces can be utilized efficiently at all times as combination music practice–dressing rooms. Figure 14.7 is self-explanatory. The music areas shown in this cluster should be designed and located so that the sounds emanating from them do not interfere with quiet activities in the auditorium or in other instructional areas.

The gymnasium cluster.   In addition to what is shown in Figure 14.8, it should be pointed out that no driveways should be interposed between the gymnasium and the play areas of the school. Also, pupils should be able to travel directly from the locker and shower area to the out-of-doors without walking through the gymnasium.

A few special requirements of this area are worth noting. Each teaching area of the gymnasium should be provided with a storage room and instructor's office. At least two corrective rooms should be included directly off the floor of the main gymnasium, one for the girls and one for the boys. Drinking fountains should not be installed in the main gymnasium area, but in an alcove of the gymnasium or in a corridor. In the Midwest, architects ingeniously provide additional teaching stations by locating supplementary spaces on balconies that are also used as seating capacity when

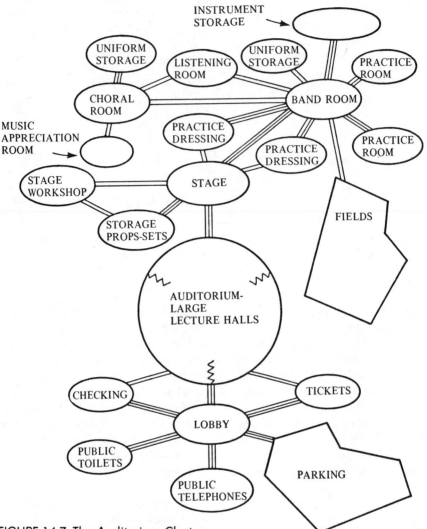

FIGURE 14.7 The Auditorium Cluster

folding bleachers are open. In the closed position, the bleachers form a partial wall between the upper main gymnasium and the auxiliary balcony gymnasium.

The homemaking cluster.   The specific location of this cluster (Figure 14.9) is not very critical. However, if a nursery program is to be served by this cluster, it is essential that it be located at ground level adjacent to a play area for the four-year-old children who participate in the program.

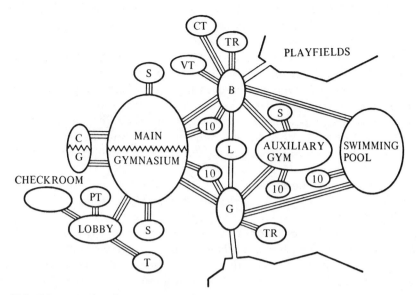

FIGURE 14.8 The Gymnasium Cluster

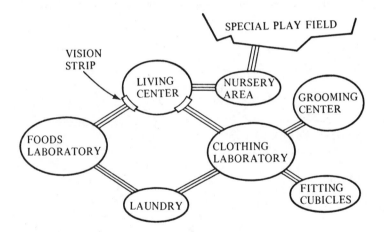

FIGURE 14.9 The Homemaking Cluster

In the past, some school planners have insisted that the homemaking cluster be located next to the cafeteria. There is little basis for this contention. The homemaking suite serves an instructional function while the cafeteria is a pupil service. Some school people argue that the homemaking teacher should be near the cafeteria so that she can supervise the cafeteria personnel. Such an added duty overburdens the homemaking teacher and "shortchanges" the pupils. To avoid this questionable practice, it might be desirable to remove the homemaking cluster from the vicinity of the cafeteria, as is customary in many conventional secondary schools.

The cafeteria cluster. The individual elements in the cafeteria cluster are shown in Figure 14.10. Of primary importance in this regard is the strategic location of the kitchen, dishwashing area, and storage room. Two flow charts should be prepared when this cluster is being planned. One chart should show the pupil circulation from the point where he enters the cafeteria to the point where he leaves the area after dining. The other chart should indicate the flow of food from the storage room to the preparation area, the preparation and cooking point, and to the serving counter. The chart should also show the movement of dishes from the clean-dish storage to the serving areas, to the dishwashing machine, and back to the point of origin.

The location of the service drive is critical to the kitchen function. The delivery zone should be designed so that bulk foods may be easily unloaded at the storage areas. And there should be provision for the storage and removal of trash from this area, a feature that is usually overlooked in planning a kitchen area. Empty food cans are unsightly and usually attract flies. It is suggested that a special screened-in can wash and storage area be provided in a location convenient to the service drive.

The service cluster. The basic feature of this cluster of spaces is its location next to the service drive. Very few schools provide adequately for

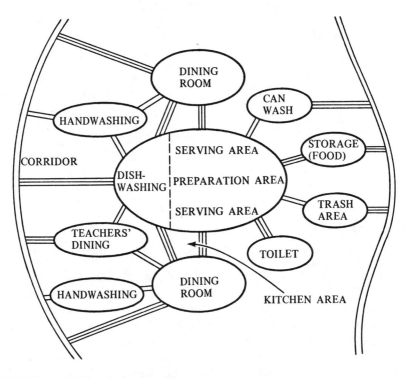

FIGURE 14.10 The Cafeteria Cluster

receiving and storage of supplies and for maintenance facilities. Storage often seems to be located wherever the architect has excess space rather than where it is needed. It is true, of course, that a few odd spaces cannot be avoided in any school plan. The use of such spaces for storage is most acceptable. In addition to these spaces, however, special-purpose storage spaces are needed in specific areas properly related to other spaces. Figure 14.11 indicates the type of spaces that should be located in the service cluster.

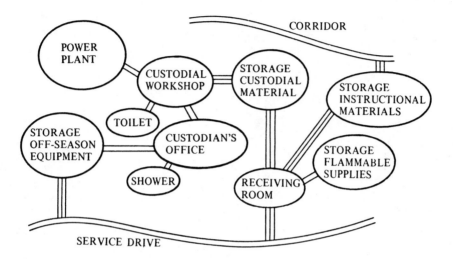

FIGURE 14.11 The Service Cluster

CHAPTER 15

Postplanning Procedures and Construction Costs

After architectural plans have been developed to the satisfaction of the planning team and the board of trustees or board of education, they must be translated into a school building by the cooperative efforts of the architect and the builder. The conversion from plans to building is a crucial part of school plant planning. It includes bidding, supervision, and a good working relationship between architect and general contractor.

PRUDENTIAL CONTRACT STIPULATIONS

Construction Time and Penalty Clauses in the Contract

It is generally agreed that the number of working days allowed for construction should be stated in the contract. If the expected completion date of the project is clearly specified, the contractor will not be tempted to shift his work force from one project to another of higher priority and thus postpone the completion of the building.

In specifying a completion date, however, both parties should agree that the length of time allowed for construction is reasonable, whether or not penalties are involved.

Penalty Clauses in the Contract

The insertion of penalty clauses in a construction contract is not an unmixed blessing to the owner. Generally, where penalties are imposed upon the contractor on a per diem basis for exceeding the stipulated construction time, he is allowed a stated bonus for each day in advance of the specified completion date that he completes his work. Unless the allocated construction time is reasonable, a penalty clause in the contract is likely to cause a significant increase in the contract price of the job.

Even where a penalty clause exists, there is really no positive assurance that the contractor will be legally penalized for not completing the project on time. In most situations, change orders of one form or another are bound to be made. If penalties are involved, the contractor will always seek time extension whenever a change order is requested. In one instance, a contractor requested a 10-day extension of time to move two electrical outlets from one part of a wall to another. The owner has little choice under such circumstances. If he wants the change, he must accept the extension of time. In a state project having an area of about 120,000 square feet, the contractor requested and received a total time extension of 240 calendar days as a result of numerous change orders. The penalty clause in the contract was never invoked, although about 1,000 students were deprived of the use of the facility for an additional academic year.

The Liquidated Damage Clause

Under this clause, the builder agrees to complete the project on a given date, but the owner does not automatically receive payment in the event that he fails to do so. The owner must prove damages directly resulting from the delay in completion of the project in order to collect damages. As a rule, it is difficult to prove that damages are directly traceable to the builder's failure to comply with the contract. For this reason, the liquidated damage clause is not always effective in assuring completion of educational facilities on time.

Insurance

In any contract between a school district or college board and the builder, provision should be made for various types of insurance. The liability insurance is usually carried by the contractor and the fire insurance by the owner. A northern Illinois school district found that it was less expensive for the district to carry both the liability and fire insurance. As a result, it requested the contractor not to include the cost of liability insurance in his bid price. It is suggested that boards of education or boards of trustees explore these alternatives and select the one that provides adequate insurance coverage at least cost.

Performance Bond

According to Strevell and Burke,[1] "This (performance bond) is an assurance that the person or firm to whom the contract is awarded will faithfully per-

---

[1]Wallace H. Strevell and Arvid J. Burke, *Administration of the School Building Program* (New York: McGraw-Hill, 1959), p. 411.

form the contract including all provisions of plans and specifications." The performance bond should not be executed prior to the execution of the construction contract. The terms of the performance bond must meet with the approval of the owner. The premium for this bond may be paid by either the owner or the contractor. It is important, therefore, that the owner specify who will pay the premium for this bond at the time bids are requested.

BIDDING PROCEDURES

The accepted method for selecting a contractor is competitive bidding. This procedure, generally followed by private enterprise, is almost always required by state and local statutes for the construction of public buildings. Bids are not always given to the lowest bidder. Most laws simply require that contracts be awarded to the lowest responsible bidder.

The usual procedure is to invite bidders to submit a proposal and then to supply them with plans and specifications to use in preparing cost estimates. Invitations are usually issued through the press or construction publications. Such invitations include the name of the project and the time and source from which plans and specifications may be obtained. The announcement must also state when and where the bids must be filed and the documents returned, and whether or not a deposit is required for the drawings. Very frequently the bidders must give some assurance that they will accept the bid if it is offered. This assurance usually takes the form of a deposit of a certified check or the filing of a bid bond. The amount of the deposit is usually specified in the statutes.

Time for preparing the bid. The contractor should be allowed ample time to make cost determinations and prepare his bid. Usually a period of about four weeks is allowed, but in less complicated projects two weeks is generally sufficient. Sometimes, extension of bidding time is necessary. In such cases, all bidders should be notified of the extension at least 48 hours before the original opening time. At times, the architect may be required to issue explanations and clarifications during the bidding period. When such action is necessary, he should be sure to issue all supplementary information to all the bidders.

Opening of bids. In general, bids are opened at the appointed time in public and are tabulated by the architect. After prices and alternatives are carefully weighed and compared, the successful bidder is selected. Before receiving the contract for the project, however, the successful bidder is usually required to post a performance bond for the full amount of the contract. This bond serves as a guarantee that should the contractor fail to complete his work satisfactorily, the bonding company will assume the financial obligation for the completion of the building.

Awarding of the contract.   The contract for the construction of the school is signed by both the awarding authority and the contractor. It is strongly suggested that legal advice be sought at this point to make certain that the document is properly prepared and fully protects all concerned, and that persons signing the contract are legally authorized to do so.

Upon signing the contract, the builder is customarily required to submit to the architect a breakdown of his estimates concerning items set forth for the work of the various building trades listed in the specifications. He also submits a schedule of dates for the completion of the various aspects of the construction project, such as footings, foundations, electrical roughing, plumbing, and heating.

BUILDING THE EDUCATIONAL FACILITY

Once the contract is let, the builder must commence construction within the time specified in the contract. The building of a school, as mentioned earlier, is basically a cooperative effort on the part of both the contractor and the architect. In order to be sure that work is performed in accordance with specifications, continuous supervision should be provided. Unless the project is fairly large, in excess of, let us say $200,000, it is difficult to justify the employment of a full-time clerk-of-the-works, even though the employment of such a person is highly desirable in any project.

The supervisory responsibility of the architect.   Contrary to popular belief, the architect is *not* responsible for continuous supervision on the job, unless this is specifically stated in the contract. On the other hand, the supervision provided by the architect should be sufficient to insure that the building is constructed according to specifications. On small projects, the architect may supervise the work as infrequently as one afternoon per week, while on a multi-million dollar project he might provide a full-time resident architect or engineer.

The builder cannot deviate from the plans and specifications without the approval of the architect. Neither can he devise his own method of construction unless it is approved by the architect. Oftentimes, the architect is called upon to verify shop drawings produced by fabricators of the several components of construction. Also, the owner makes no payments to the builder without the authorization of the architect.

The clerk-of-the-works.   In fairly large projects, a clerk-of-the-works is employed by the owner to supervise and inspect every detail of the construction on a full-time basis. He reports any irregularities to the architect, who then takes the necessary corrective action.

The clerk-of-the-works is often worth many times his salary. He makes certain that the contractor delivers a full measure in materials and workmanship. The writer had an experience that clearly demonstrates the value of a component clerk-of-the-works. While visiting a school building under construction, he was conversing briefly with the clerk-of-the-works. In the middle of the conversation, the clerk-of-the-works departed abruptly and climbed a ladder leading to the roof where a workman was installing a flashing around the chimney. Upon his return, he stated, "Just as I thought, they were using ¾-inch copper nails instead of the required inch and a half." When he was asked how he had detected this deficiency at a distance of 300 feet, he answered, "Whoever heard of driving a one-and-one-half-inch roofing nail with a single blow of the hammer?"

Change orders.   A change order is defined as a change made in the plans of a building while construction is in progress. The number of change orders should be kept to a minimum, but where the function of a school plant can be substantially improved, or serious deficiencies corrected, change orders should be made.

In general, change orders are more costly than the same changes would have been if they had been included in the original working drawings. They need not be so costly, but because of the very nature of competitive bidding, the contractor's profit is often not included in a deductive change order. On the other hand, an additive change order is often treated as a single project without competitive bidding. Thus, the amount that is added to the contract is ordinarily greater than it would be if competitive bidding entered the cost estimate. For example, a school district in central Illinois had awarded a substantial contract to a contractor for pointing the mortar joints in the exterior of a fairly large junior high school. While work was in progress, it was discovered that the parapet was loose and constituted a safety hazard. The board of education voted to remove it from the building. The contractor was asked to quote a price on a "change order" basis for the removal of the parapet, on the assumption that he was already on the job and his price would probably be lower than others. As a matter of academic interest, one of the board members suggested that several other quotations be sought. To the surprise of all concerned, the price of the contractor on the job was about 25 percent higher than that supplied by others! Needless to say, no change order was issued.

Relationship between the contractor and school officials.   Generally speaking, there is no direct relationship between the owner and the contractor. The owner deals with the contractor through the architect. It is true, of course, that the owner retains his right to inspect the work during construction, but the builder is usually not required to take orders directly from him.

It should be pointed out, however, that the builder generally has complete jurisdiction within the contract limits of his project during construction. He almost always has the authority to prevent anyone from trespassing within his contract limits. Builders are reluctant to permit persons not having official business in the construction zone because of legal liability in case of accidents.

MANUAL FOR ADMINISTRATION AND STAFF

The normal procedure after school facility is ready for occupancy is relatively simple. The board of education accepts the building. The contractor turns the keys of the building over to school officials and, at some early future date, an open house is held for the public under the auspices of the board of education. Speeches are made, the taxpayers are congratulated, and the school band plays on. This marks the end of the major construction works, on the part of the contractor, the architect, and educational consultants. Of course, all parties may be called in to correct problems that may arise during the "shake down" period of the building operation.

Eventually, all parties responsible for the planning and construction of a building will become disassociated with the occupied school facility. And after a decade or so, very few people will know who these parties were, without reading the bronze plaque that is usually affixed to one of the walls in the lobby area of the building. There is nothing improper or unusual about this sequence of events. However, the administration and staff assigned to the building inherit a complicated educational facility which they are required to operate for many years in the future. In some instances, no one will remember or know the intended function for each space in the building nor how the mechanical and electrical equipment should be maintained and operated.

In order to avoid this situation, it is suggested that the architect be required to prepare a manual regarding the maintenance and operation of the school building. The manual shoud describe:

1. How each space was intended to be used when the building was planned.
2. All of the lighting, heating, and ventilating controls, where they are located, and what they control.
3. How each critical building or working surface and each piece of mechanical equipment should be maintained, including cautionary statements as to "what not to do."
4. How the building is planned for expansion and the specific points in the electrical, mechanical, and architectural systems where extensions can be made.

The manual should also show the "as built" plans in logical segments on several pages of the booklet, so that future modifications of the building can be made economically and intelligently.

COMPARISONS OF CONSTRUCTION COSTS

As many architects and educators readily admit, comparing the unit cost of one school with that of another is meaningless and often misleading. Costs simply indicate the number of dollars that are spent for a unit area, volume, or student. This much of the comparison is quite specific and definite. On the other hand, there are several aspects of a school plant that are not revealed in unit cost figures. In computing any type of unit cost, there is only one figure that is certain, namely, the total cost. For this reason, unit costs in school construction are really quite vague. Unit costs are determined by dividing cost by another item, usually number of students, number of square feet, number of cubic feet, or number of classrooms. Since only the numerator or cost figure is definite, the unit cost loses much of its significance.

Inadequacy of Unit Cost Comparisons

Unit cost figures alone are quite meaningless in making cost comparisons. There are several shortcomings inherent in all unit cost figures applicable to school buildings; others are peculiar only to certain unit costs.

Inadequacies common to all unit cost figures.   A cost of a school building per square foot, per cubic foot, per classroom, or per student cannot be used by itself in comparing school building costs sensibly for the reasons listed below.

1. It does not indicate what is actually included in the building in terms of unusual spaces, laboratory units, and special built-in equipment.
2. It does not reveal the quality of the construction materials selected by the architect and educational boards.
3. It does not tell anything about extraordinary site conditions.
4. It fails to indicate the type, extent, or quality of mechanical equipment used in the building.
5. It neglects to provide an index of economy regarding the cost of operation and maintenance of the building after it is completed.
6. It omits any information regarding the educational efficiency of the structure.
7. It does not reveal the extent to which the building may be over-planned for future expansion.
8. It fails to indicate how much site development and educational equipment are included in the cost figure.
9. It does not reveal how efficiently the space within the building can be utilized.

Additional shortcomings peculiar to the use of cost per square foot or per cubic foot of school buildings.　　　(Such a unit cost is also deficient for the reasons listed below.

1. It fails to indicate what areas or volumes included in obtaining the total areas or volumes. For example, is attic space included in the volume? Are pipe trenches counted as area or volume?
2. It does not reveal how overhangs, enclosed walkways, and covered walks have been treated in the computation.

Shortcomings of the use of the cost per class room or per student.　　　These unit costs are even less reliable than those listed above, for several obvious reasons.

1. The capacity of a school building is not fixed or uniform for every school of the same type. There is no standard of measuring building capacity. In most cases, it is simply an "educated guess."
2. The cost figures do not reveal the number of square feet in a school building per student or per classroom. Clearly, a building with inadequate instructional spaces costs less to construct than one with adequate spaces.

How to Make Reliable and Meaningful Unit Cost Comparisons

The view of unit cost comparisons expressed in the previous paragraphs is not altogether dismal. Up to this point, it has been assumed that a board of education or board of trustees seeks to compare simply by reviewing unit costs supplied by architects, school personnel, or educational consultants. Such figures, as indicated earlier, are quite meaningless, except in making crude estimates of school building costs. Unit costs can be extremely valuable, however, when they are compiled by a central statistical agency.

Which is the most reliable unit cost figure?　　　The author made a study of two of the unit costs in common use. One hundred and twenty-nine elementary units were included in the study. Costs were derived from the official records of the Massachusetts School Building Assistance Commission. A coefficient of correlation was computed between the construction cost of a school and (a) the cost per square foot and (b) the cost per student. It was found that the coefficient of correlation between cost per square foot and total construction cost was 0.92, and the coefficient of correlation between cost per student and total construction cost was 0.71. Obviously, the cost per square foot is a more accurate predictor of the total cost of a building. This fact is not surprising. Architects have used this method since the beginning of architectural costs analysis.

Obtaining reliable cost figures.   Sensible cost comparison using cost per square foot can be made if the instructions listed below are followed.

1. Start with the basic data. Use working drawings of the various buildings and request a breakdown of the costs involved.
2. In measuring areas, observe the following rules:
   (a) Use all outside dimensions of the buildings.
   (b) Include only usable floor spaces. For example, storage rooms in the basement would be considered part of the area of the building, while unfinished spaces and pipe trenches would not.
   (c) Divide the areas of all covered walks and overhangs by three before adding them to the area of the rest of the building.
   (d) Divide enclosed corridors by two before adding them to the area of the rest of the building.
   (e) Staircases should be included at each level at full value for each level.
   (f) The area of elevator shafts should be included only once, but the wall thickness at all levels should be included in the spaces surrounding the elevator shaft.
3. Costs should be treated as follows:
   (a) Construction cost should include the cost of the structure, all equipment attached to the building, and the cost of site development for about 25 feet around the building. Care should be taken in comparing costs of buildings in which expensive laboratory equipment or air-conditioning is installed. In these cases, be sure that buildings compared are similar. Otherwise, the cost of the highly specialized equipment must be omitted from the total cost.
   (b) Exclude architectural, legal, and other fees.
   (c) Exclude the cost of the site development and site acquisition.

If these guides are observed, any central office can accumulate a reliable set of cost figures for both predicting and comparing school building costs. This service can best be rendered to school districts by the various state departments of education and by the statistical branch of the U.S. Office of Education.

4

Modernizing, Maintaining, and Operating an Existing Facility

CHAPTER 16

Modernization of Educational Facilities

The terms *rehabilitation, remodeling,* and *modernization* are common in the parlance of schoolpeople, but they often have different meanings to different people. As used in this text, *rehabilitation* is a form of deferred maintenance. The school building is simply restored to the same condition as it was when it was built. Old equipment and worn parts are replaced. The interior walls, floors, and ceilings are repainted and refinished and the exterior of the building is reconstructed wherever necessary in order to make it weather-proof again. These changes are essentially cosmetic. *Remodelling* goes one step beyond rehabilitation. It also includes changes in the size or shape of any space within the building.

To this extent, a remodelled school facility could improve its function as an education tool. And finally, the term *modernization* as defined in this text is a process whereby an existing school facility is brought up-to-date structurally, educationally, and environmentally. In this process, certain spaces within the school building may be reshaped in order to accommodate modern educational practices. Worn mechanical equipment, weathered parts of the structure, and unsightly and unsafe interior surfaces may be restored to their original state. Modernization also includes the installation of more efficient mechanical and electrical equipment and the addition of energy-efficient materials to the exterior walls and roof. And finally, modernization accommodates a forward-looking educational program, improving the health and safety of the students occupying the building and provides for special education services as described in *A Guide for Planning New and Renovated Schools.*[1]

[1]Allen C. Abend, Micheal J. Bednar, Vera J. Froelinger, Yale Stenzler, Education Services, Council for Exceptional Children, Reston, Va., 1979.

AN OVERVIEW OF SCHOOL FACILITY MODERNIZATION

School facility modernization is a more complex and time-consuming task than planning a new facility. It is much easier to change lines on paper than it is to move partitions, reroute electric wires, cut and rejoin pipes, and redesign the structural members of an existing building. On the other hand, educational facility planners and architects are presented with both a challenge and an opportunity to transform an obsolete school buildng into one that is educationally efficient, structurally safe, and environmentally healthful. Several aspects of school facility modernization are outlined in the following sections.

IMPROVEMENTS IN EDUCATIONAL FUNCTION, ENERGY CONSERVATION, AND ENVIRONMENTAL QUALITY

The interrelated improvements in a school facility can be illustrated best by introducing a hypothetical situation involving the Smith Elementary School which is typical of those built in 1923. It is a two-story building with a flat roof and parapet. It contains eight classrooms, and features a principal's office on the second floor over the main entrance. It has a brick exterior, wooden sash and frames, and two basement play areas with toilets adjoining each room. The classrooms are fairly large, each containing slightly over 900 square feet. A cloakroom about 10 feet wide and 22 feet long adjoins each classroom. The central corridors and lobbies in this building are constructed of fire-resistant materials. The ceilings and walls are plaster on wooden lath, except in the corridors and exterior walls where plaster is applied directly to the brick walls. The lighting system in each room consists of four suspended globe-type fixtures furnished with 200-watt incandescent bulbs. The heating system consists of a coal-fired steam boiler and cast-iron radiators in the classrooms and corridors. The ventilating system is capable of providing about 25 cubic feet of fresh air per pupil per minute.

After a review of the findings of a school survey recently completed by a team of educational consultants from Home State University, the board of education decided to follow the recommendation in the long-range plan calling for modernization of the Smith Elementary School. The study described some of the school's shortcomings as follows: "The wooden floors in the corridors and classrooms are dark, warped, and creaky. The window sashes are loose and in need of repair. There is no suitable place for physical education and assembly. There is also no health room or workroom for the teachers. The building, as a whole, is in excellent structural condition but the atmosphere found in the classrooms is not conducive to effective learning. . . ." On the basis of this report and a study of the curriculum, educational specifications were developed and the following was accomplished.

In addition to a face-lifting around the front entrance and main lobby, the Smith Elementary School was modernized as follows:

1. The foundation was examined, repaired wherever necessary, and insulated with panels of styrofoam or equivalent structural insulating materials.

2. A gas hot water heater, separate from the boiler, was installed in the boiler room and piped through insulated pipes to the cafeteria, adjoining lavatories, and to the multipurpose room. A small, self-contained electric hot water heater was installed near the principal's office and teachers' lounge. (This eliminated long hot-water pipe lines from the central hot water heater.)

3. A gas hot-water heater was installed in the boiler room and hot water piped to all lavatories.

4. Two cloakrooms on each floor were converted to modern toilet rooms, one for boys and one for girls. Ceramic tile was installed on the floor and walls, and new lighting and improved ventilation were provided. Wall-hung fixtures were used throughout, and foot control, single-spigot faucets with tempered water were introduced.

5. A new base was installed on all of the wooden floors in the corridors and classrooms, and light-colored vinyl asbestos tile was laid over it.

6. The upper part of all classroom and corridor walls was repainted in pastel colors. A warm wood-toned formica-type material was installed on the lower walls of the classrooms.

7. The ceilings in all of the classrooms and corridors were lowered to a height of about 10 feet, using a mechanical steel grid system. Acoustical tile was installed on all ceilings.

8. The lighting in corridor and classroom areas was replaced by continuous-strip fluorescent fixtures. The school was completely rewired.

9. The wooden window sashes and frames were replaced with modern anodized aluminum units with insulating glass.

10. The parapet was removed and new flashing was installed to give the building a modern, sleek appearance and to correct a leaking roof.

11. The three outside doors were replaced with modern glass doors.

12. All stairs were resurfaced using abrasive, nonslip materials.

13. The single wooden handrail was replaced by a modern, metal double handrail set at two heights.

14. Cloak closets with vertically sliding panel doors were built in the classrooms along the corridor walls.
15. The gray slate chalkboards were removed, and the walls beneath were replastered, refinished, and painted. Vertical standards four feet apart were installed in all areas where chalkboard and tackboard were needed. Movable, metal chalkboard panels were hung on these standards. The two chalkboard panels in front of each room were equipped with a source of ultraviolet light so that luminous chalk could be used.
16. Similar standards were installed in the main lobby to support display cabinets and shelves.
17. The lower walls in all corridors were sprayed with plastic-type paint to a height of about four feet.
18. At least two duplex electrical outlets were installed on the opposite walls of each classroom and in strategic locations in the corridors.
19. The old shades in the classrooms were replaced by vertical-type venetian blinds for improved light control.
20. Eight solar hot water heating panels, each having an area of about forty square feet, were installed on the roof facing south and tilted at an angle from the horizontal, approximating the latitude on which the Smith School was located. This unit was tied into the new gas hot-water heater.
21. One cloakroom on each floor was converted to a remedial room for speech therapy, reading, and arithmetic.
22. The remaining cloakroom on the first floor was used for storage of instructional and custodial materials. Locks were installed on the doors.
23. The principal's office on the second floor was enlarged, refinished, relighted, paneled in birch, and converted into a teacher's lounge. All of the floor was carpeted except the area surrounding the work space and the sink-refrigerator-range combination, where vinyl tile was used. This space was enlarged by removing the wall between the principal's office and the adjoining cloakroom. Part of the cloak area was added to the teachers' lounge and part of it was designed as a workroom.
24. The two basement playrooms with relatively high ceilings were converted into a kitchen and cafeteria for the hot-lunch program. The ceiling was dropped about 6 inches below the former ceiling and covered with acoustical tile. Surface-type, plastic-covered fluorescent strips were attached to the ceiling. Wooden paneling was used on the walls and gaily colored vinyl asbestos tile was installed on the floor. A movable raised platform was placed at one end of this space.

25. Modern, movable, colorful plastic chairs and plastic-surfaced tables were provided.
26. Lounge furniture and a comfortable work table were provided in the teachers' room.
27. The two large toilet areas in the basement were reduced in size and completely restyled with new fixtures, ceramic tile floors and walls, better lighting, and improved ventilation.
28. A general storage area for instructional materials was developed in the basement of the building.
29. A fire-resistant area for storage of cleaning agents was built in the basement area.
30. New partitions were installed in the basement areas to separate the kitchen from the dining area, the boiler room from the rest of the basement, and the storage spaces from the spaces around them.
31. The walls between four pairs of classrooms were replaced with movable partitions having a rated sound transmission loss of about 40 decibels.
32. The bricks on the exterior walls were steam-cleaned and re-pointed. The outside walls and the roof were insulated and the basement walls were repaired and waterproofed.
33. An addition to the Smith Elementary School was also built. The new section was connected to the side entrance by an attractive carpeted corridor. The addition was designed so that it could stand by itself architecturally and structurally if the main building were to be demolished at a later date.
34. The new addition contained the following spaces:
    (a) One 1,200-square-foot kindergarten room of modern design with wall-to-wall carpeting, except in the dressing space and in the wet work areas.
    (b) One library room having an area of about 1,500 square feet, plus space for storing audiovisual equipment.
    (c) Four regular classrooms, each about 950 square feet in net area. Wall-to-wall carpeting was installed in all except wet work areas.
    (d) A multipurpose room having an area of about 2,500 square feet, plus space for a stage and chair storage room.
    (e) A clerk and principal's office and a health suite with office and examination room. A toilet and hospital-type sink were also located in this area. These areas also had wall-to-wall carpeting.
35. The four regular classrooms mentioned in item 34 were located in circular cluster so that movable partitions between them could be opened to produce a single unified space for about 120 pupils.

36. Television reception jacks were installed in both the new and original classrooms of the Smith Elementary School.
37. A special conference room was located adjacent to the library. It was directly connected to the library for the convenience of team teachers using this space in the preparation of their work. It was furnished with comfortable chairs and trapezoidal tables.

Thus, Smith Elementary School in Hometown, U.S.A. was extensively modernized. The cost? Hundreds of thousands of dollars. Was it worth it? Probably not. A formula will be presented in the latter part of this chapter to assist shool planners in making this crucial decision.

HEALTH RELATED IMPROVEMENTS

The modernization process demands that educational facility planners concentrate heavily on matters related to the safety and health of the occupants of a building. Lighting, temperature and humidity control, sound pollution, water quality, ventilation, fire protection, and potentially dangerous situations should be improved to the maximum possible degree. Any flaw in the design of the building or construction material that may have a deleterious effect on the health of the occupants must be corrected in its entirety, notwithstanding economic considerations. One example of this type of health hazard is cited in the next paragraph.

Medical research scientists have discovered that asbestos is a cancer-producing agent. Immediately following World War II, asbestos was widely used in the construction industry because of its excellent thermal properties. It was fireproof and a good heat-insulator. It appeared in several forms. It was pulverized and made into a cement-like substance that was plastered around boilers or steam pipes. Often, the asbestos insulating tubes were covered with fabric. During this period, the walls and ceilings were constructed of materials containing asbestos. Sometimes, asbestos and other sound absorbing materials were sprayed on ceilings for accoustical and insulating purposes. School administrators should not wait until a school building suspected of containing asbestos is modernized. All asbestos materials should be replaced immediately with noncarcinogenic materials. In situations where asbestos materials cannot be removed immediately, a temporary solution may be considered once the mechanics of the asbestos danger are understood. As long as the asbestos remains where it was installed, there is no real danger from it. But, since it is a cementous substance, it ultimately pulverizes in time and becomes airborne. When such air is inhaled, the danger of developing cancer is real and imminent. There are currently on the market resinous sprays that can be applied to the surface of materials containing asbestos. This treatment seals the asbestos-laden material temporarily and prevents the asbestos powder from becoming airborne. A word of caution is in order. This is not a permanent solution to the asbestos problem in school facilities. Funds should be provided to remove asbestos materials from a school building as soon as possible.

MODERNIZED FACILITIES FOR SPECIAL EDUCATION SERVICES

In Chapter 6, a few guidelines were presented in relation to the planning of new facilities for the needs of exceptional students suffering from physical impediments and learning disabilities. The same goals and objectives apply to modernized educational facilities. Accordingly, all special features and design characteristics planned for exceptional students in new school facilities should be embodied in the plans of a modernized school facility. It is suggested that the publication, *Facilities for Special Education Services*[2] which has been cited earlier, be perused from cover to cover before planning facilities for exceptional students. It is replete with extremely valuable information on the needs of these students. It is further suggested that the sections in Chapter 6 dealing with facilities for special students needs be reviewed during the design stages of school facilities that are being modernized.

TO MODERNIZE OR TO REPLACE

One of the most perplexing questions confronting citizens within a school district is whether or not the existing school facility should be modernized or replaced. Many approaches are possible but there seems to be no single line of reasoning that will satisfy everyone.

Paradox and Controversy

For various reasons, the issue of modernization or replacement is often fraught with paradox and controversy. There seems to be a natural tendency among many citizens to favor modernization over replacement for two reasons. They may feel a sense of loyalty to the grand old school that served them and their predecessors well in the past. There seems to be a common belief that modernization automatically means greater economy because part of the old structure is preserved. Unfortunately, the average citizen sees only part of the picture. He seems to be unaware that school buildings, like his automobile, become functionally obsolete. Too few citizens realize that the educational process of today is considerably different

[2]*Ibid.*

from what it was when they attended school. Consequently, when citizens' committees examine today's school buildings, they often fail to perceive the presence of educational obsolescence. Under these circumstances, they cannot be expected to make valid judgments of the educational worth of an existing school building. Nonetheless, citizens do make judgments about their schools, arrive at conclusions, true or false, and act accordingly. Sometimes they make unwise decisions without realizing it. Having convinced themselves, with or without a valid basis for judgment, that a building is educationally useful, citizens frequently presume without additional study that it is unquestionably more economical to modernize it than to replace it. To such citizens, this conclusion is axiomatic. This line of reasoning is perfectly understandable from the standpoint of the taxpayer. After all, he sees before him an apparently useful educational structure that represents a real value in dollars and cents. Why abandon it only to replace it with another structure? During a recent controversy regarding the question of modernization or replacement, the mayor of a large, conservative New England city said, "The city has no use whatsoever for that (high school) building except as an educational facility. There's been talk of turning it into a new City Hall, but it would cost millions to turn classrooms into office space. Abandoning that building as a school would be abandoning a facility valued at some $6,000,000, private assessors have told me." This statement or one similar to it is quite familiar to educators in all parts of the country. Whenever the question of modernization versus replacement arises, someone is almost certain to remind the voters of the replacement value of that wonderful old school building in the middle of town. This subtle emotional appeal and the desire for economy lend considerable power to such statements. This argument places economy above educational values, and it is very difficult to combat it with reason, logic, common sense, or a promise of a better educational program for all of the children of all of the people.

Modernization is both a blessing and a curse. When modernization is warranted in terms of the criteria presented in this chapter, it is usually easier to "sell" to the public than other proposals. On the other hand, when new construction is preferable to modernization, the issue may become highly emotional and controversial. The resistance to new construction seems to stem from the feeling of some citizens that a perfectly good building is being abandoned only to be replaced by a new one on the same or on another site.

MODERNIZATION OR NEW CONSTRUCTION

The decision whether or not to modernize a given building requires time, study, vision, and courage. A comprehensive study of all aspects of the problem is a necessary first step. Time and imagination are needed to identify and explore alternatives and to study and evaluate the consequences and educational returns associated with them. A hasty and ill-conceived decision to modernize a school may penalize the education of children yet unborn. School officials and members of boards of education should identify the real issues and act in the best interest of the public and the school district.

The Castaldi Generalized Formula for School Modernization

A thorough search of the literature of school modernization uncovered virtually no information about what factors should determine whether or not a school should be modernized. The author asked himself the question that at some time or other has confronted all school planners, "When should or should not a school be modernized?" Only two rules of thumb were discovered. They are as follows:

1. According to Linn, the decision to modernize a building is questionable if the cost of modernization exceeds 50 percent of the cost of a new project. He suggests that a 40 percent figure would be more realistic.[3]
2. The second rule of thumb was proposed by building experts who believe that when any two of the following items are required, modernization should be questioned. The items include major replacement of plumbing and heating; total replacement of electrical wiring; basic structural changes involving space arrangements; complete replacement of roofing; or complete revamping of the fenestration pattern.

There is, to be sure, much merit in both of these guidelines to modernization. Both statements focus upon economic considerations, but the Linn statement is more precisely related to the actual expenditure that may be required for modernization. The rule of the building experts, on the other hand does not require that the cost of modernization be converted into dollars before a decision is made. Also, since the decision whether or not to modernize is based upon the need for any two of the major projects noted above, the actual cost that serves as the determinant in making the decision may vary over fairly wide limits. This does not mean that the second rule of thumb is of little value. The rule of the building experts serves a most important function in alerting boards of education and school planners to take a second and even a third hard look at the advisability of modernizing an existing school.

Another approach to the financial aspect of modernization is proposed here. In developing the generalized formula for school moderniza-

[3]Henry Linn, "Modernizing School Buildings," *American School and University,* 24 (1952), p. 401.

tion presented in this book, the author has sought to set forth a mathematical expression that:

1. Separates, insofar as possible, the total cost of modernization into its major component parts, namely, cost for educational improvements, cost for improvements in healthfulness, and cost for improvements in safety.
2. Takes into account the educational adequacy of the modernized school, which also includes the school site.
3. Clearly indicates whether or not modernization would be of financial advantage to the school district over an extended period of time.
4. Places replacement cost and modernization cost on a comparable basis.

This formula is based upon the rate-of-depreciation concept, and contains both a determinant and a hypothesis (underlying the formula).

The fundamental determinant in the proposed formula for school modernization is the annual rate of depreciation of school facilities. It is hypothesized that the lower the effective rate of depreciation[4]—represented primarily by the amount of capital required to provide a school plant that is adequate in every respect—the sounder the expenditure of public funds. It is postulated, therefore, that the determinant of financial advantage on the part of a school district is not the initial cost, but the *rate* at which the initial cost is likely to depreciate over a period of years.

The general formula is stated as follows: Modernization is justifiable if:

$$\frac{(C_E + C_H + C_S)}{(L_M)(I_A)} < \frac{R}{L_R}$$

where
C_E = Total cost of educational improvements
C_H = Total cost for improvements in healthfulness (physical, aesthetic, and psychological)
C_S = Total cost for improvements in safety
I_A = Estimated index of educational adequacy (0–1)
L_M = Estimated useful life of the modernized school
R = Cost of replacement of school considered for modernization
L_R = Estimated life of new building

Discussion of the general formula.   The three terms in the parenthesis include many items that are not readily apparent. For example, C_E may include, in addition to remodeling, the expansion of the site, new wiring for

[4]Effective depreciation includes both educational adequacy and capital outlay.

educational television, and accommodating new teaching practices. C_H may involve an improved heating system, improved lighting, redecoration, refenestration, resurfaced floors and ceilings, and better ventilation. And finally, C_S may cover items such as structural repairs, fireproofing corridors and stairways, elimination of loose plaster, or repairing loose shingles.

I_A is an index of educational adequacy, ranging in value from 0-1, that is applied to the school for which modernization is being proposed. The value of the index is determined in relation to the educational adequacy of a replacement for the school in question. Often, when a school is modernized, compromises must be accepted. They may appear in the form of inconveniences to pupils and teachers or as restrictions of the educational function of the school. The school site is a case in point. The author does not hold that an inadequate site, per se, is sufficient reason for arbitrarily deciding that a school can neither be replaced nor modernized at a given location. The size of a school site is an important factor, but it is only one of many that must be considered in deciding where a school should be located. In situations where school sites do not meet desired standards, the site deficiency should be reflected in the index of educational adequacy unless the replacement school would also be located on an inadequate site. It is important to bear in mind, however, that the index of educational adequacy applies to the entire school plant, of which the site is only one element. Since the index of educational adequacy is determined subjectively and represents a professional judgment, it might be desirable to obtain an evaluation of educational adequacy both from professional persons within the school system and from one or two qualified professionals outside of the school district.

L_M refers to the estimated number of years of useful life remaining in the school in question after it is modernized. It is quite possible that under certain circumstances, the expected life of the modernized building can be extended through structural improvements.

R and L_R represent the cost of a school that would replace the building under consideration and the number of years it is likely to remain in operation, respectively. Admittedly, both the modernized school and a new building would require maintenance over an extended period of time. And it might even be argued that the average annual cost of maintenance could differ considerably between the modernized school and its replacement. For the purpose of the generalized formula, it is assumed that the average annual cost of maintenance for the modernized building is the same as that for its replacement. It should be pointed out, however, that a well-designed modern school may have a greater life expectancy than the building designed in the past.

Application of the formula.   The figures required in the formula should be determined as accurately as possible and entered in their proper places in the formula. If the left side of the formula is numerically smaller than the right, modernization would be financially advantageous to the school district. The smaller the numerical value of the left side in comparison with the value of the right, the greater would be the financial advantage of modernization to the school district. If both sides are approximately equal, the author would favor replacement over modernization. A word of caution is in order, however. The formula should be the determining factor only if the prerequisites mentioned later are met.

Comparison of the Linn rule of thumb with results from the generalized formula.   It will be remembered that Linn suggested that modernization may be justified if the cost of modernization is about 40 percent of the cost of replacement. It will also be recalled that in the life cycle of a building, forty seems to be the age at which most schools are considered for modernization. Let us assume that a school building is forty years old and is estimated to have a remaining life of thirty years after modernization. Let us further assume that the modernized school would contain a few unavoidable compromises so that its educational adequacy is judged to be about 90 percent of that expected for its replacement. It is also assumed that the replacement would have an expected life of sixty-five years.

$$\frac{(\text{cost of modernization})}{(30)(0.90)} < ? \frac{(\text{cost of replacement})}{65}$$

But according to the Linn hypothesis, if cost of modernization equals 0.40 (cost of replacement), modernization is justifiable. Let us test the Linn hypothesis in the general formula for the situation in this example. Substituting 0.4 (cost of replacement) for the cost of modernization in the general formula, we have,

$$\frac{0.4 \ (\text{cost of replacement})}{(30)(0.90)} < ? \frac{(\text{cost of replacement})}{65}$$

$$\frac{0.4}{(30)(0.90)} < \frac{1}{65}$$

$$0.0148 < 0.0154$$

Since the left side of the expression is less than the right, modernization is justifiable according to the generalized formula. It can be concluded, therefore, that the Linn hypothesis is a special case of the general formula presented in this report, and is valid for schools similar to the one described above. It should be noted, however, that the Linn hypothesis would not agree with the generalized formula when the school considered for modernization is more than forty-five years old.

REQUISITE CONDITIONS FOR MODERNIZATION

Before modernization can be justified as the best expenditure of public funds in any school district, the answer to *every* question listed below must be *in the affirmative*. It cannot be overemphasized that a negative response to any *one* of the criteria listed below is a sufficient reason for rejecting a proposal to modernize a given building. These statements may appear to be exacting and uncompromising. They are meant to be just that. School officials and boards of education cannot afford to yield to selfish pressures when the welfare and education of pupils are at stake and when tax funds would be used inefficiently.

1. *Is the school building under consideration needed in its present location for at least 75 percent of its remaining useful life after moderization?* Stated differently, the question might be, "Why spend money to modernize a building that will be phased out of operation in the very near future?"

2. *Is it impractical to distribute the pupil load of the school considered for modernization among other nearby adequate schools?* In some instances in large cities, it is possible to abandon an obsolete school building after reassigning its pupils to other schools. This alternative, when feasible, should take precedence over modernization.

3. *Does the structure lend itself to improvement, alteration, remodeling, and expansion?* If the answer is "no," the cost of remodeling or expanding such a building could be unreasonably high and/or the educational function could be restricted because of the technical impracticability of accomplishing certain necessary structural changes.

4. *Does the modernized building fit into a well-conceived long-range plan?* There are situations in which a modernized building can be justified on all counts on a short-range basis it does provide for an immediate and predictable need. But a short-term perspective is sometimes costly where modernization is concerned.

Let us illustrate this point. A northern Illinois school district was operating a single, centrally located high school enrolling about 1,000 students. The building was about thirty years old and in fairly good repair, but it was situated in the middle of the city on a site of about 4 acres. The site was hemmed in by business enterprises on three sides and was bounded by homes in the rear. The school district was confronted with the problem of providing space for an anticipated increase in enrollment of approximately 1,100 pupils within three years. The district had several alternatives: (1) it could change the grade organization so that it could house the lower level of the secondary school in the existing building with only a few modifications and construct a new building for the upper level on an adequate site; (2) it could sell the school for use as an office building and construct a single large high school on a site of about 30 acres located less than one-half mile from the existing school; or (3) it could modernize and expand the existing school.

After a great deal of controversy, the school district chose to modernize and expand the existing building. Although this action satisfied a number of criteria favoring modernization, it failed to pass the test of fitting into a plan designed to meet the long-range needs of the school district. Nevertheless, the adjoining block of houses was acquired by the board of education for the expansion of the school. This addition pushed the rear boundary of the site back to a railroad track which served as a major railroad trunk line.

Two years after the project was completed, it became obvious that the expanded school lacked sufficient capacity to house an additional 400 pupils. The board of education found itself in a dilemma. It did not feel that it could justify construction of a separate high school for this enrollment, but there was no free space on the already crowded 7½-acre site to construct the needed facility. Furthermore, the board of education realized that the present site was already severely overloaded. It recognized, too, that it would be folly to add pupil capacity to an already inadequate site and simultaneously reduce its land area still further by placing another structure on it.

This unwelcome situation could have been avoided if the electorate had been better informed when the decision to modernize was made. At least two of the criteria for modernization discussed here were not met. Indeed, the site could not be expanded to the minimum size needed for the ultimate enrollment, and the modernized building did not fit into a long-range plan for the school district. Nonetheless, in this particular instance, the board of education recommended—and the electorate supported—the modernization and expansion of the original high school building.

5. *Can the site of the school considered for modernization be expanded to meet minimum standards for the ulitmate enrollment envisioned on the site?* In the example cited in the previous section, it was clear that the school district had not developed a long-range plan to guide its action. But the modernization proposal would have been indefensible on the basis of site considerations alone. The original building housing about 1,000 students was situated on a 4-acre site. A 3½-acre block was added to the original site. Consequently, the board recommended that a 2,100 pupil high school be situated on a 7½-acre site. When it is realized that the board of education could have purchased about 30 acres of open farmland less than half a mile from the existing high school, the case for modernization is considerably weakened.

6. *In accordance with the Castaldi Generalized Formula, is the annual cost of capital outlay for modernization less than it would be for a replacement building?* Regardless of the purported value of an existing building or the initial cost of new construction, it is the rate of consumption of capital outlay funds that is significant in the choice between moderniza-

tion and new construction. Figure 16.1 illustrates the application of balance to modernization.

7. *Has a blue-ribbon committee concluded that educational obsolescence of a given building can be substantially eliminated through the process of modernization?* A team consisting of the superintendent of schools, a member of the board of education, a qualified educational consultant, an architect, and a citizen selected by a group or person (mayor) outside of the school should be organized when a building is considered for modernization. This group should review, study, and discuss the educational aspects of the building, particularly its limitations, and then decide whether or not it is *physically* possible to correct its educational shortcomings. The team should also make an estimate of I_A, the index of educational adequacy of a modernized building. This figure should then be substituted in the Castaldi Generalized Formula.

SEQUENTIAL STEPS IN PLANNING FOR SCHOOL FACILITY MODERNIZATION

As school districts develop, expand, and reach maturity, the cumulative investment of public funds or educational facilities becomes progressively

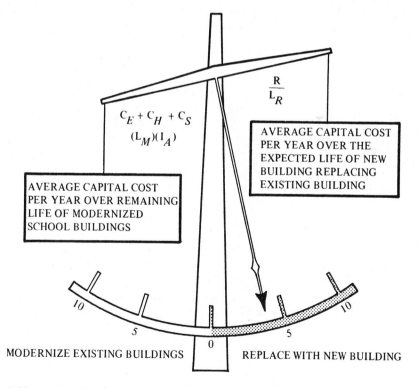

FIGURE 16.1 Modernization in Balance.

larger. It is not long before this total dollar investment in school buildings by a school district over a period of years represents an enormous accumulation of capital assets. The dollar and cents value of this investment may be quite impressive from the position of an economist, but may look quite different from the standpoint of an educator. In a few cases, the educational value of this large capital investment may even be close to zero. This low educational assessment of capital expenditures occurs when the existing school plant is no longer capable of sustaining, reinforcing, and promoting an effective program of instruction.

In many instances, school buildings become outmoded only after twenty or thirty years of occupancy. A few become obsolete even sooner, particularly if they were not designed to accomodate foreseeable changes in future educational practices. In the natural course of events, however, obsolescence ultimately sets in. This phenomenon cannot be evaded or sidestepped in spite of the imaginative and advanced feature that might have been built into a school building when it was conceived. The reason for this unavoidable outcome is quite clear. The educative process is inherently dynamic and is in a continual state of flux. School facilities, on the other hand, are rigid, fixed, and quasi-permanent. Thus, educators find themselves constantly trying to fit a changing educational activity into a static and immutable structure. As the gap between the needs of the educational program and the original design function of the building widens, it becomes more and more difficult to house the desired educational program in a building that was not planned for it. Consequently, in due time an existing school building becomes obsolete. Unfortunately, too many school buildings must be continued in operation even after they become obsolete because there is insufficient bonding capacity to replace them. This situation exists in many of the fast-growing school districts throughout the country. Hopefully, some of the suggestions presented in this chapter can help to remedy this situation at a reasonable cost.

The modernization of obsolete school buildings is perhaps one of the most controversial and difficult decisions confronting a board of education. The first basic question that must be answered is whether or not a given obsolete school facility should be remodeled or replaced. This question has already been discussed in the preceding chapter. It must be stressed again that no decision should be made to modernize an obsolete school building until it has been demonstrated beyond any doubt that such modernization is in the best interest of the school district. The criteria set forth in the preceding chapter are developed to assist school plant planners and boards of education in arriving at a decision regarding this issue.

This chapter is intended primarily for those school districts that have come to a well-reasoned conclusion that the modernization of an obsolete school building is clearly warranted. In this connection, it should be mentioned that, in most cases, modernization of obsolete school facilities is not a wise expenditure of public funds. This rule is especially true in situations where a school district has a choice between modernization and replacement. A sound rule of thumb to bear in mind is, "When in doubt, do not modernize." In some instances, however, modernization of obsolete school buildings is justifiable and appropriate. The suggestions and procedures described in this chapter are therefore dedicated to the sound planning and design of such obsolete school buildings. In presenting the practical aspects of modernization, it is presumed that an obsolete school is needed in its present location, fits into a valid long-range plan, and has the potential of being transformed into a facility that is educationally and economically equivalent to a new building.

The Need for Clear Thinking and Positive Action

School building modernization usually has great appeal to the taxpayer. It is often taken for granted, prima facie, that modernization is certainly in the best financial interest of the school district. This assumption is not always true. For this reason, it is essential that school plant planners should make every effort to follow the procedures set forth in this section. Based on the experience and insights gained from conducting several hundred school building surveys, the writer has concluded that modernization can be justified in fewer than 25 percent of the cases. Conversely, it also was quite evident that the cost of modernization can be a wise and fruitful expenditure of public funds under certain circumstances. It is important to bear in mind that as school districts reach maturity, the need for new buildings in new locations will decrease. The number of existing buildings needed in their present locations will increase in these school districts. Thus, it is expected that there will be a marked increase in the number of existing school buildings that can be justifiably modernized.

Even what appears to be a modest modernization project to the average citizen may require a fairly large expenditure of public funds. In general, modernization projects are comprehensive in scope and quite extensive in structural changes within an existing school building. Such projects almost always involve rehabilitation, remodeling, updating of the heating, cooling, ventilating, plumbing and electrical systems, and improving the energy efficiency of the building. Consequently, the decision whether or not to modernize an existing school facility is of paramount importance. It requires clear thinking, sound judgment, and positive action on the part of boards of education, school officials, citizen leadership, and educational facility planners. It is hoped that this presentation will be helpful to all concerned in dealing with school facility modernization.

A Suggested Plan of Action

At the risk of being repetitious, it is strongly recommended that all persons involved in the consideration whether or not to modernize an existing school facility concentrate heavily on Task Unit One below. This is one task that deserves as much time as is required in order to arrive at the solution that is in the best interest of the school district. Take time, think clearly and objectively, and act logically.

Task Unit I: Can the Obsolete School Building Considered for Modernization be Fully Justified Educationally, Structurally, Geographically, and Economically?

It is suggested that the section in this chapter entitled, "Requisite Conditions for Modernization" be reviewed and studied carefully. It is further suggested that each question be listed on a blank piece of paper and that the answers to each item be committed to writing by all persons contributing information related to the decision whether or not to modernize a given building. At some point in the decision-making process, such persons should meet as many times as needed to share and exchange views on the issue. If the answer to any one of the first six questions is "no," the modernization issue requires further study and analysis. The findings of the "blue ribbon" committee under question 7 should be given very serious consideration since this group recommendation is made by a majority of its members, representing citizens, school officials, experts and the board of education, which, of course, must make the official decision on the issue. It should be mentioned, that it is the people, except in some cities, that really make the final choice by supporting or not supporting a referendum authorizing funds for the modernization project.

A word of explanation regarding the answers to the questions on the modernization issue is in order at this point. A "no" answer to any one of the first six questions does not necessarily kill the project, but certainly places it in serious jeopardy. For example, if the site is inadequate and cannot be improved at a reasonable cost, it may still be advantageous to modernize an existing school facility, provided the "yes" answers to the other questions are preponderantly positive. Or, the modernization cost of an existing school may not be in the best financial interest of the school district according to the Castaldi Formula, but the school district may find itself in such financial straits that its bonding capacity is not sufficient to replace the building. Although modernization is not the ideal solution in this instance, the decision to modernization it would be more in line with the financial capability of the school district.

The modernization of a school facility should not be ruled out *a priori*. It is well known among educators that modernization is often justifiable and in the best interest of the school district. On the other hand, a modernization project should not be undertaken until every facet of the problem is studied in depth. Such a study is required under Task Unit I. In conducting this study, it is important that the first six questions mentioned earlier be fully addressed and that the recommendation made by the "blue ribbon committee," described under question 7, be positive and supportive of the modernization proposal. If, upon completion of this investigation, a decision is made to modernize an existing school facility, proceed to Task Unit II.

Task Unit II: Developing a Set of Ideal Educational Specifications

At this point in the planning process, it is assumed that the decision has been made to modernize a given building for a specified capacity and a stated grade grouping. For example, "The Jones Elementary School shall be modernized to serve 750 pupils in Grades 5 through 8." Once these two elements have been stipulated, educational planners should develop educational specifications for a school facility designed to house the desired educational program. Modernization should be temporarily disregarded. It should be stressed that one of the premises leading to a decision to modernize was that the modernized building would approximate the function of a new facility. In order to achieve this goal, it is essential that the educational specifications be exactly the same as those prepared for a new building. Obviously, compromise will need to be made in a later stage of the planning, but it is imperative that an ideal set of educational specifications be prepared at this stage.

It is suggested that the procedure described in Chapter 10, be reviewed and followed as much as possible. Information contained in Chapters 6, 13, 14, and 15 will also have a direct bearing on the preparation of educational specifications.

Task Unit III: Fitting Available Spaces in the Existing Building into the Ideal Educational Specifications

This is one of the most difficult and crucial steps in modernizing an existing school building. Obviously, the present structure does not contain very many spaces that conform to the educational specifications. If it did, the existing structure would not be considered obsolete. The major objective at this point in the planning is to search for the most effective use of existing spaces in relation to the spaces specified in the educational specifications prepared under Task Unit II. Before attempting to develop a variety of options designed to satisfy the educational specifications—more or less—it is suggested that the next section of this chapter, entitled "Practical Considerations in School Modernization," be read very carefully. This section provides helpful approaches designed to assist school plant planners in developing a multitude of options for consideration by the board of education.

Task Unit IV: Preparing a Revised Set of Educational Specifications

After completing the time-consuming procedure suggested under Task Unit II, the board of education is in a position to approve the combination of options that make the most effective use of existing spaces. Once these options are defined, the educational consultant or some designated school official should revise the original specifications and rewrite them in relation to the building to be modernized.

Let us cite an example illustrating the nature and type of revision.

"The ideal educational specifications for the learning resources center call for a total area of 7,000 square feet distributed as follows:

Reading area	3,500 sq. ft.
Librarian's office	250 " "
Librarian's workroom	300 " "
Audiovisual storage	500 " "
Audiovisual workroom	350 " "
Television workroom	350 " "
Television studio	750 " "
Self-instructional area	500 " "
Conference Room	500 " "

The present auditorium containing 5,000 square feet will be converted as part of the learning resources center. The three regular classrooms across the corridor from the present auditorium, together with the intervening corridor, will become part of the learning resources center. The architect will develop various schemes of this area incorporating the space relationships described in the ideal specifications. Existing walls may remain. Vision strips should be installed in all walls separating operational units in the learning resources center. Such vision strips shall be approximately three feet high. The bottom edge of the strip should be about three feet above the floor. Where vision strips cannot be installed, supervision will be conducted using closed-circuit television."

The instructions to the architect should be as flexible as possible. Specifics should be included only when they have educational significance. Otherwise, the architect should be given as much freedom as possible. For example, in the above illustration, the upper edge of the vision strip is specified at a level about six feet above the floor. There is a specific functional reason for this. It is extremely annoying to a person when an obstruction is located in a vision strip at eye level. A person finds himself subconsciously either standing on his toes trying to look over the obstruction or bending down to look under it. Such annoyance is not conducive to effective teaching or learning. The remedy is simple and not costly. Educationally important details should be clearly stated in the educational specifications. This is the only way that the architect will know what is desired.

Task Unit V: Architectural Planning of the Modernized Building

The revised educational specifications described in the previous section become the basic educational requirements which the architect will make every effort to satisfy. As plans develop, the architect will discover a large number of previously unknown obstacles. For example, he may find that a major waste line is imbedded in the wall that was scheduled for removal. As these problems arise, the consultant, school officials, and the architect will convene and discuss alternatives, arriving at the best resolution in each instance.

The general procedure from this stage to the awarding of the bids for a modernized building is similar to the one described in Chapter 10 beginning with step 10. It will be the responsibility of the consultant to make certain that the plans conform to the requirements stated in the educational specifications. From this standpoint, the consultant will be devoting far more time to a modernized building than he would to a new one. Under new construction, lines can be changed quickly and easily. In a modernized building, it is definitely more difficult to move or remove existing walls.

Task Unit VI: Generating Public Support

The importance of gaining public support for any school project has already been discussed in Chapter 10. There is no evidence showing that it is easier to win a bond referendum for modernization than it is for a new building. Whenever public funds are being expended, it can be anticipated that opposition to such expenditures will develop. The extent of such opposition, however, is unpredictable. It is therefore essential that early attention be given to the matter of public support.

It might be helpful to review the section in Chapter 10 dealing with public support and the strategies that might be used to develop a favorable attitude toward the project among the citizens. Unless this support can be generated prior to the referendum, the project may be doomed to failure.

PRACTICAL CONSIDERATIONS IN SCHOOL MODERNIZATIONS

The modernization of an existing school plant is far more complex and time-consuming than planning a new school building for the same educational program and capacity. The design, construction, and structural system of an existing school facility often impose serious physical constraints upon the architect. Some of these obstacles are frequently difficult, if not impossible, to overcome. To say that school modernization is a challenge to ingenuity of school plant planners is an understatement of high order. The best that can be expected in the modernization of a school building is finding a solution that contains the lowest number of least harmful compromises. For this reason, school planners often develop several options that are designed to satisfy the educational specifications. In most cases, none of the options completely meet the requirements of the educational program. Consequently, choices are usually made so that each compromise solution has the smallest negative effect on the educational program. A number of guidelines are presented in this section to assist planners in the search for solutions that are least harmful to the educational function.

1. *The modernized school facility should be equivalent to a new building housing the same educational program.* When a decision is made by school officials to modernize an existing school building instead of replacing it by a new one, the implied assumption is that the modernized facility is equivalent to a new building that would be constructed to replace it. Very rarely do school officials feel that this equivalency cannot be achieved when the decision is made. The decision to modernize is usually made in good faith with the full expectation that such equivalency is possible.

In the real world of planning, however, it is almost impossible to modernize an existing school building without making a number of significant compromises. The validity of this premise is well recognized by most school plant planners. Thus, the architect often presents several options to a board of education. It is suggested that the principle of "least educational compromise" be kept clearly in mind when choices are being made among a number of reasonable solutions to a modernization problem.

2. *The least costly conversion from one space use to another is one that requires only a change in room label.* In the interest of economy, school plant planners should actively seek out spaces that can be used effectively almost as they are, for one or more instructional purposes. There are frequently many spaces in an existing building that can be well utilized for functions different from those currently housed in them. For example, a large regular classroom can be used as a drafting room. A large typewriting room can be utilized for large-group instruction. A shop planning room can be converted to a room for small-group discussion. The educational specifications should be scanned to identify existing spaces that meet the physical requirements of the desired educational program.

Decisions of how to best utilize existing spaces, however, require extreme care and sound educational judgment. When the educational specifications are compared with the physical features of existing spaces, it is often quite possible to find a number of existing spaces that satisfy the size requirement stated in the specifications. Many of these properly sized spaces, however, cannot be used effectively in a modernized building, because they may not be well related to other spaces functionally associated with them. For example, the small-group discussion room mentioned in the preceding paragraph may be isolated at the end of a wing of a building. Thus, even though it meets all other criteria for a small-group discussion room, it lacks the proper functional relationship to other associated instructional activities.

On the other hand, it is frequently quite surprising to discover how many of the existing spaces can be utilized for other uses without making any major changes in the spaces. Oftentimes, when two or three spaces in a given area of an existing building are remodeled and converted to specialized uses, they may be surrounded by a cluster of spaces that could be adapted for functions associated with the remodeled area. In some instances, these related spaces may be adequate and suitable as they are. Consequently, the decision of which rooms to remodel in an existing building becomes quite crucial. It is important, therefore, to look for clusters of spaces that are logically associated with the spaces considered for major modernization. This precaution could result in substantial savings through a more efficient utilization of existing spaces.

3. *The conversion of existing large spaces into smaller ones can be financially rewarding.* It is frequently advantageous to subdivide a large space in an existing building into smaller ones. Obviously, any space, large or small, that can be utilized effectively in its original location and design should be continued in operation with minimal changes. There are many instances, however, when existing large spaces are no longer adequate, suitable, or needed in their present form. Oftentimes, such spaces are replaced by new additions to the modernized structure. Consequently, there are situations when a large existing space can be considered for new educational uses.

The subdivision of large spaces into effective smaller instructional areas is an important aspect of school modernization. The multitude of potential uses of large spaces presents a wide variety of exciting options in the redesigned version of a modernized school building. In order to explore a large number of possibilities, it is suggested that the total usable area of each existing large space destined for conversion be determined and recorded, and that the total area included in each cluster of related spaces be computed from an analysis of the educational specifications. All clusters that contain areas approximating the areas of the various large spaces should be given further study. School plant planners should prepare several options in which combinations of related functions can be housed in existing large spaces. Each combination should then be evaluated in terms of educational effectiveness, considering both the advantages and disadvantages of each proposed use of available space.

There are a few common uses of large spaces that are worthy of note. They are mentioned only as ideas that will hopefully suggest many other possible solutions to local school planners. An obsolete assembly hall, for example, has a number of possible uses. It can be converted into a library on two levels. The lower level might contain bookshelves, together with carrels, a librarian's office and workroom, a television center, and an audiovisual center. The second level could be designed as a mezzanine for expanded library services. It may be possible to include remedial rooms for speech, reading, and mathematics on the mezzanine level, with direct entry to such spaces from the second-floor level in a two-story building. This same large space could be converted into a two-story classroom area. A 6,000–square foot assembly hall, for example, could be converted into approximately ten classrooms, five rooms on each floor. It may be possible to use certain large spaces for one or more clusters of related specialized rooms, such as science, homemaking, art, and business programs. Large spaces can also be subdivided into offices for administration, health, guidance, and faculty work stations (offices).

Sometimes one large space function can be substituted for another. For example, an outmoded gymnasium with a relatively high ceiling (20'–22') could easily be converted to a sloping floor auditorium, particularly if it was originally designed as a gymnasium-auditorium with a stage and proscenium opening. Cafeterias can frequently be converted into multi-sized teaching areas for large-group–small-group instruction through the ingenious use of interlocking movable partitions. Shop areas are usually large, single-story, high-ceiling enclosures. If these areas become available, it is often advantageous to consider using these spaces for specialized classrooms that require water, gas, and electricity. The functions that might be most appropriate for these areas are homemaking, art, drafting, business programs, and science. In school districts that provide student activity-type facilities, a properly located large space can often be converted into spaces for student lounge, quiet study areas, television viewing areas, and small film projection viewing rooms. These facilities are essential in secondary schools where the "open-campus" concept is embraced by the school philosophy. Under this concept, students are free to leave the campus whenever they are not in scheduled class activities. In some instances, students do not leave the campus but congregate in the corridors and lobbies when no other facilities are available. Under these circumstances, the corridors become sources of distracting noise and teachers have found it difficult to conduct classes in adjoining classrooms. Consequently, when the "open-campus concept" is adopted, student activity centers are basic to the success of the open-campus plan.

4. *Housing large-space functions in a cluster of small spaces.* Although it is much simpler to convert a large space into a number of smaller ones, it is sometimes possible to house large-space functions within a constellation of smaller spaces. The learning resources center function is one that can often be accommodated in a cluster of smaller spaces. Let us illustrate the application of this concept by citing an example. In this illustration, it is assumed that the educational specifications call for 5,000 square feet of space for the learning resources center. What is needed in this instance is essentially a 5,000-square foot block of spaces that can become a self-contained operational unit of the school. This large block of space might be located at the end of a wing or it might occupy a major part of one floor level in an existing building. If such an isolated area cannot be found, it may be possible to remodel the existing building slightly to create this condition. Normally, a 5,000-square foot block of space in an existing school building contains several classrooms, a small storage room or two, a main corridor, and possibly toilet areas. The boundaries of this block of spaces should be clearly outlined on a plan of the existing building in pencil or ink. Hopefully, in designing the learning resources area, this main corridor can be "dead-ended" and become an integral part of the learning

resources center. Entrance to one end of this center can be gained from the terminus of the remaining corridors through a set of doors at that point. In this situation, it is not necessary to remove entire walls to create the feeling of a library. It may be advantageous to simply install vision strips in the intervening walls so that the bottom of the vision strip is about three feet above the floor. The height of the top of the vision strip should be not less that six feet above the floor. Such vision strips provide visual coherence to the area and simplify supervision of the area. Obviously, it may not be possible to install such strips in all walls because of the location of utility pipes and wires in some partitions. Closed-circuit television can be utilized for supervision in these instances. In spaces where privacy is needed at certain times, it is a simple and inexpensive matter to install draw-curtains across the vision strips. If double glazing is used on the vision strips, each cubicle or room can be acoustically insulated from adjoining spaces, thus making it possible to use different audiovisual materials for group viewing in adjoining rooms.

In some existing buildings it might be possible to convert classrooms, corridors, and small storage spaces into a cafeteria. If a sufficiently large block of space could be found with one end of it easily accessible to the service drive of the school, it might be feasible to convert this block of space to cafeteria uses. The cafeteria effect can be created through the judicious use of vision strips. There may be some decided aesthetic and functional advantage in using a series of smaller spaces in contrast to the usual institutional-type cafeteria. Special attention should be given to the circulation patterns established under this concept. Generally, classrooms already have two means of egress. These can be incorporated into the traffic flow pattern of the cafeteria function, which would be housed in a series of adjoining spaces.

5. *From the standpoint of cost and structural considerations, the removal of load-bearing partitions should be kept to the absolute minimum.* In school buildings constructed prior to World War II, many of the interior walls of the building were load-bearing. This was particularly true of the walls on both sides of the main corridor. In addition to being load bearing, these corridor walls were also constructed of fire-resistant materials. The question is frequently asked as to whether or not a load-bearing wall can be removed. In some instances, it can be removed entirely; in others, it can be eliminated only partially. Technically, walls can be removed and a new structural system can be substituted for the original wall in most situations. Indeed, all this can be accomplished but usually at an enormous cost to the owner. Is such a tremendous cost justifiable? Not very often. These high costs can be supported only in rare cases where no other alternative is possible.

As a practical matter, therefore, it is suggested that the removal of load-bearing interior partitions be avoided as much as possible. Vision strips or closed-circuit television, as described in the preceding section, often solve the problem of visual contact very inexpensively. Nonbearing partitions, of course, do not present serious structural problems, except when utility pipes are located within them. The cost of removing nonbearing walls is often quite reasonable and justifiable. When vision strips do not serve an educational function, the cost of removing a nonload-bearing partition should be compared with the cost of installing a vision strip. In some instances, it could actually be less expensive to tear down the wall, remove the rubble from the premises, and patch the ceiling, floor, and walls than it would be to install a vision strip.

6. *If the modernized building is to be expanded, it might be advantageous to plan large and specialized spaces under the new construction.* There are many reasons why existing school buildings become obsolete. The rooms may be too small for modern educational practices. There may be no provision for water, electricity, or gas in certain areas. The space for physical education may be too small. There may be no suitable space in which to install automated instructional equipment. Most often, however, the reason that most school buildings are considered obsolete stems from the absence of adequate and suitable specialized classrooms and the lack of sufficiently large spaces for large-group activities such as assembly and physical education. Frequently, spaces that were originally designed for specialized uses can no longer support the more sophisticated teaching practices that require more space and more advanced equipment. These deficiencies must be taken into account during the modernization process. Consequently, the plans of the modernized facility must contain design elements that correct such deficiencies.

When modernization also includes new construction, it is often financially rewarding to locate specialized classrooms and large-space functions within the new construction. The benefits resulting from this suggestion are twofold. Since many of the specialized spaces in the original building are usually nothing more than oversized classrooms, it is educationally sound to use these existing spaces as regular classrooms. Also, most of these spaces can be used without any appreciable expenditure of capital outlay. In many instances, the conversion of a former specialized space to a regular classroom requires simply changing the label on the door. This type of modernization is inexpensive and educationally sound. The reason for including large-space activities under new construction, however, is usually more a matter of necessity than choice. Generally speaking, there are usually no spaces within an obsolete building that can be expanded or converted into suitable large-space use. For this reason, many additions to school buildings frequently include a gymnasium, an auditorium, and a cafeteria. Of these three, the gymnasium is the space that is most often included in new construction.

7. *Rehabilitation of obsolete school buildings.* It is important to bear in mind that obsolete school buildings have often been occupied for several decades. During this long period of time, it is highly probable that the

electrical, mechanical, plumbing, and heating systems in the building will require special attention when the building is modernized. It is also anticipated that there will be a certain amount of deferred annual maintenance that can be dealt with at the same time.

As mentioned earlier in this chapter, modernization is comprehensive in scope. It includes both remodeling and rehabilitation. Several aspects of remodeling have already been discussed in the preceding six sections. Rehabilitation alone does not produce a modernized building. It simply brings the physical plant to the same level of appearance and function that it possessed when the building was occupied for the first time. Thus, when a building constructed in 1940 is rehabilitated in 1975, it improves physically but not educationally. It is the combination of remodeling and rehabilitation that transforms an obsolete school building to one that is aesthetically pleasing, mechanically functional, and educationally effective.

Rehabilitation is primarily concerned with the restoration of the physical plant to its original condition. Consequently, all spaces and equipment within a school building are subject to rehabilitation, regardless of whether or not it was remodeled. Ceilings and walls may need to be repaired or replaced. Floors may require resurfacing. Lighting fixtures may need to be replaced with more efficient units. Interior surfaces will undoubtedly need to be cleaned and redecorated. Masonry must be examined for evidence of deterioration, and corrective measures must be taken. Plumbing fixtures may be in need of repair or replacement. The heating system may be obsolete and inefficient. There may be a need to change from one form of heating energy to another because of changes in the cost of various sources of energy, such as gas, oil, coal, and electricity. Ventilation equipment may require new motors and control systems. These are only a few of the many items that could be included under rehabilitation. In rare cases, the total cost of rehabilitation may well exceed that of remodeling. The writer has observed on several occasions involving modernization, that members of boards of education were frequently surprised to learn that the cost of rehabilitation was sometimes as high as 40 percent of the cost of modernization. This is especially true when the architect is trying to bring the level of the modernized building up to the standards of a new building.

Remodeling without rehabilitation leaves much to be desired. Although the educational function of certain spaces will be improved, the general atmosphere within the school may not be conducive to effective learning. The cost of rehabilitation varies over a wide range. In school districts where there is a systematic program of maintenance and upgrading, the cost of rehabilitating an obsolete school building is relatively small. Unfortunately, when a school district must operate within budgetary cutbacks, funds for maintenance are among the first to be deleted from the budget. As a result, the cost of rehabilitation rises in direct proportion to the amount of deferred maintenance accumulated over a number of years. In spite of these situations, every effort should be made to fully rehabilitate a building that is scheduled for modernization. To do less means that the modernized building is not equivalent to a new structure that could have replaced it.

CHAPTER 17

Maintenance and Operation

School officials and boards of education have realized for a long time that the construction and operation of a school building involve a substantial expenditure of public funds. The investment for construction represents only the initial cost of a school facility. Operational costs for power, maintenance, and custodial staff become an important item in the annual budget. The sequence of events is quite familiar to all educators. Once the building is completed, the keys are turned over to school officials. Power and fuel are supplied to the building and, for the first time, are charged directly to the school district as school expenses. The switches are activated, and the building—hopefully—provides a comfortable and inspiring environment for learning. Ideally, once energized, all systems and equipment should operate flawlessly. In practice, this situation almost never occurs. In most cases, there is a "shake-down" period when all equipment and controls are adjusted, rebalanced, or replaced. In due time, however, the new or modernized building becomes operative and begins to fulfill its intended purpose.

As soon as the teachers, students, administrators, and physical plant staff begin to function normally within the spaces specifically designed for them, the building is said to be "operational." This is the point in the life of a school building when the aging process sets in. The materials and surfaces of the structure begin to deteriorate very slowly, and each piece of mechanical equipment starts to wear out at its own predictable rate. The aging process is natural, universal, and inevitable. It cannot be eliminated. For this reason, a well-conceived program of maintenance is an integral part of the daily operation of a school building. The details concerning the development of such a program are presented in this chapter. A number of promising practices dealing with the periodic care and maintenance of school buildings are also included in this chapter.

Several publications have been prepared on the routine maintenance of school buildings. They contain a large number of details pertaining to a wide variety of daily housekeeping duties normally performed in a school building. A discussion of these matters is not within the scope of this book. Consequently, this chapter will deal primarily with the major concepts on school building maintenance covered in such texts. One of the earliest publications in this field was entitled "Housekeeping Handbook," written by Dr. Henry H. Linn at Columbia University. Dr. O. Barker Harrison prepared a comprehensive handbook for custodians dealing with both the building maintenance and the care of mechanical controls and devices in a school building. There is no scarcity of custodial handbooks. Many of the larger school districts and most state departments of education publish handbooks for custodians for the purpose of prolonging the life of a building and improving the environment for learning.

According to Harrison[1],

> The school custodian is co-responsible with the principal for a building worth many thousands of dollars, its care and operation, and indirectly responsible for the priceless lives of hundreds of children and their teachers, as their lives relate to the proper operation of the school plant.

The great contribution made by physical plant personnel in maintaining a comfortable and healthful environment in a school building is rarely recognized by school officials, boards of education, and the general public. Admittedly, the work of the school custodian is physical, time-consuming, and not particularly glamorous. Nevertheless, an alert and knowledgeable custodian can save the school district thousands of dollars in future maintenance costs by paying attention to the "little things," such as water leaks, lubrication of equipment, erosion of soils adjacent to the building, excessive condensation of humidity around cold pipes, and replacement of defective temperature controls.

The men and women in the physical plant work force also play an important part in the educational function of the school. It is these men and women who provide and maintain an environment that is conducive to effective learning. And they do all this without interfering with the educational process. These dedicated people do most of their work after the teachers and students have left the building for the day or before they return to it in the morning. This often-unseen work force performs an indispensable service that benefits the students, teachers, administrators, clerical personnel, and the taxpayers. It is this group of people that improves learning by providing a proper environment and saves the taxpayers thousands of dollars over the life of a school building by giving immediate and prompt attention to the "little things" before they become big and costly problems.

[1]O. Barker Harrison, *Suggested Methods to Custodians for the Routine Care of Schools* (Nashville, Tenn.: Yearwood and Johnson, 1973).

THE ROLE OF CENTRAL ADMINISTRATION IN OPERATION AND MAINTENANCE

The central administration of a school district has an important part to play in the operation and maintenance of all of the school buildings within its jurisdiction. It develops district-wide policies concerning the working conditions of physical plant personnel, their rate of pay, fringe benefits, and other forms of compensation. It sets work standards and procedures that are implemented by the individual school principals. And it develops instructions designed to help the entire physical plant staff to better preserve and maintain the school buildings to which they are assigned.

Determining the Size of the Work Force

The central administration of a school district has the basic responsibility of making certain that custodial personnel are not being overworked. It also has an obligation to the taxpayers of the school district to keep the number of personnel at a minimum. There are currently several "rules of thumb" that can be used to compute the number of custodians normally required in a given school building. Any one of them could be used to determine the "theoretical" custodial staffing required in a school. One of the nationally accepted methods, known as the "factoring formula," is presented in this section. Although this rule of thumb is completely empirical, it does give the superintendent of schools or his assistants a valuable point of departure. In applying the formula, one should bear in mind that there may indeed be situations where the conditions within a particular school building make it necessary to assign more personnel to it than the formula would indicate. For example, the building may be old and hard to keep clean and maintain, or it may be a new building that is severely overcrowded and used more hours per day than is customary. On the other hand, any staffing in existing school buildings that deviates substantially—too high or too low—from the theoretical staffing computation described previously should be studied and justified by the central administration. If the present staffing is too low compared to the theoretical result, the custodial staff is probably overloaded and relief for them should be sought. On the other hand, if the present staffing exceeds the theoretical need, such additional personnel should be justified on the basis of extenuating circumstances. If this cannot be done, the excessive staff should be reassigned to school buildings where staff deficiencies may exist. A work sheet for implementing the "Factoring Formula" is presented in Table 17.1.

There is another rule of thumb for determining the number of needed cleaning personnel, which is simpler and not as analytical as the "Factoring Formula." According to this unsophisticated approach, the number of cleaning personnel needed is simply one cleaning person for each eight or

TABLE 17.1   Work sheet for estimating custodial staffing using the factoring formula

Factor 1	Number of teaching stations* divided by 11.		
	$$\frac{\text{(No. of T.S.) (\quad)}}{11} = \underline{\hspace{2cm}}$$		Line 1
Factor 2	Number of teachers divided by 8.		
	$$\frac{\text{(No. of Teachers) (\quad)}}{8} = \underline{\hspace{2cm}}$$		Line 2
Factor 3	Building capacity divided by 25.		
	$$\frac{\text{(Bldg. Capacity) (\quad)}}{25} = \underline{\hspace{2cm}}$$		Line 3
Factor 4	Gross area of building divided by 15,000.		
	$$\frac{\text{(Bldg. Area (\quad)}}{15,000} = \underline{\hspace{2cm}}$$		Line 4
Factor 5	Area of site in acres divided by 2.		
	$$\frac{\text{(Site in Acres) (\quad)}}{2} = \underline{\hspace{2cm}}$$		Line 5
Factorial Sum	(Add Lines 1–5) _____		Line 6
Final Computation of Staff Need	Divide Factorial Sum by 5.		
	$$\frac{\text{(Enter Line 6) (\quad)}}{5} = \underline{\hspace{2cm}}$$		Custodians Needed (Round off to next higher whole number.)

*A teaching station is equivalent to about 900 square feet in which teaching is conducted. Divide area of gymnasium floor by 1,000 to determine the number of teaching stations for it.

nine teachers assigned to the school building. The weaknesses inherent in this formula are obvious. It disregards student load, which contributes directly to the work of the custodian. It ignores the condition, number, and size of teaching areas in the school. It does not take into account the size of the school site and school walks. And it makes no provision for the amount of custodial work required due to the overall size of the building. In spite of these shortcomings, this formula does offer a simple first approximation to the staffing need in a given building.

In addition to adjusting the custodial staff load for each school building, the central administration can also utilize information regarding the number of physical plant personnel needed in each building for purposes of planning, budgeting, and reassignment of custodians within the school district. If a study of custodial needs within the total school district reveals that the number of existing staff is too small, the central administration has two options. It may choose to employ additional custodians to correct the overloaded conditions. Or, if funds are not available for additional staff, it can reassign personnel among the various schools in order to distribute the overload equitably among all of the custodians on the work force.

Selection of Custodial Personnel

The central administration establishes the qualifications for hiring custodial personnel. It conducts the search for qualified candidates for existing vacancies, and sets up a screening procedure to identify the best candidates. In many school districts, the final selection is made jointly by the central administration and the school principal where the vacancy exists.

Qualifications.   School districts should develop a set of job qualifications tailored for their particular situation. Some districts may have special needs, such as the requirement of custodians to be bilingual. There are, however, a number of qualifications that would apply to most school districts. These are presented below in outline form for the purpose of assisting local school districts in preparing their own job specifications for custodial positions. The set of qualifications given below contains items that would apply to most school districts. This list[2] should be revised, expanded, or shortened according to the specific requirements of a given school district. Hopefully, it will serve to suggest other pertinent qualifications.

The candidate:

1. Should be physically capable of performing duties required by the position.
2. Should be of good moral character, clean habits, and clean speech.
3. Should possess sufficient ability to carry out duties in an intelligent manner.
4. Should at least be able to read and write and should have a ninth-grade education.
5. Must be free from communicable diseases and should be free from chronic disturbances that could cause him to be absent from his job excessively.
6. Shall present a neat, clean appearance.
7. Should be dependable, able to get along with people—teachers, principal, and patrons.

[2]*Ibid.*, p. 55.

8. Should be orderly and willing to learn new techniques for house-keeping.
9. Must be able to plan and organize his work and the work of his staff, and to supervise the efforts of his staff in the proper house-keeping of the plant.
10. Should be even-tempered and possess a good disposition.

Maintenance and Operation Budget

In addition to staffing, the central administration is responsible for providing funds for custodial supplies, cleaning and maintenance equipment, normal wear and tear of mechanical equipment, and preventive maintenance. Unfortunately, these are usually items of low priority in the school budget. It is true, of course, that when funds are limited, these expenditures can often be deferred without penalizing the educational function of the school. But this relief is only temporary. Sometimes the cost of deferral is much greater than providing the funds when they can do the most good. For example, it may be possible to postpone the replacement of boiler tubes for a year or two on the premise that "we'll just have to make do." In the meantime, the school district will be spending more money for fuel because the old tubes are not as efficient as new ones in transmitting heat from the combustion chamber to the water or steam flowing through the tubes. Thus, in the long run, the school district is paying a penalty for such a postponement.

Procurement and use of custodial supplies.   In this connection, the central administration has two major responsibilities. The first one, obviously, is to include sufficient funds in the school budget to purchase custodial supplies. The second and equally important obligation, on the part of central administration, is to make certain that the most efficient and least damaging cleaning agents are provided for each school building in the district. Some person in the central staff should be charged with the responsibility of conducting the necessary study and research regarding the proper selection and appropriate use of various maintenance supplies and cleaning agents. The importance of this task cannot be overstated. For example, one coat of ordinary paint over an acoustical plaster ceiling can destroy most of its sound-absorbing capability. The daily or prolonged use of abrasive powders on glazed materials, stainless steel, and chromium-plated fixtures can permanently damage their surfaces. The application of acid solutions on ceramic-tiled floors tends to weaken the mortar joints between each tile unless the floor is sealed perfectly. Consequently, the improper use of cleaning agents can be very costly to a school district over a period of time.

The selection and proper use of cleaning agents is usually the responsibility of the superintendent of buildings or the director of plant operations in large school districts. In the smaller school districts, however, this function is often delegated to the head custodian of the building. Obviously, the superintendent of schools in these small school districts cannot be expected to conduct the necessary study and research pertaining to the selection and use of cleaning agents. The best protection for the school district, in these cases, is to employ a high-level, well-trained, and well-paid head custodian with at least ten years of experience in a large school district working under the supervision of a director of physical plant.

Hiring a competent custodian, however, does not completely solve the maintenance problems of the small school district. The superindendent of schools in such districts cannot afford to give a low priority to the maintenance and care of school facilities on the grounds that he simply does not have time for it. Admittedly, his time is limited and other duties are more pressing. There are a few measures that he can take, however. He can make arrangements with his counterparts in the larger school districts in his area to have his head custodian participate in training sessions held in the larger school districts. He may be able to purchase approved lists of cleaning agents researched and prepared by the larger school districts. And finally, he may be able to obtain a copy of a custodian's handbook from one or two of the larger school districts at a nominal cost. Armed with this material, the school superintendent in a small school district can feel fairly secure in the choice and proper use of cleaning agents, if he has selected an experienced and competent head custodian trained to use them appropriately.

Although it is simply good business to procure custodial supplies through a central purchasing office, care should be exercised to make certain that the needs of each building are reflected in the unified purchasing process. Centralization does not imply uniformity of need in each building in the school district. Each building should be considered unique regarding the type and amount of supplies. There are, to be sure, a wide variety of supplies common to all buildings. There are a few supplies that are needed in all buildings but in different quantities depending upon the age, size, and type of construction of the building, and there are certain supplies that may be peculiar to a given school building. For example, a school building that uses energy pumps for heating and cooling may require a small supply of refrigerant to recharge the system, while other buildings may have no need for such material.

Normal Wear and Tear of Mechanical Equipment

Seldom, if ever, does one find a school district that has been able to set aside funds in advance to replace all equipment that is completely worn out through normal use. The practice of establishing reserve funds for equipment depreciation is commonly found in business. It is a financially sound policy. In many states, however, school districts are prevented by law from establishing reserve funds. This may be the reason why school districts have generally not become involved in reserve or sinking funds commonly found in business.

Nevertheless, it is both economically sound and financially wise to anticipate the replacement of sometimes costly equipment. If each piece of equipment were classified in terms of its normal life expectancy, it would be possible to determine its rate of depreciation in terms of dollars per year. Then, it would be relatively simple to determine the total cost of depreciation for mechanical equipment each year. If this amount of money, representing the total cost of depreciation, could be placed in a reserve fund, all of the mechanical equipment owned by the school district could be replaced when it was no longer operable. This practice would apply to items such as water circulators, motors in the ventilating system, motor vehicles, power equipment, fuel burners, electric resistance-type heaters, vacuum cleaners, machine scrubbers, typewriters, business machines, and photocopiers. If this practice were instituted, the tax levy each year would include a proportional amount of money for equipment replacement. Thus, the cost of replacing mechanical equipment would be spread over the expected life of the item, rather than having the entire cost of such items fall upon the taxpayers in a single year.

If laws prohibit the establishment of reserve funds for equipment depreciation, every effort should be made to have them changed. If business finds this practice sound and in its own best long-range interest, it would seem reasonable and proper that public agencies be allowed to engage in the same healthy fiscal practice.

It might be possible, even under existing laws, to develop a program of planned replacement. It is suggested that the rate of depreciation be determined for each mechanical item and that the total annual cost of depreciation be computed for the entire school district. The next step in this suggested process is to examine the condition of each piece of mechanical equipment and set forth the cost of equipment that needs to be replaced or will require replacement sometime during the next fiscal year. Find the total cost of equipment that should be replaced. Compare this total replacement cost with the total annual cost of depreciation. If they are approximately equal, simply include the cost of equipment replacement in the budget. If the cost of depreciation is greater than the total replacement cost, include at least the replacement cost in the budget. This type of imbalance occurs whenever replacement of worn equipment has been deferred in the past. Under the reserve plan practiced by business, this circumstance would never occur because the accumulated reserves would balance out the cases where the cost of replacement would exceed the total annual depreciation figure.

The above suggestion does not solve the depreciation problem. It simply eases it by focusing attention on the need for replacing mechanical equipment on an annual basis. Through this procedure, there would be an opportunity to include funds for equipment replacement each year on a systematic basis. Without this approach, or one like it, school districts would find themselves replacing worn crucial equipment from time to time on an emergency basis. Mechanical equipment of lower priority would probably be continued in use at a high maintenance cost to the school district. Such practice is certainly not prudent from the standpoint of economic efficiency. It represents an unnecessary waste of public funds. It can be corrected only when educators make responsible legislators aware of the situation.

THE ROLE OF THE SCHOOL PRINCIPAL IN OPERATION AND MAINTENANCE

The school principal is the key person in the school district responsible for the operation and maintenance of the school building to which he is assigned. He is the direct operational supervisor of all physical plant personnel assigned to his building. In some school districts, the custodian has a dual administrative responsibility. He reports to the school principal for all functional matters associated with the operation and maintenance of the school building to which he is assigned, and is accountable to central administration for all technical matters related to his work. For example, the custodian may be responsible to the principal for scrubbing a certain classroom floor at a given time on a specified day, but he may be responsible to the central office staff for the type of cleaning agents he uses and the procedures to be followed. Thus, he is functionally responsible to the principal and technically responsible to the central administration. These two responsibilities are compatible, easily differentiated, and administratively consistent.

Custodial Obligations

In the daily operation of a school building, the principal can reasonably expect that his custodian will fulfill these requirements:[3]

1. Have a knowledge of the principles of heating, ventilating, sanitation, and care of school buildings.
2. Have a knowledge of the best tools, materials, cleaning agents, and methods to use in various phases of custodial work.
3. Have a knowledge of the correct use of mechanical equipment of school buildings.
4. Have skill in using proper tools, materials, cleaning agents, and methods of procedure for the different kinds of custodial jobs under various conditions.

[3]*Ibid.*, p. 56.

5. Possess a scientific attitude toward the study of various phases of custodial services, in order to effect the greatest efficiency and economy of time and energy.
6. Possess attitudes that will lead to serious whole-hearted and unselfish attention to the duties of custodial service.
7. Possess attitudes that make for harmonious cooperation with pupils and with the administrative, educational, and custodial forces.
8. Have ideas of what constitutes good custodial service and of the importance of the service to both the educational work of the school and the protection of the school property.
9. Have an appreciation of beauty, harmony, and cleanliness in and about the school grounds.

Maintenance and Operational Responsibilities of the Custodial Staff

The school principal has the right to expect his custodial force to perform the duties listed below. They are presented in two groups. The first category deals with tasks related to the maintenance of the school building. The second group includes routine operational responsibilities subdivided into three classifications—daily operations, weekly operations, and periodic operations. The principal may hold the custodians responsible for the performance of these tasks.

A. *Maintenance responsibilities*[4]
1. Replace broken door and window glass.
2. Make minor repairs to locks, hinges, door closers, etc.
3. Repair and adjust faulty window shades.
4. Keep stair handrails tightly in place.
5. Make minor repairs to pupils' and teachers' lockers.
6. Replace faulty lamps, fuses, etc.
7. Keep all fire-fighting equipment securely in place.
8. Maintain towel racks, soap dispensers, and tissue racks.
9. Maintain pupils' and teachers' furniture.
10. Render minor repairs to heating and plumbing equipment.
11. Make minor repairs to playground equipment.
12. Repair or replace pencil sharpeners as needed.
13. Lubricate heating and ventilating fixtures.
14. Paint rusting and corroding metal surfaces with inhibitors in small areas. Report large-scale rusting or corrosion to the principal.
15. Correct minor leak problems and report major leaks to the principal.

[4]*Ibid.*, p. 159.

B. *Operational responsibilities*
    1. Daily operations
        a. Displaying the flag as weather permits.
        b. Cleaning and dusting all classroom areas.
        c. Cleaning and dusting all administrative areas.
        d. Cleaning and dusting all stairway and corridor areas.
        e. Cleaning and servicing all restroom areas.
        f. Cleaning of chalkboards and erasers.
        g. Care of all entrances, walks, and drives as weather permits.
        h. Cleaning and servicing of physical education and auditorium areas.
        i. Inspection and care of playground equipment.
        j. Disposal of trash, waste, and ashes.
        k. Cleaning and care of custodial rooms, supplies, etc.
        l. Care and servicing of heating plant area.
        m. Cleaning of drinking fountains.
    2. Weekly Operations
        a. Cleaning or dusting of doors and door glass.
        b. "Spot cleaning" of soiled floor and wall area.
        c. Cleaning of restroom walls, doors, and partitions.
        d. Polishing of floor areas as assigned or scheduled.
        e. Cleaning inside glass as assigned or scheduled.
        f. Cleaning of furniture as assigned or scheduled.
    3. Periodic Operations
        a. Clean, finish, and polish floor areas.
        b. Clean window glass inside and outside.
        c. Clean or dust window shades.
        d. Clean ceiling, walls, bulletin boards, and trim.
        e. Clean lighting and heating fixtures.
        f. Care of yard and ground area.
        g. Inspection, cleaning, and care of storage areas.
        h. Attend to custodial maintenance functions listed under section A.

TIME STANDARDS, SCHEDULING AND DESCRIPTION OF CUSTODIAL DUTIES

The general duties of the custodial force were listed in outline form in the preceding section. No reference was made to the allocation of these tasks among the custodial work force, nor to the operational features of a care and maintenance program for a given school building. In order to accomplish this task, it is necessary to make a job analysis of the individual custodial tasks together with the time required to complete each one of them.

Time Standards for Selected Custodial Tasks

It is helpful to both the principal and the head custodian to know how much time is normally required to complete a number of specific custodial tasks. It is also important to establish the frequency with which these jobs must be repeated in maintaining a high level of custodial services. Table 17.2 contains a list of jobs normally performed by most custodians assigned to a school building. It also includes the frequency of each task and the time normally required to perform it.

Custodial Work Load

The time standards and frequency with which each task is to be repeated form the basis for determining a reasonable work load for the custodian. In developing a custodial work schedule, it should be remembered that the time standards listed in Table 17.2 do not include preparation time. For example, the time required to mop and rinse a 900–square foot class room is 40 minutes. Additional time is required by the custodian to fill a water bucket, add detergent to it, place the container with the cleaning agent back on the shelf, locate the mop, and carry these materials from the custodial closet to the classroom. The time standard of 40 minutes does not include the time necessary for the custodian to return to the custodial closet, clean the mop(s), dispose of the dirty water, and rinse out the buckets. Depending upon the location of the custodial closet with respect to the classroom, the additional time required could easily be 10 percent higher than the standards would indicate. It should also be borne in mind that it takes the custodian time to reach the custodial closet from some other part of the building. Thus, the time standards should be used judiciously. They serve as starting points. The other conditions related to each task should be taken into account and the time requirement should be adjusted accordingly.

Custodial Work Schedule

The schedule of work for each custodian should be structured so that it interferes minimally with the educational function. Custodial tasks are dovetailed with the instructional uses of the building. For example, classrooms can be dusted and swept before school, after school, and when they are not in use during the school day. For this reason, some school systems stagger the hours on which the custodians report for work. In general, most of the custodians are on duty at the close of the school day when the bulk of the cleaning tasks can be accomplished.

Barker Harrison[5] has developed a sample daily schedule that could be adapted in many school buildings. This example applies to a school

[5]*Ibid.*

TABLE 17.2   Time normally required to complete selected custodial tasks

Task	Frequency	Time Required
Classroom (Assumed area of 900 square feet)		
a. Dusting	Daily	5 min. per rm.
b. Sweeping	Daily	12 min. per rm.
c. Damp mopping	As needed	23 min. per rm.
d. Wet mop and rinse	As needed	40 min. per rm.
e. Machine scrubbing	As needed	25 min. per rm.
f. Machine polishing	As needed	15 min. per rm.
g. Wet vacuum pickup	As needed	14 min. per rm.
Servicing classroom	Daily	15 min. per rm.
a. Removing waste paper		
b. Sweeping floor with treated mop		
c. Dusting chalk tray, window sills, etc.		
d. Closing windows and adjusting shades		
e. Adjusting temperature controls		
f. Making note of needed repairs		
Servicing men's lavatory	Daily	35 min. per lav.
Servicing women's lavatory	Daily	38 min. per lav.
Lavatory area		
a. Cleaning lavatory	Daily	1 min. per fixture
b. Cleaning toilet bowl and seat	Daily	1 min. per fixture
c. Cleaning urinals	Daily	2 min. per fixture
d. Cleaning urinal trap	Weekly	2 min. per fixture
e. Cleaning wash sink	Daily	2 min. per fixture
f. Mopping toilet floors	Daily	2 min. per 100 sq. ft.
Stairways		
a. Damp mopping	Weekly	4 min. per flight
b. Sweeping	Twice Daily	6 min. per flight
Other		
a. Cleaning drinking fountains	Daily	1 min. per fixture
b. Dusting fluorescent tubes	Monthly	12 tubes per min.
c. Sweeping auditorium	Daily	15 min. per 1,000 sq. ft.

TABLE 17.2   (Continued)

Task	Frequency	Time Required
d. Sweeping corridors	Twice Daily	8 min. per 1,000 sq. ft.
e. Sweeping gymnasium floor	Daily	5 min. per 1,000 sq. ft.
f. Washing glass	As needed	1 min. per 10 sq. ft.
g. Buffing and reconditioning plastic-finished floors	As needed	50 min. per 1,000 sq. ft.
h. Machine scrubbing traffic areas		
1. Light-soil areas	8–24 months	90 min. per 1,000 sq. ft.
2. Medium-soil areas	Every 6 months	100 min. per 1,000 sq. ft.
3. Heavy-soil areas	Every 3 months	110 min. per 1,000 sq. ft.
i. Refinishing floors (wax-less finish)	As needed	20 min. per 1,000

building employing a head custodian, a helper, and a maid. This building would house twenty to twenty-five secondary school teachers and serve between 550 and 600 students depending upon the grade level and class-size policies. The sample schedule is presented in Table 17.3. This schedule applies to a relatively small school building where all custodial staff are employed during the day. In some of the larger schools, this schedule might have to be changed substantially if night crews are hired to perform some of the work listed in the sample schedule. Regardless of the time when each member of the custodial staff reports for work, however, it is essential that each person be scheduled for his or her entire eight-hour tour of duty.

Preventive Maintenance Program

Boards of education are often not aware of the potential savings that could accrue to a school district by instituting a well-defined plan of preventive maintenance. Over an extended period of time, it is economically advantageous to avoid the complete breakdown of mechanical equipment and the serious deterioration of the physical elements of a school building. It is far better, for example, to repair a hairline crack on the exterior surface of

TABLE 17.3   A sample custodial schedule

Time	Custodian	Helper	Maid
7:00–7:30	Raise flag Open building Check heating plant Check fire bells Check building		

7:30–8:00	Dust all class-
	  rooms, princi-
	  pal's and secre-
	  tary's offices,
	  library, and any
	  other room to be
	  used during the
	  day.
		Same	Same

8:00–10:00	Sweep sidewalks
	
	Check with office
	Install glass if
	  needed
	
	Check heating
	  plant
	
	Make minor
	  repairs
		Wash sweeping
		  mops
			Begin dusting in
			  corridors
			
			Clean some
			  inside hall
			  glass
			Sweep stairs and
			  corridors if
			  needed

10:00–10:30	High School—
	  Check all toilet
	  rooms—see that
	  all fixtures are
	  flushed, if
	  needed
	Insure proper
	  ventilation
	Pick up paper from
	  floor
	Replenish towels,
	  paper, and hand
	  soap as needed
	Elementary School
	  —Same as H.S.
	  but completed
	  immediately
	  following the
	  morning recess
		Same	Same

TABLE 17.3   (CONTINUED)

Time	Custodian	Helper	Maid
10:30–11:00	Check boiler Check with office Walk building to check for needed repairs	Return to dusting and cleaning in halls	Same as helper
11:00–12:00	Check toilet rooms Shake out doormats	Lunch	Check drinking fountains and wash sinks (clean and replenish soap and towels)
12:00–1:00	Lunch	Brush and pick up papers in corridors Clean sweeping brooms and mops	Lunch
1:00–1:30	All toilet rooms—same as 10:00–10:30	Same	Same
1:30–2:40	Check drinking fountains and wash sinks Burn (dispose of) paper and rubbish collected during day Clean some inside door glass and any writing from walls (In H.S., right after noon recess)		
2:40–3:00	Ready equipment and materials for afternoon cleaning Give help 5-minute rest period	Same	Same
3:00–5:00	All classrooms and halls to be swept	Same	Same

TABLE 17.3   (CONTINUED)

Time	Custodian	Helper	Maid
	Clean all toilets Mop toilet floors Carry out trash and paper Empty pencil sharpeners		
	Custodian is to begin checking behind help so entire building is checked prior to day's end	Classrooms No. _____, _____, _____, ten rooms with halls and other areas and two toilets	Same
	Secure building Take down flag		

the roof when it is barely visible and is still harmless, than it would be to do it later. In time, the extreme changes in temperature, the repeated melting and freezing of ice, can enlarge the crack to such an extent that water can seep into the building and discolor ceiling tiles in a classroom directly below the deteriorated roof. Under these conditions, the lack of preventive maintenance could subject the school district to the cost of redecorating a classroom ceiling at best, and the possible replacement of the entire ceiling under less favorable circumstances.

Developing a preventive maintenance plan.   The creation of an effective plan of preventive maintenance is highly technical. It is not something that can be delegated to the school principal or head custodian. The central administrative staff should take an active role in the development of such a plan. Except in very large school districts, the necessary expertise will not be available to create a maintenance prevention plan. The accomplishment of this task requires the talents of an architect, a heating and plumbing engineer, an electrical engineer, and a structural engineer. These services should be secured by the school district on a per diem basis. When a new building is being planned and constructed, the architectural firm can supply these services gratis or at a nominal fee because each expert is intimately familiar with all of the materials and systems included in the new building. Although the breadth of the talents required to produce a maintenance prevention plan is wide, the amount of time required by each expert is quite minimal. Each expert should be able to list the items requiring preventive maintenance in a given situation within a period of one or two days. The basic question to each one of these experts should be, "What can I do on a regularly scheduled program to extend the life of each piece of major mechanical equipment, and to preserve the physical properties and function of the building itself?"

Once the plan is developed, it is the responsibility of the building principal to implement it. The custodian or his assistants are required to perform all of the work called for in the preventive maintenance program. The principal should hold the head custodian accountable for the proper execution of the plan. The success of this program depends largely upon the commitment of the building principal to it. If he carefully supervises the work of the custodians and maintains some form of check on whether or not certain work has been performed, the success of the plan is assured. And with such success, the school district can reap rich financial rewards in the form of reduced cost of school building maintenance.

Implementing the preventive maintenance plan.   In any prescribed maintenance program, the list of tasks to be performed is described in detail. The frequency and nature of the work are clearly stated. The materials to be used are specified in considerable depth. And the manner in which the work is to be accomplished is expressed in simple language.

It is suggested that the head custodian develop a reliable system for accomplishing all of the required work. He may wish to record each task to be performed on a card. This may include a description of the task and the tools and materials to be used. These cards may well serve as a "tickler file" or a reminder to the custodian as to when the task should be completed. He should note on the card the date of the next time when the work is required and file all of the cards chronologically by date, starting with the current date. In this way, the custodian will know at a glance what needs to be completed within a given month, week, or day. Once the work is completed, he can record what was done on the back of the card. The principal can scan through these cards from time to time to assure himself that the preventive maintenance program in his building is effective and in full operation. He may also wish to compare the work described on the card with that stated in the preventive maintenance plan developed under the auspices of the central administration.

Appendices

A

How to Make an Enrollment Projection Using the Percentage of Survival Method

The "Percentage-of-Survival Method" involves a relatively simple concept that is illustrated in the following example. Let us assume that during the past fifteen years it was found that, on the average, 95 percent of the pupils enrolled in the first grade appeared in the second grade a year later, and that 98 percent of the pupils enrolled in the second grade entered the third grade in the following year. Then, if there are now 100 pupils in the first grade, it can be anticipated that 95 of them will appear in the second grade next year. And, of these 95, it can be reasonably expected that 93 (98 percent of 95) will be enrolled in the third grade in the following year.

Basic Assumptions

In the "Percentage-of-Survival Method," it is assumed that the following factors will continue in the future as they have averaged during the past (usually fifteen years).

> Death rate of children
> Migration of pupils (both in and out)
> Retardation policy
> Dropouts
> Influx from private to public schools and vice versa

Modification of Results

The future enrollments predicted by the "Percentage-of-Survival" technique should be scrutinized in terms of the above assumptions. Any evidence that changes one or more of the five assumptions listed above should be carefully considered in determining future school enrollments. Adjustments in final enrollment figures should be made judiciously where necessary. For example, a community that has experienced rapid population growth during the past five years would have more pupils than would be indicated by the projection based on the past fifteen years. On the other hand, the recent construction of a new private school in the community would result in an actual enrollment lower than the predicted figure. Also, if it is known that a real estate development of several hundred homes is being planned in a certain area, modifications in the projected enrollment should be made prudently in the light of this evidence.

Limitations

A total enrollment in grades kindergarten through 6 can be predicted only five years in advance. However, due to the ease with which an enrollment projection of this type can be kept up-to-date on a yearly basis, this limitation is not considered serious. it should be pointed out that this method is *not* reliable for communities where the rate of change of school population is erratic, as for example a community adjacent to a military establishment. In this case the results of this enrollment projection should be modified in accordance with the best judgment of the local school authorities.

Enrollment Projection by Study Areas or Zones

In addition to a community-wide enrollment projection, school authorities may wish to compute anticipated enrollments in several sections of their town or city. These zonal or area projections are extremely useful in locating school sites near centers of school-age population. When sectional projections are made, it is suggested that barriers such as rivers, lakes, main highways, and railroad tracks be given serious consideration. In fact, such barriers may become zonal boundaries.

Attention: *Do not use* the instructions in this section for very small school systems where the yearly births and grade-by-grade enrollments are less than twenty. A grouping technique must be used. Seek the advice of an educational consultant.

Caution:

Make each zone as large as possible, but not so large that the zonal projection loses its usefulness.

Do not use the sum of zonal projections for determining future *town-wide* enrollments. Zonal projections tend to be less reliable than town-wide projections because population growth in each section of the community is apt to be more erratic than in the town as a whole.

Supplementary Enrollment Projection for Communities Experiencing Rapid Growth

A supplemental enrollment projection should be made for communities that have experienced a large change in pupil population within recent years. The only difference between this and the ordinary projection is that a past experience of *five* years instead of the usual fifteen years is used.

ENROLLMENT PROJECTION BY STUDY AREAS

Otherwise, the same instructions apply to both projections. For communities that have recently experienced a rapid growth, the figures in this enrollment projection will give the local school authorities a basis for revising the original enrollment projection. The following statements should be borne in mind when revisions are made:

1. The original enrollment projection assumes that the school population will continue to change in the future as it has during the past fifteen years.
2. The supplementary projection is based on the assumption that the school population will continue to change in the future as it has during the past five years.
3. In a community that has grown very rapidly during the past five years, the actual future enrollmment may lie between the original and supplementary figures.

Caution:

Before entering basic data on Form A2, make double sure that birth and enrollment figurees are *accurate*.

Be certain that the sources of information are reliable.

Check to see that the information received is exactly that which is required.

Although work sheets A1 or A2 may at first glance seem somewhat complicated, it is relatively simple to compute future enrollments if the instructions are followed step by step.

Assemble Basic Data and Record on Form A1

List births. Compile a year-by-year listing for the past twenty years of children born to parents who reside within the community, and record on Form A1. Some parents choose to have their children born in communities other than the one in which they reside, but nevertheless most of these children will probably be on your school register five or six years later. This information may be obtained from the local recorder of vital statistics or from the superintendent of schools.

Record year-by-year, grade-by-grade enrollments.   Collect the year-by-year (as of a given date, usually October 1st), grade-by-grade enrollments for the past sixteen years, and record these figures on Form A1. These data may be obtained from the superintendent of schools.

Step 1.   Fill in dates in Form A2, column (1), corresponding to the various years.

Start with "current year," and enter past years serially on the upper section of Form A2 labeled "past experience."

Start with "current year" in the lower section and proceed serially in the future.

Step 2.   Fill in birth data.

Using information on Form A1, enter births five years earlier in column (2) of Form A2 provided the school entrance age is approximately 5.

Step 3.   Fill in enrollment data.

Using information from Form A1, fill in year-by-year, grade-by-grade enrollments for the various years and corresponding grades in columns (4), (6), (8), (10), etc. on Form A2.

Step 4.   Compute survival ratio of the number of pupils appearing in kindergarten to the number of children born five years earlier.

Divide figure in column (4) by the corresponding figure in column (2) on Form A2.

Record the result in column (3).

Repeat this procedure for each year under "past experience."

Step 5.   Compute grade-by-grade, year-by-year survival ratios.

Divide the enrollment for a given year and grade by the number of pupils enrolled in the previous year in the preceding grade. (These two figures lie on a diagonal line between the given year and the preceding year.)

Record the result in the space between the two figures that were used to obtain the survival ratio.

Repeat this procedure for all years listed under "past experience."

$$A \div B = C \qquad 120 \div 125 = .96$$
$$D \div E = F \qquad 95 \div 110 = .86$$
$$G \div H = I \qquad 112 \div 120 = .93 \text{ etc.}$$

BASIC DATA FOR ENROLLMENT PROJECTION

Form A-1

RESIDENT BIRTHS

Year	
19__	
1967	115
1968	105
1969	130
1970	140
1971	150
1972	145
1973	150
1974	156
CURRENT YEAR 1975	

PAST ENROLLMENT BY GRADES AND YEARS

PAST SCHOOL YEARS	K	GRADE 1	2	3	4	5	6	7
19__								
19__								
19__								
19__								
1973	120	110	80	95	82	85	80	
1974	130	112	95	100	95	90	85	
CURRENT YEAR 1975	146	115	100	105	100	95	90	

Form A-1

BASIC DATA FOR ENROLLMENT PROJECTION

RESIDENT BIRTHS

PAST CALENDAR YEARS	NUMBER
19 _	
19 _	
19 _	

PAST SCHOOL YEARS

PAST ENROLLMENT BY GRADES AND YEARS (AS OF A CERTAIN DATE)

COMMENCING	K	GRADE 1	2	3	4	5	6	7	8	9	10	11	12		
19 _															
19 _															
19 _															
19 _															
19 _															
19 _															
19 _															
19 _															
19 _															
19 _															
19 _															
19 _															
CURRENT YEAR 19 _															

CAUTION:

1. Be sure the source is reliable.
2. Make certain the figures are accurate.

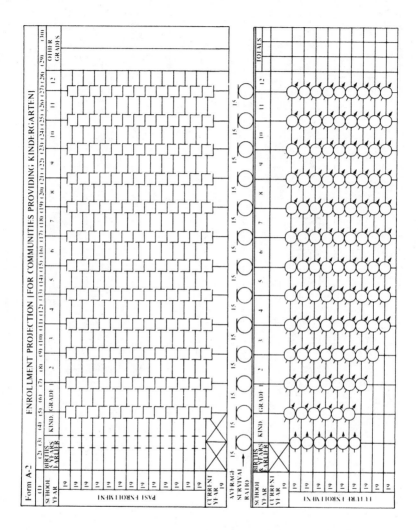

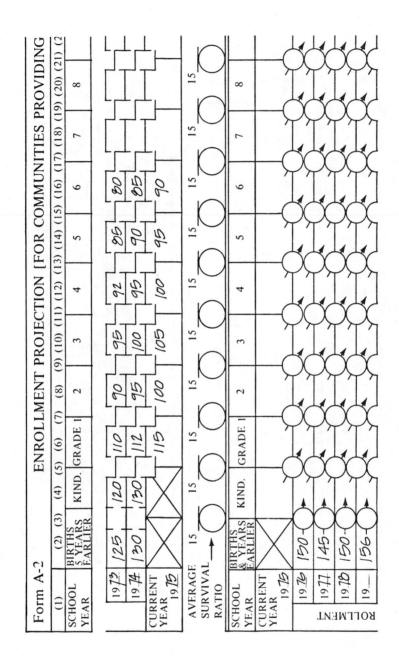

EXAMPLE (Illustrating Steps 1, 2, and 3)

Step 6.   Find average survival ratios.

Find the arithmetic average of each column of ratios (columns [3], [5], [7], [9], [11], etc.) and record the result in the circles labeled average survival ratio corresponding to each column.

Also record the average survival ratio for each column in each of the circles in the corresponding vertical line (as indicated by the arrow leading from the circles containing the respective average survival ratios).

Caution:

Scan each column of survival ratios for any figures that are obviously "out of line." These irregularities may be due to faulty data or to some unusual situation in that particular year. These obviously incorrect ratios should not be included in computing the average. For example, if three figures are considered incorrect, add the remaining 12 ratios and divide by 12.

Look for abrupt pattern changes. If such a change is detected, use only the figures after the change occurred in computing the average. For example, if a private school was opened ten years ago, an abrupt pattern change would take place at that time. Therefore, only the figures following that change should be used to predict future enrollments.

Step 7.   Compute future grade-by-grade, year-by-year enrollments. Record the current grade-by-grade enrollments in lower section of Form A2 opposite "current year."

Record resident births five years earlier in column (2) for the years already entered in lower section of Form A2.

Multiply each number of births recorded in column (2) by its corresponding average survival factor (in circle), and record the result in column (4) in the direction of the arrow (horizontally).

Multiply the number of pupils in a given grade and year by the survival factor within the circle through which the arrow passes, and record the result in the space indicated by the tip of the arrow.

The list below indicates how figures illustrating Step 7 were obtained:

1. Current-year enrollment figures are known and recorded in the appropriate columns.
2. Kindergarten figures $A \times B = C$ or $156 \times .98 = 153$
3. First-grade figures $D \times E = F$ or $153 \times .91 = 139$ ("Round off" to the closest whole number.)
4. Second-grade figures $G \times H = I$ or $139 \times .88 = 122$ etc.

| Form A-2 | ENROLLMENT PROJECTION [FOR COMMUNITIES PROVIDING |

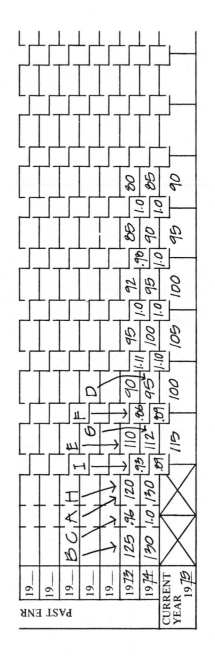

EXAMPLE (Illustrating Step 4 and Step 5)

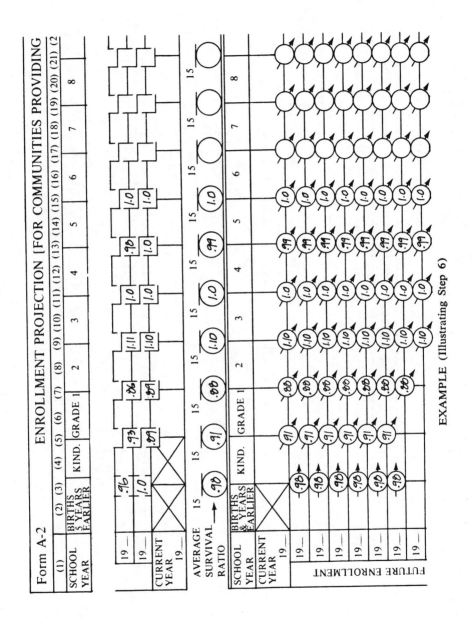

EXAMPLE (Illustrating Step 6)

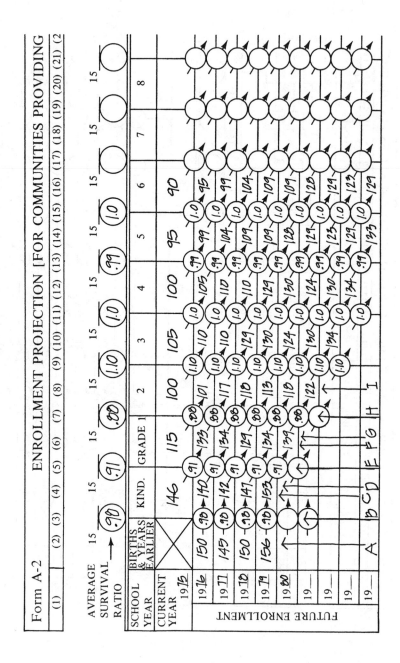

EXAMPLE (Illustrating Step 7)

The completed form now shows the anticipated enrollment year by year and grade by grade. On the extreme right of the enrollment projection form are three columns labeled "totals." These may be used for grouping grades by year. For example, it may be necessary to know how many pupils are expected in Grades K–6, 7–9, and 10–12 within the next few years. These columns can be used for such purpose. The actual groupings will depend upon local policy regarding grade organization.

B

Technique for Determining the Approximate Location and Capacity of New Construction Employing an Indirect Approach

In utilizing the indirect approach for determining the location and capacity of needed facilities when accurate census data are not available, it is suggested that:

1. An enrollment projection of the entire school district be made using the percent-of-survival technique or its equivalent, and the desired grade organization be established for the school district by the board of eduction.
2. The capacity of each serviceable building that would make most effective use of each school be determined by use of techniques discussed in Chapter 5.
3. The total available capacity in the school district for each grade grouping be computed and deducted from the total projected enrollment in the respective grade groupings for the key planning year. The difference, then, represents the additional capacity that should be provided somewhere in the school district for the respective grade groupings.
4. The present attendance areas be drawn on a map of the school district, and present enrollment and the capacity of the respective buildings in each area be shown in each attendance area.
5. A qualitative estimate be made regarding the likely increase or decline of pupil population in each attendance area, and each area be shaded in by distinctive colors or cross-hatching indicating the extent of the estimated change.

6. Present enrollment in each attendance area plus estimated increases of enrollment in the future as determined by the percent of expected population change, be compared with the present capacity in each attendance area, and a symbol be entered in each area showing whether an excess or deficiency of capacity is expected in each attendance area.

7. Attendance areas be revised as follows:
   (a) Excess and deficient capacity areas should be balanced as much as possible through minor adjustments of attendance lines, or by transporting pupils from one area to the other.
   (b) Attendance lines should be adjusted if possible, to shift pupil population from insufficient areas to those with excess-capacity.
   (c) When deficient capacities exist in several adjoining attendance areas, attendance lines should be altered so that the total deficiency is concentrated in an area where present facilities or availability of sites offers a logical solution to the problem of increased capacity for that general area.

8. After attendance line adjustments have been made according to paragraph 7 above, the amount of the additional capacity and its possible location be determined for each reconstructed attendance area. Where excess capacity is available, its location should be noted for possible use later in formulating the final long-range plan.

9. The sum of the additional capacity envisioned for each attendance area under paragraph 8 above be subtracted from the overall district capacity deficiency computed in paragraph 3. In school districts that are relatively stable, a balance between the sum of area needs and the overall district capacity needs may be reached at this point. If balance is not achieved, readjust the estimates of growth within the attendance areas accordingly.

10. In growing school districts, the areas of potential population growths be defined and drawn on a map of the school district. Priorities as to areas where the most rapid growth is likely to occur should be indicated on the map. New facilities should be strategically located in these areas of potential growth.

11. The long-range building program provides for the construction of schools in locations specified under paragraph 10 above, and a balance between total capacity and expected enrollment in the key year be attained.

It is realized, of course, that this procedure for determining the location of additional capacity in a school district is more qualitative than quantitative. A scientific approach to this problem would require that the school district be subdivided into small permanent census tracts without regard for attendance areas, and further, that an annual census be taken of pre-school and in-school pupils. The reason for taking a census of pupils who are in school as well as those below school age is to provide a check on the validity of the pre-school data. By comparing the number of pupils in the first grade, for example, with the number of first-grade pupils reported by the census-takers, it is possible to determine the percent of under-enumeration and thus provide a basis for adjusting the pre-school figures.

INDEX